A Strengths-based Approach to International Development

Praise for this book

'Somehow in one book Winterford, Rhodes and Dureau have managed to weave together all the strands of theory and practice that have coalesced into a strengths-based approach to development. A wonderful history of how and why the approach emerged, its philosophical underpinnings and its implication for the future of development practice and policy are grounded by the inclusion of 21 wonderful case studies that give the reader a worm's eye view of how a strengths-based approach is being used by practitioners all over the world.'

Gord Cunningham, Former Executive Director of the Coady Institute

'For several decades Papua New Guinea's local development workers were inspired by a Constitution that endorsed a strengths-based approach to local and national development. They facilitated relationships of solidarity, mutual learning and exchange and hope in building the future they had envisioned. But the emergence of a global development industry has turned all that on its head. The focus, energy, capacities and hope of communities swept away by the tides of needs-based approaches that have inflated the power and purse of (too) many external agents. The authors provide us with a wealth of knowledge, evidence and analysis, making a reader-friendly, cogent, irrefutable and timely case for 'A strength-based approach to international development'. This text will inform and inspire at every level – from national and bilateral planners and policy makers to the universities and into the field where the best of NGOs have the commitment and capacity to restore agency and voice to local citizens and their leaders, working together locally and cross country, for the future they want.'

Elizabeth Cox, PNG/Pacific ally, and development worker since 1973

'This book is a breath of fresh-air to the trappings of international development. The strengths-based approach challenges the status quo, equalizes the power-imbalance and shifts the dial in favour of the so-called recipients of aid and beneficiaries of international development. A must read!'

Setareki S. Macanawai, Chief Executive Officer, Pacific Disability Forum

A Strengths-based Approach for International Development
Reframing aid

Keren Winterford, Deborah Rhodes and Christopher Dureau

Practical Action Publishing Ltd
25 Albert Street, Rugby, Warwickshire, CV21 2SD, UK
www.practicalactionpublishing.com

© Keren Winterford, Deborah Rhodes and Christopher Dureau, 2023

The moral right of the authors to be identified as authors of the work has been asserted under sections 77 and 78 of the Copyright Design and Patents Act 1988.

All rights reserved. No part of this publication may be reprinted or reproduced or utilized in any form or by any electronic, mechanical, or other means, now known or hereafter invented, including photocopying and recording, or in any information storage or retrieval system, without the written permission of the publishers.

Product or corporate names may be trademarks or registered trademarks, and are used only for identification and explanation without intent to infringe.

A catalogue record for this book is available from the British Library.

A catalogue record for this book has been requested from the Library of Congress.

ISBN 978-1-78853-236-5 Paperback
ISBN 978-1-78853-237-2 Hardback
ISBN 978-1-78853-238-9 Electronic book

Citation: Winterford, K., Rhodes, D., and Dureau, C. (2023): *A Strengths-based Approach for International Development: Reframing aid*. Rugby, UK: Practical Action Publishing <http://doi.org/10.3362/9781788532389>.

Since 1974, Practical Action Publishing has published and disseminated books and information in support of international development work throughout the world. Practical Action Publishing is a trading name of Practical Action Publishing Ltd (Company Reg. No. 1159018), the wholly owned publishing company of Practical Action. Practical Action Publishing trades only in support of its parent charity objectives and any profits are covenanted back to Practical Action (Charity Reg. No. 247257, Group VAT Registration No. 880 9924 76).

The views and opinions in this publication are those of the authors and do not represent those of Practical Action Publishing Ltd or its parent charity Practical Action.

Reasonable efforts have been made to publish reliable data and information, but the authors and publisher cannot assume responsibility for the validity of all materials or for the consequences of their use.

Cover design by Katarzyna Markowska, Practical Action Publishing
Typeset by vPrompt eServices, India

Contents

List of tables, figures, and case studies ix
List of abbreviations xiii
Acknowledgements xv
Preface xvii

Part A: Introducing a strengths-based approach

1. Why a strengths-based approach in international development? 3
   Development 3
   Waves of development practice 5
   The fundamental problem 7
   Signposts to the alternative 9
   The importance of a strengths-based approach – now and beyond 19

2. Philosophical underpinnings of a strengths-based approach 23
   Values underpinning a strengths-based approach 23
   As a reaction to and critique of deficit-based change 32

3. What is a strengths-based approach? 35
   Common processes 36
   Examples of strengths-based practice 46
   Acknowledging critiques of strengths-based practice 66

4. How change happens within a strengths-based approach 73
   Conceptual framework 73

Part B: Exploring a strengths-based approach

5. Perspectives on power 87
   Negative view of power within international development discourse 87
   Alternative views of power for a strengths-based approach 89
   Power in a strengths-based approach 94

6. Culture and a strengths-based approach 99
   Cultural value differences 99
   A strengths-based approach and the value of culture 102

7. Psychology and a strengths-based approach   113
   Positive psychology   114
   Positive emotions   115
   Flourishing   118
   Motivation   120
   Character strengths   121

8. The development worker   123
   Mindset shift   123
   Identity, role, and knowledge   124
   New ways of working   129

Part C: Application of a strengths-based approach in international development

9. A strengths-based approach and the programme cycle 143
   Policy and strategy in international development   146
   Programme/project planning and design   149
   Programme implementation   153
   Managing risk   155

10. Rethinking monitoring, evaluation and research   157
    Monitoring, evaluation, and research in international development   157
    Monitoring, evaluation and research through a strengths-based approach   162
    How to assess a strengths-based practice   168

11. A strengths-based approach and development themes 171
    Geo-political relationships   172
    Partnerships   175
    Capacity development   176
    Community development   181
    Gender and social inclusion   185
    Governance   190

12. A strengths-based approach and development sectors 197
    Climate change action and disaster risk reduction 199
    Economic development   202
    Education   205
    Food security and agriculture   209
    Gender-based violence, domestic violence, and child protection   211

Governance and social accountability	215
Health systems strengthening and health security	217
Humanitarian responses and recovery after disasters	221
Law and justice	225
Water, sanitation, and hygiene	226
13. Conclusion	231
Websites and training manuals applying strengths-based approaches	237
References	241
Index	263

List of tables, figures, and case studies

List of tables

Table 1.1	Simple, complicated, complex	15
Table 3.1	Comparing a strengths-based and problem-based approach in international development	43
Table 3.2	Pathology versus strengths	60
Table 3.3	Connecting common processes to strengths-based practices	67
Table 11.1	Strengths-based processes used in ACCESS II in Indonesia	193

List of figures

Figure 1.1	Framing development	9
Figure 1.2	The movement of strengths-based practice in international development	17
Figure 2.1	Philosophical underpinnings of a strengths-based approach	23
Figure 2.2	Glass half-empty or glass half-full	24
Figure 2.3	A choice to make	25
Figure 2.4	Heliotropic effect	29
Figure 2.5	Rear view into the past	31
Figure 3.1	Common processes, methods, and tools of a strengths-based approach	36
Figure 3.2	Example of asset-based community development mapping	47
Figure 3.3	Steps in ABCD	47
Figure 3.4	The Appreciative Inquiry cycle	51
Figure 3.5	Positive Deviance: five basic steps	56
Figure 3.6	The futures triangle	65

Figure 4.1   Framework for how change happens within
             a strengths-based approach   74

Figure 5.1   Inherent power, collective power, expanding power   90

Figure 7.1   Broaden-and-build theory of positive emotions   116

Figure 7.2   Five factors of flourishing   119

Figure 7.3   Character strengths   122

Figure 10.1 Action research cycle   169

List of expanded case studies

Case Study 1   Strengths-based approaches are the way of the future   20

Case Study 2   Designed to engage with and learn from local initiatives
               in Solomon Islands   44

Case Study 3   ABCD in the Philippines   48

Case Study 4   Appreciative Inquiry Summit in Indonesia   53

Case Study 5   Recognizing traditional wisdom in health care in India
               and Timor-Leste   58

Case Study 6   Engagement between traditional and modern education
               in Indonesia   63

Case Study 7   Transformative change for a safe community
               in South Africa   81

Case Study 8   Improving health through collective action in Indonesia   92

Case Study 9   Collective and expanding power in responding to
               a natural disaster   95

Case Study 10 Take your ego out of the equation   127

Case Study 11 Learning to listen   135

Case Study 12 Trial project leads to whole organizational approach
               for Caritas Australia   144

Case Study 13 Designing to maximize a strengths-based approach
               across Africa   151

Case Study 14 Research that gives back in rural Papua New Guinea   164

Case Study 15	A government–citizen partnership using ABCD in Vietnam	183
Case Study 16	Strengthening civil society for improved governance in Indonesia	191
Case Study 17	Using local assets to improve school infrastructure in Papua New Guinea	207
Case Study 18	Generative change in addressing gender-based violence in Kenya	213
Case Study 19	Positive Deviance study of health clinics in eastern Indonesia	219
Case Study 20	Rebuilding with the community after a natural disaster in Indonesia	223
Case Study 21	Value for money in a WASH project in Tanzania	228

List of abbreviations

AACES	Australia Africa Community Engagement Scheme
ABCD	Asset-Based Community Development
ABM	Anglican Board of Mission
ACCESS	Australian Community Development and Civil Society Strengthening Scheme
ACIAR	Australian Centre for International Agricultural Research
AI	Appreciative Inquiry
AOA	Anglican Overseas Aid
CRPD	Convention on the Rights of Persons with Disabilities
DAC	Development Assistance Committee
DCEP	District Citizen Engagement Plan
DFAT	Department of Foreign Affairs and Trade, Australian Government
DSR	Department of Social Responsibility, Anglican Diocese of Grahamstown, South Africa
EWB	Engineers Without Borders
FAO	Food and Agriculture Organization
LAPIS	Learning Assistance Program for Islamic Schools
LOGICA	Local Governance and Infrastructure for Communities in Aceh
M&E	monitoring and evaluation
MoE	Ministry of Education
NGO	non-governmental organization
ODA	Official Development Assistance
OECD	Organisation for Economic Co-operation and Development
OPD	organization of persons with disabilities
SDG	Sustainable Development Goal
SINPA	Solomon Islands NGO Partnership Agreement
SLA	Sustainable Livelihoods Approach
UNICEF	United Nations Children's Fund
WASH	water, sanitation, and hygiene

Acknowledgements

An Acknowledgement of Country is a practice in Australia that allows for any individual to pay their respects to Aboriginal and Torres Strait Islander people, country, culture, heritage, and their ongoing relationship with the land. We acknowledge the traditional custodians of the land on which we live and work – the Gadigal of the Eora Nation, Wurundjeri and Wadawurrung of the Kulin Nation – and pay our respects to elders past and present, and extend our respects to all Aboriginal and Torres Strait Islander people in Australia and all Indigenous communities around the world.

We acknowledge the privileged contexts in which we have lived and worked, with considerable opportunities for learning, good resource bases, and engagement with supportive institutions and communities. We recognize we have the opportunity and power to influence others in the international development system and wish to use this to enable people who currently have not been able to express their voice in this context, to do so. We consider that when people's voices are both expressed and listened to, the international development system will be better and people whose development is most important will be able to realize their own vision strengthened by their own resources and local assets.

We are grateful to the 37 generous people who shared their reflections, experiences, and stories with us in interviews, for this book. They come from many different countries, mainly in the African, Asian, and Pacific regions. They hold diverse roles in civil society, donor agencies, private sector, and research institutions, work in many different sectors, and are at various stages in their careers and lives. They all share an interest in and commitment to contributing to a better world, including through the use of a strengths-based approach. Those interviewed were: Alice McGrath; Alison Preston; Anna Gero; Anne Wuijts; Anton M. Indrianto; Barbara Pamphilon; Bernadette Whitelum; Casterns Mulume; Christa Dewi; Erin Anderson; Florence Nderita; Genevieve Timmons; Godwin Yidana; Ian Cunningham; Ivy Khoury; James Senjura; Jayne Curnow; Karen McNamara; Lina Magallanas; Lisa Cleary; Lisa McMurray; Martha Hebi; Martin Wanjohi; Millicent Wambugu; Mohammad Najib; Paul Boon; Rebecca Spratt; Sarah McCana; Scott Martin; Setareki Macanawai; Shinko Tana; Soli Middleby; Stefanus Segu; Sulis Seda; Tony Schnell; Vicki Vaartjes; and Vinh Nguyen.

Keren: Thanks to my Mum and Dad, and David for their expanding support and love. I would also like to thank and acknowledge all the people in my life, and those I have worked with, and met along the way, who have inspired and shaped my thinking over multiple decades.

Deborah: Thanks to Ernie, Sebastian, and Jacob for their support and patience. Thanks to the people I have collaborated with over 35 years, who have taught me about this rich, complex, and extraordinary world, and steered me towards understanding people's inherent strengths.

Chris: Thanks Christine for your consistent encouragement and ongoing advice. Thank you to all the people I have had the privilege of interviewing for this book and those I have worked with during the past 20 years.

Special thanks also to the wonderful Jess McArthur for her expertise in designing the figures and tables for this book.

Preface

> *A strengths-based approach ... reframes how people engage with the world, which is essentially what life and work are all about (Soli Middleby)*

In the 21st century, a paradigm for international development which reflects contemporary understanding of the world is necessary. This includes a way of thinking which recognizes the interconnectedness of humanity, shared development challenges, and collective priorities. Recognition that no single person, development programme, discipline or country 'has the solutions' to another's issues, should underpin current practice. A way of working that expands the size of the power pie so that more people have agency over their development future, rather than just shifting power from 'donors' to 'recipients', is relevant in this dynamic and interconnected world. An approach which is about 'us all' bringing about change for 'us all', rather than 'us' bringing change to 'them' is required. A strengths-based approach is a means to respond to all of these opportunities and priorities.

This book makes a timely contribution at an early stage of the new decade. Significant global shifts have occurred, which, combined with decades of global concern for injustice and inequality, has meant many people feel overwhelmed by the enormity of the world's challenges and many institutions face significant change. This book offers a way forward, based on a feasible, practical, and proven approach. On its own, it is not a promise to change the world, but a means for people to do so, collectively, confidently, and optimistically.

Just as the world is rapidly changing and facing new and more complex challenges, such as a global COVID-19 pandemic which started in 2020 and has exposed and exacerbated social injustice, the international development sector is also changing. Traditional donor frameworks are weakening and new groupings and voices are gaining prominence. There is a clear opportunity to contribute to new ways of working. The development sector is increasingly engaged with movements and ideas originating in countries that have traditionally been the 'recipient' locations of donor-funded development programmes. Alternative voices are being heard. They are demanding to be heard more and for the status quo to be disrupted. In countries which have traditionally been classified as 'donor countries' there is increasing recognition of the reality that we live on a shared planet, with a shared future. In particular, there are calls to decolonize development systems and practice. Localizing humanitarian action, decolonizing 'knowledge' about the concept of development, and challenging the dominant power of leaders from a narrow demographic range are all part of this major shift. A strengths-based approach, which emphasizes and mobilizes the strengths that exist in every context, and gives voice to communities, leaders, and organizations in their own development, is well-aligned with this shift.

The jigsaw of different approaches to international development has continually changed since official development assistance (ODA) systems were first created after World War II. A core premise, however, has remained relatively constant: international development seeks to address or solve problems in 'developing countries' or now more commonly termed lower- and middle-income countries (LMICs). Consistent with this problem-based paradigm is the expectation that countries should follow a trajectory towards the achievement of economic and political benchmarks set out in the 'developed world'. The process of addressing poverty and inequality is thus understood as an exercise in exploring the pathology of poverty and a scientific undertaking to fix the situation. A large proportion of people currently working in international development consider such premises to be absurdly simplistic and flawed to various degrees, but as a dominant paradigm, the deficits perspective remains a major influence on the systems which underpin development practice.

Why now?

A redirection from a problem-based approach to a strengths-based approach is the paradigm shift that is necessary for all aspects of development practice in the 21st century. A strengths-based approach contributes to better collaboration at all levels, between countries and people, because it enables recognition of the potential contribution of all. Dialogue and collaboration are processes of sharing ideas from different perspectives, asking questions and stimulating new frames of reference or practices, all essential for people to achieve change. Strengths-based collaboration is thus central to the achievement of developmental benefits, that is, positive change that is relevant, locally led, successful, and sustainable. Importantly, it enables groups of people working together to achieve not just simply the 'solution to a problem', but a better future, beyond that which can be determined through a problem-based or needs-based approach.

While this may be one of the first books which directly links a strengths-based approach with the international development sector, the approach is not new: it has been applied by many actors in international development in the past two decades. Luckily, therefore, there is a substantial body of evidence about its use and benefits. This book describes the approach and where it comes from, considers contexts in which it is useful and shares stories that have emerged from those who have used it across the world. In particular, the book discusses conditions under which a strengths-based approach works, as well as the enablers for effective processes and outcomes.

A strengths-based approach is not a method, but a philosophy and way of thinking which generates a suite of methods and tools for facilitating positive change. Those who adopt this way of thinking, from development programme leaders to village community members, describe its invigorating and life-changing impact. The authors recognize that the adoption of a strengths-based approach represents a departure from commonly used problem-solving approaches; any transition between the two is not necessarily linear nor easy for many who are used to control and prediction as part of problem-solving approaches.

The authors strongly appreciate that context matters. We know that people and elements unique to each place and each collaboration shape the prospects for that context (Pritchett and Sandefur, 2014), and propose a strengths-based approach as a means to surface these in every context. We therefore include stories of experience from various contexts. Since every development activity inevitably involves cross-cultural interaction, the benefits of a strengths-based approach in strengthening cross-cultural understanding and respect are particularly highlighted.

The authors have used a strengths-based approach in international development practice for more than two decades, in some ways 'under the radar'. This has often been the case despite the dominant systems which demand a problem- or needs-based approach. We started with doubts, but with extensive experience in applying, studying, and reflecting on the approach, both confidence and conviction about its value have strengthened over time. This book is the culmination of our respective experiences and reflections.

In the traditional context of ODA, few government donor agencies of the past half century remain independent: they have moved into ministries and departments of foreign affairs and trade. International relationships are now dominated by diplomacy, stability, risk management, investment, and a focus on commercial benefits. Different world-views are therefore brought into determining ODA policies, budgets, and approaches, commonly ignoring the lessons learned from decades of experience as well as alternative voices. The consequences of this change are still emerging, making the opportunity for a paradigm shift, portrayed in this book, even more timely.

Who are we?

The authors worked together in the early 2000s at International Development Support Services (IDSS), which at the time was the consulting arm of Oxfam Australia. We informally 'picked up' and applied ideas related to a strengths-based approach for various programmes in Asian and Pacific countries. IDSS ceased operations and we went our separate ways, each working with diverse organizations and programmes in many countries in various roles since. Keren undertook a doctorate in strengths-based practice in social accountability, in relation to World Vision's Citizen Voice and Action approach, using case studies from Uganda and Armenia. Chris incorporated Appreciative Inquiry, Asset-Based Community Development, and other strengths-based methods into the programmes he managed or supported in many Pacific, Asian, and African countries, at community and national levels and in many sectors. Deborah incorporated the approach into her programme design and evaluation work, as well as in cross-cultural training, advising thousands of development workers that a strengths-based approach was an effective way to work cross-culturally in diverse sectors from disability inclusion to policing. In 2019, the authors re-grouped and recognized it was time to pool our diverse experiences and share these with the development sector. With seismic shifts in the world during 2020, the opportunity to write became feasible and the value of such a book became even more obvious.

All three of us acknowledge our privilege, as citizens of a wealthy country: we have had extraordinary opportunities to travel and learn. We share a commitment to centring the voices of people we work with – villagers, officials of government agencies, staff of civil society organizations, and others – in relation to their own development. We consider ourselves facilitators (rather than experts) and have sought within this book to promote the voices of other development workers who have also used a strengths-based approach in their own international work.

Where we started

Keren: I had a memorable formative experience using a strengths-based approach in Swaziland as a new Country Program Coordinator for World Vision Australia in 2004. My role was to monitor programmes funded from Australia as well as strengthen staff capacity, with a focus on sustainability of programme benefits.

On my second visit to Swaziland, I organized a workshop with the Program Director, to explore community development outcomes, World Vision's contribution, and how to achieve and sustain more success. I started the day with an overview of Appreciative Inquiry, both the process and assumptions that underpin the approach. To enable people to practise appreciation, we identified personal strengths that we brought to our roles in World Vision. Paired interviews were then organized to discover past successes, using questions such as 'What is the most exciting community achievement you can recall, that produced the most enduring benefits?' and 'What makes it so sustainable?'

Over tea at the morning break, the Program Director told me he did not like the process and asked that it should change. 'There was too much talking', he said. 'What did the staff really know and have to contribute about sustainability?' he asked. His experience of the morning session and my own were very different. I was excited about the noise in the room and the energy of the group. From my perspective, everyone in the room was equally valued for their contribution, but I understood his reaction to be a response to the highly participatory and democratic process. I tried to convince him to keep going, asking, 'shall we just see what happens in the next session before lunch?' I trusted the process, and more importantly the knowledge of staff about how to strengthen sustainability of outcomes in their programmes. At the same time, I also had niggling doubts. Was the Appreciative Inquiry process really going to work, especially in this context that was still foreign to me? We continued with the process. Participants generated important insights about how to strengthen World Vision's community development programmes, identifying initiatives and practical actions to strengthen sustainability of change outcomes. They suggested more attention be given to facilitation (rather than implementation) and building better links with other resources, such as government service providers. The Program Director was impressed that so many practical and achievable ideas had been revealed.

My experience that day gave me practical insights into the value of a strengths-based approach and fuelled my trust in the process and the people who are central to leading their own change process.

Deborah: My first experience of using a strengths-based approach was in 2006, when I was asked by the Australian High Commission in Vanuatu to design a new governance programme. The design process included chiefs from the *Malvatumauri*, an advisory body of chiefs recognized by the Constitution of the Republic of Vanuatu, plus academics from University of Queensland and aid officials. The programme did not respond to a 'problem', but was seen as an opportunity to support community level discussions about the interface between traditional (*kastom*) and introduced government systems. A standard problem-based or needs-based approach was not appropriate, and my colleague at the time Keren Winterford suggested I might use a strengths-based approach. She explained Appreciative Inquiry and waved me off with the line 'trust the process'. I integrated Appreciative Inquiry into a three-day workshop to suit the Vanuatu context, including group discussions, use of symbols to convey ideas, and time for rich discussions.

By all measures, the workshop was a success: participants said they felt valued, included, and respected. Focus on what had already worked well and envisioning a new future were particularly effective. Sessions generated a sense of positive energy, enthusiasm, and momentum I had not previously witnessed. After three days, we had agreed objectives, a common purpose plus a neat set of actions to which all partners were enthusiastically committed, and, importantly, a strong level of mutual cooperation and trust. To top it off, one chief told me the process used to underpin the workshop could be replicated by chiefs across Vanuatu as a way to strengthen communities.

A design document was approved (with no problem-analysis) and in the early period of implementation, efforts were made to sustain a strengths-based approach. Informally I visited the *Malvatumauri* office two years later: the positive energy was palpable. Officials said two of the main reasons the programme had worked so well were the respect shown for Vanuatu culture and high level of trust. Some chiefs said these two elements helped them open up to new ideas: they began to collaborate with Vanuatu women's groups for the first time, a significant change that could not have been successfully imposed from outside. My witnessing of major shifts in mindset, significantly different dynamics, and obvious empowerment effects of using a strengths-based approach in Vanuatu has influenced my entire consulting practice since!

Chris: In 2002, I was Director of the Australian Community Development and Civil Society Strengthening Scheme (ACCESS) in the eastern islands of Indonesia. The Scheme moved away from provision of community grants towards promotion of community-driven development and gender empowerment. The Scheme's experience of embedding a community-led assessment and planning process helped realize the potential of communities to design and manage their development aspirations and contribute to achieving them. Phase II of ACCESS (2006–2014) specifically called for a strengths-based approach in implementation. My contribution in this phase was to incorporate this approach across the whole Scheme. Eventually this included participation by 70 civil society organizations and 3,500 citizen associations; overall, the Scheme reached 1,118 village communities in 20 districts.

Previously, with colleagues, I had applied a strengths-based approach to mobilize communities to improve 2,000 primary schools in Papua New Guinea, and to respond to an earthquake disaster in Yogyakarta, Indonesia, both with overwhelming success. In ACCESS II, with enthusiastic staff, we used Appreciative Inquiry interviews to identify people who were committed to be change agents, regardless of their official rank or role. Each person identified the ingredients of past successes and potential assets their organization or community could contribute. We then organized District Level Appreciative Summits, week-long workshops with representatives from the whole system, including senior government officials and community leaders. Appreciative Inquiry's '5D' process was introduced in these workshops, to enable leaders to identify a district level vision and action areas. These led to numerous examples of communities controlling their own assets and collaborating with government to achieve mutually agreed development goals (see Case Studies in this book).

On reflection, perhaps the most significant contribution of ACCESS II was its part in the passing of Village Law (Law No.6/2014 on Villages) which recognizes the legitimacy and effectiveness of citizen-led development across all 75,000 villages of Indonesia. ACCESS II also developed tools to assist village-led planning, implementation, and monitoring of their own engagement in development. It was clear to all that villages had both capacity and resources to lead their own development as well as tools to do so effectively.

In my experience, the core purpose of any strengths-based approach is to amplify the space for those most affected by change to be the drivers of that change. This has been a key tenet of all my work since, in many countries and contexts.

How we approached writing the book

Once we agreed to write the book together, we developed an overall plan, collating our diverse networks, knowledge of resources, and experience of the practical and theoretical aspects of a strengths-based approach. We compiled lists of potential interviewees, case studies, and literature. We then conducted 37 interviews, read huge numbers of resources, and developed

40 case studies. We present in this book half of the case studies we collected in order to represent different regions, contexts, and sectors. We drafted chapters, using each other as peer reviewers. We held weekly conversations about initial drafts, emerging themes and topics. These conversations also provided an opportunity to think critically and deeply and link ideas. The COVID pandemic gave us more focused time and opportunities to bring our collective knowledge and experience together. Finally, we allocated case studies to different chapters to highlight the most pertinent of the book's key messages. We modified the draft text in response to feedback from each other, from our analysis of interview transcripts and case studies, and from publisher reviews.

Who is the expected audience?

Any person engaged in the international development and humanitarian sector is a potential reader of this book. You may be a young person volunteering to raise funds for a school building or a senior diplomat involved in negotiating the scope of a multi-million-dollar ODA programme to address gender inequality in the water and sanitation sector. You may be a village leader in Indonesia tasked with developing a plan to improve the lives and livelihoods of communities. You may be a board member of an NGO with long-held partnerships with faith-based organizations in Africa, Asia, South America or the Pacific. You may be a health specialist involved in training nurses or doctors in pandemic responses or an education specialist contracted to strengthen school quality systems or literacy. You may be organizing a humanitarian response to a climate change-related disaster. You may be the head of a UN agency or a ministry official working in partnership with international colleagues on nation-building, strengthening accountability systems or reporting on compliance with aspirational goals in global treaties. Put simply, a strengths-based approach has value for anyone and any organization working collaboratively to bring about positive change; our interest is to explore and explain a strengths-based approach in international development for these multiple audiences.

Readers are assumed to be people who are interested in supporting change processes as well as those who may be questioning dominant problem-based or needs-based approaches in international development. Those who seek to contribute to or support change in ways which maximize the quality and relevance of collaboration will find this book helpful. Stories included in this book are from people who have used and experienced the benefits of a strengths-based approach in their development practice in many locations, organizations, and sectors. These examples may connect with readers' similar experiences across the world: the universality of the approach is a key feature.

The book sets out a philosophy of a strengths-based approach which underpins practical application, relevant and valuable in almost all contexts.

It seeks to communicate the story of a strengths-based approach and illustrate its value and benefits in the international development context. The book presents the need for a paradigm shift in international development. Such a shift has already occurred in other disciplines, such as organizational change management and psychology. International development practice will be significantly improved and manifestly more in line with processes of localization and democratization of knowledge if a strengths-based philosophy is applied and if strengths-based practices are used.

Many individuals and organizations are already using the philosophy and practice, and they do so in different ways around the world. Some are fully committed to the philosophical aspects while others use the techniques in some aspects of their work but not others. A mixed practice of a strengths-based approach, that is, more like a SWOT analysis (strengths-weakness-opportunity-threats) misses the potential and transformative opportunity of a strengths-based approach. In particular, we sought to address the issue that many people are partly or 'inaccurately' using the approach.

Rather than provide guidance on how to use strengths-based tools in a step-by-step way (though some references are offered in an annex), the book offers an alternative perspective on international development and a set of alternative practices. The strengths-based philosophy contrasts squarely with the premise that aid donors can and should identify a problem in a different context, plan an expert-led response, and expect to deliver sustainable results. Therefore, this book directly contrasts with the myriad guides on how external people can bring about change in different places.

International development policy developers and practitioners consistently promote the importance of effective cooperation and partnership in contemporary practice. This book will illustrate the value of a strengths-based approach for enabling and sustaining any kind of collaborative arrangement. Leaders and staff of organizations who partner internationally will find the approach is particularly useful in multicultural contexts. The examples provided will illustrate that use of a strengths-based approach contributes to respectful communications and collaboration, to community coherence, and many other positive changes. We hope that the book will contribute to increased respect for different world-views and forms of knowledge and thus a more inclusive approach to international development.

PART A
Introducing a strengths-based approach

> *A strengths-based approach is the only and the best way to solve any problem* (Lisa Cleary)

Part A introduces a strengths-based approach and its philosophical underpinnings. A strengths-based approach for international development has a strong theoretical and practical basis informed by established fields beyond this sector. This part of the book provides a summary of the history of its emergence in various disciplines.

A strengths-based approach is not only a set of methods or tools to carry out, but a way of thinking and being. Given that international development is primarily focused on bringing about positive change, this part of the book also brings together the value of a strengths-based approach to concepts related to change and to contemporary processes associated with facilitating change in international development.

This is one of very few books that connects a strengths-based approach to international development concepts and practices. It provides a compelling set of reasons for its value in international development. It builds on and extends the work of at least two others (Mathie and Cunningham, 2008; Dureau, 2014). While there is much written about the approach in other contexts and many guides and resources on how to use it in practice, this book makes the case for its application at all levels of international development thinking and practice.

Chapter 1 explains why a strengths-based approach is so critical in international development. It highlights the dominant problem-based concepts which have shaped approaches to international development for decades and describes signposts to an alternative.

Chapter 2 provides a summary of the philosophical underpinnings and values associated with a strengths-based approach, describing key features and making foundational concepts accessible to the reader. In particular, the chapter synthesizes literature about the core elements of the approach and begins to illustrate how relevant they are to contemporary approaches and practices used in international development.

Chapter 3 provides an explanation of core processes and descriptions of the most commonly and widely used practices, such as Appreciative Inquiry and Asset-Based Community Development. Describing the shared aspects of multiple aligned practices, this chapter helps the reader make sense of how a strengths-based approach works within international development. Importantly, this chapter acknowledges and responds to critiques of a strengths-based approach.

Chapter 4 delves into the connections between the ideas and processes associated with change itself and how change happens through the lens of a strengths-based approach. Since achieving positive change is the focus of all development practice, understanding how change happens within a strengths-based approach is crucial. The chapter confirms a strengths-based approach's focus on the future, in contrast with approaches which look to solve problems of the past. This chapter leads into the next part of the book, which explores central elements of how a strengths-based approach contributes to positive change in more detail.

CHAPTER 1
Why a strengths-based approach in international development?

> *It's about focusing on what is working and what a different future might be – not on what is missing or what needs to be fixed – that really changes the dynamic in international development and fuels collective action for sustained and meaningful change* (Keren Winterford)

A strengths-based approach seeks to reveal assets, strengths, or what is working within an individual, group, community, or organization, then elevates and amplifies them, as a means to achieve a preferred future. The term 'a strengths-based approach' is used as an umbrella term in this book to capture a way of thinking and practice. It is informed by complementary practices used across various disciplines: organizational change in the public and private sectors; community development; social services; education; health and psychology. These established practices frame inquiry to focus on what is working and what is good as a means to enable positive change.

This book offers a reframing of international development. For many, this is a radical or even revolutionary shift, but for others, the writing is already on the wall and the shift away from a deficit or problem-solving approach is already happening and long overdue. This book offers the thinking, practical action, and evidence-base to inform a sector-wide transformation.

Development

The development agenda has been premised on a view that certain countries are problems to be solved and comprise deficits to be addressed or needs to be met. The agenda has been driven by leaders and institutions in countries where interests and resources exist to provide contributions to other 'eligible' countries. This book proposes both an alternative view and a contrary practice in international development.

Many cite the inauguration speech by US President Harry Truman in 1949 as the first use of the term 'development' to describe the process of addressing global poverty and inequality between countries. In his speech, he divided the world into 'developed' and 'underdeveloped' countries. Following World War II and in response to the emerging Cold War, Truman stated:

> We must embark on a bold new program for making the benefits of our scientific advances and industrial progress available for the improvement

and growth of underdeveloped areas. More than half the people of the world are living in conditions approaching misery. Their food is inadequate. They are victims of disease. Their economic life is primitive and stagnant. Their poverty is a handicap and a threat both to them and to more prosperous areas. For the first time in history, humanity possesses the knowledge and the skill to relieve the suffering of these people (Truman, 1949).

This agenda for poverty reduction and improved global wellbeing through 'development' remains, more than 70 years later. The Sustainable Development Goals (SDGs) and the 2030 Agenda of action for people, planet, and prosperity maintain the language. In 2015, national governments within the framework of the United Nations committed to the SDGs:

We resolve, between now and 2030, to end poverty and hunger everywhere; to combat inequalities within and among countries; to build peaceful, just and inclusive societies; to protect human rights and promote gender equality and the empowerment of women and girls; and to ensure the lasting protection of the planet and its natural resources. We resolve also to create conditions for sustainable, inclusive and sustained economic growth, shared prosperity and decent work for all, taking into account different levels of national development and capacities (United Nations, 2015).

This view of a world separated into 'developed' and 'underdeveloped' has spawned an industry to address 'the problem'. Within international development, there are countless approaches, tools, and methods to support needs assessment, problem and gap analysis. A professional practice of 'international development' has been established, whereby the problem of underdevelopment is addressed by managers or facilitators who administer programmes using deficit-based approaches, tools, and methods. The separation between 'us' and 'them' is clear: the experts *do* development and people in countries where programmes are implemented are their *beneficiaries*.

The distinction between *us* and *them* is blurring as a result of an increasingly interconnected world, with shared experiences of inequality, poverty, and environmental sustainability. However, development practice has largely not taken this on board. This view is echoed by others (Horner, 2020).

There is no doubt that an agenda focused on reducing poverty, inequity, and social injustice remains critically important. However, we argue there is a better path to achieving positive outcomes than the deficits-based and problem-solving practice of previous decades: we describe this as a strengths-based approach to international development.

Waves of development practice

Over the last 70 years, different approaches to development have emerged, rarely in a linear way. There have been discernible patterns and evolution in development discourse and practice, often with one approach developed in reaction to the limitations of the previous wave. However, the concept of 'fixing the problem of underdeveloped or lower-income' countries has remained.

Early official development assistance (ODA) programmes responded to a perceived problem that low-income countries lacked resources, particularly after the widespread destruction caused by World War II. Government aid programmes therefore largely comprised funding for infrastructure, equipment, and provision of technical specialists. It became clear that donor governments and development banks simply could not afford to build infrastructure for all low-income countries, and the problem was reframed as a lack of 'basic needs'. Programmes thus shifted to the provision of food, housing, and basic education and similar 'basics'. In reaction to the inevitable limits of this approach, another shift occurred. The problem of 'developing countries' began to be framed as weak institutions. In response, foreign experts were tasked with delivering health, education, and other government services in many countries, and later to train others how to do so.

Another dominant wave has been a focus on the transfer of skills and knowledge about governance reforms and public service delivery, on the assumption that the 'problem' is a lack of capacity, largely defined as a lack of skills and knowledge. Ideas about the importance of capacity development emerged in the late 1990s as a reaction against ideas that external organizations or countries could deliver development results themselves. The concept of capacity development and the merits of various approaches to changing capacity have been discussed and widely contested since then (for example, see the Learning Network on Capacity Development website). From early in the 21st century, another shift has taken place, based on the view that the 'real' problem is the negative influence of politics and poor governance and leadership in development decision-making. Thus, many bilateral and global development agencies have shifted attention from capacity development approaches to political economy analysis.

Non-governmental organizations (NGOs) or the civil society sector involved in development programmes have in part followed their own paths, shifting understandings of the 'real' problems underpinning poverty, inequality, and injustice over time. While framed in various sets of values, overall, a shift has occurred from helping communities through provision of goods and services to supporting them to determine and achieve their own priorities and engage with their own governments. Not all NGOs have followed this path or made the shift: the extent to which NGOs have engaged with different levels of understanding and their consequences of practice varies widely, so generalizations are not really possible. However, a dominant message from NGOs, at least in their fundraising pitches, is that people in 'developing countries' need the assistance they offer, with funding provided by private donors, government agencies, or the general public in 'developed' countries. A small proportion of NGOs challenge the basic premise that countries where donor programmes operate are 'problems to be fixed', for example, by promoting the importance of global partnerships to address shared priorities.

The waves of development discourse and practice described above are often reactions against previous approaches which are deemed to have failed or been inadequate to solve particular identified problems, big and small. Of course, significant geo-political, social, and economic changes have also occurred over this period, and changes in approaches and practice have been influenced by these, too. Intervals between the emergence of new approaches seem to be shorter, with insufficient time between new approaches for many people to work out what they mean, let alone determine whether the previous one was effective or a failure before moving to the next approach. Given the diversity of workers and thinkers in international development, many different approaches also prevail at the same time, with some organizations practising ideas from several waves ago, while others are innovating the next wave.

The global COVID-19 pandemic provides another opportunity to consider a potential new wave of international development approaches. Already, greater attention to localization of programme management of emergency responses has emerged but it's too early to say how the sector might have changed as a result of the global pandemic overall. It is possible that lessons learned from previous experience could be lost in any shifts to a new approach, thereby missing out on positive benefits from previous practice.

It may be easy to dismiss strengths-based thinking as just another reaction or just another short-lived wave in international development. However, we believe a strengths-based approach is a way of thinking that shifts the basic premise and notions underpinning international development. Numerous examples of how a strengths-based approach has already been applied over the last two decades described in this book also highlight that while a deficit, problem-based perspective currently defines international development, there is a more constructive and practical alternative.

Framing development

Use of a deficit-based perspective to justify funding for international development has a long and ongoing legacy. Stereotypes of poverty reinforce funding campaigns grounded in the idea of 'white saviours', whereby a white person (or an organization comprising white people) rescues, frees, or uplifts a non-white person (or society of non-white people). This is grounded in centuries-old perspectives which underpin colonialization (Giotis, 2022). Critiques of this framing also refer to 'poverty porn'. International development campaigns in the 1980s were critiqued as exploitative and devoid of dignity, especially for children and their mothers. This framing of development has been increasingly questioned, but still dominates. A problem-based approach has been central to how development is communicated. Audiences for this communication include those who practise development, citizens of countries where development programmes are implemented, as well as the general public and the political sphere in countries where funds are sourced.

A deficit framing of development creates separation between country contexts, separation of people as 'us' and 'them', as well as 'othering' of different contexts. Yet the world's people experience issues that are shared globally, such as growing inequality, gender-based violence, climate change, and the COVID-19 pandemic. More than ever, countries and people are increasingly connected through communications, media, and sharing of cultural practices and languages in multicultural countries and organizations. A simple divide between 'developed' and 'underdeveloped' countries makes little sense in the 21st century and misses the complexities associated with connections and divisions among people.

The fundamental problem

Implications of a deficits-based approach in international development are potentially catastrophic to individuals, groups, communities, or organizations. Identification of problems in effect regards those at the centre of focus as problems to be fixed and the external programmes or projects as means by which to fix the problems (Elliott, 1999). To be defined within a problem analysis denies dignity and the innate human potential of individuals, groups, and communities. Ngunjiri (1998) wrote:

> Asking people to say what their problems are, using all sorts of participatory methodologies, is tantamount to asking them to say how useless, weak, empty, powerless, and worthless they are in order for them to qualify to be helped (Ngunjiri, 1998: 468).

Various theories give voice to the negative consequences of current paradigms in international development. Learned helplessness (Hiroto and Seligman, 1975) describes dynamics whereby 'subjects' of international development feel disempowered, useless, and have a sense of hopelessness for the future. Illich (1973) developed a general theory of how the 'helping professions' (e.g. doctors, nurses, lawyers, psychologists, teachers, ministers, aid workers, and social workers in general), each with their own professional associations, can provide counter-productive help that generates as many 'needs' as it resolves. This thinking was further developed by McKnight (1995) using the notion of 'disabling help'. The helping professions depend on needs, disability, incapacity, and helplessness in order to make their living, so this puts them in the paradoxical position of working to eliminate their own jobs, at least when they actually try to help people help themselves. Ellerman (2007) wrote 'there are essentially two ways that the helper's will can supplant the doer's will to thwart autonomy and self-help: (1) the helper, by professionally guided programmes of social engineering, deliberately tries to impose his will on the doer; (2) the helper, by benevolent aid, replaces the doer's will with her will, perhaps inadvertently' (p. 564). In the international development context, the 'helper' can be a development worker and the 'doer' can be individuals, groups, communities, or organizations in a change process. This description may seem extreme for some, but it has been the basis of practice for decades.

This book explores the value of development workers stepping back from a position of helping, having control over and prediction of the development agenda, and instead enabling locally led change fuelled by local strengths and assets, informed by locally defined agendas for change.

Post-development theorists also critique the deficit-discourse paradigm. Mwenda (2012) noted during a TED Talk (Radio Hour):

> We need to reframe the challenge that is facing Africa, from a challenge of despair to a challenge of hope. That is 'worth creation'. The challenge facing all those who are interested in Africa is not the challenge of reducing poverty. It should be a challenge of creating wealth.

Post-development thinking critiques the concept and practice of international development. It suggests that development is informed by European colonial perspectives and discourse, situating the 'north' (northern hemisphere) as advanced and the 'south' (southern hemisphere) as backward. Post-development theorists reject previous development theory and practice, considering that development initiatives, on the whole, have done more harm than good. They call for 'alternatives to development'. Post-development theory surfaces fundamental problems with the dominant paradigm of deficit-discourse. Who decides about problems or needs is based on Eurocentric hierarchy, which defines non-western, non-modern, non-industrialized ways of life as inferior and in need of development (Esteva, 1992). Post-development theorists question Eurocentrism and Eurocentric standards as universal standards imposed on all country contexts (Elgström, 2009; Sachs, 1997). As discussed in Chapter 6, a strengths-based approach shifts perspectives about what is at 'the centre' and intrinsically recognizes and respects cultural values and cultural diversity by prioritizing strengths and assets and leadership of change in each specific context where change happens.

Figure 1.1 highlights the critical importance and power of framing international development. As illustrated, international development often focuses inquiry and action on one part of any situation, the deficits or needs to be addressed. It is unable to see assets, strengths, or resources which can be used to catalyse change. For example, one of the book's authors participated in an NGO staff induction training programme many years ago, where the question was asked 'why is this child poor?' This framing is erroneous, potentially harmful to children and their families, and demonstrates the blinkered perspective of the dominant deficit-based approach. Figure 1.1 illustrates that if we only inquire, look for, and ask questions about needs and problems,

Figure 1.1 Framing development

that is the only thing we find. If we look solely at a child, we may miss the broader family and community support that enriches and sustains aspects of the child's experience. A strengths-based approach recognizes a broader perspective. Furthermore, it values this broader perspective, appreciating strengths or assets as a means of catalysing future change.

Signposts to the alternative

This book offers a more constructive, respectful, collaborative, and practical alternative for international development. A strengths-based approach is informed by evidence from many sources. These include: the authors' experience and that of many other development workers cited in this book; insights from other disciplines and perspectives; the trajectory of current approaches within international development; and contemporary discourse on development. These are discussed below and further explored throughout the book.

Our experience

The authors' use of a strengths-based approach over several decades, together with many other development workers cited in this book, demonstrates the real benefits and practical potential that a strengths-based approach offers. Like many, we have reacted negatively to the use of problem analyses and needs assessment tools and recognized that a strengths-based approach offers more positive processes and outcomes. We have seen the negative consequences of problem-based and deficit perspectives in many settings and countries. Our collective experience demonstrates the opportunity that a strengths-based approach offers to the practice of international development. Importantly, it confirms the approach's ability to realize development and social justice outcomes in many different contexts.

There is a common thread in our experience. It often started with dissatisfaction or discomfort with the deficit perspective. Then followed a chance encounter with a strengths-based method or practice. This experience revealed that a focus on what is working well, local assets and capabilities, creates better and lasting outcomes. It confirmed that a strengths-based approach provides the framework and language for a way of working we had been intuitively searching for in our work. Experience of a strengths-based approach is not an isolated event. It is increasingly common to find 'strengths-based approach' terminology in policy and programme documents, though details of the theory and practice are often not well understood. Our interest in writing this book is to provide the foundations for defining a strengths-based approach for international development.

Insights from other disciplines and perspectives

A strengths-based approach is not yet a dominant feature in international development, but it has established credentials in other disciplines and professions. Extensive writing and theorizing about the underlying philosophy, world-views, and principles as well as exploration of practice are evident in many fields. These include organizational management, community development, social services, education, health, and psychology. The next chapter draws on insights offered from other disciplines and encourages application to the international development sector.

Gaining insights from other disciplines and professions is not new for international development. The sector has borrowed from more established disciplines and fields of practice including engineering, health, education, organizational management, and community development. Disciplinary insights and dominant perspectives are evident in the 'waves' described above. There is great value in international development workers and organizations learning from and being informed by a strengths-based perspective from other disciplines, as explained below.

Alignment with contemporary discourse of international development

A strengths-based approach aligns with many contemporary concepts and agendas in international development thinking and practice. Development discourse has evolved since its inception, yet the problem-solving deficit paradigm does not reflect these current perspectives on development. Descriptions of 'aid' have often been replaced with new language. While the term 'development' is still used as a descriptor of the broad agenda of work focused on poverty reduction, social justice, and equality, the language to describe much of this work has also changed. We explore alignment between contemporary concepts and a strengths-based approach below.

Capability

The capability approach defines the development agenda as one in which individuals exercise their capability to realize their own wellbeing. The approach was conceived in the 1980s by Amartya Sen (1985, 2001) who promoted the idea of enhancing the freedom of individuals to be active agents of change, rather than passive recipients of services. Sen won the Nobel Prize in Economic Sciences in 1998 and the capability approach can be described as both a philosophy and a theory in economics.

A range of key terms are relevant to the capability approach, which align with a strengths-based approach. *Capability* is realized through *functionings* and *freedoms*. *Functionings* are defined as the 'beings' or 'doings' of individuals and determined by an individual's own choice. Substantive *freedoms* describe the ability to choose how to be or act (functioning). The focus here is on the freedom that a person actually has to do this or be that – things that one may value doing or being. *Capabilities* are viewed as inherent to each individual, informed by your own characteristics; people around you; resources and services you can draw on and the rights you can access; as well as institutions and structures and the legal framework of society. The notion of *capabilities* is also key to a strengths-based approach which focuses on inherent capabilities as well as broader sets of resources which can be drawn on to achieve individual and collective wellbeing.

Key to the capability approach are *freedoms* and *agency* which align with a strengths-based approach. A strengths-based approach prioritizes the agency of individuals to express and act on what they value, informed by their own contexts and cultural preferences. The capability approach is 'people-centred', putting human agency rather than organizations, markets, or government at the centre. The aim of development, within this approach, is to expand human *agency* and *freedoms* through increased social opportunities. While the capability approach may seem orientated to an individualistic perspective, the options that a person has depend on relations with others as well as broader societal and institutional situations. A strengths-based approach similarly includes focus on both individual and broader societal perspectives on what is important and valued. The capability approach includes both subjective and objective outcomes and, like the strengths-based approach, prioritizes individuals' values about what is important.

The focus of the capability approach, like a strengths-based approach, is on creating an enabling environment for people themselves to act, informed by their own choices and preferences and what they value as important for their futures. This is particularly relevant to the role of development workers within a strengths-based approach (see Chapter 9) to step back and enable individuals, groups, and organizations in their own contexts to lead the development agenda. A strengths-based approach emphasizes revealing what is most valued in each context, and how these values inform and shape action towards preferred futures.

Localization

The concept of 'localization' is an increasingly important agenda in the humanitarian sector, and has become more prevalent and relevant to broader development practice especially in light of COVID-19. The World Humanitarian Summit in 2016 confirmed the agenda of localization. The Grand Bargain (World Humanitarian Summit, 2016), agreed at the Summit, set out a commitment from the largest humanitarian donors and aid organizations to ensure national and local partners are involved in decision-making processes in any humanitarian response. The notion of localization is inherent in a strengths-based approach, since it emphasizes place-based development, whereby agendas and priorities are decided by local actors in any given context, and change processes are fuelled by the bringing together of local strengths and assets. A strengths-based approach inherently embodies the localization agenda.

Acknowledging that the term 'local' can be interpreted in several ways, including to imply 'lower level', the localization movement and this book uses the definition that emphasizes the specific geographical context in which change is sought, as in 'improvements in community participation in rural Thailand' or 'strengthening citizen-government relations in northern Solomon Islands'.

While efforts are still under way to achieve the Grand Bargain's 51 commitments for humanitarian response, the term has taken on a life of its own in the development sector. For example, the START Network, comprising global and national humanitarian agencies, developed a framework for understanding localization that articulates seven dimensions: funding, partnerships, capacity, participation, coordination mechanisms, visibility, and policy influence. The localization agenda seeks to shift practice within each of these dimensions such as:

- more equitable relationships (partnerships);
- stop undermining local capacity (capacity);
- participation of crisis-affected communities (participation revolution);
- coordination mechanisms (national actors have greater presence and influence);
- visibility (roles, results, and innovations by national actors);
- policy (national actors' greater presence and influence in international policy debates).

The strengths-based approach embodies all these characteristics. It starts with explicit recognition and respect of local capacity, participation of those involved in the development agenda, and leadership of local actors, and by its nature embodies localization. A strengths-based approach invokes equitable relationships and ensures that external actors work in a way that is driven and led by local agendas and priorities. It is not just about shifting practice to enable a localization agenda and then ensuring a strengths-based approach. A strengths-based approach enacts localization, since at its core it starts with leadership in any given context. It is fuelled by capacity and assets situated within the context relevant to the change agenda, whether they be at community, group, or institutional levels. A strengths-based approach by its nature fulfils the localization agenda.

Decolonizing knowledge

In line with post-development critiques introduced earlier, the agenda of decolonizing knowledge questions and seeks to shift dominant Eurocentric notions of development agendas and practice. As noted by Sultana (2019: 34) 'decolonizing development means disrupting the deeply-rooted hierarchies, asymmetric power structures, the universalization of western knowledge, the privileging of whiteness, and the taken-for-granted Othering of the majority world'. Importantly this movement identifies and challenges the continuation of hegemonic western perspectives in development. The process of decolonizing knowledge raises questions about where knowledge comes from and the power implicit in creation and control of knowledge. Within the decolonization agenda, local knowledge and perspectives are premised to disrupt dominant paradigms and the basis of knowledge which informs development. With a focus on inquiry into local strengths and assets and local leadership of change agendas, a strengths-based approach provides both an ideological basis as well as practical means by which to decolonize knowledge. A Pacific leader, Setareki Macanawai, interviewed for this book illustrated this when he said, 'A strengths-based approach is particularly relevant to former colonized countries, where the cultural assets were largely ignored or portrayed as a weakness not a strength. The approach contrasts this, by focusing on what countries have, and often their cultural values are central.'

Many authors who write on decolonization (Gronemeyer, 1992; Shiva, 1997; Henkel and Stirrat, 2001; Kothari, 2005; Escobar, 2007) have made the case that power is vested in knowledge and those who control knowledge have power. Within a strengths-based approach, power is inherently vested in actors in each context where change is expected or sought. A strengths-based approach assumes the power and potential of local knowledge to inform preferred futures decided by local actors. The concept of power for a strengths-based approach is addressed further in Chapter 5.

A strengths-based approach counters the dominance of external knowledge and prioritizes the importance of knowledge within each context. Local values, perspectives, and actions are at the forefront of a strengths-based approach. It is through the prioritization of local perspectives and agendas that an externally derived universal vision of the future and linear path to development is countered.

A strengths-based approach includes processes which enable multiple types of knowledge to be expressed and valued. A strengths-based approach includes an inherent appreciation of cultural values and information relevant to each context. It makes possible a move towards intercultural communication and genuine exchanges of experiences. This means that people whose lives are affected by development are central to discussions and decision-making processes, and people are empowered to lead their development from within their own context. Chapter 6 addresses the cultural relevance of a strengths-based approach. We explore knowledge within a strengths-based approach throughout the book, including through an exploration of power in Chapter 5, as well as the role of the development worker in Chapter 8.

Complexity

Complexity is another key concept central to contemporary thinking and practice of international development, which aligns with and is a useful way to describe how change happens within a strengths-based approach.

For many decades the change process within development was taken for granted and the view that there could be different types of change processes was largely ignored. Since the 2000s, notions of different types of change emerged in development discourse, including the notion of complexity.

The idea that changes can be 'simple, complicated or complex' can be used to distinguish between different organizing properties, situations or systems and types of change in international development. The typology is described in slightly different ways by various authors as they emphasize particular characteristics to make a distinction between the three. Patton (2011) drew on the earlier work of Zimmerman et al. (1998) to emphasize a distinction in terms of 'the extent to which cause and effect is or can be known' (p. 92). In simple interventions, cause and effect are known, so interventions and their consequences are highly predictable and controllable. In complicated interventions, cause and effect are knowable over time. The presence of a large number of variables makes prediction and control difficult. In complex interventions, cause and effect are unknown and unknowable until after the effect has emerged (Patton, 2011). Complexity thinking is a way of understanding how elements of systems interact and change over time, often leading to the emergence of unpredictable outcomes. Complexity thinking has applications in a range of fields such as ecology, biology, economics, physics, and some fields of social studies.

Donald Rumsfeld, former United States Secretary of Defense in 2002 infamously described complexity thinking in a press briefing which won him the 2003 'Foot in Mouth' award from the Plain English Campaign:

> Reports that say that something hasn't happened are always interesting to me, because as we know, there are known knowns; there are things

we know we know. We also know there are known unknowns; that is to say we know there are some things we do not know. But there are also unknown unknowns – the ones we don't know we don't know.

In his convoluted statement, Rumsfeld described the difference between simple (known knowns), complicated (known unknowns), and complex (unknown unknowns) situations. Another common way to describe the difference is: baking a cake is simple; sending a rocket to the moon is complicated, and raising a child is complex (Table 1.1).

International development has predominantly been informed by a 'simple' perspective on how change happens. It emerged from the tradition of project management for engineering projects and has been applied to all other forms of activity including social change. This style of management emphasizes control and prediction, rather than recognizing that the real world is infinitely more unpredictable, with endless variables that cannot be controlled. It is erroneous to think development processes can be planned and controlled. It is also unethical to think that people can be controlled and change predicted on their behalf. A strengths-based approach aligns with understanding about the complexity of contexts in which development and change processes occur.

Complexity thinking has been applied by several authors who use it to both describe and inform international development. For example, Ramalingam (2013), Burns and Worsley (2015), and Boulton et al. (2015) all discuss this phenomenon. Ramalingam (2013) cites Positive Deviance (see Chapter 3) as 'the way aid could work', informed by the framework of complexity thinking.

Table 1.1 Simple, complicated, complex

Simple	Complicated	Complex
Baking a cake	Sending a rocket to the moon	Raising a child
The recipe is essential	Formulae are critical and necessary	Formulae have limited application
Recipes are tested to assure easy replication	Sending one rocket increases assurance that the next will be OK	Raising one child provides experience but no assurance of success with the next
No particular expertise is required. But cooking expertise increases success rate	High levels of expertise in a variety of fields are necessary for success	Expertise can contribute but is neither necessary or sufficient to assure success
Recipes produce standardized products	Rockets are similar in critical ways	Every child is unique and must be understood as an individual
The best recipes give good results every time	There is a high degree of certainty of outcome	Uncertainty of outcome remains
Optimistic approach to problem possible	Optimistic approach to problem possible	Optimistic approach to problem possible

Source: Glouberman and Zimmerman, 2002

A strengths-based approach aligns with and fulfils the agenda of complexity thinking. It acknowledges that we can start a process but cannot know the outcome. We cannot predict and control a situation if all the parts move and shift in their own direction. Complexity thinking recognizes that once a person, group, community, organization or institution engages in a change process, the situation changes, to inform a new inquiry and change process. We explore this notion of how change happens further in Chapter 4.

Trajectory towards a strengths-based approach

In this book we advocate for an exclusive focus on strengths, assets, and what is working well, to fuel change and development outcomes, rather than a mixed approach. A strengths-based approach is often implied within a balanced inquiry of strengths and weaknesses, for example through a SWOT analysis (strengths-weaknesses-opportunities-threats). The authors and other development workers cited in this book have used balanced approaches as well as approaches which are exclusively strengths-based. An exclusive focus might be controversial for some or confusing for others, but our intention is to provide clarity on thinking and practice of a strengths-based approach. Our intentional focus is informed by evidence of the value of an exclusive inquiry on the positive as a means for catalysing change.

The implications of an exclusive (rather than balanced) focus on strengths are significant. At the strategic level, international programming will not begin with an external analysis of problems and weaknesses through a foreigner's lens, but of strengths and assets from the perspective of the people whose lives and institutions are changing. At the planning level, programmes will define changes sought (e.g. objectives, outcomes, results) to reflect the desires and expectations of those whose lives and organizations will change. At the level of development processes, partnerships, and monitoring, discussions will focus on what is working well and how to best achieve intended changes as people achieve change themselves, collaborate, and learn more. An exclusive strengths-based approach situates power and control and motivation to those at the centre of the change agenda. As described in other parts of this book, the alternative of defining needs and deficits is to label, stigmatize, and demotivate those at the centre of development.

We recognize there is a variety of approaches in the development sector which share a trajectory towards a strengths-based approach and give further insights into what is and is not a strengths-based approach. Below, we explain why some approaches, such as the sustainable livelihoods approach and generic participatory approaches, are not necessarily strengths-based, even though they share some features. We also consider the implications of such a categorization.

Figure 1.2 provides a summary of waves of international development practice over many decades since the term development was first used in the post-World

WHY A STRENGTHS-BASED APPROACH IN INTERNATIONAL DEVELOPMENT?   17

Overseas development assistance to governments for infrastructure development.

Neo liberalism agenda - dominated by the World Bank and IMF – focus on structural adjustment and the shrinking of government and the public service.

Sustainable Development Goals 2015 – 2030

Millennium Development Goals 2000 – 2015

Use of the term international 'development' Truman **1949**

Focus on 'poverty agenda' and rise of the role of NGOs

A 'poverty agenda' dominates inclusive of the 'Make Poverty History campaign' - 2005

| 1940s | 1950s | 1960s | 1970s | 1980s | 1990s | 2000s | 2010s | 2020s |

Foresight – futures studies – multiple authors from 18th century to today

Co-production
Elinor Ostrom - 1978

Participatory rural appraisal (PRA)
Robert Chambers - 1984

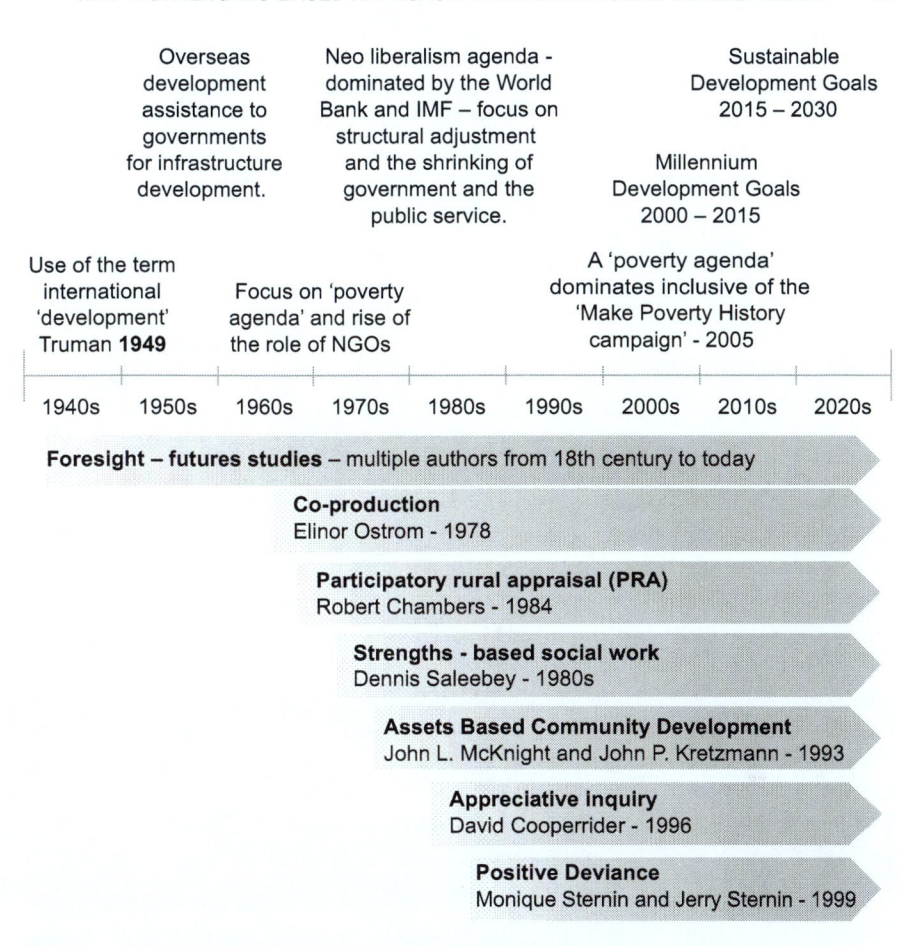

Strengths - based social work
Dennis Saleebey - 1980s

Assets Based Community Development
John L. McKnight and John P. Kretzmann - 1993

Appreciative inquiry
David Cooperrider - 1996

Positive Deviance
Monique Sternin and Jerry Sternin - 1999

Figure 1.2 The movement of strengths-based practice in international development

War II period, highlighting changes in discourse and practice, trajectory towards a strengths-based approach, and a variety of strengths-based practices. The text along the top of the figure summarizes major types and periods of discourse and practice which have influenced development. The text below the timeline indicates different types of strengths-based practices that have developed in different fields of practice and are introduced in Chapter 3.

Participatory approaches

The notion of participation has evolved within development discourse and practice: participatory approaches are now a core feature. Robert Chambers' (1997) seminal work *Whose Reality Counts? Putting the First Last* championed a new development practice, describing participatory rural appraisal as a means for professionals to 'hand over the stick' to invite local knowledge to inform and shape development programmes.

While participatory approaches focus on people at the centre of their own development and premise capacity and agency of individuals and communities to inform their own future, the overarching inquiry is often still framed through a deficit perspective. For example, numerous participatory methods informed by participatory rural appraisal include the identification of needs to be addressed through a development programme or project. Community members are facilitated through various methods to identify issues, problems, or needs in their communities. This information is then used to design and plan a development initiative. As discussed above and throughout this book, the negative framing of a context or situation can have harmful consequences.

Sustainable livelihoods approach (SLA)

The concept of sustainable livelihoods evolved from the work of Robert Chambers and others in the 1980s in the context of participatory approaches. The sustainable livelihoods approach (SLA) was introduced in the early 1990s, with a focus on using stronger assets – or 'capital' – as a way to address weaker assets or deficiencies that could lead to poverty and dependence. In the late 1990s, the UK Department for International Development, assisted by the UK Institute for Development Studies, developed the concepts into a specific approach to development. Organizations such as United Nations Development Programme (UNDP), CARE (USA), Oxfam (UK), and Canada's International Institute for Sustainable Development were pioneers in using this approach. While assets are emphasized in SLA, the approach is underpinned by a deficit perspective as described in guidance:

> The framework depicts stakeholders as operating in a context of vulnerability, within which they have access to certain assets. Assets gain weight and value through the prevailing social, institutional and organizational environment (policies, institutions and processes). This context decisively shapes the livelihood strategies that are open to people in pursuit of their self-defined beneficial livelihood outcomes (Kollmair and Gamper, 2002: 4–5).

SLA was also one of the first international development approaches to deliberately identify categories that could be used to document an inventory of assets. Building on strengths is included within its core principles:

> Building on strengths: A central issue of the approach is the recognition of everyone's inherent potential for his/her removal of constraints and realisation of potentials. Identifying these strengths rather than the needs and problems is the starting point of this approach, in order to contribute to the stakeholders' robustness and ability to achieve their own objectives (Kollmair and Gamper, 2002: 4).

The SLA is underpinned by core principles which align with a strengths-based approach, such as identifying existing assets and building on these 'strengths'; it is 'people-centred', 'holistic', and 'dynamic' but it also has a focus on exposing vulnerability. It is not defined as a strengths-based approach in this book, but rather a balanced inquiry and approach. It has a focus on the vulnerability context including 'shocks, trends, seasonality' which may surface negative drivers to change. In contrast to the SLA, which focuses inquiry on the past, a strengths-based approach is future-orientated and focuses inquiry and action towards preferred futures and visions for change. This future orientation also aligns with futures or foresight thinking explained in Chapter 3.

The importance of a strengths-based approach – now and beyond

As noted in the Preface, with a rapidly changing world and more complex challenges emerging, there is an opportunity to apply a strengths-based approach widely. COVID-19 has revealed and exacerbated existing inequality and injustice within and between countries. The pandemic has stretched health systems and tested political options to manage economic and health indicators. With unexpected, increased, and more complex challenges to social justice emerging in many corners of the world, there is a need for effective, adaptable new approaches. More than ever, a strengths-based approach provides a means to address the many critical challenges, and signs of its potential are clear in the many stories collated for this book.

A key message in this book is that a strengths-based approach does not deny inequalities, injustices, and problems: it offers an alternative perspective on how these issues can be addressed. It seeks to address these through an orientation and focus on action towards preferred futures, rather than defining needs, problem-solving, and filling gaps.

A strengths-based approach seeks to elevate the potential and power of ordinary people to contribute and be part of transformative futures. Barack Obama in his book *A Promised Land* wrote about how ordinary people can and do transform their own futures and the potential for change. He wrote:

> I saw the possibility of practicing the values my mother had taught me; how you could build power not by putting others down but by lifting them up. This was true democracy at work – democracy not as a gift from on high, or a division of spoils between interest groups, but rather democracy that was earned, the work of everybody. The result was not just a change in material conditions, but a sense of dignity for people and communities, a bond between those who had once seemed far apart (Obama, 2020: 11).

Case Study 1 Strengths-based approaches are the way of the future

Jayne Curnow was the Social Science and Research Program Manager at Australian Centre for International Agricultural Research (ACIAR). Here she reflects on her role at ACIAR and use of a strengths-based approach.

1. Do you recall how you came across a strengths-based approach?

   Following on from project management roles in Timor-Leste a friend told me about a PhD scholarship to conduct applied research on a different approach to development practice being offered at Australian National University. In the field I had found there was quite a bit of rhetoric about social capital but little practical guidance on how to marshal this for people-centred development. The scholarship was tied to a project which addressed what I had been looking for in the field. As part of an Australian Research Council Linkage Grant, the research was to trial a strengths-based approach to Community Economies in Southeast Asia. I joined a team at the Australian National University Research School of Pacific and Asian Studies (now Crawford School) led by Professor Katherine Gibson. The project offered an opportunity to answer the questions I was asking at the time such as:

   - How do you empower people to drive development?
   - How do we share power to define the aim and approach to development?
   - How can the design of development projects acknowledge that the community often has the know-how?
   - What is the best approach to supporting people to make their own decisions?

   My PhD analysed Asset-Based Community Development (ABCD) in the context of the diverse economy in Flores, Indonesia.

2. Do you mainly use a particular tool within a strengths-based approach framework? If so, how do you locate that with other approaches?

   ACIAR is an agricultural research for development donor agency, a statutory authority in DFAT. At ACIAR my role was less applied and more strategic. I worked to influence and direct project designs away from deficit thinking and leverage changes that are more focused on strengths-based approaches.

   In the social sciences portfolio, there are three projects that exemplify the use of strengths-based approaches at ACIAR. These are:

   - Improving the methods and impacts of agricultural extension in conflict-affected zones of Mindanao, Philippines. The improved method of extension works through Landcare to apply ABCD in engagement with farming communities to introduce different agricultural practices and diversify incomes.
   - Family Farm Teams (FFT), which improves opportunities for economic development for women and men smallholders in rural Papua New Guinea. The Appreciative Inquiry and Asset-Based Community Development approaches engage the whole family to work more equitably and effectively. This successful approach is improving livelihoods drawing

(Continued)

Case Study 1 Continued

        especially on local knowledge and multiple, diverse use of social and physical assets.
- Improving agricultural development opportunities for smallholders in rural Solomon Islands. This draws on the FFT success in Papua New Guinea and applies the same approach to another Melanesian context.

The tools used in all of these, and forthcoming projects are a combination of Appreciative Inquiry to value local success and create shared visions of what the future might be, and ABCD to engage local people in identifying, mapping, and mobilizing available assets to bring about productive change.

3. What is it about a strengths-based approach that you have found helpful, positive or useful?
All the projects that are using strengths-based approaches are working really well and there is a lot of excitement about the results. I like how the use of strengths-based approaches enables transformation in gender relations, not by imposing or forcing ideas, but by revealing gender inequity through a process of discovery. Strengths-based approaches are the way of the future because they engage more directly with communities, share decision-making power, and are more fitting for establishing the sorts of partnerships we want to foster.

4. What differences are made by a strengths-based approach, that you think contrast them with other approaches?
The Family Farms Team project is into a third generation and we are now commissioning research on the same approach in the Solomon Islands. We continue to commission and expand this applied research because we can see the success of what is happening. It provides us with an assurance that ACIAR commissioned research is beneficial for the community now and into the future. It creates genuine partnership in learning within the communities themselves. In contrast to other approaches, it invites more active, equitable participation.

5. Where do you think a strengths-based approach fits best in the world of international development?
I would say I am a true believer in strengths-based approaches having experienced many 'ah-ha' moments both in the field and in commissioning research. Although it is still not the dominant paradigm, it is the most effective approach to international development that I have seen to date.

6. What reactions do you get from others when you apply a strengths-based approach?
Through regular communication and collaboration with my colleagues and many university research teams there is a growing appreciation of the value of a strengths-based approach and how to build this into ACIAR commissioned research projects. I enjoy seeing others have their 'ah-ha' moments. The challenge is conveying that this is a particular philosophy of development, not just a way to structure an activity log frame.

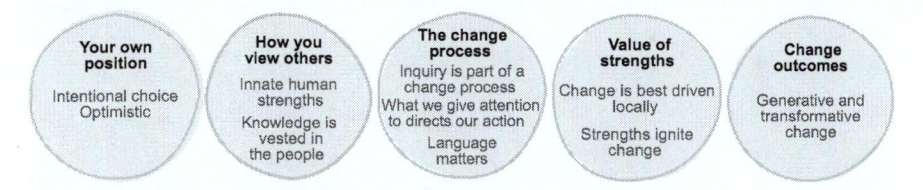

CHAPTER 2
Philosophical underpinnings of a strengths-based approach

The power of a strengths-based approach is in the philosophy as much as the tools. People could use the tools without understanding the philosophy, but it won't have the same effect (Dr Ian Cunningham)

Values underpinning a strengths-based approach

A strengths-based approach is not simply a set of activities to carry out or a tool to employ, but a way of viewing the world and considering one's own position in relation to others. Taking a strengths-based approach encompasses a way of 'being' just as much as a way of 'doing'. This chapter draws on literature related to strengths-based practice and international development discourse to set out the philosophical underpinnings of a strengths-based approach.

Many markers of a strengths-based approach can be identified in international development practice itself (as explored in the previous chapter), in strengths-based practice (explored in the next chapter), and in multiple philosophical views. A strengths-based approach for international development draws on this existing theory and practice and weaves them together to provide a coherent paradigm or model. Figure 2.1 sets out the fundamental beliefs or values which underpin a strengths-based approach and are detailed below.

Your own position	How you view others	The change process	Value of strengths	Change outcomes
Intentional choice Optimistic	Innate human strengths Knowledge is vested in the people	Inquiry is part of a change process What we give attention to directs our action Language matters	Change is best driven locally Strengths ignite change	Generative and transformative change

Figure 2.1 Philosophical underpinnings of a strengths-based approach

For those interested in philosophical terminology, a strengths-based change process is informed by a foundation of beliefs or values which include one's own view of the world; how one views others (ontological position); how inquiry is understood; and how knowledge is used (epistemological view). These beliefs provide the basis of how change is understood to happen within a strengths-based approach which is explored in more detail in Chapter 4. They also inform the philosophical underpinnings set out in this chapter.

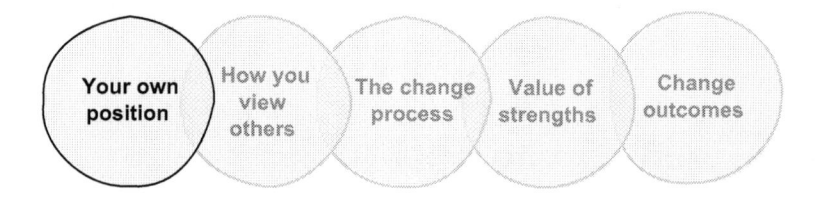

Intentional choice

A strengths-based approach requires acceptance that there can be different ways one can see the world. This is the starting point of a strengths-based approach and while it is easily accepted for some, an alternative to problem-solving perspectives might be unsettling for others. A metaphor commonly used to describe a strengths-based approach presents this choice: to see a glass half-empty or to see that same glass half-full, illustrated in Figure 2.2. When this analogy is applied to international development, one's perspective is framed to see the local context as either empty or lacking (problems to be solved, needs to be fulfilled, weaknesses to be fixed) or occupied (with strengths, assets, and resources), which provides the starting point from which to ignite positive change.

To take a strengths-based approach is to make an intentional choice. As Kretzmann and McKnight (1993: 1) described, there are 'two divergent paths' to creating change: 'to focus on a community's needs, deficiencies and problems' or to 'begin with a clear commitment to discovering a community's capacity and assets'. Kretzmann and McKnight (1993) initiated Asset-Based Community Development (ABCD), a strengths-based practice detailed in the next chapter. Proponents of a strengths-based approach argue that individually and collectively we have a choice about what to focus on in order to inform change, as illustrated in Figure 2.3, and that this focus has serious implications for the quality of change outcomes achieved.

A strengths-based approach intentionally seeks out what is working well, to reveal existing strengths, assets, or resources as a means to generate desired change.

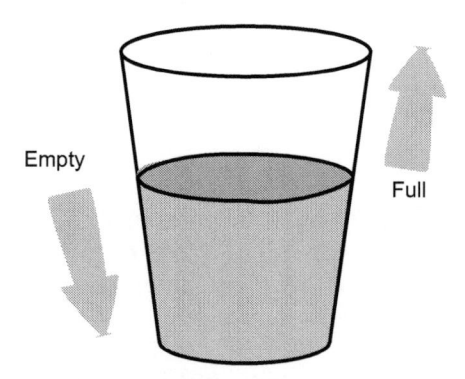

Figure 2.2 Glass half-empty or glass half-full

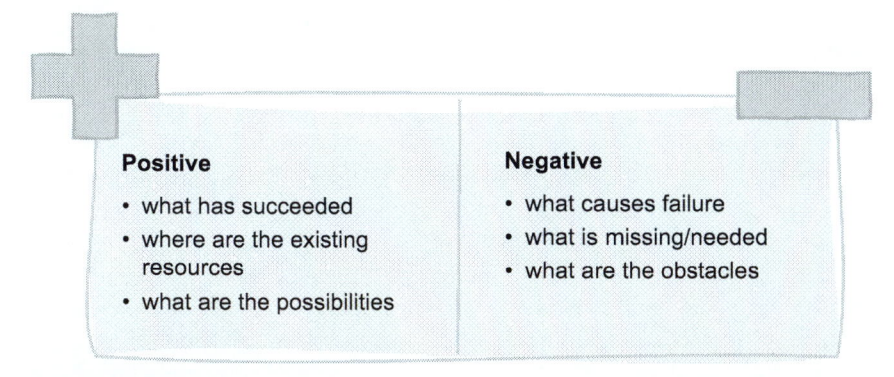

PHILOSOPHICAL UNDERPINNINGS OF A STRENGTHS-BASED APPROACH

Positive
- what has succeeded
- where are the existing resources
- what are the possibilities

Negative
- what causes failure
- what is missing/needed
- what are the obstacles

Figure 2.3 A choice to make

Optimistic

The strengths-based approach requires an optimistic stance. Saleebey (2009), who wrote about strengths-based social work, described in the next chapter, best summarizes this:

> No matter how subordinated, marginalized, and oppressed individuals and communities may appear, people individually and collectively, can find nourishment for their hopes and dreams, tools for their realisation somewhere. These tools may be damaged, hidden, or out of circulation, but whatever their condition, they are awaiting discovery and/or expression (Saleebey, 2009: 284).

An optimistic view of the world advocates that constructive change towards a more preferred, better, and positive future is possible. When people choose to accept the possibility of a positive and desirable future, their actions are drawn to making this a reality (Zander and Zander, 2000). An optimist views the potential of change through the practice of a strengths-based approach. As discussed in this book, a strengths-based approach does not deny problems or challenges of individuals, groups, or communities, but proposes the best way to achieve change is through catalysing strengths and identifying preferred futures.

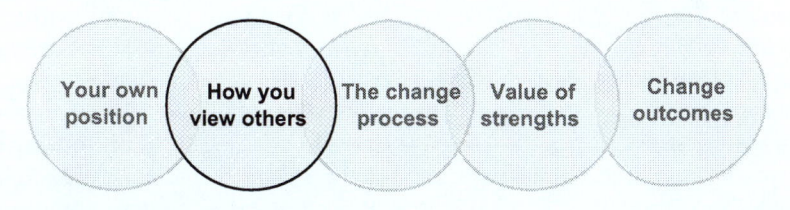

Your own position — **How you view others** — The change process — Value of strengths — Change outcomes

Innate human and contextual strengths

A fundamental belief of a strengths-based approach is that every individual has innate capacities, characteristics, and life experiences that can contribute to creating change for themselves or others. We assume there are strengths, assets, resources to reveal in any context. It is assumed that something is good and working, which can be drawn upon to catalyse change. This can be described as a 'consciousness' orientated towards valuing the presence of strengths (Bushe, 2001; Cooperrider and Whitney, 2007).

The term 'strengths' is used to describe a broad range of positive attributes within any given context. At the individual level, strengths are assumed to be intrinsic to every human being: 'people have credible, though often untapped or unknown resources for transformation and development' (Saleebey, 1992: 176). Strengths are described as the talents, resources, desires, and aspirations within each individual and are drawn from 'physical, emotional, cognitive, interpersonal, social and spiritual energies, resources and competencies' of each individual (Saleebey, 1992: 6). Some describe the inherent human qualities as 'the giftedness of every individual' (Kretzmann and McKnight, 1993: 6). Strengths also encompass 'what works well' with a recognition that 'these strengths can be the starting point for creating positive change' (Cooperrider et al., 2008: 3). Strengths are also embedded in spiritual values and norms that help a society consider what is good and how they move towards a desirable future.

At the level of groups, teams, organizations, sectors, and networks, a strengths-based approach also assumes there are always existing or previous strengths, assets or qualities. This is of particular interest in international development, since programming largely addresses change at these levels. For example, a group or team will have various human resource strengths, collective experience, prior successes, or access to other forms of support. Organizations and networks will also have a mix of assets, experiences, abilities, or other strengths, which can form the basis for future effort. An organization's strengths can include a wide range of elements, from leaders and values to physical infrastructure natural resources, or relationships.

It is assumed that strengths are representative of the innate power within individuals, groups, societies, and institutions. For example, strengths-based social work practitioners speak about the value of strengths. They note a strengths perspective is not based on 'returning power to the people, but on discovering the power within people individually and collectively' (Saleebey, 1992: 8). Similarly, Paulo Freire's (1970) seminal work, *Pedagogy of the Oppressed*, which focuses on educational theory, refers to innate strengths within all individuals. He critiques the 'banking form' of education where knowledge is deposited into empty, passive students and teachers are deemed to be the sole owners of knowledge, and pre-existing knowledge is ignored. His alternative is to view students with prior knowledge that can be capitalized on for learning outcomes. This same belief is shared by a strengths-based approach and provides the foundation and basis on which all practices are structured.

Knowledge vested in people

A strengths-based approach premises knowledge of those individuals who are situated in the change process, in contrast to prioritizing external expert opinion. The approach values the knowledge of those closest to each context who know the past and can best articulate aspirations for and potential of the future. It is in this context that the renowned African anthropologist and linguist, Harold C. Fleming, once famously stated: 'The wisdom of the community always exceeds the knowledge of the experts'.

Within international development, there is an array of different and often contradictory perspectives on whose knowledge counts or whose knowledge is intentionally heard and informs decision-making. Robert Chambers (1997) formulated participatory rural appraisal approaches in response to questions about whose knowledge counts. Critiques of participation since the 2000s, such as Cooke and Kothari (2001) and Hickey and Mohan (2005), continue to question the practice of participatory development and the extent to which these practices have indeed shifted the basis of knowledge in international development. They contend that knowledge is still held by dominant institutions and organizations such as donors and international NGOs. For example, this is evident in the Organisation for Economic Co-operation and Development Development Assistance Committee (OECD DAC) quality standards for development evaluation. The standards describe evaluations as best carried out by evaluators 'independent from the development intervention, including its policy, operations and management function, as well as intended beneficiaries' (OECD, 2010: 11). Knowledge of local actors is not prioritized in these quality evaluation standards. This issue is explored more in Chapter 10.

A strengths-based approach views knowledge as constructed through human interactions. For example, Appreciative Inquiry, underpinned by a strengths perspective (explored in more detail in the next chapter) defines social constructionism as a core philosophical foundation. Social constructionism views social knowledge as not 'out there in nature to be discovered through detached value-free observational methods' but rather, 'created, maintained and put to use by the human group' (Cooperrider et al., 2008: 15). Valuing of context-specific knowledge respects processes through which knowledge is formed, created, and re-created. The value of local knowledge also premises and informs the potential for locally led change.

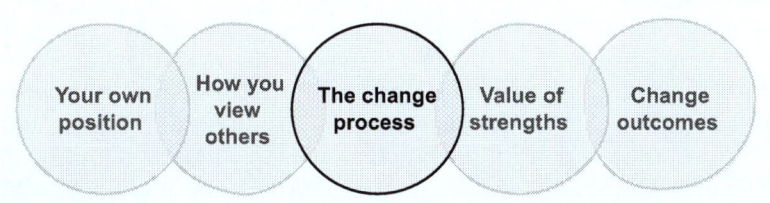

Your own position | How you view others | **The change process** | Value of strengths | Change outcomes

Language matters

A strengths-based approach uses language intentionally, recognizing that words shape understanding of the world. It considers that questions asked inform answers given, what will be learned about the past, and what guides people to the future. This view is informed by social constructionism, which, as noted above, recognizes that reality is shared by meaning and understandings of words and language gained through collective, group, and relational processes (Gergen, 1982, 1999, 2009; Burr, 1995; Schwandt, 2000). As expressed by McNamee and Gergen (1999: xi), 'meaningful language is generated within processes of relationship'.

Proponents of a strengths-based approach argue that an inquiry which is informed by deficit-based language has a detrimental effect on creating change. This view is expressed by Saleebey (2009: 9) who confirms 'language and words have power. They can elevate and inspire or demoralize and destroy'. The choice of language is a key theme of a strengths-based approach, referenced throughout this book.

Inquiry is part of the change process

A strengths-based approach considers that the moment we ask a question, we are engaging in a change process. If we accept that language matters and shapes the world we live in, then the inquiry and the type of questions we ask inform the change process. Concerned with how meaning and knowledge are created through language, a strengths-based approach is underpinned by the view that the 'questions we ask largely determine what we find' (Cooperrider and Srivastva, 1987: 164). If we ask an individual or group to share problems or needs, then that is what we will learn about. If we are seeking to offer potential for transformative change, then we need to intentionally ask questions that invite that potential. We need to ask questions that value and give momentum to the type of change sought.

What we give attention to directs our action

A strengths-based approach recognizes that people move in the direction to which they give attention. Recognizing that the questions we ask will determine what we find, and potentially what action we might take, questions within a strengths-based approach are purposively framed to enable the creation of a positive image of the future and to foster action towards achieving this change.

The phenomenon of focusing attention on a particular direction is not simply a belief system, but informed by scientific evidence known as the Pygmalion effect. This describes the phenomenon of how individuals' actions and the reality constructed can be influenced by expectations, projections, and images. For example, studies by Rosenthal and Jacobson (1992) showed this effect within a classroom setting. At the start of their study, they told teachers that a certain cohort of students were expected to be 'intellectual bloomers', yet these students were all randomly chosen with no particular difference from other students. At the end of the study, these students out-performed others in the class. Teachers' expectations of

PHILOSOPHICAL UNDERPINNINGS OF A STRENGTHS-BASED APPROACH   29

Figure 2.4 Heliotropic effect

these students had projected onto the students, and they had performed in line with the image they had of themselves, as supported by the teachers' views. Applied in the international development context, a strengths-based approach can inspire and motivate action, informed by individuals', groups' or communities' images of themselves and their aspirations for the future.

The heliotropic effect (Figure 2.4) is used by Appreciative Inquiry theorists to describe this effect of moving in the direction to which we give attention. This effect describes the ability of plants to grow towards light and is employed to explain the value of inquiry focused on exploring strengths and positive images of the future for groups to work towards (Cooperrider, 1990; Bushe, 2001; Rogers and Fraser, 2003; Whitney and Trosten-Bloom, 2003). The focus on what is working well, and the vision of a preferred future, direct attention and action towards positive change.

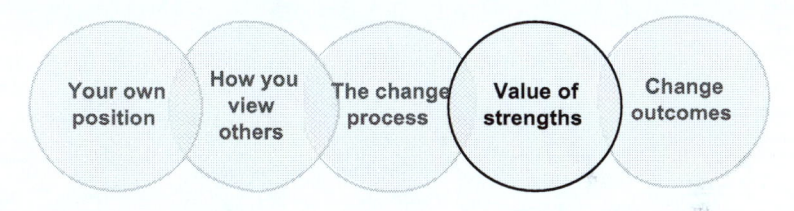

Your own position | How you view others | The change process | **Value of strengths** | Change outcomes

Strengths ignite change

In a strengths-based approach, innate strengths within each and every individual and context are the catalyst to effect change. A strengths-based approach intentionally seeks to reveal current and past strengths as fuel to realize the future potential of change. Questions are focused to reveal the positive in any given situation. A strengths-based approach seeks to reveal, elevate, and use or ignite these strengths to power change. Depending on the context, strengths are connected together to maximize potential for change. Strengths within a community, group, organization, or network/sector can be connected together to complement and leverage with others.

Past success also provides the energy for future change. When people become aware of their own past successes, they can find both the energy and motivation to make future changes.

As presented in latter parts of the book, the view that change creation is best enabled by revealing strengths is substantiated by other fields. For example, the value of encouraging motivation through identifying strengths is evident through positive psychology research (see Chapter 7). The contrasting practice and outcomes associated with identifying problems which reveal faults, and often create divisions between those who could work together to create change, are explored below.

Change is best driven locally

A strengths-based approach believes that change is best driven by those at the centre of the change agenda. This includes a few elements. First, since individuals, groups, or organizations are best equipped to know the change they seek, they can decide the direction they wish to follow. Second, individuals and their peers know their own strengths, and these are informed by their own local values. Third, drawing from these local strengths, change happens at the centre closer to those involved, and extends outward to gain contributions from others in widening and broadening concentric circles. Linked to this point, change is driven by individuals themselves who are the experts in determining change priorities and the best ways to achieve these changes. People at the centre draw on additional resources from external actors to achieve priorities, defined within the specific context. Involving multiple stakeholders in the change agenda can bring about systems-level change, whereby all relevant stakeholders are engaged in inquiry and relevant assets are drawn upon to catalyse change.

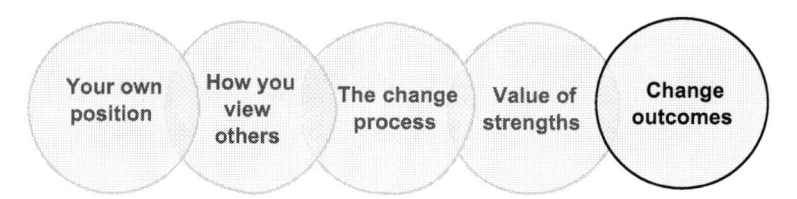

Your own position | How you view others | The change process | Value of strengths | Change outcomes

Generative change towards a preferred future

A strengths-based approach values generative and transformative change, rather than being solely focused on solving current or previous problems. It does this by seeking to express alternative and preferred futures. Several authors have likened the difference between a problem-solving approach and a strengths-based approach to looking into a car's rear-view mirror to solve the problems of the past, rather than looking to the open road ahead to see the possibility and vision of a transformed future (Figure 2.5).

Figure 2.5 Rear view into the past

Generative change is focused on challenging the status quo and assumptions which underpin the status quo. It involves the 'capacity to challenge the guiding assumptions of the culture, to raise fundamental questions regarding contemporary social life, to foster reconsideration of that which is "taken for granted" and thereby provide new alternatives for social actions' (Gergen, 1978: 1346). Schön (1979: 138) similarly described generativity as 'nothing less than how we come to see things in new ways'. A strengths-based approach purposively structures inquiry and action to foster generative change. The approach seeks to enable questioning of that which is taken for granted, to see the world anew and inspire alternative futures. Bushe (2013: 89) described generativity 'as the creation of new images, metaphors, physical representations, and so on, that have two qualities: they change how people think so that new options for decisions and/or actions become available to them, and they are compelling images that people want to act on'. Notions of generative and transformative change are explored in further detail in Chapters 3 and 4.

These philosophical underpinnings presented in this chapter have informed practical action by the authors and also many development workers interviewed for this book. For example, Casterns Mulume, Director of Social Development for Episcopal Conference of Malawi, and with extensive experience in non-governmental organizations, explained why he was convinced to use a strengths-based approach in all internationally funded activities across the whole country:

> For me the change to a strengths-based approach was not just about another way of doing development, but a completely different mindset, a radically different concept – a new way of life for us as an agency and for the communities we worked with.
>
> The use of locally available resources, the turnaround in people's thinking about their role in development activities and the visioning were so radically different from traditional approaches.
>
> I became convinced by the enormous increase in stakeholder involvement, the extent and intensity of the linkages that were created, the

advocacy opportunities that opened up for the people themselves and all this led to a much stronger sense of ownership of both the process and the objectives. And in the end, these were the only projects that continued well beyond the inputs we provided. This continuity represents sustainability, the end goal of any development activity.

As a reaction to and critique of deficit-based change

The beliefs or values which underpin a strengths-based approach can be seen in contrast with deficit-based perspectives. Strengths-based practices have emerged as a reaction to processes which attempt to create change by identifying and solving problems, deficits, and weaknesses within individuals, communities, and organizations. Exploring the critique and reaction to the deficit-based perspective offers further insights into the fundamental beliefs or values which underpin a strengths-based approach. Common concerns about deficit-based change described in the literature are also echoed by the many international development workers interviewed for this book.

Deficit-focused inquiries create negative mental images or labels

Through a deficit-based inquiry, the individual, organization, or community in effect becomes the problem to be solved. This can be demoralizing and demotivating as part of a change creation process. This concern is raised by authors describing different strengths-based practices. Saleebey (1992: 3) writing on strengths-based social work suggests that 'the diction and symbolism of weakness, failure and deficit shape how others regard clients and how clients regard themselves'. Likewise, Kretzmann and McKnight (1993) writing in relation to Asset-Based Community Development argue that through needs mapping, communities 'begin to see themselves as people with special needs that can only be met by outsiders' (p. 2). The focus of a strengths-based approach on values such as 'language matters' and also 'inquiry as part of a change process' are key responses to the concern about negative mental images or labels as a consequence of deficit-focused inquires.

Many development workers interviewed for this book also raised concerns about the way in which a deficit-based approach creates negative mental images for individuals, groups, and communities. For example, commenting on programmes in the Philippines, Lina Magallanas, International Program Manager for Anglican Board of Mission, compared strengths-based and deficits-based approaches and their consequences:

> The key difference to a traditional aid program is the way this approach changes the idea of agency and ownership. With Asset-Based Community Development (ABCD) [explored in Chapter 3], the participants understand that they have resources, they have their own plan, and they are leading

the process. If a course of action or a focus on a particular activity emerges from the initial discussions, they know and we know that it has come from them, not from outside.

This is achieved probably more than anything else when they realize they have gifts (of the head, hands, heart) and when they start to map their available assets and describe themselves as asset rich.

Before they would say: 'We are poor: we can't do anything ourselves' but after asset-mapping, they realize that they cannot have that image of themselves. They are now enabled and have the resources to at least get started.

Another development worker, Ian Cunningham, reflected: 'a deficit approach is very de-motivating: it often focuses on incremental problem solving and doesn't take us very far. When I train volunteer engineers, I often show them an assets map and deficits map and get them to notice how the two make them feel inside. There is a palpable difference in the mood in the room in response to the two maps'.

Moncrieffe (2006) similarly wrote about the negative consequences of labels:

We inevitably make assumptions about individuals and categorize and label them based on our own socially acquired preferences and perceptions and/or based on the (mis)information we obtain ... stigmatized individuals and groups are often so discredited – 'reduced in our minds from whole and usual persons to tainted, discounted ones' (Goffman 1963: 12) – that they are excluded from the spaces that would allow for encounters and from real opportunities to contest. Notably, persons who accept or feel unable to confront the stigma may opt to exclude themselves (Moncrieffe, 2006: 38).

Deficit-focused inquiries create a distorted view

Negative images of individuals and communities generated through deficit-based inquiry commonly become the whole truth rather than being seen as only part of a total picture. This focus can skew perspectives and priorities, limiting potential for local agendas to surface and local action to be motivated for change. Sullivan and Rapp (2009), who wrote about strengths-based social work, suggested within a deficit-based approach there is an 'overemphasis on the deficits or toxic elements in the social environment' (p. 222). Kretzmann and McKnight (1993: 2) also raised the concern that 'images of needy, problematic and deficient people often convey part of the truth about actual conditions of a troubled community. But they are not regarded as part of the truth, they are regarded as the whole truth'. A strengths-based approach seeks to counter these concerns by emphasis on valuing 'inquiry as part of a change process' and also that 'we give attention to what directs our action'. By intentionally focusing on strengths and assets within a local context and by visioning a preferred future, a strengths-based approach seeks to draw on local capabilities and resources to direct positive change.

Deficit-focused inquiries create cultures of blame and defensiveness

A strengths-based approach is concerned that deficit approaches can lead to division rather than coalesce people in a change creation process. Deficit-based inquiries can easily create cultures of blame, defensiveness, and the erosion of trust, as people distance themselves from each other and the problem (Whitney and Trosten-Bloom, 2003). Needs assessments create competitiveness rather than cooperation because everyone's needs are primarily their own and with limited resources they must be prioritized and assessed for support. In contrast, an inquiry which is focused on revealing strengths which can be shared, brings multiple strengths together and maximizes them to achieve future visions. Defensive positions can act as barriers to learning and thinking about ways to act. A strengths-based approach alternatively provides opportunities to think anew about the world and new alternatives for social action and organization (Barrett and Cooperrider, 1990; Bushe, 1995; Finegold et al., 2002).

Barbara Pamphilon, interviewed for this book, described her view of the negative consequences associated with a needs perspective:

> Sometimes I ask the donor to come along for the journey when explaining the weaknesses of deficit language: 'Think about what you would feel if someone came into your community to do a gap analysis or a needs assessment and then walked away with this information alone. Then compare this with an appreciative approach in which we find a much richer database of what exists and what is possible'.

This chapter introduces fundamental beliefs or values which underpin a strengths-based approach. It describes the positionality and viewpoint of a strengths-based practitioner (who has a choice of inquiry and whether to be optimistic); their view of others (belief in inherent human strengths and that knowledge is vested in collective groups); and interest in a change creation process (where language matters; the inquiry one takes is part of a change process; and the questions we ask direct our future action). A strengths-based approach values the role of strengths in igniting change and locally led processes to lead to generative and transformative change. Beliefs and values of a strengths-based approach were born from a reaction to deficit-based approaches. A strengths-based approach is a way of viewing the world and considering one's own position in relation to others. This mindset is the foundation from which strengths-based processes are enabled. The next chapter introduces strengths-based practices and processes for international development.

CHAPTER 3
What is a strengths-based approach?

> *People feel confident and energized to move into the future when they can bring with them experiences that have given them a sense of pride about their abilities in the past* (Chris Dureau)

In this book, we employ the term 'a strengths-based approach' as an umbrella term to include thinking and practice which premises an inquiry into strengths as a means for catalysing change. In the late 1980s and early 1990s, various practices emerged in parallel in different disciplines including organizational management, community development, social services, education, health, and psychology. These practices responded to common concerns and critiques of deficit-based perspectives and shared a focus on strengths as a means to create change. Since 2000, these ideas have permeated across different fields of practice, and have also been embraced by many academics and international development workers, as illustrated in this book.

This chapter provides an overview of a range of practices with similar characteristics, common processes, or methods which can be defined as core to a strengths-based approach and resonate in international development. Seven established practices have been chosen to demonstrate the range of options: Asset-Based Community Development (ABCD), Appreciative Inquiry, Positive Deviance, Endogenous Development, strengths-based social work, Co-production, and Foresight thinking/Futures Studies. We recognize that these practices are not all equal. Some are based on values which align directly with the strengths-based approach presented in this book. Others, while aligned with the strengths-based approach, have not emerged from a critique of problem-solving approaches. Instead, they emphasize localized ownership of change processes and futures orientation which are at the heart of a strengths-based approach in international development. The broad suite of practices presented in this chapter highlights both the theoretical and practical foundations on which a strengths-based approach for international development sits.

The introduction to these diverse strengths-based practices is intentionally limited as there is a wealth of literature available. Here, we provide an overview and acknowledge sources of each practice, the rich basis from which it has developed, and consider applications to international development. Also, we deliberately avoid the provision of step-by-step guidance for carrying out a strengths-based approach, but offer references and a resource list for the many existing guides (see Websites and training manuals applying strengths-based approaches, before References).

Common processes

Before introducing seven different strengths-based practices, it is useful to identify the processes they have in common. While these elements are not shared consistently across all practices, there is ample similarity and coherence to create a meaningful picture of a strengths-based approach. Different terminology is sometimes used, processes are not necessarily set out in the same specific sequence, and there are subtle distinctions between practices. These processes or methods, while not dominant within the development sector, have been applied in many country and sector contexts. Examples are provided, drawn from experiences of development workers around the world.

As described in Chapter 1, processes within a strengths-based approach do not deny that problems exist or that there are experiences of inequity or social injustice. Rather, they seek to address them by analysing what can be built on or used in any context, and identifying a preferred future and actions to achieve this future. A strengths-based approach explores the factors that individuals and groups value and which shape their world and uses them as levers for change. Change is catalysed by deciding visions and preferences for the future, rather than through an investigation of problems to be fixed. Problems are solved by this approach, as action is orientated towards achieving preferred futures. In effect, problems dissolve as contexts are changed and transformed.

It is of course important to acknowledge individual and collective experiences of problems, challenges, trauma, or inequity within a strengths-based approach. Practices such as Appreciative Inquiry or strengths-based social work described in this chapter recognize the importance of any development worker listening with empathy and concern. However, the focus of inquiry within these practices is not on exploration of the details of the problems in order to create change, but instead to focus on a preferred future and how to achieve this.

Five common processes at the core of a strengths-based approach for international development are listed in Figure 3.1 and described below. Terminology is purposely vague to refer to 'process' since what is described is both a broad suite of actions or activities as well as discrete and specific actions as part of a strengths-based approach. As will become evident, there is no prescription

1	2	3	4	5
Inquiry into the positive	Imagine a preferred future	Collective inquiry and action	Orientated locally	Facilitation only

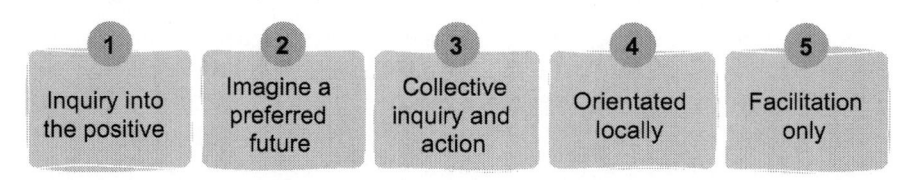

Figure 3.1 Common processes, methods, and tools of a strengths-based approach

or simple recipe to carry out a strengths-based approach. Processes must be considered in and shaped by the context in which they are applied.

1. Inquiry into the positive as the basis for change creation

A village leader in Malaita, the Solomon Islands, cried in front of his people following the session on mapping existing assets. 'For all these many years', he said, 'I have thought we were poor and could not do anything ourselves. But now that I am about to retire, I realize I have not led you well. I now see that we have all these strengths and resources we could have been using but did not. We are not poor. We just did not realize how many things we have already that we could have used to improve ourselves' (Lucas et al., 2016).

Strengths-based practices all include an exclusive focus on revealing strengths, assets, local resources, or what is working well as the basis for creating change. Identification of these elements is achieved through a variety of methods, such as 'appreciative questions', 'asset-mapping' or 'asset-surveys'. These are used for the purpose of 'revealing', 'discovering', 'un-tapping', 'mapping', or 'tracking' strengths as the primary means of creating change. This inquiry is the foundation of a strengths-based approach and is carried out at the start of any initiative.

Importantly, this process is not just about identifying strengths or what is working well, but also understanding enablers of what worked well in the past. These are used to catalyse positive change in the future. In addition, the discovery of these strengths by the participants themselves is a process of self-discovery, confidence-building, and empowerment. Tony Schnell, the Director of the Department for Social Responsibility of the Archdiocese of Grahamstown, Eastern Cape, South Africa has practised a strengths-based approach for many years. He told us:

> For a community to discover its own strengths is no small achievement. It takes time for them to come to the realisation that they actually already possess lots of assets they could be using and it's one of the hardest mindsets changes we help them to come through. We are tempted to rush this process, but it is a mark of our respect for them to go slowly through this with them and repeat it many times over.

2. Imagine a preferred future

A priority concern for a strengths-based approach is creating change towards a preferred and better future. There are several processes and methods to support this. An image of a preferred future provides a generative metaphor that enables individuals and groups to see the world anew and a practical basis to frame action to achieve change in that direction. The notion of seeing the world anew is an important outcome of a strengths-based inquiry (Barrett and Cooperrider, 1990; Kretzmann and McKnight, 1993; Blundo, 2009; Saleebey, 2009) and the use of creative and imaginative methods to identify the vision or dream is a key feature of the process.

In international development contexts, 'a preferred and better future' may be understood as the 'objective statement' of a programme, that is, the change that is envisaged. Importantly, a strengths-based approach ensures that it responds to an analysis of the strengths in the particular context and the statement comes from those for whom the change is central. For example, a ministry of health focused programme may include an objective of 'responsive health systems supporting the provision of quality services in rural areas', which could be understood as a statement of a preferred future, *if* the statement reflected a mapping of strengths by all relevant stakeholders and a vision formulated by leaders and personnel. In another example, 'transparent and timely accountability between citizens and public service agencies' could be a legitimate programme objective following a strengths-based approach. What is important is that the objective statements describe the preferred future, a new transformed status quo, which is informed by multiple stakeholder perspectives and enriched by appreciation of what is already present that can be used and leveraged to achieve this change.

An image of a preferred future acts as a coalescing force that motivates, inspires, and binds people together for collective action. Through a strengths-based approach to creating change, 'new impressions and judgements' are formed and 'social solidarity' is built which enables 'a renewed capacity to collectively imagine a new and better future' (Barrett and Cooperrider, 1990: 220).

The primary processes to imagine and articulate preferred futures include 'visioning', 'dreaming', 'goal-orientation', and 'scenario-building' by individuals and as a collective. This means that the role of people in individually and collectively identifying their past achievements and imagining a different future is critical. The imagination engages the more creative functions of the brain and often is evoked through metaphor, play acting, drawing, and song. In contrast, problem-based approaches place more emphasis on evidence, data, analysis, and external determinations of what should happen, informed by the problems to be solved.

The value of emphasizing preferred futures is illustrated in most case studies in this book. In particular, Case Study 13 describes processes whereby community visioning for change processes lasted well beyond the life of the project that was initially funded through the Australia Africa Community Engagement Scheme (AACES). For example, a Caritas Australia officer, Scott Martin, returned to a community in Tanzania four years after leaving and found the community still engaged and organized in mobilizing assets and achieving their collective visions for a variety of changes.

3. Collective inquiry and action

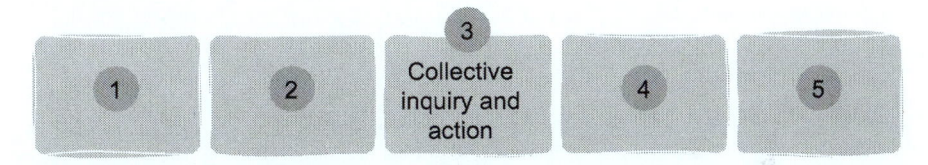

A common feature of a strengths-based approach is an interest in bringing together a range of different individuals and stakeholders in the inquiry process, so they can develop shared imagined preferred futures and then act together to achieve change.

There are multiple ways to bring people, groups, communities, and organizations together, including in systems-level change, through a strengths-based approach. For example, paired interviews between different actors in any context or small group exercises can be used to identify divergent views and perspectives and share emerging insights. A whole system summit (see Case Study 4) is another option. In order to maximize connections between strengths and assets, a strengths perspective prioritizes the inclusion of 'the whole system' in the change process. Emphasis is placed on encouraging participation from all stakeholders such that the change effort can benefit from the multiplicity and connection of these resources. A stakeholder mapping exercise can help to identify all relevant actors who can contribute to change. These processes intentionally seek to strengthen relations between different actor groups. Below we explore in depth how this happens with a particular emphasis on inclusion.

From a strengths perspective, change is supported by connecting strengths, resources, and assets within the given context. The key is to 'locate all the available local assets, to begin connecting them with one another in ways that multiply their power and effectiveness' (Kretzmann and McKnight,

1993: 6). Attention is focused on ensuring the inclusion of those who are often excluded. The notion of synergy describes the outcomes of connecting strengths: 'The synergistic perspective assumes that when phenomena (including people) are brought into interrelationship they create new and often unexpected patterns and resources that typically exceed the complexity of their individual constituents' (Saleebey, 1992: 11).

Strengthening relations is another important consequence of a collective inquiry and action process. A strengths perspective stresses 'the importance of relationship-building for every person and group in the community ... and the necessity of basing those relationships always upon the strengths and capacities of the parties involved, never on the weaknesses and needs' (Kretzmann and McKnight, 1993: 10). Informed by an appreciative process of inquiry, a strengths-based approach breaks down existing stereotypes and defences between individuals and groups, which offers opportunity for a collective commitment to change (Barrett and Cooperrider, 1990). Increased mutual understanding and trust are viewed as important consequences of a strengths-based inquiry. See Chapter 4 for an explanation of how change happens, even when there is no consensus on preferred futures.

From a strengths perspective, change is enabled through building and rebuilding relationships. While an emphasis on relationships is not unique to a strengths-based approach, efforts are made to 'constantly build and rebuild the relationships between and among local residents, local associations and local institutions' (Kretzmann and McKnight, 1993: 9) as a means of connecting strengths, assets, and resources and enabling and sustaining collective efforts for change.

One consequence of engaging in a strengths-based process is that different groups discover a new-found respect for each other. For example, elders can describe when and how the community used to be more self-sufficient, how practices of mutual cooperation within communities were the norm, and how long-standing traditional methods of food production are still relevant. Or from an organizational perspective, the process can reveal how different departments operate and work to achieve similar goals. Every group, community, or organization has something to be proud of, and when this is expressed, the potential for change is realized.

A strengths-based approach offers a space for those who are often not listened to be heard. What worked well in the past is often found in the 'knowledge bank' of elders. Through this process of collective inquiry, elders become more respected and listened to by younger generations. When women are provided with the opportunity to describe their contribution to both family and community life, men become more respectful and more willing to listen. This has been commonly reported by those working with women smallholders in horticulture in Papua New Guinea for example (Pamphilon and Mikhailovich, 2017).

Similarly, in programmes that engage people with disabilities, this usually marginalized group in the community can become key to its future success. Chris Dureau recalls from his time working with Solomon Islands NGOs that in one community, copra production began to wane because none of the younger generation wanted to sit all day to de-husk coconuts. A strengths-based workshop called for everyone to identify their strengths and one community member, who had a mobility impairment, offered his services. 'I sit around all day and people think of me as useless', he said, 'de-husking is something I could do beside the pile of coconuts just as easily'.

In another example from Yogyakarta in Indonesia, following the introduction of a strengths approach after a devastating earthquake, a group of people with disabilities who said they had never before been asked to make a contribution for the common good, invented a special way of harvesting rice and also a new computerized monitoring tool that became universally used by all project partners.

4. Orientated locally

Local orientation is enabled through a series of steps. First, local strengths are identified. Second, preferred futures are decided. Third, informed by this vision of the future, local assets and strengths are capitalized on to achieve change. This approach emphasizes the internal catalyst for change, but does not exclude external resources and expertise, such as evidence of success from other contexts. Fourth, external resources are sourced to complement local strengths and visions of preferred futures. From a strengths perspective, external resources 'will be more effectively used if the local community is itself fully mobilized and invested, and if it can define the agenda for which additional resources must be obtained' (Kretzmann and McKnight, 1993: 8).

From a strengths perspective, change starts from existing strengths and continues to employ new and emerging strengths over time. The notion of strengths as 'renewable and expandable resources' (Saleebey, 2009: 11) means that while change is initiated by using existing strengths, over time strengths within individuals or organizations also grow, and these strengths can be continually employed to create change. Continued processes of inquiry and action enable the wealth of emerging strengths and assets to be identified and used for change.

5. Facilitation only

Common to the main strengths-based practices is a preference for external contributors to play a limited facilitation role rather than one of control or coordination. There is not a clear agenda for the development worker, other than to facilitate leadership of local actors in the process of inquiry into the positive; visioning preferred futures; collective inquiry and action; and ensuring inclusion of locally orientated change. Chapter 8 describes this further.

Facilitation of a strengths-based approach requires trust in the process and those involved in the change process, such as citizens, participants, and leaders. For many development workers, especially in the early days of using a strengths-based approach, this experience may be uncomfortable as it might be they feel 'not in control'. This is consistent with the concept that development workers should not be at the centre of the development agenda, but rather those at the centre of the change agenda should be driving change. It is through the intentional though minimal facilitation efforts of development workers that this is possible (Rhodes, 2022).

Case Study 2, below, an example from the Solomon Islands, describes a programme that explicitly sought to engage with and learn from national initiatives, using a strengths-based approach. The case study illustrates the critical roles of facilitation for providing opportunities for organizations and communities to reflect, identify their strengths and assets, and determine their own change-related objectives. As part of this programme, the Solomon Islands NGO Partnership Agreement (SINPA), author Chris Dureau facilitated an annual monitoring and learning workshop for the NGO participants. In one of these workshops the following story was related. An Adventist Development and Relief Agency extension worker became afraid after attending the initial strengths-based training workshop run by Chris. There she learned that her job was to facilitate a process of identifying assets and determining a desired future for participating communities. She reasoned that if she helped the community have a vision for the future, this would mean many issues and aspirations would emerge. Her concern was that with such an 'open-menu' approach, she would leave the village with multiple demands upon her which she knew her agency would most certainly not be able to meet. Six months later, at the interagency review, she reported that she realized that once the community had been through the whole process of the strengths-based approach, it was not her agency that the community looked to but rather themselves and their available assets to fuel their desired change. They saw the whole change process as owned and managed by themselves, rather than her. She became aware that instead of meeting needs, her agency's main role was to facilitate a process of the community's self-discovery. She discovered that whole communities had set themselves multi-faceted visions of their own future and that the role of Adventist Development and Relief Agency, beyond initiating the change process, was incidental to much of what the community wanted to achieve for themselves.

Another example of the agenda of locally led change enabled through facilitation is the Basic Education Development Program in Papua New Guinea (see Case Study 17 in Chapter 12). The monitoring process for that programme noted that the way local volunteer facilitators worked, meant that sustainable benefits for communities were much larger than the achievement of objectives set by the programme itself.

Another documented case study that emerged from the Australian Community Development and Civil Society Strengthening Scheme (ACCESS) in Indonesia (see Case Study 16), noted that programme managers were not mentioned in any of the interviews with community members and local government. One respondent noted that 'if ACCESS would be at the forefront and at the centre of the action that would not be good, it would mean that the project has failed'. ACCESS's role had been to suggest innovative ways of working, such as Appreciative Inquiry and Outcome Mapping and other tools, as well as providing inputs in terms of capacity development for developing a monitoring framework to assess changes (Pellini et al. 2014).

Table 3.1 describes differences between a traditional problem-solving approach and strengths-based approach to international development using the five processes outlined above.

Table 3.1 Comparing a strengths-based and problem-based approach in international development

	Common process	Problem-based	Strengths-based
1	Inquiry into the positive as the basis for change creation	Identify felt needs of beneficiary Evaluate the result and leave	Discover what works well now and then Engage in continuous learning from initial successes and improved mobilization of assets
2	Imagine a preferred future	Design a planned solution: 'The Project'	Describe the ideal future/vision of success (what is important locally)
3	Collective inquiry and action	Enlist beneficiary support Implement the plan	Mobilize and connect local strengths Design a plan of action for initial phase
4	Orientated locally	Analyse the causes remotely Source external funding Recruit an implementing agency	Identify currently available assets, skills, and values Focus on preferred future and orientate action from local strengths and connect external resources to support local agenda and action

(Continued)

Table 3.1 Continued

Common process	Problem-based	Strengths-based
5 Facilitation only	Manage an intervention to address a beneficiary-felt need	Facilitator role seen as external, and emphasis given to locally led change
	The donor and partners manage a process	Facilitation focuses on supporting continuous learning about the use of local assets and strengths
		Donors and partners facilitate mutual learning

Case Study 2 Designed to engage with and learn from local initiatives in Solomon Islands

This case study is an example of a major bilateral programme in which the implementation team deliberately set out to engage local capacity and learn from local initiatives. The emphasis was on what could be learned from a citizen-led development process in order to reveal and catalyse existing strengths.

Between 2009 and 2015, six Australian NGOs and their local partner NGOs in the Solomon Islands were selected as part of an Australian Government programme to improve the wellbeing of rural and vulnerable communities, especially women and youth. The A$22.6 million Solomon Islands NGO Partnership Agreement (SINPA) included an initial four-month consultation with participating communities, annual collective reflections, and a taskforce to collate and formulate lessons learned. At the initial consultation, NGOs chose to use a strengths-based approach across all activities. Joint training and individual coaching were provided by Chris Dureau, drawing from the theory and practice of ABCD, Appreciative Inquiry, and Positive Deviance.

In contrast with the usual way of proceeding, most NGO partners engaged the whole community to focus on each specific project objective. Projects addressed issues such as greater engagement of young people, empowering women, climate resilience and improving livelihoods. In line with the principle of increasing localization and cultural relevance, the initial consultation stage involved communities being given an opportunity to fully understand the process and to begin their own story-telling, asset-mapping, and visioning. At the end of this consultation period, each community had their own management committee, a clear vision, and a deep appreciation of all their potentially available assets and strengths. In most cases it became clear to communities that they had under-used their own access to power, their women in public leadership, and the contributions of people with disabilities.

Use of a strengths-based approach led to some unexpected timing and scope issues. While the lengthy initial consultations focused on long-term change, it was not uncommon for individuals and groups to engage in 'quick wins' such as carrying out much-needed repairs or building a community hall in just three days (Willetts et al., 2014: 361). Changes carried out by some communities were well beyond anticipated outcomes. In one community, villagers all decided to dig a new dam for water retention, realign and repair all the houses, and introduce improved sanitation practices. They also asked a local tourist resort to buy fish and vegetables from them rather than from the more distant urban centre, and resurrected a business carting

(Continued)

Case Study 2 Continued

and reselling petrol which engaged several unemployed youth. In another community, after having waited for years for an access road to be built by the government, villagers realized there was a retired roads engineer living in the community and they had all the materials they needed to build the access road themselves.

A research paper on the effectiveness of a strengths-based approach used in SINPA was commissioned midway through the programme (Willetts et al., 2014) to critically reflect on the practice and philosophy. The study found a strong belief among almost all participating NGOs in the following:

- the ability of individual capacity and skills to contribute to development;
- the availability of community resources;
- being facilitators rather than experts;
- the importance of nurturing strengths;
- the benefits of focusing on revealing strengths rather than analysing problems;
- that communities should own and direct the change process.

In relation to the practice of a strengths-based approach among NGOs, the study found the following:

- Most NGOs revealed community strengths through applying their own mix of Appreciative Inquiry, ABCD, and Sustainable Livelihoods.
- There were multiple examples of how one individual or family's use of their strengths led to many other sections of the community taking up similar initiatives.
- The approach led to improved internal cohesion and external relationships with service provider agencies, which in turn led to sharing of resources between NGOs and their communities and enhanced avenues for advocating greater government involvement.
- This approach leads to immediate and short-term gains by communities which create motivation for ongoing strengths-based change.
- In the discovery of strengths of every member of the community and in the implementation of projects by different gender and youth groups, the community grew in their appreciation of the value of inclusion. Men grew in appreciation of women's abilities and wanted to replicate their successes. Youth learned to seek out and appreciate the contributions of the whole community, including the elders.

This research concluded that in addition to many tangible outcomes, 'the intangible outcomes of increased confidence, self-esteem, motivation and hope bode well for stimulating the ongoing generative processes referred to in the SBA literature' (Willetts et al., 2014: 367).

The final independent evaluation of SINPA carried out in 2016 reported that 'the strengths-based approach was ... a key factor in helping communities realize that they can solve their own development challenges. The Partnership has led to lasting improvements in the lives of communities, particularly women and young people...' It also concluded that 'the strengths-based approach undertaken by SINPA was an effective approach to building resilience in communities ... It was also a key factor in helping communities realize that they can solve their own development challenges' (Lucas et al., 2016: iv).

Examples of strengths-based practice

A range of practices is described below, which share elements of the philosophical underpinnings explained in the previous chapter as well as processes described above. We have chosen seven established practices to demonstrate the range of strengths-based practices: ABCD, Appreciative Inquiry; Positive Deviance; Endogenous Development; strengths-based social work; Co-production; and Foresight/Futures Thinking. For each practice we describe core features; history and current practice; reaction to deficit-based approaches relevant to its discipline; and application and examples in international development. Further examples are provided throughout the book. Some of the practices chosen for this overview are an explicit reaction to a deficit-based approach, while others have emerged from a strong orientation to localization and futures perspectives in international development. A range of practices are deliberately included to highlight that a strengths-based approach is not new but has a significant body of evidence to substantiate relevance and value, and should be taken seriously as an alternative paradigm to current international development practice.

Asset-Based Community Development

Asset-Based Community Development (ABCD) is an established community development practice employed in many diverse contexts globally, including within international development for the last two decades. ABCD is derived from the field of community development, informed by work in Chicago, USA neighbourhoods in the 1980s, and first described in a book authored by Jody Kretzmann and John McKnight from the Northwestern University in Illinois titled *Building Communities from the Inside Out* (1993). There are now various champions and dedicated organizations of ABCD such as the Coady International Institute; St Francis Xavier University; and the ABCD Institute based at the Steans Center for Community-Based Service Learning at DePaul University. An ABCD Asia-Pacific Network established in 2007 gathers practitioners to share their skills, talents, and passions to support communities to discover and mobilize local assets.

ABCD is premised on the view that in every community there are existing assets which can be used for community development. Through this approach, change is driven by community assets, defined as capacities, abilities, and competences, which are situated within the community (Kretzmann and McKnight, 1993, 1997; McKnight and Russell, 2018). The role of a community development worker is to enable the community to lead a mapping exercise to identify assets (see Figure 3.2) and to mobilize and connect assets. A collective visioning process is used to direct action towards a preferred future.

ABCD was developed as a reaction to needs-based community development approaches. Proponents of ABCD argue that through government, non-government, or university supported programmes which use a deficit

WHAT IS A STRENGTHS-BASED APPROACH? 47

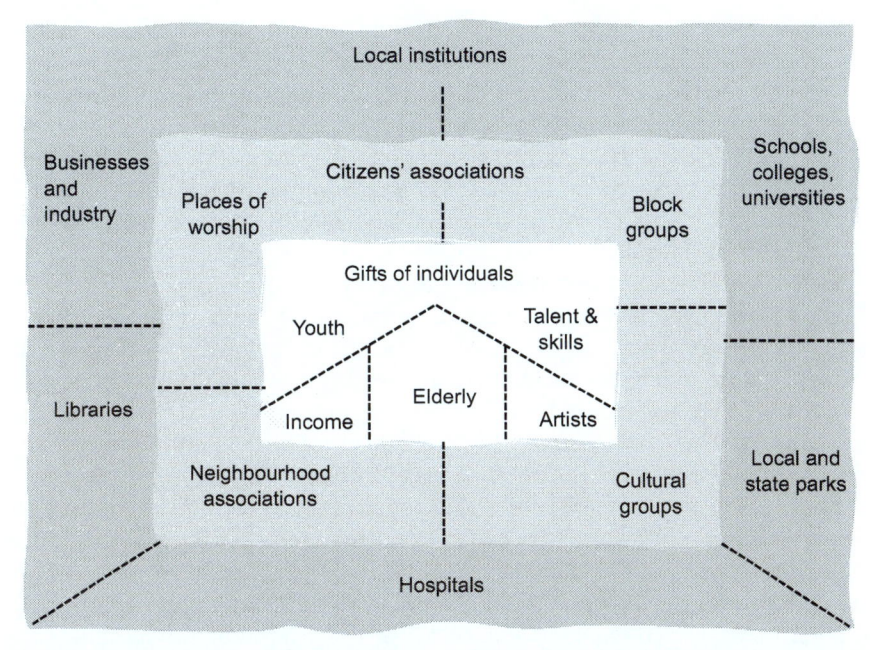

Figure 3.2 Example of asset-based community development mapping
Source: Kretzmann and McKnight, 1993: 7

approach, residents of neighbourhoods come to see themselves as consumers of services, passive and reliant on outsiders. If neighbourhoods see themselves as clients, they supress their own potential for transformational change. Kretzmann and McKnight (1993) note that there are two paths 'to rebuilding troubled communities'. One is focused on a community's needs, deficiencies, and problems while the other is focused on discovering a community's capacities and assets. The practitioners argue the former creates 'images of needy and problematic and deficient neighbourhoods populated by needy and problematic and deficient people' (p. 2). They note that a 'needs map' does not just become part of the truth, but the whole truth. Communities themselves start to see their neighbourhoods as deficient, requiring external resources and expertise to fix them. The alternative is a process focused on community development informed by capacity and strengths. Kretzmann and McKnight (1993) set out the following five steps summarized in Figure 3.3.

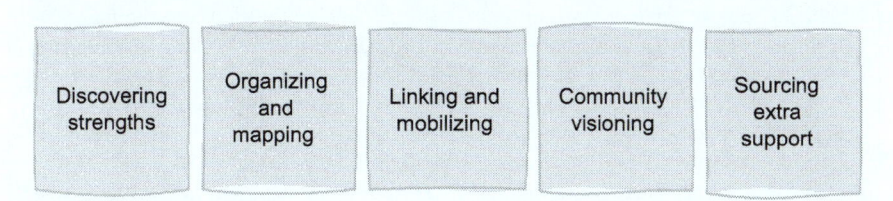

Discovering strengths | Organizing and mapping | Linking and mobilizing | Community visioning | Sourcing extra support

Figure 3.3 Steps in ABCD

Step 1 involves methods to map and mobilize community assets, situated within individuals, associations and organizations, and institutions.

Step 2 is focused on building relationships among the community's assets. Change is understood to be 'relationship driven' and efforts are made to 'build and rebuild relationships' in order to maximize the connection of local assets.

Step 3 is focused on mobilizing the community's assets to develop the local economy and strengthen the neighbourhood's capacity to shape and exchange information.

Step 4 is convening the community to develop a vision of the future.

Step 5 involves leveraging outside resources to support locally driven development. Efforts are made to connect assets from within the community with each other to create change before accessing external resources.

The role of ABCD facilitators is to support locally led inquiry and action. Importantly, ABCD recognizes power and control within communities and promotes leadership and control by communities.

There is extensive use of ABCD in international development in multiple country contexts with a focus on a diverse range of social and economic wellbeing outcomes. The practice of ABCD is explicitly included in half of the case studies in this book (Case Studies 2, 3, 4, 9, 12, 13, 15, 16 and 17). In particular, the rich experience of each of the ABCD steps is evident in Case Study 3 below, from the Philippines.

Case Study 3 ABCD in the Philippines

Asset-based approaches have been part of community development work across the Philippines since the early 2000s. In northern Mindanao, following the founding inspiration of Father William Masterson, SJ, the Southeast Asia Rural Social Leadership Institute (SEARSOLIN) (now part of the Xavier University College of Agriculture) introduced ABCD in 2002 as the key approach to rural leadership training. In the following year, a formal association with the Coady Institute in Nova Scotia, Canada established an accredited degree course in ABCD at Xavier University. Since then and through the continuing work of SEARSOLIN, ABCD has been introduced to more than 100 communities in the Philippines and several other Southeast Asian countries including Cambodia, Laos, and Myanmar (Mathie and Cunningham, 2008).

Research by the Department of Human Geography in the Research School of Pacific and Asian Studies at the Australian National University also included asset-mapping in their application of the Community Economies Collective (Gibson-Graham, 2008) in several parts of the Philippines (http://www.communityeconomies.org/). Dr Amanda Cahill, the principal researcher at that time, started working in Jagna and Bohol provinces in the Philippines in 2003. Using the ABCD approach and Diverse Economies Framework to support the development of new livelihoods and income-generating opportunities, her team found considerable success in developing four community-owned enterprises, two of which continued for many years.

Another example of this transformative change in development work was promoted by the Sydney (Australia) Archdiocese of the Anglican Church's community

(Continued)

Case Study 3 Continued

outreach work. After 20 years of grant-seeking and use of a needs-based approach, the Community-Based Development Program of the Episcopal Church of the Philippines revised its approach to a more inclusive, positive, and sustainable way of working. Since then, the E-Care Foundation, as it then became known, has adopted a strengths-based approach which incorporates lessons from ABCD, Appreciative Inquiry, and Community Economies. This approach has been very successful for E-Care and its major funder the Anglican Board of Mission (ABM) in Australia, with its partner communities and other associations and organizations.

In 2017, ABM Program Officer Kate Winney visited Benguet and Mountain Provinces in the north of the Philippines and asked community members to describe changes following their training in ABCD by E-Care. Many described a much more inclusive and unified community resulting from collectively identifying their strengths and assets. Others described how they had reclaimed unproductive land to increase production and income resulting in further education for their children. One member described the process of ABCD as 'transformative, not just informative' (Anglican Board of Mission, 2018).

Further to the south in the Philippines, another organization that has partnered with ABM for over 10 years is IFI-VIMROD. This organization works in 30 communities across central Visayas. The story of the Marikaban's shell-craft makers is one example of the use of ABCD. The fishing community became increasingly dependent on handouts as fish stocks decreased. With the support of the Church of the Philippines programme VIMROD, they identified shell-craft making as one of their traditional community skills and together realized that this was a significant income-generating activity if properly managed and marketed. The community tells its story of how the approach has helped many members of the community including people with disabilities and single parents in a video produced by the Anglican Board of Mission Australia (2018).

Like other NGOs, ABM has gradually realized that approaches like ABCD have much more and longer-term impact than needs-based approaches. Lina Magallanas explained,

> I am really passionate about this approach. I think it's the way to go because it validates local agency or ownership and is consistent with what is considered desirable. For example, when we talk about sustainability, ABCD is much more likely to achieve this. When we talk about localization, again people learning about, owning and mobilizing their own assets is the best expression of a localized approach.

Appreciative Inquiry

Appreciative Inquiry originated in the field of organizational management and change. It represents a reaction against the emphasis of a problem-solving approach on what is wrong and needs to be fixed. Appreciative Inquiry was first proposed by David Cooperrider, within his post-doctoral research. His thinking was in part informed by Peter Drucker, a management specialist, who said 'The task of leadership is to create an alignment of strengths in ways that make a system's weaknesses irrelevant'. Since the first article about

Appreciative Inquiry (Cooperrider and Srivastva, 1987), the approach has been written about extensively by practitioners and academics. Authors describe Appreciative Inquiry's principles, philosophical underpinnings as well as practice in multiple sectors and country contexts in numerous books and papers. Appreciative Inquiry has been applied in management, change management (Lewis et al., 2008), leadership, coaching, research (Reed 2007), evaluation (Preskill, 2003; van der Haar and Hosking, 2004; Preskill and Catsambas, 2006), and everyday living (Kelm 2015). An extensive set of resources can be found on the 'AI Commons' website (see Resources list), as well as numerous texts and explanations such as Ludema (2002) and Cooperrider et al. (2005).

Appreciative Inquiry literature consistently cites the negative impacts of a pathology-based approach which identifies symptoms, diagnosis, and treatment. Issues of blame, defensiveness, and lack of motivation are raised when people, groups, and organizations are identified as problems to be fixed.

At the core of Appreciative Inquiry is what was originally known as a 4-D cycle. Some practitioners have added a fifth element, resulting in a 5-D cycle comprising:

- *Define* – decide the topic/focus – affirmative topic choice
- *Discover* – appreciate the best of what is
- *Dream* – imagine what could be
- *Design* – determine what should be, planning and prioritizing
- *Deliver* (or destiny) – creating what will be, by delivery of the plan

Figure 3.4 illustrates the cycle, with the first D for 'define' or 'definition' described as 'affirmative topic choice' at the centre. To start the cycle, the topic of inquiry is chosen: this shapes the focus of inquiry and the expected change outcome to be achieved. The topic of inquiry is framed in the affirmative or as a positive and desirable outcome rather than as a topic for overcoming a problem or filling a gap. The inquiry is a deliberate search to explore how to achieve a successful outcome. For example, in the international development context, a topic could be 'strong and responsive accountability in Ministry X', 'extensive outreach for NGO Y' or 'inclusive economic activity in Province Z'. Affirmative topic choices described in the literature include British Airways' decision to reframe their topic from 'reduce lost and damaged baggage claims' to 'exceptional arrival experiences' (Whitney and Trosten-Bloom, 2003: 133–36); and the US Navy's change from referring to 'retention' to 'engaged and empowered leaders at every level' (Cooperrider et al., 2008: vii). The local government in Cleveland, Ohio identified their affirmative topic as 'building an economic engine empowering a Green City on a Blue Lake' to focus on revitalization of the economy through a focus on sustainability (Glavas et al., 2010). The affirmative topic choice focuses on action towards the expected positive change.

The second D for 'discover' entails participatory processes (usually one-on-one interviews either in groups as part of a workshop or individually with representatives of every part of an organization or system), which enable

WHAT IS A STRENGTHS-BASED APPROACH?

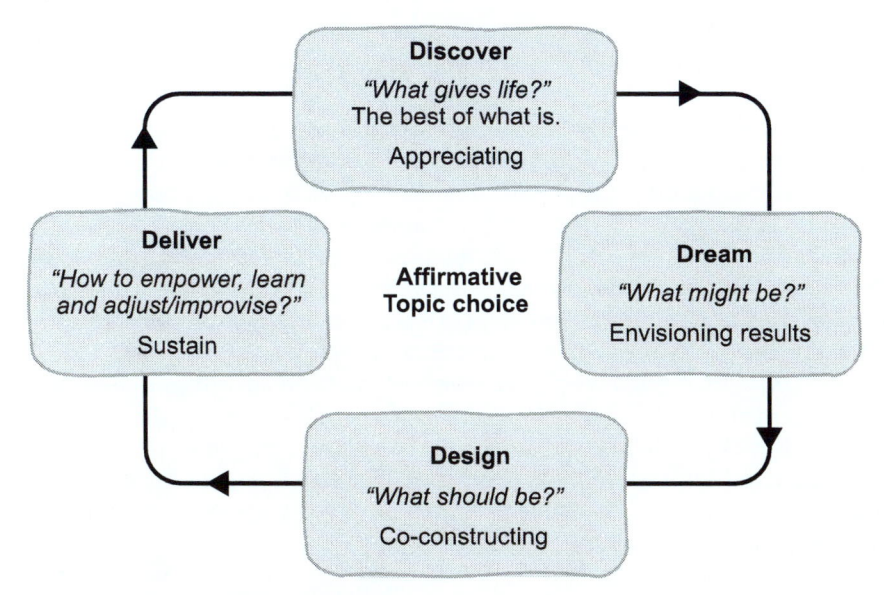

```
                    Discover
                "What gives life?"
                 The best of what is.
                   Appreciating

    Deliver                                    Dream
"How to empower, learn      Affirmative    "What might be?"
 and adjust/improvise?"    Topic choice    Envisioning results
       Sustain

                     Design
                "What should be?"
                  Co-constructing
```

Figure 3.4 The Appreciative Inquiry cycle
Source: Cooperrider and Whitney, 2005: 16.

people to identify, reflect on, and discuss what have been their peak moments of success in their context, including what is working or has worked well (described under 'inquiry into the past' in 'Common processes' section above). The process encourages the interviewer to assist the interviewed to find those moments of success that they are most proud of in their work history or communal life. The interviews or group inquiry are followed by a synthesis of stories of success and key enablers of these. Examples of these enablers or strengths in the international development sector will vary widely in nature and scope: participants might suggest 'supportive and respected leaders', 'effective communications systems', 'trust-based support networks', 'trained/skilled people' or 'specific technology, assets or equipment'. In a more local context, it could be proactive actions of nurses or women's groups which enable a health system to work well or collective practices and communal efforts which enable farmers to have a good harvest.

The third D for 'dream' involves participants' efforts to imagine, identify, and define their collective preferred future (see 'imagine a preferred future' in 'Common processes' section above). This is where statements are generated which describe what the future looks like not just for the donor-funded activity but for the whole system – a new and better state of things. Statements evoke a leap forward from the present state. This stage concludes with a collective agreement on a statement or goal for the future. They must provoke or encourage the desirable direction of change. For this reason, they are more imaginative (hence dreaming) than practical or rational objectives. In international development, examples could include any level of change: 'abundant water supply for everyone's health and hygiene', 'inclusive and accessible health services for all', 'fully accountable governance' or 'more equal political representation.'

The fourth D for 'design' enables groups of people to negotiate and agree on steps to take to achieve their preferred future (see 'collective inquiry and action' and 'oriented locally' in 'Common processes' section above). In international development contexts, this includes people who best understand the context and field(s) of practice coming together, navigating the complexities and opportunities, brainstorming and agreeing on appropriate sets of plans and responsibilities. Design processes can produce any type of 'design product' including theories of change and action, principles and approaches to be applied, and/or steps that can be taken, along with timelines and resource lists for example.

The fifth D for 'deliver' covers the process of putting plans into action. In Appreciative Inquiry, emphasis is on people collaborating and delivering for themselves, mobilizing available resources, with any external partners playing a limited facilitation role (see 'facilitation only' section above).

While the practice of Appreciative Inquiry has remained predominantly uniform since its inception, there have been some innovations. Since the 1990s, Appreciative Inquiry has been linked to systems thinking with the development of the Appreciative Inquiry Summit. The Appreciative Inquiry Summit recognizes the value of 'whole system positive change'. Ludema et al. (2003: 42) noted 'having the whole system in the room also brings an ecological perspective: all the pieces of the puzzle come together in one place and everyone can gain an appreciation for the whole. The unique perspective of each person, when combined with the perspectives of others, creates new possibilities for action, possibilities that previously lay dormant or undiscovered'. Appreciative Inquiry Summits might take the form of mass gatherings or a process of gathering insights and perspectives prior to a representative collective process. While the intention is to achieve 'the whole story in the room', a representative process may obviate the need to include every relevant individual. Whole system change provides the means for generative and transformative change described in the next chapter.

Appreciative Inquiry shares elements with other strengths-based practices and includes all five of the common processes described above. It starts with a focus on identifying what is working well in any situation. It presumes that even in a place of dysfunction, there is something that is working well or strengths that can be understood and used to generate change. Like other strengths-based practices, Appreciative Inquiry is participatory, whereby participants lead and own the inquiry and its outcomes. It prioritizes inquiry and change as a relational process, which enables expression of different views and perspectives and shared understanding to inform the direction and actions for change. Like other strengths-based practices, creation of a vision for the future acts as a catalyst for change. Uniquely for Appreciative Inquiry, the affirmative topic choice is a provocative statement, metaphor, or image of the future, usually defined collectively, which frames the focus of inquiry and leads the direction of change.

Application of Appreciative Inquiry in international development is cited numerous times in this book and included in nearly half of the case studies (numbered 2, 3, 4, 8, 9, 12, 16 and 17). In particular, Case Study 4 (Appreciative Inquiry Summit) below illustrates widespread use of the method in Indonesia at the interface between local government and communities. These examples demonstrate the practice's relevance across a range of different contexts and purposes. Appreciative Inquiry has been used successfully to inform programme design and implementation as well as international development evaluation and research (Michael, 2005).

Case Study 4 Appreciative Inquiry Summit in Indonesia

The Australian Community Development and Civil Society Strengthening Program Phase 2 (ACCESS II) used Appreciative Inquiry extensively over six years (2006–2012) and at all levels. The previous Director of ACCESS Paul Boon stated in an interview for this book, 'Appreciative Inquiry proved to be an approach that triggered a wide and diverse array of people to initiate action and believe in their ability to address issues within their district. It instilled a sense of enthusiasm to work together on change previously thought of as impossible'.

One example of the application of Appreciative Inquiry was the initiation of Appreciative Summits or Appreciative Citizen Engagement Workshops. ACCESS facilitated such gatherings for one week in each of 20 different districts across eastern Indonesia. Summit delegates included representatives from all levels of society, including senior government officials, community change agents, religious leaders, civil society and village leaders, academics, and representatives from the private sector. Delegates were chosen from among those who had proven to be champions for change, with a positive vision for the future. Such champions demonstrated existing strengths or human resources that included their knowledge of the local context, proven experience as a motivator, representation of existing local institutions, and shared values in line with ACCESS (including gender and social inclusion, transparency and accountability, and use of an asset-based approach).

The Summits combined three key elements of the Appreciative Inquiry model for organizational change: an emphasis on engaging local assets; a focus on participants' ownership of vision; and action plans that incorporated strengthening relationships between civil society organizations, government, media, and private sector (Munggoro and Kismadi, 2013).

The workshops began with obtaining an agreed definition of the Appreciative Inquiry process relevant for each district. The next step involved use of Appreciative Inquiry interviews, drawing on participants' own experience to map human, social, physical, cultural, political, and economic assets. This was a journey of 'discovery' of their own strengths and those of their communities. Many were surprised to find even the poorest environments have many sources of strength and potential.

(Continued)

Case Study 4 Continued

The workshop groups each prepared a statement about the relevance of these assets for their context.

The 'dream' or visioning stage was carried out in four steps. The first involved groups creating visions for their own district. The second step collated these into a collective vision. This was followed by a breakdown of the vision into subcategories or 'elements' of success (step three). These mini descriptions of success were usually relevant to the four main themes of ACCESS, namely 1) participatory planning; 2) local economic development; 3) community-led natural resource management; and 4) improved public services through citizen participation. Finally, each group again described the vision in their own words and in creative ways, such as a letter to a friend, a poem, a song or a dance or simply a strong and provocative statement.

Typically, vision statements were described in positive and engaging terms. For example, in Jeneponto, South Sulawesi, where the overriding priority is to improve access to water in the long dry season, the vision agreed was for 'A Green and Prosperous Jeneponto', achieved by: the creative mobilization of local assets; full participation of all members and groupings in society; economic development through enhancing the informal sector; and improved public service delivery in quality and management.

Following the formulation of the vision, the District Citizen Engagement Plan (DCEP) was debated, prioritized, and collated. The emerging concept designs were to be carried out by citizen associations and civil society organizations in collaboration with district government activities.

The development of DCEPs respected participants' own capacity for constructive self-determination. The visioning exercise was inclusive of all levels of actors in the district and encouraged citizens and government to collectively propose a desirable positive future (in contrast with a statement which would address core problems). The DCEP also embraced many creative solutions in a context where multiple paths are appropriate to achieve desired social, political, and economic change.

Participants in the District Appreciative Summits become an interim or 'ad hoc' group of citizens who had already shown their willingness and ability to be change agents or champions. Their task following the Summit was to conduct AI-style multi-stakeholder meetings at the community level with those who have power (senior government officials) and influence (community, business, and religious leaders) to design specific activities in support of the District Vision, to be funded either by local government or local contributions. Support for civil society organizations was funded by ACCESS to facilitate the process of design and implementation by local actions.

The Appreciative Summit provided the blueprint for collective action at multiple levels where people drew from their own assets and resources to design and implement local initiatives in support of overall District Plans. The government used this framework as the basis for their own district level planning. One governor told Irene Insandjaja (personal communication): 'I am confident in sending this plan to central government and that the funds will be of real benefit, because for the first time I can say that this is truly the plan of the people, by the people and with the people'.

(Continued)

Case Study 4 Continued

The staff of ACCESS II and many participants remain connected via a very active WhatsApp group. Within the group, one participant, Sulis Seda, now Program Manager of a large regional NGO, stated that 'after ACCESS II, Appreciative Inquiry became the basis for all subsequent organizational capacity building and multi-sector socio-economic change programs carried out by our organization (Yayasan Social Donkers)'. And another, Stefanus Segu, Director of Yayasan Harapan Sumba, reported that 'Appreciative Inquiry and ABCD have become the basis for our cooperation with Save the Children and for all our training activities, including a community development course at Universitas Kristin Wira Wacana Sumba'.

Positive Deviance

Positive Deviance is a practice with a specific interest in revealing and amplifying existing strengths in local contexts. The practice is based on the central premise that in any given context there are individuals 'whose deviation from the norm generates innovative solutions to their local problems' (Ochieng, 2007: 458).

The practice was first developed in relation to child nutrition (Zeitlin et al., 1990) but has since been applied across a wide range of health, education, and social change issues (Pascale et al., 2010). The first application of the practice in contexts of poor child nutrition highlighted that some children were less malnourished than others despite living in the same context and with access to the same resources. The practice sought to reveal the reasons why some children are these 'positive deviants'. The inquiry explored the behaviours of families with less malnourished children with the intention to scale up or replicate these practices in other families in the community.

Positive Deviance methodology comprises five basic steps, listed below and illustrated in Figure 3.5:

1. Define the issue, current perceived causes, challenges and constraints, common practices, and desired outcomes.
2. Determine the presence of positive deviant individuals or groups.
3. Discover uncommon but successful behaviours and strategies through inquiry and observation.
4. Design activities to allow community members to practise the discovered behaviours.
5. Monitor and evaluate the resulting project or initiative which further fuels change by documenting and sharing improvements as they occur, and help the community discern the effectiveness of the initiative (The Positive Deviance Initiative, 2010: 6).

Unlike other strengths-based practices described in this chapter, this practice originated within international development work (Mackintosh et al., 2002). It purposely sought to avoid the normal practice of international development which applies external solutions to local problems. The premise instead is that the best solutions to an issue can be locally sourced. The results associated

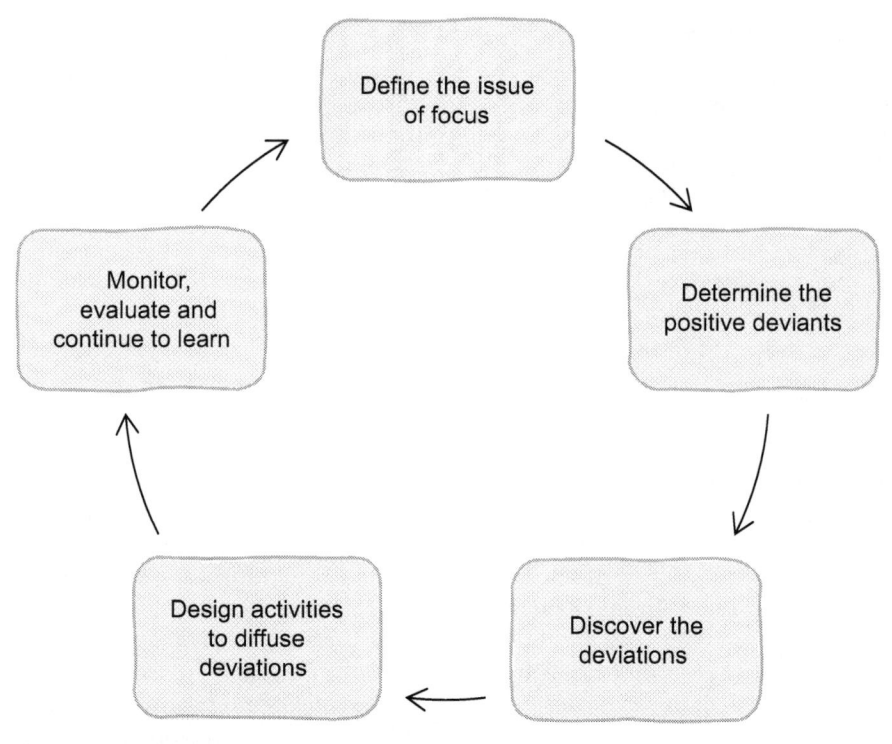

Figure 3.5 Positive Deviance: five basic steps

- Define the issue of focus
- Determine the positive deviants
- Discover the deviations
- Design activities to diffuse deviations
- Monitor, evaluate and continue to learn

with the practice have been impressive, with numerous evaluations citing continued benefit of innovative behaviours which have been revealed and scaled up with this approach (Mackintosh et al., 2002; Herington and van de Fliert, 2018).

Positive Deviance shares common elements with other strengths-based practices. It starts with an appreciation of strengths that can be used to fuel change. Its inquiry is unconditionally focused on the positive as a means to inform change. When applied to child nutrition, the practice was critiqued as being labour-intensive and time-consuming, though multiple applications and examples have demonstrated its applicability and adaption to diverse contexts, issues, and styles of facilitation and implementation.

Examples of the application of Positive Deviance are referenced in Case Studies 3 and 16. Another example is found in a rural community outside the town of Ballantyne in southern Malawi, where a group of farmers were considering how to improve food security as part of the AACES programme managed by Caritas Australia (see Case Studies 12 and 13). The local government agricultural extension officer was also present at farmer meetings. He explained that it was government policy to promote diverse cropping and livestock. Government extension officers had been trying for some years to support this shift, but with limited success.

Using a Positive Deviance practice, author Chris Dureau, as facilitator, asked the community to nominate who among them were the most successful farmers. They all pointed to one man in particular. He then explained to the group that he had adopted the government's suggestions and had improved his living standard and now had the funds to send his children to secondary school. He said he had also learned to plant early and re-plant if any crop died early in the season to ensure that he had a full crop of beans, peanuts, and vegetables in addition to the traditional corn crop. He was then able to work out a way to have goats and chickens as supplements.

The facilitator asked the nominated successful farmer and several others to become members of a technical advisory group to systematically train all other farmers in the community. Other farmers were happy with this arrangement as they often wondered why and how this particular farmer could be so much more successful than them. The government's agricultural extension officer visited more often and used this group to reach the community. He later explained that it was much easier to relate to the community on a regular basis because they had formed themselves into a peer education group and additional government support was provided. Two years later, when Chris returned to conduct a mid-term monitoring visit, the whole group of farmers and their families reported many positive changes had occurred, with urban centre traders coming to the village to pick up farm-related supplies, including vegetables, beans, and goats' cheese (DFAT, 2014b).

Endogenous Development

Endogenous Development is the term used for a strengths-based practice that emerged from the experience of many grassroots organizations in Latin America, Africa, and India. It is also relevant to and draws inspiration from collaborations with First Nations people and more traditional societies. This approach is grounded in an appreciation of cultural and biodiversity found in the material, social, and spiritual resources of indigenous communities (COMPAS, 2007; Van't Hooft, 2010).

Proponents of this approach claim that contemporary development contains an implicit bias towards material or physical improvements without due consideration of cultural values and traditional ways. Endogenous Development seeks to overcome this bias by prioritizing people's world-views and traditional livelihood strategies as starting points for development. These world-views and value systems are then integrated with modern knowledge. While not a reaction to deficit-based approaches, this approach is critical of expert, externally driven ways of working which premise western knowledge and world-views. Like other strengths-based practices, it highlights the importance and value of locally led change processes.

A wide range of case studies collated by Van Otterloo-Butler (2007) illustrate key elements of this approach. These include local control of the development process; building upon what already exists; taking cultural values seriously as a key locally available asset; appreciating and integrating the wisdom and world-view of the local community, including both beliefs and practices as well as the way learning is acquired; integrating the desired vision with this traditional world-view; and finding a balance between local and external resources in developing a plan of action.

With its focus on the development worker spending time to learn how ideas are communicated and how learning occurs before engaging in activities or improving services in various contexts, this approach deliberately locates the change process in the hands of those most affected by change. For example, Solomon Islanders frequently use living creatures to describe development concepts to each other – the crab, the eagle, the fish, and coral. These local meanings are used to communicate community insights and perspectives on the future.

Also, through revitalizing ancestorial wisdom, Endogenous Development helps any community or group of people to select those external resources and technical knowledge that best fit their conditions. Van't Hooft (2010) demonstrates that use of Endogenous Development contributes to increased bio- and cultural diversity, reduces environmental degradation, and promotes regional exchange.

An example of the application of Endogenous Development is included in Case Study 5 below, about the recognition of traditional wisdom in health care in India and Timor-Leste.

Case Study 5 Recognizing traditional wisdom in health care in India and Timor-Leste

This case study documents the relevance and value of working with traditional health practitioners and drawing out potential contributions of traditional medicines in carrying out modern health care. The principle of starting with and building upon traditional values and spiritual beliefs is at the heart of Endogenous Development.

Use of this approach to health care has been pioneered by the Institute of Ayurveda and Integrative Medicine (I-AIM) in Bangalore, India. Since 2001, I-AIM has documented and assessed local health traditions to make effective primary health care services available for rural households. Between 2006 and 2010, I-AIM surveyed 82 traditional healers about their traditional anti-malarial practices in the states of Orissa, Andhra Pradesh, and Karnataka. Promising treatment procedures were selected, analysed, and tested by botanists, doctors, and malaria experts. A decoction taken from the plants and herbs used by traditional healers was trialled in four clinical studies of 1,788 people carried out in close collaboration with the National Institute of Malaria Research of India. The study found that of those who were given the treatment only 45 people (2.5 per cent) contracted malaria compared with 215 (12 per cent) people from the control group (Prakash, 2011: 22).

What is relevant in this case study is that traditional medicines are more readily available and more likely to be used than many of the prophylactic or treatment medication found in clinics. Modern approaches to primary health care in low-resource communities often fail to recognize the experience and contribution of traditional healers and their understanding of the value of traditional medicines.

(Continued)

Case Study 5 Continued

A strengths-based approach begins with the assumption that traditional methods of health care do have value especially when they complement modern medicine. Any health-related engagement using a strengths-based approach begins by appreciatively enquiring about how traditional health-related practices may become the basis for a more comprehensive health care programme.

In Timor-Leste, both traditional and modern medicine are used to contribute to healing. Associate Professor Dr Lisa Palmer from University of Melbourne, Australia, is a human geographer researching human-environment relations and indigenous approaches to social issues. In a short film entitled *Holding Tightly – Custom and Healing in Timor-Leste*, Dr Palmer interviewed Health Clinic Director Domingos Reinaldo Guterres from Venilale in Baucau. The Health Director advised that encouraging the use of traditional healers and forest medicine has become an integral part of the healing process alongside modern medicine. 'Patients place their trust and faith in traditional practices, so working to complement with sensitivity and awareness rather than competing or denying traditional practice provides the best health outcomes' (Palmer and Barnes, 2021).

In her short film, Dr Palmer also documented interviews with traditional healers from Baucau, Timor-Leste, whose work complements the efforts of the modern health system. For example: Januario da Silva, a bone-healer, uses massage and 11 botanical spices from the forest; Joaquin and Palmira, a husband-and-wife team, treat patients who had first sought treatment unsuccessfully from the clinic, using a variety of forest medicines to complement what they had received from the clinic; and Almeida, a retired nurse, finds ways to better engage traditional practices alongside practices used in the formal health system (Palmer and Barnes, 2021).

The Director of the Venelali Health Clinic, servicing this part of Baucau, Domingos Reinaldo Guterres, acknowledges and encourages the use of traditional healers and forest medicine as an integral part of the healing process for patients. He knows that collaboration between traditional and modern healing methods is more effective, saying in the film 'we can work together for the best outcomes when we collaborate with sensitivity and awareness'.

Strengths-based social work

As its name suggests, strengths-based social work is a field of practice that purposely seeks to use strengths and counters a deficit perspective as part of traditional case-management practice. It began in the early 1980s at the University of Kansas School of Social Welfare. In 1989, Weick, Rapp, Sullivan, and Kishardt coined the term 'strengths perspective' which recognizes the assets and authority of clients in determining their own future.

Strengths-based social work reflects the view that despite challenges, issues, or problems that individuals might be facing, they have inherent strengths which can be drawn on to improve their lives. The intention of strengths-based social work is to appreciate and tap the potential of inherent individual strengths in order to create change. Client motivation and action towards creating change are encouraged by fostering client strengths. In strengths-based social work, change is driven both by individual client strengths and by connecting these strengths with other resources in the local environment. Hammond and Zimmerman (2012) provide an excellent summary of a strengths-based approach, focusing on youth work. They note 'the problem is the problem – not the youth' (p. 3). Like others, they question the effective role of needs assessments and negative consequences of labelling. A strengths-based approach is described as 'offering a genuine basis for addressing the primary mandate of community and mental health services – people taking control of their own lives in healthy, meaningful and sustainable ways' (p. 5).

Like other approaches in this chapter, strengths-based social work is a reaction to the deficit-based model dominant in its sector. Saleebey (2009) wrote that 'social work, like other helping professions, has not been immune to the contagion of disease-and-disorder-based thinking' (p. 3). Saleebey adds:

> the lexicon of pathology gives voice to a number of assumptions and these in turn have painted pictures of clients in vivid but not very flattering tones:
> - The person is the problem or pathology named.
> - The language of pessimism and doubt; the sway of professional cynicism.
> - Distance, power inequality, control and manipulation mark the relationship between helper and helped.
> - Context stripping: denying the power of context.
> - The supposition of disease assumes a cause for the disorder and thus, a solution (Saleebey, 2009: 3–6).

Table 3.2 compares strengths-based and traditional approaches to social work. This table illustrates broader consequences of strengths-based and deficit-based perspectives.

Table 3.2 Pathology versus strengths

Pathology	Strengths
Person is defined as a case; symptoms add up to a diagnosis	Person is defined as unique and their talents and resources add up to strengths
Theory is problem-focused	Theory is possibility focused
Category/classification	Client's desired outcome
Emphasis is on solutions to match problems	Emphasis on exceptions, past successes
Worker as the expert	Client as the expert
Resources for the work are the knowledge and skills of the worker	Resources for the work are the strengths, capacities of the client
Good/bad, black/white	Different alternatives
Intervention	Collaboration
Question: what is the problem?	Question: in what situation is the client?

Source: Adapted from Saleebey, 1996: 298

Strengths-based social work shares common elements with other strengths-based practices. It uses strengths assessments and promotes the role of the social workers as supporting and facilitating clients to realize their own strengths and potential, and enabling these to be connected with untapped external resources. Like other strengths-based practices, goal orientation is critical to guide individuals' action towards change and preferred futures. External resources are identified to complement individuals' assets and support achievement of self-identified goals. These two elements, goal orientation and strengths assessment, can both be sequenced first. In the process of strengths-based social work, each person is deemed an expert on their strengths, resources, and aspirations for the future. It is the practitioner's role to encourage informed decisions and support individual action.

Strengths-based social work is not as relevant to international development as other practices described above, since it has an orientation towards individuals rather than communities, organizations, or systems. There is little written on its application outside high-income contexts. However, the theory and practice associated with strengths-based social work offers valuable insights relevant for a strengths-based approach for international development. Extensive literature is available on application of strengths-based social work in the UK, USA, Canada, and Australia.

Co-production

Co-production describes the process of active citizen involvement in change processes, most notably in design, production, or delivery of public services. The concept of Co-production was introduced and developed by Elinor Ostrom in the 1970s and has since been expanded and applied to numerous country and sector contexts, mostly in western countries. Ostrom's work was originally applied to policing in Chicago USA, though the thinking is relevant to community-based management of services in other country contexts. Her observation was that police efficacy was increased with community involvement. She noted that effective policing requires citizen assets, experience, knowledge, and efforts as much as the expertise of professional service providers. She noted that active participation of citizens such as through neighbourhood watch and crime reporting enhanced police operations and community safety. As noted by Ostrom (1996: 1073), 'co-production implies that citizens can play an active role in producing public goods and services of consequence to them'. Since the 1970s more theorists have used and explored the practice of Co-production in many sectors of public service delivery, including health, education, and social services.

Co-production is a reaction to externally driven, expert-led change which is a common feature of strengths-based practices. While not explicitly a reaction to deficit-based approaches like others described above, Co-production recognizes and values the capacities, knowledge, and interests of those involved in the change process, to best lead the change themselves.

For many, the notion of Co-production goes beyond perspectives of consultation or participation to embody a broader recognition of the assets of individuals, the value of these, and their use in the delivery of public services. Key aspects of Co-production cited in literature (Cahn, 2004) include: recognition of assets and capabilities of service users; strategies that support genuine coming together and respecting each other's (service users and service providers) expertise; and processes to enable joint decision-making. Everyone who has a stake in a project or service is involved from the start to design the whole process of development. Therefore, participation starts early and is an effective strategy to enable active roles in decision-making. Participation defines joint power and joint decision-making.

The term Co-production is often used erroneously to describe merely consultation of citizens in a design process or the abandonment of state responsibility for the delivery of public services. These criticisms highlight the risk and challenge of Co-production. Like other strengths-based practices, Co-production necessitates the recognition of individual assets, strengths, and capabilities. The role of public service workers is to become facilitators and catalysts of the Co-production process and outcomes. Responsibility and authority are devolved through joint decision-making processes.

Ostrom (1996) highlights that Co-production is not relevant for all contexts and provides a set of conditions necessary for its practice:

- 'bringing together of genuine citizen assets relevant to the service;
- legal authority to make decisions together;
- credible commitments to one another, and where inputs change from one side, the other changes;
- incentives to encourage commitment and building opportunities for shared understandings' (p. 1082).

Some common processes and methods of a strengths-based approach are evidenced in Co-production. A key priority is a locally led agenda for change, enabled by the strengths and resources of local actors. These are then combined with external resources and expertise. There is extensive literature on Co-production in high-income countries, such as use by the UK Government (Public Health UK, 2018), though to date there is little written about it in lower- and middle-income countries.

Case Study 6 below is an example of the application of Co-production in the education sector in Indonesia. It illustrates the benefits of bringing together people with expertise and experience in the contexts where changes are sought. It confirms that ongoing collaborative reflection and planning processes are both necessary and feasible in a large-scale programme, rather than following predetermined, externally defined and fixed plans.

Another example, described in Case Study 16, is the Australian Community Development and Civil Society Strengthening Scheme (ACCESS) in Indonesia, which included training for more than 10,000 village facilitators between

2006 and 2014. Those trained were directly involved in Co-production, and the following examples illustrate the power of this particular approach.

In Muna, south-east Sulawesi, Saidah organized a campaign to stop fishermen using bombs to catch fish on coral reefs. Her success in banning the use of bombing not only led to substantial increases in local production of seafood and seaweed but also led the government to pass legislation to promote a range of measures designed to increase the likelihood of sustainable fishing. In Jeneponto, South Sulawesi, the community organized themselves into an alliance of 27 productive water user groups to manage a much fairer distribution of water for rice irrigation. The government took notice and realized that using its resources to support this initiative would lead to a much more equitable and sustainable use of this scarce resource. The government demonstrated its support with funding for improved infrastructure and stronger legislation. In Sumba, East Nusatengara, the farming community decided to plant candle nut trees on their more barren uplands, organizing themselves into cooperatives. Their success attracted the attention of the government who have invested further resources into this and a number of other income-generating initiatives, including fish ponds and infrastructure for improved marketing of produce.

Case Study 6 Engagement between traditional and modern education in Indonesia

This case study describes a programme that built upon existing capacity and successful networks to improve the learning environment of traditional Madrasah schools in Indonesia. Two of the authors of this book were members of the advisory team.

Learning Assistance Program for Islamic Schools (LAPIS) was a programme funded by the Australian Government (A$33.5 m) between 2004 and 2011. More than 1,800 middle level traditional Islamic schools (Madrasah) were invited to work with the National Ministry of Religious Affairs and the National Ministry of Education to raise the standard of teaching and educational outcomes. By the end of the programme, almost 200,000 students and teachers had benefited, with some selected studies finding 94 per cent of stakeholders reporting significant improvements in student results (Robert Kingham, previous Program Director, interviewed for this book).

Although not specifically defined as such, LAPIS contained many aspects of a strengths-based approach. Robert Kingham reflected: 'The whole purpose of LAPIS was getting Madrasah school communities to be proud of what they have done and encourage them to do it better'. The main objectives of the programme reflected this orientation. These included:

- Map and mobilize existing social capital, relationships, and networks around Islamic schools and related institutions at every level to enhance their capacity.

(Continued)

Case Study 6 Continued

- Provide local organizations with small grants that build upon current initiatives and available assets and stimulate immediate activities designed to improve the school environment, teacher education, and the quality of the curriculum.
- Facilitate the collaboration of other readily available resource organizations and programmes to enhance gender equity, curriculum, and teaching methods.
- Create learning exchange forums for mutual learning and more strategic planning.

Enhancing existing associations and networks is a key step in a strengths-based approach. In 2009, national accreditation was mandated for all schools. Building on existing capacities and mutual support through these associations and networks, LAPIS trialled accreditation with 90 Madrasah schools in three provinces using locally available advisers. The pilot was successful, with over 90 per cent of Madrasah achieving accreditation. This pilot became the basis for the Madrasah Accreditation component of the subsequent Australian Government funded Education Partnership 2011–2016.

During the first and exploratory stage of LAPIS, over 100 remote rural school communities were provided with small grants to 'make an immediate impact' on basic education. Typically these grants were used to improve the Life Skills Development subject and community engagement. In one village, every household grew two extra papaya trees in their own backyard. The fruit from one would be for the local school and the fruit from the other, sold to pay for their own child's educational costs. The LAPIS grant was to establish a nursery and provide educational inputs on how to grow and market the resulting crops. In another village, everyone learned to breed budgerigars, both as a life skill as well as using the enterprise to teach maths, biology, and science.

LAPIS staff and field workers saw themselves as facilitating a process of learning by bringing together those with expertise and those with experience drawn from the immediate activities. Each new stage of the programme was not a predetermined input, but rather the result of reflection and subsequent strategic planning.

The independent completion report for LAPIS included comments from Indonesian stakeholders about the results, highlighting the particular approaches used. Examples include: 'we feel that our human resources in Madrasah were empowered by LAPIS' and 'in my opinion the strategy of trust-building was quite amazing. I learned a lot from LAPIS from how they approached institutions, and key individuals within institutions, and discussed ideas, and then expanded these ideas' (AusAID, 2010b: 12).

Kingham continues to maintain contact with the sector. He said that although the support of the Australian Government for this programme concluded in 2011, the Ministry of Religious Affairs continues to pay the salaries of facilitators in Provincial Madrasah Education Centres and apply the model across almost all of Indonesia.

Foresight Thinking/Futures Studies

Foresight thinking, also known as futures studies, considers how to use a focus on the future to inform thinking, action, and decision-making. There is no single framework or approach shared across foresight thinking but rather different authors (Schwartz, 1998; Meadows et al., 2004; Slaughter, 2008; Inayatullah, 2008) who present their own unique, though complementary, frameworks. They share an emphasis on exploring options for the future. Foresight thinking is focused on long-term futures (at least 10 years in the future) and alternative futures, not just what is currently the present or likely to be the future. Distinctions are often made between different likely futures. For example, Inayatullah (2008) makes a distinction between possible ('push of the present'), probable ('weight of history'), and preferable futures ('pull of the future'), in his 'futures triangle' in Figure 3.6.

The work of Donella Meadows (1999) is another example of futures thinking. She proposes the value of considering change in relation to leverage points (12 points) that can be used to intervene in the existing system from micro-details such as mechanistic characteristics to underpinnings of values, goals, and world-views.

Within foresight or futures thinking there is a strong focus on the possibility of the future. A key concept is 'building the future', a philosophy based on seeing the future as 'a realm of freedom, power and will' (de Jouvenel 2004: 10). Foresight thinking includes a process to generate images of the future, with an interest in expanding perspectives of new possibilities, alternative futures,

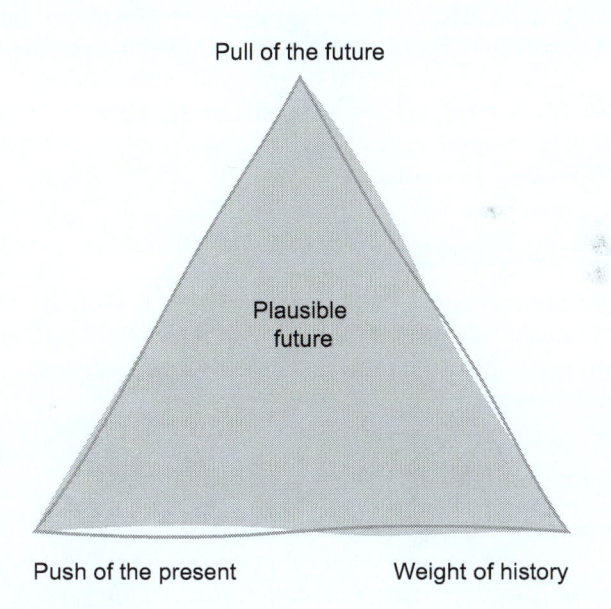

Figure 3.6 The futures triangle
Source: Inayatullah, 2008.

as contexts change over time. Foresight thinking allows for a prospective stance towards the future, so that the new and novel can be realized.

Another key feature of foresight thinking is its perspective on the process of inquiry. Reality is viewed as layered and consists of deeper structures that shape perspectives on what is real. Different forms of inquiry and participatory processes are used to inform the inquiry. Foresight thinking provides a structured way to perceive the future and engage practically in alternative futures and to take action now, in the present, to achieve future change. Inquiry is also influenced by notions of complexity. Ongoing shifts mean that long-term future changes are often unforeseeable, informed by dynamic changes of the present and more immediate futures.

Foresight thinking aligns with common processes and methods of a strengths-based approach. Common methods are employed within foresight thinking, and could be categorized as: scanning; mapping; analysing trends; scenario planning; scenario development; and visioning. Most particularly the focus on imagining futures with a long-term focus and clear horizon is akin to a strengths-based approach. Recognition that the process of exploring future possibilities surfaces and reveals values and perspectives is also central to why a strengths-based approach is interested in a collective and inclusive process.

Foresight thinking has been applied in international development in ad hoc but relatively limited ways. Bingley (2014) noted that this practice remains on the margins of international development practice. Manuals such as the UNDP (2018) *Foresight Manual: Empowered Futures for the 2030 Agenda* demonstrate more recent interest.

Foresight thinking does not necessarily have an interest in debunking deficit-based approaches like other practices included in this chapter; it simply reorientates the focus, to prioritize energy and resources on questions and inquiry about the future, not the past. Like other strengths-based practices described in this chapter, foresight thinking premises the transformative potential of a futures orientation.

Comparison between seven practices

The seven practices described above have common elements that connect them and nuances that differentiate them relevant to a strengths-based approach for international development. The common areas of focus are summarized in Table 3.3.

Acknowledging critiques of strengths-based practice

Critiques of strengths-based practice are acknowledged – the authors have heard and read about them often. Our concern is that these critiques often demonstrate a missed understanding of a strengths-based approach. The common critiques are summarized and addressed below. Concerns are often raised about specific practices, but may be relevant more broadly to a strengths-based

Table 3.3 Connecting common processes to strengths-based practices

Strengths-based practice	Asset-Based Community Development	Appreciative Inquiry	Positive Deviance	Endogenous Development	Strengths-based social work	Co-production	Foresight/Futures thinking
Common processes							
1 Inquiry into the positive as the basis for change creation	✓	✓	✓	✓	✓		
2 Imagine a preferred future	✓	✓		✓	✓	✓	✓
3 Collective inquiry and action	✓	✓		✓		✓	
4 Orientated locally	✓	✓	✓	✓	✓	✓	
5 Facilitation only	✓	✓	✓		✓	✓	

approach for international development. As described here and in other parts of this book, the authors, based on decades of experience and also informed by many development workers we interviewed, have trusted and been witness to multiple transformative outcomes. In simple terms, a strengths-based approach universally catalyses change. We acknowledge the critiques in order to better make sense of this approach and realize the potential of a strengths-based approach for international development.

There is a place for problem analysis and problem-solving. When the car stops, the roof leaks, or a tap in a water system is broken, it is natural and appropriate to look for the problem. Problem-solving is suitable for mechanical, engineering or health issues where it is possible to identify a single and relatively simple resolution. These are technical contexts requiring mechanical type fixes. At the lowest level of aid delivery, identifying the absence of a basic need or resolving a construction issue may be all that is required. When human interaction is involved and behaviour change required, or when multiple systems are interacting and multiple solutions are potentially available, or when the emphasis is on the capacity to address bigger issues in future, then applying a strengths-based approach is more effective for achieving a useful and sustainable outcome.

A commonly asked question raised by people when they first hear of the approach is 'yes – but what about the problems?' Reason (2020: 10) suggests that 'in its emphasis on the positive, Appreciative Inquiry is in danger of ignoring the shadow'. However, a strengths-based approach both reveals the problems and provides means and processes to address them as groups articulate and then act towards preferred futures. Within Appreciative Inquiry, problems are revealed in the difference between the 'best of what is' within the discovery stage, and 'envisioning the ideal future' within the dream phase. Preskill and Catsambas (2006: 26) noted that 'issues, challenges, problems and conflict' are addressed 'by shifting the focus and language from one of deficits to one of hope and possibilities based on what has worked in the past'. As Patton (2003: 92) noted, 'existing weaknesses' are identified in 'wishes' or 'dreams' of participants. It is in the comparison of the current state and preferred future where problems or weaknesses are identified. It is in action taken to achieve the dream where problems are addressed. For a strengths-based approach, energy is focused on achieving the preferred future rather than on solving problems of the past. A simple but effective analogy is the focusing and moving towards the future of an open road rather than looking in the rear-view mirror (of a car) and trying to solve problems of the past (see Figure 2.5).

Keren Winterford used a strengths-based approach to review a sanitation programme in Nepal in 2012. The evaluation commissioners, SNV (Netherlands Development Organization), mandated a strengths-based approach in the review Terms of Reference, though this approach was unfamiliar to Nepalese Government officials. Initially the officials were concerned to know what was not working and needed to change. During a presentation of review findings to key stakeholders (from SNV, the Nepalese Government, and UNICEF) Keren provided assurance the findings showed 'areas of weakness, problems, issues and constraints'. Within a strengths-based perspective, these insights on problems to address were found in the comparison between 'success of the past and key enablers' and 'vision of preferred future'. The learning from the review highlighted that the strengths-based approach enables a constructive and safe space for everyone to express enablers of success, as well as practical guidance and recommendations for changes for the future.

The same concern about problems was expressed to Keren during training on Appreciative Inquiry for a research organization in Cambodia. As the week-long training started, many individuals highlighted the need to focus on problems. Keren allayed participants' fears, noting they will see the problems, but not in a direct way. 'Trust the process' was a common phrase used in the training. Once the group had practised all stages of Appreciative Inquiry, they came to realize that the problems and what needed to be fixed were embedded in the dream statements of the group. These statements described the change required, and their identification of success of the past, and enablers of these provided them with effective resources to make these changes.

Also linked to the concern about not addressing problems is the view that a strengths-based approach does not acknowledge or seeks to repress or deny problems or challenges of individuals, groups or communities. This critique is summarized by Bushe (2011) who highlights what is positive for some may be negative for others. A strengths-based approach does not dismiss accounts of conflict, problems, or stress. As Whitney and Trosten-Bloom (2003: 18) wrote: 'we simply do not use them as the basis of analysis or action'. Negative experiences are validated by strengths-based approaches, but are not used as the focus to inquire and analyse as a means to create change. The emphasis on creating change through coalescing and bringing together multiple strengths, assets, and resources is an important distinction of a strengths-based approach.

The view that bad behaviour and/or what is not working needs to be called out as part of a change agenda has often been expressed as a critique of a strengths-based approach. In cases where illegal practices or criminal activity have occurred, then clearly these need to be called out and addressed. From a strengths perspective, this action does not catalyse or sustain change. It may offer a reset of the baseline but no insights into transformative change so that bad or illegal behaviour does not continue in the future, including at a systemic level. Problem analysis by outsiders who are not experiencing the problem, can narrow the perspective of what needs to change and how that change might occur.

Linked to the concern that a strengths-based approach does not deal with problems is the view that these approaches create simply feel-good 'Pollyanna' moments and do not enable critical or balanced exploration. Fitzgerald et al. (2010) highlight the view that Appreciative Inquiry is dismissed as 'the proverbial group hug' (p. 224). Rogers and Fraser (2003) also were concerned that by 'highlighting the positive there is a risk that Appreciative Inquiry may encourage unrealistic and dysfunctional perceptions, attitudes and behaviours' (p. 77).

This critique highlights two important distinctions and nuances of a strengths-based approach. First, strengths-based approaches are orientated towards creating change, not simply focused on revealing 'positives' within current situations. The change process seeks to create alternative futures by drawing on what is working in the present, by revealing and amplifying these in order to create change. It is the 'appreciative stance' which harnesses the strengths of the past and potential of the future for change. Second, change is not simply about fixing the present, but is orientated towards transformative change, that is, new situations, contexts in which individuals, groups, or organizations can operate (see Chapter 4 for a detailed description on transformative change). The future orientation and focus on transformative change are important distinctions of the change process in a strengths-based approach.

Another criticism of the strengths-based approach is that it ignores dynamics of power. Gray (2011: 8) raises concerns about 'an uncritical adoption of community development theory, which takes an overly optimistic view of communities as forces for good'. Mathie and Cunningham (2003: 483) note: 'Neither ABCD nor Appreciative Inquiry directly confronts the issue of unequal power and its attendant oppressions; instead, both tend to appeal to the higher motive of using power to act in the shared interests of the common good, and to uncover the strengths of those who might otherwise be less valued'. Aldred (2009) also raises concern about use of Appreciative Inquiry in contexts of unequal power relations.

The concern regarding power and inclusion is well-founded and the call for more guidance on effective engagement of a broad spectrum of stakeholders, 'including addressing power issues' (Rogers and Fraser 2003: 78) has been addressed by a variety of strengths-based practices. For example, as noted by Mathie and Cunningham (2003: 482), 'a central theme of ABCD is the relocation of power to communities – power that has otherwise been held by external agencies'. Also emphasized through Co-production, through effective facilitation, the power to control inquiry and to decide on action to take should be in the hands of participants. Elliott (1999) writing about Appreciative Inquiry, highlights the importance of ensuring collaboration across a broad spectrum of stakeholders. Similarly, Cooperrider et al. (2008) emphasize the importance of 'engaging the whole' within an Appreciative Inquiry process. The Appreciative Inquiry Summit (Ludema et al., 2003), as discussed earlier, is an approach which emphasizes a systems approach to change and seeks to 'get the whole system in the room' as a means of equalizing power of different stakeholders.

Another concern about a strengths-based approach is that it does not address broader structural or systemic inequalities such as race, class, or gender discrimination. Gray (2011: 8) argues 'that the agenda of participation and self-responsibility comes dangerously close to the political project of the conservative New Right, which critics see as devolving social responsibility from neoliberal governments onto local people – poor individuals and families and, more often than not, women – who bear the brunt of the burden of participation'. Friedli (2013: 140) also questions the role of assets-based approaches and failure to distinguish between a radical critique of welfare, one that is firmly linked to an analysis of neoliberal economics and the neoliberal attack on welfare. She noted 'If the strength of the assets movement is that it has generated discussion about re-dressing the balance of power between the public sector, public services and local communities, its fatal weakness has been the failure to question the balance of power between public services, communities and corporate interests' (Friedli, 2013: 140).

Yet proponents of ABCD argue that the approach 'has the potential to encourage active citizenship in the sense of citizen-to-citizen ties, while simultaneously strengthening the capacity of people as citizens to claim their rights of access to assets on which they depend for their livelihood' (Mathie and Cunningham, 2003: 475). Experience of the authors and those interviewed for this book confirms multiple ways in which a strengths-based approach enacts the role of citizens and through this, calls to account roles and responsibilities of governments and ensures the protection of rights. A strengths-based approach is not a claim for self-reliance, but a means to engage and activate individual, group, and community strengths to connect with each other and with external actors to achieve entitled human rights and their own preferred futures.

A strengths-based approach may not be appropriate or effective in every single international development context. In general, a strengths-based approach is relevant in organizational and social environments where there are multiple actors, complexities, and possible options for achieving change. As noted above, there is no use applying strengths-based approaches to simple mechanical or engineering problems like a leaking roof, a broken pipe, or a car that will not start. Setting aside these obvious misfits, there are several contexts in international development where strengths-based approaches are not likely to be effective. Here are three: when the invitation is rejected; when funders do not allow sufficient time or space for collective efforts; and when the political climate is intolerant of such an approach.

First, choosing to use a strengths-based approach is an invitation to all who participate to look for and contribute strengths, including competencies, assets, resources, or relationships. The development worker begins a relationship with a particular group, community, organisation or institution, and enters into a social contract in which the participants are ready to make a significant contribution to addressing issues they care about.

Informed by decades of aid discourse, where the poorer and more vulnerable you can appear, the more likely you are to qualify for aid, the request for mutuality of contribution is a shock. Sometimes government or community leaders can be so taken aback by the concepts of asset contribution, they may decline to participate. This has been a common experience of those who have been using approaches like Appreciative Inquiry, ABCD, and Positive Deviance, all of which demand that there is a strong equity in contribution by those who are hoping for change. Barbara Pamphilon, whose research work is described in Case Study 14, explains that in her work with village communities in Papua New Guinea, not every community leader or family is initially willing to participate. She said strengths-based approaches invite people to participate voluntarily and are happy to accept that some may not want to do so. However, our research for development programme found that it only takes five to six families initially to participate and benefit before, as people see the changes for themselves, many then want to join in willingly'.

Second, a strengths-based approach demands that programmes and donors provide sufficient space and time for essential groundwork in consultation, asset-mapping, and building appropriate networks or associations. This type of engagement should continue through the life of a programme. In traditional project design, this sort of engagement is supposed to be part of the initial design process and completed by the time the project starts. In a strengths-based approach, design and implementation are part of the change process. Once a question is asked, the change process has begun. The process of 'project implementation' is also part of the ongoing inquiry, learning, and planning process for ongoing objectives (preferred futures). For more traditional donors, engaging with communities or organizations is a short-term process before implementation.

Finally, sometimes the culture of aid dependence is so strong that any attempt to build a programme around the mobilization of local strengths is seen as both unnecessary and even insulting. Why ask the community or local government to contribute, when there is so much money available that there is far greater urgency to distribute funds than to engage participants? For a long time, the term community development was understood to be 'finding ways to ensure the funds are properly distributed'. One of the largest community projects of the World Bank, incorrectly titled 'Community Driven Development', provides subsidies to local communities whose contribution is to identify how they are going to use the funds and account for them properly. Traditionally, bilateral programme negotiations in such environments have been about sharing the 'pie' of need between donors. There may be little interest in recognizing local strengths and assets. Sometimes a country has suffered so much from natural or civil disasters that donors are only thinking of how they can come in and do whatever is needed for the people. In some contexts, governments may consider that a politically-appropriate response to offers of international development is to accept it, with little connection to locally-determined strengths and priorities.

The analysis in this chapter in part helps to explain why development agencies have persisted with problem-based, expert-driven approaches even when they have proven to be ineffective. If the programming system requires a full externally driven analysis of a 'problem' before funding is approved, then allowing for more iterative, locally driven reflections is a challenge to the system. Similarly, if funding decision-making processes are based largely on a justification of how 'bad' a problem is, and how convincing the proposed solution is, any analysis of existing strengths and self-determined strategies in a particular context, does not 'fit' the format. If efforts are made to consider how to best spend the money rather than how best to support localized agendas of change, building from local strengths and assets, then a strengths-based approach does not fit either.

Despite these three circumstances noted above, there is strong applicability of a strengths-based approach to international development as demonstrated through this book. Part C explores the relevance of a strengths-based approach to international development practice in more detail, reflecting on key concepts within contemporary practice. It showcases many examples that demonstrate the approach's relevance and value and also its potential for international development more broadly.

This chapter introduced common processes and methods associated with a strengths-based approach and seven well-established strengths-based practices. These practices demonstrate the strong foundations on which a strengths-based approach to international development stands. While not yet mainstream in international development practice, this thinking and practice is not new and much can be learned from other fields and disciplines. A strengths-based approach has both a real theoretical and practical basis for uptake in international development.

The next chapter explores how change happens within a strengths-based approach confirming the value and potential of the approach for international development.

CHAPTER 4
How change happens within a strengths-based approach

> *A strengths-based approach helps us to think holistically about any initiative, so we don't just see something as a funded project, but a broad effort which combines our expertise and resources, with the funding that comes in from outside. It reminds us to focus on our competence and contribution as part of the overall effort to bring about change* (Setareki Macanawai, CEO of Pacific Disability Forum)
>
> *How much better the world can be and how much energy can be generated when a strengths-based approach is used* (Soli Middleby)

A strengths-based approach offers a paradigm shift in how change is understood. While this can be applied to any change process, our interest is to explore and explain change from a strengths-based perspective within international development. This chapter provides a framework to describe how change happens within a strengths-based approach and how this framework connects to dimensions of change which are central to international development.

There has been a long-running interest in how change happens within international development. Notions of change in international development have evolved over time, with new offerings commonly reacting to previous practice. The use of complexity thinking (see Chapter 1) (Ramalingam, 2013; Burns and Worsley, 2015; Boulton et al., 2015) or a systems perspective (Green, 2016) have been offered to make sense of, and inform development outcomes. A strengths-based approach complements these notions of change and provides a practical means to not only understand how change happens but enable enriching and long-lasting social justice and equality outcomes.

Conceptual framework

To summarize how change happens within a strengths-based approach, one of this book's authors developed a conceptual framework (Winterford 2013), which has been further refined for this book. Refinement has been informed by conversations on key development concepts over time and the variety of development workers interviewed for the book. While the framework is orientated to international development, it could be applied to other socially orientated fields of practice.

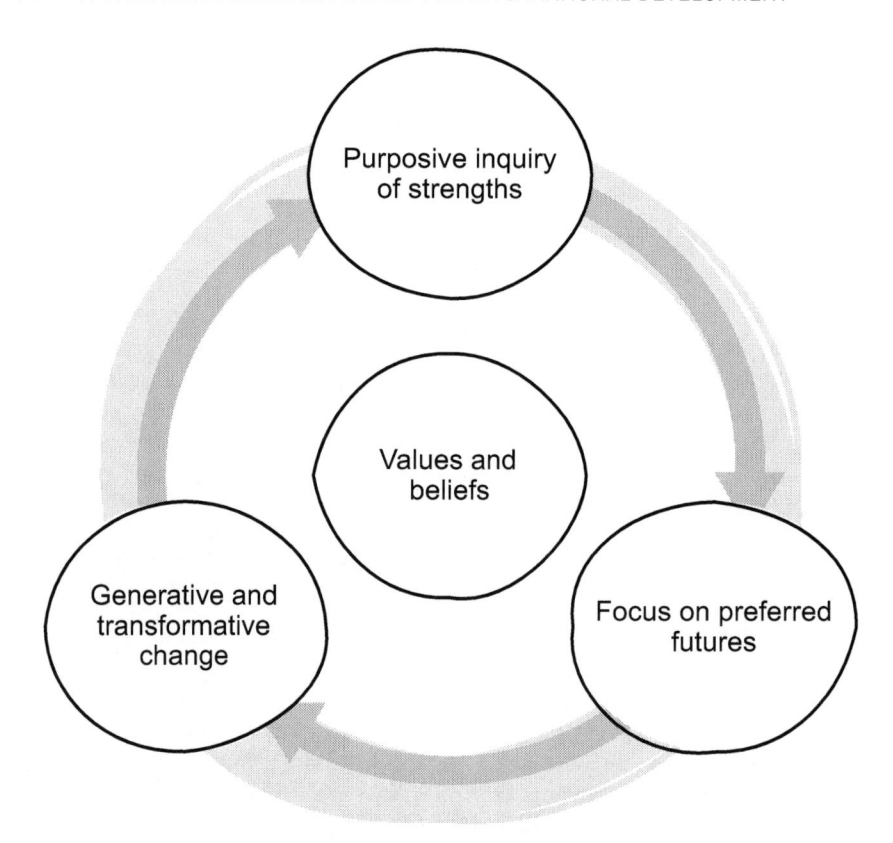

Figure 4.1 Framework for how change happens within a strengths-based approach

Figure 4.1 summarizes the framework and includes four interrelated areas, details of which are also explained in other chapters:

- values or philosophical underpinnings (see Chapter 2);
- purposive inquiry focused on strengths, assets, local resources, and what is working well (see Chapter 3);
- focus on preferred futures (see Chapter 3);
- expected broad set of change outcomes (see Chapter 1 and explanation below).

1. Values and beliefs

A change process orientated through a strengths-based approach is informed by a foundation of beliefs or values which include: positionality of oneself; one's own view on the world; how one views others; how inquiry is understood to inform change processes; and the value of strengths to support change. These fundamental beliefs or values both underpin understanding about how change happens in a strengths-based approach, as well as define appreciation of differences in socio-cultural values across the world (see Chapter 6).

The framework assumes that there is always something of value or worth or something which is working, even as the exception, which can be drawn on to catalyse change (Saleebey, 1992; Kretzmann and McKnight, 1993; Bushe, 2001; Whitney and Trosten-Bloom, 2003). From a strengths perspective, what is already working well or the strengths which are already present, are the source from which change is created. The value of strengths, assets, or resources existing in any context is the foundation of how change happens within a strengths-based approach.

2. Purposive inquiry of strengths

A strengths-based approach uses a unique form of inquiry for identifying strengths to facilitate change. The form of inquiry deliberately seeks to reveal strengths, what is working and valued in each setting. A strengths-based inquiry can reveal two types of strengths. First, strengths, assets, or resources are revealed within individuals, groups, organizations, or communities. Second, exceptional experiences, behaviours, or practices are revealed within a group, community, or organization. In this second form, the inquiry seeks to identify the factors that have enabled high points or exceptional experiences to occur in order that they may be amplified and replicated in future. Bushe (2001) described this inquiry and the process of change associated with Appreciative Inquiry as 'tracking and fanning' whereby: 'tracking is a state of mind where one is constantly looking for what one wants more of. It begins with the assumption that whatever one wants more of already exists, even if in small amounts. Fanning is any action that amplifies, encourages, and helps you to get more of whatever you are looking for' (Bushe, 2001: 6).

While not unique to strengths-based thinking, a highly participatory process is valued to inform an inquiry. This ensures that a greater breadth and depth of understanding of the local context is generated. Within a strengths perspective, knowledge of individuals themselves is valued 'and treated as a natural resource' (Weick 1992: 24). Individuals, groups, and communities know best their own strengths and assets. Knowledge generated from the purposive inquiry is owned and used by individuals and groups to create change.

3. Focus on preferred futures

The knowledge generated and insights supported by this inquiry help individuals, communities, and organizations to define the current situation and imagine the future in new and novel ways.

As described in Chapter 3, a range of strengths-based practices have been developed and applied in various disciplines and areas of work to catalyse preferred futures. These practices share three distinct elements in how their focus of inquiry catalyses change: they start by inquiry into existing strengths; the inquiry seeks to connect strengths, resources, and assets within the given context; and then they build and rebuild relationships in which dialogue is continually fostered.

Start with existing strengths

Within a strengths perspective, change starts from what is already present, in this case, strengths and assets of the people, community, or organization, as well as exceptional experiences and successful behaviours, or practices. Strengths are fostered and catalysed while exceptional experiences are elevated and amplified so they become 'new norms'.

Starting change with existing strengths means that this is the starting point, from within the local context, rather than resources from outside directing change. The notion of 'crowding out' is also helpful to describe this change. Fowler and Biekart (2008) describe crowding out in relation to citizen-driven change: 'the imagined future is one where, over the course of time citizen driven change crowds out uncivic norms and behaviours' (p. 180). The notion of 'crowding out' is central to how change happens within a strengths-based approach. Through revealing and catalysing existing strengths, and defining preferred futures and actions to achieve change, the status quo is effectively crowded out through alternative perceptions, aspirations, and action.

Numerous examples of crowding out were identified by Keren Winterford in her research (2013) on Citizen Voice and Action, a social accountability approach employed by World Vision (see Chapter 12 for more details). Through the approach, service users, providers, and local government come together to explore how to improve experiences of basic services such as health or education. The approach deals with corrupt or lazy service provision, by crowding out those who behave in this way, through a collective expectation that accountable and hard work are expected by the community and inappropriate behaviour of government officials or service providers is no longer tolerated. For example, nurses are expected to turn up on time and doctors are expected to provide free service as per government standards. Crowding out takes place when the majority of staff act in this way and those who want to continue to provide poor service are excluded, leave, or change their ways: their old ways of working are no longer accepted by community and other service providers. This way of creating change establishes new norms and behavioural expectations. In the instances where criminal action was identified through Citizen Voice and Action, individuals were referred to local police for follow-up action.

The notion of strengths as 'renewable and expandable resources' (Saleebey, 2009: 11) means that while change is initiated by using existing strengths, over time strengths within individuals, communities, or organizations also change and grow, and these strengths can be continually employed to create change.

Connect existing strengths

From a strengths perspective, change towards preferred futures is supported by connecting strengths, resources, and assets within the given context. The key is to 'locate all the available local assets, to begin connecting them with one another in ways that multiply their power and effectiveness' (Kretzmann and McKnight, 1993: 6). Efforts are made to 'match and develop the inherent strengths of people *and* the social environment' (Sullivan and Rapp, 2009: 221). The notion of synergy describes the outcomes of connecting strengths: 'The synergistic perspective assumes that when phenomena (including people) are brought into interrelationship they create new and often unexpected patterns and resources that typically exceed the complexity of their individual constituents' (Saleebey, 1992: 11). In order to maximize the connections of strengths and assets, a strengths perspective prioritizes the inclusion of 'the whole system' in the change process. Emphasis is placed on encouraging participation from all stakeholders so that the change effort can benefit from the multiplicity and connection of these resources.

Build and rebuild relationships

From a strengths perspective, change towards preferred futures is enabled through building and rebuilding relationships. While an emphasis on relationships is not unique to a strengths-based approach, relationships are defined as a means to catalyse change. Efforts are made to 'constantly build and rebuild the relationships between and among local residents, local associations and local institutions' (Kretzmann and McKnight, 1993: 9). These connections provide an enabling environment to connect strengths, assets, and resources. Strengthening relationships provides a way of enabling and sustaining efforts for change. In a strengths-based approach, while emphasis is on the internal focus of change, external resources and expertise to support and augment internally defined change objectives are also not valued. From a strengths perspective, change towards preferred futures starts from existing strengths and continues to employ other external strengths over time.

A strengths-based approach seeks to create a safe space for different types of groups to engage in a change process. Effort should be made to ensure the negative aspects of politics or personality do not dominate and that any power between different actor groups is equalized, to ensure that those often marginalized or silenced are core to the process of change that is relevant to their lives.

4. Potential for generative and transformative change

An important insight for how change is understood to occur in a strengths-based approach is that change is constant and there is no particular end point to be defined. This contrasts with dominant perspectives in international development which describe projects or programmes with specific end-of-programme change outcomes. In a strengths-based approach, change is uncertain and emergent, informed by earlier change outcomes. Figure 4.1 illustrates that generative and transformative change outcomes in turn fuel new cycles of inquiry and inform new perspectives on preferred futures.

Generative change

Generative change is a key feature of a strengths-based approach (introduced in Chapter 2). Schön (1979) explains that answers or responses are framed and aligned to the questions we ask. The questions asked within a strengths-based approach purposively invite generative and transformative change. Schon (1979: 268–69) wrote, 'it follows that problem setting matters. The ways in which we set social problems determine both the kinds of purposes and values we seek to realize, and the directions in which we seek solutions'. It is this basic understanding – that the questions we ask determine the answers we get – which guides a strengths-based approach to ask different types of questions.

The central visioning process within a strengths-based approach offers individuals and communities a 'generative' metaphor that inspires new decisions and actions towards preferred positive futures. As explained in Chapter 3, there are numerous methods to support groups, organizations, and communities to imagine preferred futures. Proponents of Appreciative Inquiry describe the notion of generative metaphors (Cooperrider and Srivastva, 1987) to ignite alternatives and action for change. Generative metaphors inform how we feel, think, and act, often unconsciously. Within Appreciative Inquiry, generative metaphors, 'open up new avenues of thinking and acting' (Bushe, 2013: 6). These metaphors can surprise, strengthen relations, ignite people's hearts and spirits, and force us to question the taken for granted reality and see the world anew with different and alternative possibilities. The metaphors act as a coalescing force to drive action towards preferred futures.

The power of the metaphor is present in many contexts. In a documentary about South Africa directed by Sifiso Khanyile, *A New Country*, released in 2020, the power of the metaphor is described by Adv. Tembeka Ngcukaitobi, Senior Advocate, author, and activist. His insightful message addresses the power of an image that compels people to collect and act together for a preferred future:

> We should never abandon the myth of South Africa's exceptionalism, because it is in that myth that we start believing that something bigger than us is possible, and that if we abandon that myth we also abandon dreaming. And yet we do need to dream big in order to be a better country, including the very idea of forgiving people who have not asked for forgiveness, that comes as a consequence of the idea of the myth of a better country. And so even though I identify myth-making as part and parcel of the problem I realize its sheer power in keeping us motivated about working for a better South Africa (Khanyile, 2020).

Transformative change

Connected to notions of generative change is transformative change, from which further insights about change within a strengths-based approach can be gained. Fields of practice and literature such as organizational management, ecology, and engineering use the term 'transformative change', since it recognizes that change is constant. This notion of emerging change is aligned to complexity thinking introduced in Chapter 1. Metaphors help to shift perspectives and offer opportunity for something new in transformative change. Some key characteristics of transformative change are described below.

Transformative change encompasses a paradigm shift, focused on new ways of thinking and being. First, across a variety of fields of practice and multiple authors (Levy and Merry, 1986; Mezirow, 1997; O'Brien, 2012) transformative change is underpinned by characteristics such as multi-dimensional and multi-level change which are discontinuous of the present state. Descriptors such as 'higher-order change' or 'deep-level change' are also used. Transformative change includes reflecting on and challenging existing assumptions, prevailing norms, and interests and acting in new ways.

Second, transformative change is connected to systems thinking. Transformative change is often described as systems-level change which is large-scale, holistic and recognizes the interplay with any change and other parts of the system. Importantly within systems thinking, there is recognition that there are multiple aspects or parts of a system, and that most often all different parts need to shift to enable transformation. Systems thinking recognizes that change in one part of the system will influence, intentionally or not, other parts in the system. There may be positive or negative feedback loops as a change in one part of the system drives change in other parts of the system, sometimes in the same direction, or other times in a different direction. Having a broad perspective of all aspects, including micro and macro influences towards change, is therefore necessary.

Third, transformative change can be incremental or shift quickly. Importantly, incremental change cannot be insignificant since change needs to shift the status quo. Burnes (2005) described the perspective of continuous transformational change which can be shaped through a series of small in-depth steps or small wins. Small wins contrast with quick wins, which are first-order changes where people take fast and easy steps towards change.

A key feature of transformative change is that it is not problem-solving. This way of thinking recognizes that problems are history, and rather than focusing energy on the past, focus is directed to the future. Transformative change is focused on ways to meet the preferred expectations and aspirations of the future. The focus is on creating something new, rather than fixing the past.

Challenge traditional forms or knowledge to inform change

Generative and transformative change challenge traditional forms of knowing and knowledge to inform change creation. As Gergen noted (1978: 1349), problem-solving approaches are 'primarily focused on reliable description and explanation'. Problem-solving approaches are focused on understanding, prediction, and control. This describes the project management approach included in almost all international development programming. Gergen (1978) argued that to 'recognize facts one must already possess some form of conceptual knowledge. Such preliminary knowledge is required in order for a discrimination to be made between "facts" and "non-facts" or events and their surrounding context. Yet, it may be further asked, "what is the basis of the preliminary conceptual orientation?"' (Gergen, 1978: 1348). For development workers, the question should also be posed: how can assessments, analysis, and project designs be decided through scant knowledge of local contexts and perspectives?

Generative and transformative change requires us to break free from perspectives of 'what is' to consider 'what might be'. Gergen (1978: 1354) wrote 'if the theorist considers current social patterns as fragile, temporary, and capable of alteration, theoretical analysis need not be circumscribed by a consideration of "what now exists". Rather, the theorist may be freed to consider alternatives, the advantages and disadvantages of relationships as yet unseen'. Gergen (1978) argues that change based on what is known proves detrimental to catalytic potential. This insight is also true for international development.

A strengths-based approach encourages us to see the world anew, to put aside bias and current forms of knowing to move towards new possibilities or new futures. For the development worker, this practice can be challenging, though as demonstrated in this book, it is possible. We explore more about the development worker role and knowledge in catalysing change in Chapter 8.

Another dimension of alternative forms of knowing and knowledge central to generative and transformative change, is the centrality of inclusive approaches to participation in generating knowledge. The experts' job of analysis, description, and prescription is brought into question, when local voices are centralized. The power structures which underpin a problem-solving approach are dissolved as broader sets of (multi-dimensional) participants at different levels throughout the system are brought to engage in the change process. More discussion on power is included in Chapter 5.

The five key strategies used by a strengths-based approach in relation to changing power dynamics, central to a transformative change agenda, are:

1. Amplify the use of new sources of power.
2. Crowd out the misuse of power over others by a dominant individual or a few individuals.
3. Generate forums of engagement that are appreciative, inclusive, and equitable.
4. Promote dialogue through deliberative/representative governance by discovery of new platforms for citizen voice and accountability.

5. Establish multi-stakeholder platforms where everyone or representatives of every level within a system or organization negotiate a new collective vision of reality.

As described above, change is a key feature and purpose of a strengths-based approach. Informed by a strengths perspective, change starts from the centre of the local context or situation, fuelled by local assets, strengths, or what is working well. A purposive inquiry intentionally seeks to reveal these as a means to catalyse change. Case Study 7, set in South Africa, illustrates these and related aspects of generative change over an extended period of time.

Case Study 7 Transformative change for a safe community in South Africa

The Sinakho Safe Community Network is the third stage of an outreach programme of the Department of Social Responsibility (DSR) of the Anglican Diocese of Grahamstown in Eastern Cape, South Africa (Anglican Overseas Aid, 2019).

This case study illustrates the shift in practice towards a more holistic and positive future-orientated programme as the DSR increasingly embraced a strengths-based approach. What began as an individual care response to a pandemic (HIV/AIDS) and efforts to address gender-based violence has moved to a more holistic understanding of the place of violence in culture and community practice. Encouraged by the key elements of a strengths-based practice, the programme further evolved to focus on how to achieve a 'safe community'. Exploring available strengths, assets, and effective networking practices, the programme is now introducing alternatives to institutionalized cultural practices that perpetuated violence, and promoting sustainable opportunity for greater social cohesion and sustainable livelihoods.

Director of DSR Tony Schnell, interviewed for this book, was already convinced of the value of changing from a deficit approach when he came to the position after having attended a course in Appreciative Inquiry years earlier. Through his influence and multiple staff development activities, the programme increasingly embraced a strengths-based approach. The framework for this shift was a response to the question put by Tony Schnell when he was first appointed as the Director of DSR: 'How can the whole of the community and all the support agencies, including the police, use what they do have, their strengths, assets and resources, to achieve a community vision of what they most desire, a safe and prosperous community?'

Now, this way of thinking and working is fundamental to all DSR's activities. Tony said, 'once you really understand the strengths-based approach, it informs the way you do everything, independent of who is funding us. People think it is a special DSR approach, because for them everything we do is based on this way of working'. He explained what he means by applying a strengths approach in the following terms:

1. *We do not simply follow the steps.* Just following set steps is a danger because the community needs to take time to understand what is behind each of these steps. When you ask a community about their 'resources', they need

(Continued)

Case Study 7 Continued

to think about the fact that they have never actually thought this way before. We need to spend time with them so they can 'discover' their assets or resources. For many, survival has meant doing the same thing every time, every year without variation, so the idea of being able to improve is foreign. To engage in discovering successes of the past and identifying existing resources is a big jump in thinking. We cannot rush to move to the next step. Assets and resources are not accessible to people who live in such poverty: people just surviving in life are not aware of successes or what has worked well. To learn the process of discovery becomes a very important asset for them.

2. *Ability to make a decision.* A strengths-based approach makes it possible for people to have and own their choices. A community that is just surviving has few choices. Their past experience is that they cannot or dare not choose an alternative course. Helping a community understand what has succeeded in their story and available resources means it becomes the community who is able to decide. When the process is repeated over years, the community becomes confident that different choices can lead to better outcomes.

3. *Listen for the core resource.* The core resource is what has leverage for change. This may not be seen by the community in the same way that the facilitator initially sees it. For example, when looking for the key players, the community may look to different people as their dominant drivers. We also thought initially that developing liaison with the police was a key resource for the community, but it turns out that the forum where leaders and police can learn to appreciate each other and their respective roles was the more important resource.

4. *Find the voice of the people.* A strengths-based approach is about helping people find their voice. It may be the whole community, or it may be sections of it that have not been listened to previously. This process of listening gives ownership of their opinion and experience. When people own their voice, they do not give you answers that they think you want to hear, which often happens in deficit approaches, but what they really think and feel: this is the power of finding their own voice.

5. *Expansive thinking process.* A strengths-based approach introduces an expansive thinking process that opens up the world to the community. There is never going to be one answer when we use this approach. Development agencies like 'one answer' from the community because they can then design a project around this. Single answers are about having less of one bad thing. A strengths-based approach expands thinking about each of the community's available resources. In this approach, it is not about having less of what is bad, but more of a multiple of possibilities. A strengths-based approach links a community to possibilities.

6. *Refresh.* While a strengths-based approach is about attitude change and a different way of thinking, it is not easy for a community or for field staff to stay the course without continuous refreshers and further guided reflection, so that it becomes the way of doing things for them.

(Continued)

Case Study 7 Continued

7. *A strengths-based approach is a way of processing everything.* It has become core to the way we work. We must adapt our approach in each community, otherwise it may not be meaningful to the people until they have learned to own the process themselves. We look for signs of attitude change and ownership of a different mindset: in this sense, context is primary.
8. *Turn down the speed dial.* The best advice I can give is to slow the process down so that we keep the people on board with learning how to appreciate what they have, who they are and how they can use their own resources. It is disrespectful to 'speed past'. We can show respect for the community when we let them lead the process of self-discovery.

PART B
Exploring a strengths-based approach

> *I see the value of a strengths-based approach in international development is related to the importance of understanding the links between values/frames of reference and change/outcomes for all programming* (Vicki Vaartjes)

Part B provides deeper insights into a strengths-based approach, exploring its power in reframing international development. Contemporary development practice pays more attention to power and culture than ever before, acknowledging the influence that powerful systems and people, as well as values and beliefs have over the way change happens. This Part also reminds us of the significance of psychological understanding for development practice, including positive thinking and approaches, and considers the significant implications of a different frame of reference for the lives and work of individual development workers.

Chapter 5 addresses issues associated with power, given the centrality of power to the achievement of developmental change, through a strengths-based lens. It considers different perspectives on power and aspects of empowerment and disempowerment in the conceptualization and practice of international development. This chapter applies a strengths-based approach to power, giving an alternative frame of reference to the power of people and organizations to bring about change. Understanding power through a strengths-based lens as well as applying a strengths-based lens to the application of positive power, contributes to deeper opportunities for collaboration, mobilizing positive power and joint action.

Chapter 6 delves into the reality that cultures consider strengths and change differently, and that a strengths-based approach will reveal values that will enable positive change processes to happen. The chapter discusses concepts related to different cultural values and their implications for the methods used within strengths-based thinking and practice. Also, by applying a strengths-based approach to cultural values, for example in relation to motivation and leadership, this chapter supports more attuned collaboration and practice.

Chapter 7 presents perspectives on positive psychology which provide valuable insights on why and how a strengths-based approach works. Insights into human emotions, motivations, and character strengths as enablers for change help development workers to see inside the change process which is core to international development practice.

Chapter 8 is critical for readers considering their role as development workers in this complex, messy world. It answers the question 'so what does this new concept mean for me?' It supports development workers to consider themselves and their responsibilities, and offers practical suggestions for shifting practice, which both liberate and motivate.

CHAPTER 5
Perspectives on power

> *We (people, groups and leaders) all need power to achieve change: a strengths-based approach is the means to identify and mobilise existing sources of power as well as generate new sources. The approach enables leaders to apply power in constructive ways, crowd out negative aspects of power and generate motivation to achieve positive change. Without power, little change happens, and a strengths-based approach shines light in the right direction* (Deborah Rhodes)

A strengths-based approach provides an alternative perspective on the notion of power from that commonly described in international development discourse. We know that power is important. This chapter briefly mentions common ideas associated with power such as 'changing the balance of power' and 'disempowerment/empowerment', before offering an alternative, informed by the philosophical underpinnings of a strengths-based approach. A strengths-based approach recognizes we all have power and that power can be understood in different ways. It is worthwhile to examine the dominant discourse on power in international development, through this alternative lens. The chapter also draws on earlier research by Keren Winterford (2013, 2016.)

Negative view of power within international development discourse

The notion of power is central to contemporary international development discourse and is most often framed as negative. As Chambers (2006: 102) noted, 'power is often spoken of as bad'. Power is often associated with 'authoritarianism, bossing, control, discipline, domination' and understood in terms of an 'abuse' or 'exploitation' of power (p. 100). Contemporary development practice includes efforts to strengthen or empower some people or groups as a means of shrinking the negative power of others, often state power over citizens. The notion of empowerment is discussed further below, but first the metaphors most commonly used to explain power and reinforce its negative portrayal are considered.

A four-dimension typology of power describes power over (control or influence one has over another); power to (agency or capability to decide on and take actions); power with (collective power of organization and acting together); and power within (personal confidence and self-esteem) (VeneKlasen and Miller, 2002). This was informed by earlier work by Lukes (1974) and has further informed other models and analysis of power relevant to the international development sector (Gaventa, 1980, 2006). As noted by Winterford (2016: 698) 'within political theory, philosophy, and socio-cultural writing there is an array of perspectives on power which is broader than that most often cited within development discourse'. NGOs predominantly use bottom-up processes in order to strengthen citizen power (power to, power with, and power within) to countervail (state) power over its citizens (Chambers, 2006: 100). Within international development there has also been an overemphasis on power as domination and not enough attention on the potential of expanding power through connecting and using different types of power from different stakeholder groups.

Changing the balance of power/power as domination

Redressing power inequality or asymmetry is often described as a key agenda of international development. A common phrase is 'changing the balance of power' which reinforces the negative view of power as domination. The phrase expresses an underlining view of power as a finite resource or commodity which is exchanged between actors, through contest or confrontation. For example, power may shift from state to citizen or from majority to minority groups. Chambers (2006) highlights that this dominant understanding of power confines relationships to a contest. The transfer of ownership is defined as a 'zero-sum' game, where the loss of power is balanced by the gain of power and the acquisition of power is a contest: 'those with power have to be induced to lose it' (Chambers, 2006: 102). Through this understanding of power as contested, 'confrontation and conflict are recognized as often integral to success' (Chambers, 2006: 102). This thinking does not explain the kinds of transformational change which are necessary to tackle global issues and challenges, nor does it align with a strengths-based approach, as discussed below.

Empowerment/disempowerment

The term empowerment is also commonly used in international development, though there is no single or shared definition. The underlining premise is of power as a finite entity and power as domination. As Alsop et al. (2005: 2) wrote: 'as a relational concept, empowerment often means redressing imbalances of power between those that have it and those who do not. This can also imply that empowerment is a zero-sum game – that is, one person or group gains power at the expense of another'. Luttrell et al. (2009) in setting out an overview of definitions and conceptual approaches to empowerment also emphasizes power over. Through a strengths-based lens, this framing of power contributes to lost potential for constructive change through a zero-sum game; that is, there has to be a loser in order for there to be a change. For transformational change, a new orientation of interests and actors is necessary to reprioritize everyone's interests and actions towards new and different agendas. For example, the efforts of the disability rights movement since the Convention on the Rights of Persons with Disabilities was formalized in 2006 has raised understanding that all societies are better off if people with disabilities (15 per cent of the population) are included in decision-making that affects their lives, and rights are protected, without any group 'losing power'. There is also clear understanding that gender equality outcomes not only benefit women but men also, and the broader society. Gender equality outcomes are enabled when there is change for both men and women and transformation to new ways of thinking, being, and acting.

The term 'disempowerment' is consistent with deficit thinking: naming individuals, groups, or communities as disempowered is to view them as weak, ineffectual, lacking agency, power, or authority. This identification denies inherent strengths, assets, and capabilities as premised within a strengths-based approach. Labels of disempowerment have negative consequences for those to whom this label applies. Moncrieffe (2007: 1) wrote that 'labelling can shift or sustain power relations in ways that trigger social dislocation and prejudice efforts to achieve greater equity'. She noted that terminology such as 'disempowered' may be erroneous and detrimental to individuals creating and owning positive change.

There is debate over the extent to which outsiders can actually empower others, at either an individual or group level. Many who perceive empowerment as a capacity believe that it is problematic to attempt to empower from the outside. Therefore, devising any form of external programme is problematic, owing to the danger of manipulation. However, others suggest that power relations behind disempowerment make it unrealistic for the disempowered to tackle inequality and disempowerment alone. By its very nature, disempowerment creates disadvantages through the way power relations shape choices, opportunities, and wellbeing. Owing to the internalization of oppression, the process of demanding increased rights or change cannot be expected to emerge spontaneously from within and to easily challenge entrenched inequalities, discrimination, and structural causes of disempowerment.

A strengths-based approach deals with these debates by recognizing inherent power, giving credit to individuals and groups and valuing the inherent nature of power. It is through the questions asked and creative facilitation that latent power or the potential of positive power are revealed and expressed. With a strengths-based perspective, it is known that strengths and power were always there.

Alternative views of power for a strengths-based approach

A narrow perspective on the notion of power dominates international development discourse. Key themes from broader theories about power are considered here (see also Winterford, 2016), closely aligned with a strengths-based approach; they offer potential for a different perspective for the sector and constructive insights on the value of a strengths-based approach. Below we explore power as capacity, collective power, and notions of expanding power, as illustrated in Figure 5.1. The figure represents a set of assets or strengths in the centre which combine together to expand a greater sum of power.

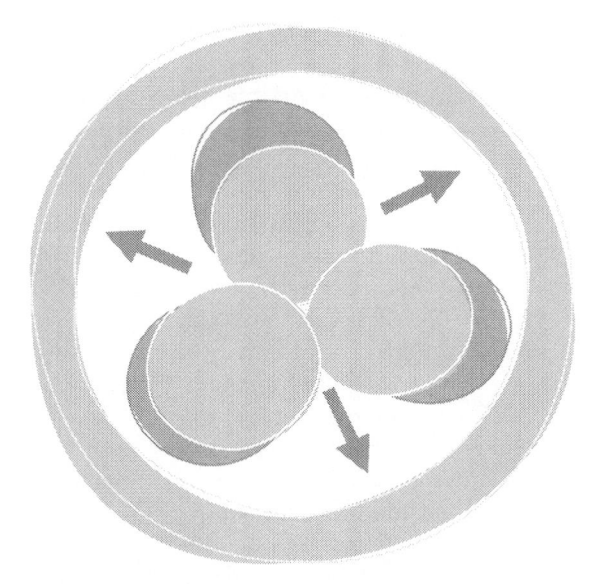

Figure 5.1 Inherent power, collective power, expanding power

Power as capacity

Power as capacity is a central tenet of a strengths-based approach, both founded in political theory and illustrated by the many examples provided by development workers interviewed for this book. As Saleebey (1992) wrote in relation to strengths-based social work, a strengths perspective is not about 'returning power to the people, but on discovering the power within people individually and collectively' (Saleebey, 1992: 8). A strengths perspective of creating change assumes that power resides in each individual: it might be latent, but once realized, has the potential to drive change.

Power can be conceived as a capacity, instead of a thing or event. Murphy (2011) distinguished internal from external perspectives on power and suggests that power 'is neither a thing (a resource or vehicle) nor an event (an exercise of power): it is a capacity' (p. 94). He noted: 'For too long, political scientists have studied power from the outside: power was understood as the cause of various observable effects ... This externalist perspective tends to reduce power to mere causal influence' (Murphy, 2011: 88). Capacity to realize one's aims 'is quite distinct from power as sheer causal influence' (p. 88). This internal perspective on power and recognition of capacity as power is aligned with a strengths-based approach which also recognizes inherent capacities of individuals.

Collective power

A key theme on power which has not been widely used in international development practice, but which offers insight into a strengths-based perspective on power is Hannah Arendt's view of collective power and her conceptualization of power as 'boundless' and 'expanding'.

Fifty years ago, Hannah Arendt emphasized the power of a collective group, noting 'power corresponds to the human ability not just to act, but to act in concert. Power is never the property of an individual; it belongs to a group and remains in existence only so long as the group keeps together' (Arendt, 1972: 143). She wrote that 'power springs up between men when they act together and vanishes the moment they disperse' (p. 200). It is through collective action that power is maintained. Power is also not necessarily conflictual, since it is generated when people work together, rather than only when they act against each other.

Arendt's focus is on 'power to' rather than 'power over'. This notion of power is evident in strengths-based practices described in this book and also in notions of transformative change which have an interest in systems change through all parts of the system, engaging in and working together for change. A strengths-based approach advocates for inclusion and participation of a variety of different actors in a change process. Power comes from people acting together. Margaret Mead is reputed to have recognized this when she wrote the famous words: 'Never doubt that a small group of thoughtful, committed citizens can change the world; indeed, it's the only thing that ever has'.

Arendt's political theory also includes a focus on relationships between citizens and the state and proposes that power of the state is legitimized by its citizens. She wrote 'it is the people's support that lends power to the institutions of a country, and this support is but the continuation of the consent that brought the laws into existence to begin with' (Arendt, 1972: 110). This is a central feature of representative government, where 'all political institutions are manifestations and materialisation of power, they petrify and decay as soon as the living power of the people ceases to uphold them' (Arendt, 1972: 111). This view of the location of power contrasts with dominant descriptions of power in international development as the 'balance of power' between citizen and the state.

Murphy (2011) extends Arendt's notion of the interplay of powers, aligned to a strengths-based perspective to consider how individuals best draw on others' capacities to expand their own power. He wrote: 'How do we learn to make use of other's capacities? First, we must learn how to make good use of our own capacities' (Murphy, 2011: 96). Relations between citizens and states are evident in this quote and the relationship between a strengths and rights-based approach. The use of a strengths-based approach often leads to the exercise of citizen claims to rights over duty bearers and as such does not deny but reinforces a rights-based approach. By drawing on one's own strengths and capacities, by engaging with others on a shared agenda, people are then able to reach out and seek protection of rights and use external resources. Practical examples are provided in Chapter 12.

Insights into connections between rights-based and strengths-based approaches are also found in literature. Peters and Landry (2018) identify a complementarity between the two. They note that while a rights-based approach places emphasis on vertical relationships (in contrast with a more horizontal relationship focus of the strengths-based approach), the notions of active citizenship, civic agency, and mutual interdependence, all relating to collective power, are central to both approaches (p. 10). Referring to papers written by Mathie and Cunningham (2008) and Mathie et al. (2017), Peters and Landry (2018) conclude that while both approaches will inevitably lead to a strong stance on advocacy for change, the use of a strengths-based approach as a starting point is less risky, more inclusive, and more comprehensive in the long run (Peters and Landry, 2018: 13–15). Collective power and combining a strengths-based approach and rights-based approach were also evident in Winterford's (2013, 2016) post-graduate research. Appreciation and use of existing strengths provide the foundation for citizens to advocate for rights.

The 'Do No Harm' approach also offers insights into the value of connections and a strengths-based approach's understanding of power. In 1999, Mary Anderson wrote a book entitled *Do No Harm: How Aid Can Support Peace – or War*. Reflecting on experiences of peace-building in the Middle East, Anderson identified ways in which aid agencies can identify and build upon what is referred to as 'local capacities for peace' (Anderson, 1999). By analysing past experiences in any conflict situation, a development worker will be able to discover patterns of behaviour, including people, places, and events, that are more inclined to promote peace-making. Development workers were encouraged to learn from this analysis of past peace-building actions and use them instead of those that are likely to escalate the conflict. These patterns or capacities that 'connect' rather than 'divide' those living in conflict could be described as peace-building assets within any given community. Mobilizing assets such as people who are strong at connecting with others or other local capacities for peace-building, represent the positive or strengths-based approach to working in conflict situations.

Case Study 8 Improving health through collective action in Indonesia

In Lombok, eastern Indonesia, an approach to strengthening citizen associations using a strengths-based approach led to improved health service delivery. This case study is an example of the impact of collective action involving both community members and government service providers and officials.

In the first stage of a large community development programme, a small number of concerned citizen organizations were established in 2006, facilitated by a local NGO *Solidaritas Perempuan*. These citizen associations functioned as community centres working with local government to improve health services, especially for women. They succeeded in establishing agreements with local Health Department Clinics about improving the quality of frontline health services.

(Continued)

Case Study 8 Continued

In the second stage of this programme (see also Case Study 16), Appreciative Inquiry was used to facilitate collaboration. As a result, stakeholders realized that there were other, more significant traditional ways to strengthen citizen–government relations. They also realized that there were other government-sponsored health programmes that had the potential to be more effective. The Appreciative Inquiry process revealed that *gawe rapah* has been the traditional and authoritative forum for community government engagement. *Gawe rapah* is a centuries-old tradition of the Sasak ethnic group in Lombok. It refers to formal meetings between citizens and public officials to discuss issues and find solutions to public services. The word *gawe* means a large meeting, while *rapah* comes from the Arabic *arafah* which means peace. Traditionally relationships between people and officials are not measured along hierarchical lines but rather in terms of values and norms such as to guard, to defend, and to work together. Consequently in 2010, a formal *gawe rapah* was organized by the network of citizen associations of West Lombok to consider how the government and community could improve health services. In response, the Government's Head of Regency (Bupati) commissioned the drawing up of a new memorandum of understanding between citizens and government which covered all the clinics of the district. A second *gawe rapah* was held in 2012 after the initial work indicated a marked improvement in the level of community satisfaction and this in turn led to a much more inclusive annual planning process of the Regional Health Department.

The Appreciative Inquiry process described above also revealed that much more could be done to invigorate existing government initiatives such as Village Ready (*Desa Siaga*) and Village Health Posts (*Posyandu*). Both these programmes were premised on greater community involvement, but little work had been done to build the trusting relationship and citizen participation required. As a result of these memoranda of understanding and the monthly meetings between citizen representatives and clinic management, both communities and government agencies benefited from a richer and more equitable partnership. Most importantly, there was a breakdown of the previous mistrust and scepticism among community members. Government health workers were more polite, more accountable, and more willing to follow announced working hours. Health information improved with better dissemination of health regulations and disease control through the community, while citizens helped resolve complaints and improved targeting of subsidies to those most in need. Services were added to address community priorities such as care for the elderly and child-minding while parents were being treated or giving birth, and to improve access to members without the 'official' documentation needed to obtain access to government services (such as those who could not show a birth certificate or returning migrant workers).

In 2014, a case study was undertaken, eight years after the initial activity, which found 45 villages had active citizen associations that worked collaboratively to co-produce improved health services through 15 health clinics of West Lombok. At its heart, this case study demonstrates that an inclusive process of all actors, collective inquiry and action in its many forms, and engaging community strengths, all help to improve decision-making and a much more satisfactory and effective health service by building upon what works (Zulkifli, 2003; Pellini et al., 2014).

Expanding power

Another perspective of a strengths-based approach to power is the idea of collective, or expanding power, as different actors with power come together. Arendt (1958) suggests that power is 'boundless' and the 'interplay of powers within their checks and balances is even liable to generate more power' (p. 201). Arendt's notion of power suggests that connecting power leads to exponential growth in power, which offers the means to achieve change which may not have seemed possible under a different understanding of competing or disconnected power.

A key element of expanding power is recognizing the value of state power and its legitimate and contributing role. This positive notion of power affirms the role of the state in creating change. This contrasts with a view of state power as domination. Green (2008: 29) noted the need for 'harnessing the state's "power over" not doing away with it'. Chambers (2006) also suggested mutual benefit can be gained by using the power of the state to support citizen and collective action for development outcomes. He wrote, 'there is extensive unrealized potential for win-win solutions through "uppers" using their "power over" to empower' (p. 104). A positive notion of power seeks to affirm and use state power in creating change. Of course, state power must be in the interests of a peaceful, just and inclusive society.

International development discourse in relation to service delivery often juxtaposes a supply side (the government) and a demand side (citizens). Implicit in this discourse is the notion that there is a provider and a beneficiary of power relations; that is, that governments have the power to deliver and citizens have the opportunity to receive. Intervention strategies are designed by donors such as the World Bank to improve the capacity of frontline service providers in education, health, and utilities for example in the hope that an efficient supply chain will lead to improved education or health outcomes. However, such an analysis assumes that citizens have no capacity or power to influence these outcomes other than to partake of them when provided. A strengths-based approach challenges this by recognizing citizens have opportunities to realize their potential contribution and exercise their inherent power to significantly improve the way government services are delivered as well as enhance services. Case studies 1, 6, 17, and 18 provide examples of this. In particular, Case Study 9 below, addresses the issue in detail.

Power in a strengths-based approach

It's important to recognize power where individuals or institutions may be predatory, or power is used to repress human rights. A strengths-based approach seeks to crowd out (see Chapter 4) such illegitimate power through collective and expanding power. Numerous examples can be found where repressive or predatory power has been exposed and debunked. For example, sexual abuse in religious institutions has been exposed and demands made for restitution to survivors through collective action and advocacy of survivors. It is only through their collective action and expanding power that change has been realized. The last century has witnessed multiple examples of collective action to redress repressive power and enact freedoms and human rights (Ackerman and Duval, 2000), and inform transformative change.

The themes of a strengths perspective on power highlight the value of power as capacity and as collective action to enable a transformative agenda. Power is not a zero-sum game, but expanding as people and groups act collectively to achieve shared visions. Opportunities for shared agendas are enabled through a strengths-based approach. These themes are provided as insights into the potential of alternative views on power which align with a strengths-based approach. Examples of practices and activities included in Part C demonstrate the benefits of using a strengths-based approach in a range of different sectors of international development.

Case Study 9 Collective and expanding power in responding to a natural disaster

This case study exemplifies how government, NGOs, and community members can work together in managing their own response to disasters, while remaining within the guidelines set out by government and international donors.

In May 2006, a major earthquake hit the southern part of Central Java in Indonesia. It left many people dead, destroyed over 300,000 buildings, and resulted in a complete collapse of livelihood opportunities. In response, the Australian Government provided funds to support the rehabilitation of homes, schools, and livelihoods. *The Yogyakarta-Central Java Community Assistance Program*, budgeted at A$30 million, started as an engineering programme based on the concept of showing people how to 'build back better' using techniques to create earthquake-resilient buildings. Model schools and houses were built as examples of reconstruction efforts.

Despite the donor's good intentions, the take-up rate was low, and the programme was not considered favourably by the Indonesian Government Relief Response Agency. A review at the end of the third year recommended that either a different approach be taken, or the programme be terminated. A minor party in the implementing agency contract, International Development Support Services (IDSS) was asked to propose an alternative.

IDSS proposed the use of a strengths-based approach. While the earthquake had left many houses and public buildings in ruins, people were still living there and they still had access to their own system of local community management, natural resources, and plenty of building materials. The approach was to engage the communities themselves, focusing on identifying and mobilizing local assets to design risk reduction strategies, rebuild using local management systems, and expand livelihood opportunities. The new design proposed that the programme work to bring the community and government into closer cooperation, rather than run in parallel with government initiatives.

The process began by bringing non-government service agencies, universities, and government leaders together for week-long workshops on various strengths-based

(Continued)

Case Study 9 Continued

methodologies and how they may apply in this context. This resulted in a comprehensive engagement strategy entitled *Assessment of Community Strengths and Assets* to be used by all operating partners in their approach to communities. The programme then provided funds and a process that gave communities control over mobilizing existing assets, relationships, and links to additional expertise, consistent with government guidelines and priorities. Each agency worked with specific communities to address their reconstruction and livelihood rehabilitation priorities.

The community engagement strategy included tools from Appreciative Inquiry, Asset-Based Community Development (ABCD), and the Sustainable Livelihoods Approach, each adapted for this context. Three key ideas were behind the use of a strengths-based approach:

- The community will be guided by local government parameters and priorities but carry out the activity in accordance with what they have to offer and their vision of the future: this strengthens the partnership between community and government.
- The whole community and its leaders are the agents for change, not the NGOs: the latter will facilitate the process and assist in the management of the grants.
- The process provides a chance for the community to recognize previous achievements and substantially improve buildings. This is achieved by adding value to frontline services, such as clinics and schools, and by linking assets and organizations together to produce something with a greater impact (see examples below).

At the end of this second phase, using a strengths-based approach, the most senior Indonesian Government official involved declared that this was the preferred approach to be used in this and any future disaster response situations. He agreed to travel to Brisbane to an International Association of Community Development conference to declare this to be so. His opinion was backed by an Independent Completion Report that stated the level of success of the development approach adopted under phase two was 'particularly impressive and far beyond the norm even when compared to longer-term development programs that have not had to negotiate the shift between emergency and development priorities' (AusAID, 2010a: 20).

Brief examples of sub-projects include:

1. An agency for people living with disability, established in Yogyakarta in the mid-1970s, explained after the initial strengths-based workshop: 'This is the first time we can remember a program actually asking us to contribute from our own insights and strengths'. The agency subsequently developed a monitoring tool for the whole programme.
2. A remote village was asked to assist in the re-design of a destroyed clinic. The community decided that a healthy community was the objective, and the clinic was just one part of this larger goal. They presented a design that included space for children to play at the clinic, two new rooms for an

(Continued)

Case Study 9 Continued

in-patient maternity ward, and consulting rooms to replace the previous visiting doctor's residence (previously a separate building). They also developed a health promotion and triage network run by the community itself to assist the Department of Health to work with the community. In this way they kept records of the health of the community, disseminated information, and prioritized the most important cases for when the doctor visited.

3. Brought together by *Yayasan Gita Pratiwi*, people involved in multiple small handicraft enterprises, such as batik cloth-making, decided to pool their respective skills and work cooperatively across multiple villages to form a much larger cooperative where each village contributed to the production and marketing process. They also used their social connections with schools and government to make uniforms for special occasions.

CHAPTER 6
Culture and a strengths-based approach

> *A strengths-based approach is far more culturally appropriate in most of the countries where we work. It doesn't ignore the challenges, but creates a sense of respect and cultural acknowledgement that then allows you to get onto the more difficult conversations (about priorities, change and collaboration)* (Erin Anderson)

International development inherently involves people and institutions from different cultures interacting and working together. Respect and trust are among the most critical factors for successful cross-cultural interaction and collaboration at any level – strategic, diplomatic, between organizations, within teams, and with people – on any topic. A strengths-based approach is particularly powerful in contributing to the kinds of respect and trust that are required for successful international and cross-cultural collaboration. This chapter considers a strengths-based approach through the lens of cultural value differences. It considers how a strengths-based approach contributes to more successful engagement, how aspects of the approach can be understood differently through different cultural lenses and how a strengths-based approach stimulates generative and transformative change beyond the confines of international development programmes.

Cultural value differences

> People across the world are capable of behaving in almost any fashion, but their preferences for one kind of behaviour over another differ from culture to culture. Characteristics that are dominant in one culture tend to be recessive in another, and vice versa (Foreword by Dean G. Pruitt, to Gelfand and Brett's *Handbook of Negotiation and Culture*, 2004).

Cultural values differ between groups of people or societies, variously defined. They are often described as the elements that distinguish one group from another. Cultural values influence beliefs, cognitive processes, and behaviour, covering all aspects of life, from the food we eat, the music we listen to, and the language we speak, to our beliefs about life and the universe. Thus, there is considerable benefit in understanding differences in cultural values when people who have been influenced by these different values work together and seek to support or bring about developmental change. This is imperative for determining what is valued, prioritized, and feasible in each setting. It also helps to inform the nature and scope of community and organizational imagination of a different future. Since international development efforts involve collaboration between individuals within a particular context (society, community, organization, or sector for example) and those from outside these contexts, this understanding is crucial.

Cultural values are the source of meaning for every interaction between people and their context. For example, a person in one culture may meet a highly trained medical professional giving advice about health-seeking behaviour at a community meeting. In a context where individualist and egalitarian values dominate, the person may believe that individuals can choose their own educational objectives and, when appointed to a particular role, have expertise in that area, but are not existentially 'higher' up in terms of power over others. They may listen and decide for themselves whether to follow the advice. In a similar scenario in a collectivist and hierarchical cultural context, a different interpretation is possible: the person may consider what group the medical professional comes from (e.g. class, language group, caste, family) as a major influence on whether they listen to the advice offered, and if they come from a 'higher' level in the hierarchy, would not consider questioning the information in any way. Alternatively, the individual might prefer to listen to peers or family members who are more trusted than an external stranger, even though the latter may have expert knowledge and experience. Responses to medical specialists during the global COVID pandemic illustrate this analysis of diverse responses.

While few people dispute the idea that there are differences between cultures, different disciplines and researchers use various models to describe or categorise these differences. The work of the Hofstedes (1980, 2005) provides a foundational categorization for comparative purposes. Hofstede's (1980) early work, *Culture's Consequences: International Differences in Work-Related Values*, identified four dimensions along which cultural values could be 'plotted' for comparison with others. Two additional dimensions were added in the 2000s, based on further research. These dimensions are:

- power distance (strength of social hierarchy) (low or high);
- individualism -collectivism;
- masculinity-femininity (task-orientation vs relationship-orientation);
- uncertainty avoidance (low or high);
- long-term vs short-term orientation;
- indulgence vs self-restraint.

To illustrate the relevance of Hofstede's cultural value dimensions for international development and for a strengths-based approach, a few examples are provided:

- In a low power distance culture, most people generally expect to be involved in decision-making about their own lives rather than be told by people who have power over them. They may also choose to be 'upwardly mobile' and this is relatively feasible and common in low power distance cultures. In comparison, in a high power distance culture, people without

much power may expect to be told by those with power (e.g. church leaders, older family members, bosses, nobles/chiefs) about what they can and cannot do, or should or should not do. They may not expect to move up the ladder of society, accepting their predetermined place in the hierarchy determined at birth or by others.
- In an individualist culture, people expect to be able to look after themselves and their immediate family members first, to decide on their own identity, and set their own goals. In contrast, people in collectivist cultures tend to have obligatory relationships with a broader group, such as an extended family, village, religious or language group, have their behaviour determined by the broader group, and consider relationships with others to be more important than their individual wellbeing.
- In a task-oriented culture, people tend to prioritize the completion of tasks and concentrate on plans, strategies, deadlines, and quality standards to achieve tasks. In contrast, people in relationship-oriented cultures place primary value on the maintenance of harmonious relationships with others, for example by avoiding events or scenarios where others might 'lose face' and placing great emphasis on ceremonies which emphasize similarities between people.
- In a low uncertainty avoidance culture, people tend to be more comfortable with the idea of change, so priority is given to planning for change, revision, reviews, restructures, risk-taking, and innovation. In contrast, high uncertainty avoidance cultures tend to promote the idea that the status quo should be maintained, that any changes should be marginal and slowly undertaken, and that uncertainty should be avoided wherever possible.
- In a culture which has long-term orientation values, people are more likely to believe that adaptation and pragmatic problem-solving are necessary to achieve prosperity. In contrast, cultures which are more short-term oriented, tend to place a great deal of emphasis on honouring traditions and holding on to long-set ideas, rather than adapting to changes in the environment or context.
- In a culture which is high on the indulgence value, people are more likely to expect freedom to follow their own desires, particularly in relation to enjoying life and having fun. In contrast, cultures which are more restrained tend to apply stricter social norms about people's behaviour, so that gratification is relatively more limited.

While there is some benefit in reflecting on how different cultural values shape people's expectations of what is good and bad, right and wrong, desired and avoided, for example, it is always important to avoid stereotyping people within particular groups and to recognize that cultural differences are relative rather than absolute. The benefits of this analysis lie in comparisons between communities and organizations and the rich discussions that can flow from shared understanding of one's own and others' cultures. There may be as many variations within a particular culture (e.g. between genders, urban and rural, and educated and less educated people) as there are between different cultures. Cultural values are dynamic and can change over time, though at social and institutional levels, usually not very quickly. Also, various disciplines express diverse ideas about whether these different dimensions hold true and whether it is even appropriate to try to categorize the differences (McSweeney, 2002 and Ailon 2008). In response to critique of Hofstede's original work, other research has sought to generate understanding of cultural value differences. The first GLOBE Study, for example (House et al., 2004), involved research in 62 countries and both confirmed and expanded the range of dimensions developed by Hofstede.

The benefit of understanding one's own cultural values and others, using Hofstede's dimensions, lies in the use of language and ideas to stimulate respectful conversations about relative differences in our views of the world. When used to express ideas about what is valued in each setting, these dimensions provide non-judgemental language to be used in conversations about how the world is and how it might be. For example, someone from a setting where collectivist values are dominant may participate in a conversation about change, thinking that change is only possible when the potential implications for all members of a group are fully taken into account. They may ask someone from a place where individualist values are dominant, how they could possibly consider making decisions based on their individual perspective only. Using the language 'individualist' and 'collectivist' the two people could seek to understand the other's perspective, without negative judgement, and to consider how the benefits of their different perspectives could be mobilized to achieve a decision which suits everyone. In an ideal scenario, this result could be better than if only one cultural value was applied.

A strengths-based approach and the value of culture

A strengths-based approach is respectful across cultures because it enables recognition and attention to be given to what is valued in each particular context; that is, what is regarded in that context as positive, successful, an asset or a highlight. In effect, a strengths-based approach gives value to the values which drive communities, societies, and organizations. A process which focuses on strengths, when conducted appropriately, can reveal the cultural values which underpin definitions of what is working well, success, and preferred futures.

Since definitions of strengths and perceptions of a positive life vary between cultures (as well as within cultures of course), the surfacing of cultural values is useful for enabling people to imagine the kinds of changes that may be sought in each context. Awareness of values and strengths-based processes can help groups of people to determine pathways which take them in the direction of their preferred future.

There is not a great deal of literature on the specific interaction between a strengths-based approach and cultural value differences, although as noted earlier, there has already been extensive use of a strengths-based approach across diverse cultural contexts. The authors' experience is that when they first used the approach in international development contexts, government leaders and officials as well as other partners expressed surprise that someone from a 'donor country' would ask about their strengths and priorities. This reflects their long experience of being asked about their weaknesses, problems, gaps, and needs. One senior government leader in Samoa replied 'do you mean our country can receive aid and still be respected?' One senior official from Papua New Guinea asked 'are you really from Australia? No-one from your country has ever acknowledged that this country has any strengths!' The cultural disrespect inherent in the use of a problem-based approach is clearly overcome by the use of a strengths-based approach.

A strengths-based approach and cross-cultural understanding intersect in many ways. The following selected aspects of particular relevance to international development are discussed below:

- Definitions of strengths and assets through different cultural lenses.
- Understanding of time (past, present, and future) through different cultural lenses.
- Opportunities provided by a strengths-based approach for the values of people and organizations from different cultural backgrounds to be recognized and respected.
- Interpretation of motivation through different cultural lenses.
- Opportunities provided by a strengths-based approach to transcend fixed ideas about what is possible within a culture and leverage the benefits of different perspectives to achieve generative and transformational change.

Strengths reveal values

A strengths-based approach is a means to surface and recognize the values that exist in any particular setting by providing an opportunity for people to express what they consider to be successful, positive, an asset, or a highlight. This expression provides potentially critical information about the values that shape people and organizations in that setting. In an international development relationship, this enables collaborating organizations to contribute to motivation and plans which are most relevant in that cultural context. For example, if a village or a work team is asked to reflect on what has worked well for them in the past, they may highlight that they had a leader who was very inclusive and treated everyone as equals (suggesting a low power distance is valued), or they may praise a leader who was very respected and wise and made the right decisions on the group's behalf (suggesting a high power distance is valued). In the first instance, facilitation of plans for the group to achieve its vision for the future should reflect the idea that participants like to work as equals, contribute their own ideas, and have them valued. In the second instance, facilitation of plans is more likely to succeed if respect is given to senior leaders within the group and value is accorded by group members to those with wisdom, high levels of education, or seniority, for example. Acknowledging that not all people in a group may respect leaders at a particular time, opportunities for nuanced expression of diverse views are promoted in a strengths-based approach.

Similarly, if participants in a consultation process give value to the idea that 'everyone was able to contribute their diverse ideas to the action plan, complete their planned tasks, and achieve a high-quality outcome', this may reflect high levels of task-oriented values. In a setting where the former ideas were noted as strengths of a previous experience, the facilitation process might focus on encouraging everyone to share their diverse ideas in setting action plans and targets. This would contrast with a strength that 'everyone respected our traditional norms, there were no arguments with the leaders, and no one lost face at the end of the day' (reflecting more relationship-oriented values). Where relationship-orientation values are prevalent, then the facilitation process may seek to emphasize processes that promote shared agreement about common goals which would not cause loss of face to anyone in the participants' defined groups, even if they are not present (e.g. village members, church leaders or people from other language groups).

Taking cultural value differences into account, it is easy to imagine that people in different contexts could define strengths in diverse ways. In international development contexts, it is common to find examples where a donor agency sees a particular strength in a process or outcome, based on the values of the donor's cultural context, while a community in a country or the leaders of an organization in another country context, sees a weakness or vice versa. For example, a donor agency may seek more inclusive leadership as a strength, whereas a community in a high power distance culture may see this as undermining the critical respect which needs to be shown to chiefs, elders, or religious leaders, for community order to be maintained. Similarly, people in a relationship-oriented culture may place great value on a facilitation process in which groups have the opportunity to find a 'broad common denominator' that suits all members of a community and does not seriously challenge anyone's obligations within the group. From the perspective of people from a task-oriented culture, this may be seen as a weakness, because ambitious goals are not set, action plans are not produced, and smart indicators are not detailed.

Surfacing different perspectives on the definition of strengths in diverse contexts is a critical element of a strengths-based approach. By facilitating processes which emphasize strengths from the perspective of participants, if participants come from different cultures, there is scope for generating shared understanding of others' values and perspectives. For example, by including participants from a donor country and from the country where programmes are being implemented, a strengths-based approach can enable participants to hear each other's views about what is valued, and with culturally savvy facilitation, can understand what these different views mean for the potential for successful collaboration and, ultimately, change.

The process of surfacing different perspectives about what is valued in each context clearly has implications for determining what success might look like at the end of a collaborative effort or development programme. There is no shortage of programmes that aim to achieve an outcome that is seen as positive from the donor's perspective but not so from another cultural perspective, or that is undertaken in a way deemed successful through a western contracting lens, but harmful, disastrous or, at minimum, a waste of time through another lens. Simply the idea of some individuals setting a high-level change-related goal, an outcome or a desired future is challenging for people in cultures which are high on uncertainty avoidance and prefer more short-term orientation. If programmes and collaborative efforts are designed in ways that recognize different cultural perspectives on change and allow for negotiations that respect different values, then it is more likely the plans will be culturally relevant and achievable.

Proponents of a strengths-based approach may be primarily interested in contributing to an organization's or community's own vision for the future and supporting members to move in directions that suit them, rather than complying with external definitions of particular developmental results. Regardless of the motivation of facilitators, the use of a strengths-based approach has much better chances of contributing to respectful collaboration across cultures than a problem-based approach.

Change, and particularly cultural change, is never linear or uniform, and there are always multiple perspectives for international development workers. A shared concept in cross-cultural research and a strengths-based approach is the necessity to work with locally determined agendas and priorities for change.

Perceptions of past, present, and future through cultural lenses

A strengths-based approach in international development is primarily associated with recognizing and drawing on past and present strengths, assets or past high-points for determining a new future, or some kind of positive change. Given this interaction with the past, present, and future, consideration of how these constructs of time may be perceived differently in different cultures is relevant to a strengths-based approach. As many international development workers will attest, perceptions of time vary between cultures, and how these are balanced against each other also differs. In particular, the ease with which people can envisage a new future and determine 'success' in achieving that future, varies widely across cultures.

Among others, Hofstede and Hofstede (2005) identified that different cultures view time differently and described relative differences between those with short- and long-term orientation. They found some cultures have values which emphasize 'living for today' while others prioritize working for tomorrow. Donor-set deadlines for major developmental changes usually reflect understanding that time is linear and that there are direct cause and effect relationships which can be planned over time. For example, international development programmes are largely designed and funded on the assumption that, first, a task will be done or activity will be undertaken, then, next, a preset output will be produced, then, next, a higher-level result will occur. Rarely is there explicit acceptance that planning for cause and effect changes over time is not linear. However, cultures in many countries in which development programmes are implemented see time in a much more circular way. In many Pacific Islands, for example, if a task is not done today, the underlying belief is that it could be done when the sun comes up the next day, or the day after that, with few concerns about the consequences. In many cultures, deep reverence for ancient events or traditional ceremonies celebrating past achievements absorbs considerable energy, resources, and effort, in ways which could be seen from another cultural perspective as detrimental to current and future prosperity. In Confucian influenced cultures, decisions are more likely to reflect an interest in future benefits, rather than current wellbeing.

Cultures which are relatively more comfortable with the concepts of change and risk management are more practised in envisioning and describing a new future or a better future, because the value given to the future dominates daily life. In Australia, for example, those working in organizations will frequently participate in restructures, strategic planning processes, and reviews, all common events in 'low uncertainty avoidance' cultures. They will be familiar with expectations that they should define objectives and expected outcomes, even at an individual level. For cultures that are relatively less comfortable with change (i.e. high on uncertainty avoidance), constructing a vision for the future is not something that necessarily comes easily. One prominent Fijian leader reported that analysing and making sense of the current complexities of a particular issue was taxing enough, let alone trying to work out what a different future might look like. In cultures with high uncertainty avoidance values, the driving force for leaders is to maintain the status quo and stability, thereby minimizing uncertainty for the population and reassuring institutions and communities that life will continue as 'normal'. While defining a specific change in terms of a development objective may not make much sense to people in this context, this does not imply that people cannot imagine moving in a direction towards a better future. This future may not be fully articulated at the outset, but may emerge over time, as people build confidence in their own strengths and ability to achieve positive change, and new ideas are stimulated from their positive experiences.

In summary, while a strengths-based approach supports participants in a change process to discover and reflect on what has succeeded in the past, it is worth keeping in mind that this is easier in some cultures than others. Thus, consideration given to understanding the perception of the past in each context is worthwhile. Similarly, a strengths-based approach supports people to form a shared vision for the future, and then potentially encourages movement towards that vision. Respecting the fact that varied cultures engage with the idea of the future in different ways is important, as is respect for the different ways that the future may be described.

Opportunities for recognition of the goodness and strengths of 'others'

When a strengths-based approach is used with participants from diverse groups, it has the potential to counter the often-negative aspects associated with 'othering'. Stereotyping of groups different from one's own is commonly based on a fear or an unfounded judgement that a whole group of people has negative qualities, behaviour, or other features *because* they are different. As noted above, this phenomenon is global, as illustrated by the significant international response to the Black Lives Matter movement. Stereotyping and racism are often initiated, entrenched, institutionalized, and exacerbated by leaders and cause massive psychological, social, political, and economic harm. The influence of these on communities' abilities to thrive and achieve positive change are clearly negative. A strengths-based approach provides an alternative paradigm.

'Othering' is a prominent feature of many aspects of modern life. It is likely derived from instinctive human tendencies to create a distance between 'us' and 'others' for safety reasons, when groups of humans first encountered different groups, competing and fighting over land and other resources. In a modern world, while contestation of ideas between groups is common, there is now plenty of evidence to confirm the benefits of collaboration with others, to overcome differences and achieve shared objectives. Given that contested behaviour and ideas occur in many contexts, activism, advocacy, and social movements are likely to continue to be needed. For example, when governments or those in power blatantly abuse human rights, a collaborative exercise to find shared objectives may seem inappropriate. In a globalized world, both contestation-based and collaborative approaches seeking to achieve positive change are more likely than ever to involve people from different cultures working together. A strengths-based approach is critical for generating respect and trust-based positive momentum for collaboration between people from different cultural backgrounds in any setting.

A strengths-based approach, if well-applied and supported, has the potential to surface and give value to the positive aspects of groups of people who are seen as 'others'. Of course, many other factors contribute to overcoming differences between people, and it is not claimed that a strengths-based approach in isolation is the answer. When facilitators and leaders are able to promote the value of differences, generate shared understanding of the fact that differences are not 'bad' per se, then collaborative approaches, across cultures, are more likely to achieve shared goals. This is consistent with contemporary international interest in 'diversity and inclusion' which recognizes better outcomes are achieved when different perspectives are applied to addressing shared issues.

Contributors to 'motivation' through different cultural lenses

As noted above, a strong feature of a strengths-based approach is its emphasis on motivating people in the direction of positive change. The nature and scope of motivation can be significantly influenced by cultural values, which differ across contexts. A strengths-based approach is a means to raise and celebrate different drivers of motivation in each setting, whether a group, community, organisation or institution.

At a basic level, for example, in an individualist culture, motivation is more likely to be based on each individual's perspective of potential benefits either for themselves or the 'public'. The concept of 'the public good' derives from more individualist cultural settings, where there are relatively low obligatory links between the individual and the whole population. While there are many people in individualist societies who are motivated to assist others and the broader public, this motivation is not necessarily obligatory in nature. In contrast, people living in relatively more collectivist cultures are more likely to be motivated by their understanding of benefits to their *particular* group or groups, rather than themselves as individuals or the 'public good'. The pull towards action for the broader public in collectivist cultures is relatively limited because of the comparative strength of the identified group obligations, for example to a village, island, extended family, language group or religious group.

Those facilitating and supporting a strengths-based approach will benefit from an awareness of different influences on individual and group motivation, and the potential for motivation in each context. In practice, this may require preparatory conversations with cultural guides and participants, to understand the particular factors which may influence motivation and the likely scope and nature of motivation. This understanding may help shape the nature of engagement and the selection of methods to suit. Alternatively, simply remaining open to different drivers which shape motivation and different manifestations of motivation, will be beneficial.

Transcending fixed ideas for generative and transformational change

As a strengths-based approach seeks to generate new ideas about what is possible in any particular setting, it has the potential to overcome the limitations of perceived 'fixed ideas' which are often associated with cultural values and norms. However, this raises a number of complexities when applied in different cultural contexts. The benefits of accessing and promoting multiple views are now widely professed under the banner of 'diversity and inclusion' in business and organizational change. However, considering ways to generate shared agreement about past highlights or strengths or visions for a better future, where people with different cultural values come together, or where the approach is applied in diverse contexts, requires care.

Three issues associated with the idea of transcending 'fixed ideas' are relevant here: the way that certain cultural values give more voice to some people than others; the extent of direct connection between cultural values and actual behaviour; and the dominance of certain groups or voices in the international development context.

By definition, cultures which have more hierarchical values give more power to the voices of some people than others. So, while applying a strengths-based approach can help generate shared visions for the future based on shared understanding of past achievements, the idea that hierarchical groups can actually or readily give equal voice to all participants is questionable. Considerable effort may be needed for this to occur, and care also taken to ensure that those with low power are not penalized by those with power (later or in less obvious ways) for raising their voice if this is seen as dissent. Thus, facilitators of a strengths-based approach need to be aware of the influence of hierarchical cultural values on the extent to which people with high and low levels of power will interact, feel safe, and potentially react, either within or outside workshop or official settings. A wide range of facilitation approaches and methods may be suitable for this purpose (Rhodes, 2022).

The extent to which cultural values influence norms and behaviour in reality is also relevant to thinking about how a strengths-based approach can overcome 'fixed cultural ideas'. There are often claims made in a culture that 'this is the way it has always been done', or 'this is our tradition so we must follow it', or 'this is a long-standing norm', when referring to a belief or practice. Polygamy in Papua New Guinea or Malaysia, domestic violence in many contexts, and other practices harmful to particular groups are often explained as 'cultural practices'. As a strengths-based approach has the potential to generate new ideas about a positive future, there is value in considering how these ideas may or may not reflect cultural values, and how closely cultural values are connected to expressions of strengths, visions for the future, and the nature of transformative change.

The international development discipline itself may help to illustrate this complexity. A number of deeply held values underpin contemporary practice, shared across many organizations, from multilateral agencies to individual development workers. These values include an emphasis on participation, local ownership and leadership of change agendas, and alignment with national priorities (expressed in the Paris Declaration on Aid Effectiveness for example), and have influenced practice since the 1970s. While the values are widely shared, accepted, espoused, and documented in official reports, many of us have experience where these values have not translated into practice. This relates to the third point below, but before leaving this point, it is worth mentioning that links between values and actual practices are certainly not always evident or consistent. So, when a group of participants reflects on a particular strength from their cultural perspective, it may not actually be the case that a positive value is practised or that a particular practice is agreed to be positive by all those involved.

A third and important element relates to the way in which certain values dominate in relationships between donor and 'receiving' cultures. It is widely agreed, despite the best intentions of the Paris Declaration, which mandated donors to work within local government systems and structures, that aid management systems reflect the dominant values of donor countries. Three decades ago, Elgström (1990) noted the 'asymmetry of power' based on his analysis of interactions between officials from European donor and African government agencies. While the localization agenda has gained particular prominence since 2015 (see Chapter 1), decision-making about international development programming is still significantly oriented to donor interests and reflects cultural values that prevail in donor countries. An abstract of a book by Malunga and Holcombe (2014) summarized the situation neatly from an African perspective:

> Development theory and practice in developing countries are dominated by the power of Western ideas, worldviews, actors, tools, models, and frameworks. Consequently, the resulting development interventions may too rarely be locally rooted, locally driven, or resonant with local context. Another reality is that theories and practice from developing countries rarely travel to the Western agencies dominating development, undermining the possibility of a beneficial synergy that could be obtained from the best of the two worlds: West and developing countries. There are many reasons why the experience of locally driven development is not communicated back to global development actors, including but not limited to the marginal role of Southern voices in global fora. (Malunga and Holcombe, 2014: 615)

While a strengths-based approach seeks to generate shared agreement about a past highlight or a vision for the future, those participating in a reflection and planning process attached to international development programming are likely to be cognizant of the power of the donor country. This awareness may influence their discussions about which particular vision could be approved by donor agencies, based on perceptions of donor values about how the world should be. The concept of Endogenous Development (see Chapter 3) championed by Malunga and Holcombe (2016) and others has the potential to overturn the power asymmetry, but there are many forces limiting its chances.

On a positive note, it is clear that a strengths-based approach can generate important, powerful, and life-changing visions for the future when used in different cultural contexts or with participants from mixed cultural backgrounds. When the process is respectfully applied in a way which reflects understanding of prevailing cultural values and connections between cultural values, norms, and practices in each context, then it is more likely that this potential will be met. The combination of a strengths-based approach and an awareness of cultural values in each setting can achieve greater results than could be achieved by using a single cultural lens.

A strengths-based approach has considerable value in generating respectful collaboration between people and organizations from different cultures, in supporting people in diverse settings to take their own journey towards positive change that makes sense in their own context, and in supporting the achievement of developmental benefits more broadly. The combination of a culturally savvy approach and a strengths-based approach in all aspects of international development practice, as described in the next chapter, make for a particularly potent way to help address the complex challenges facing the world today.

CHAPTER 7
Psychology and a strengths-based approach

> *By creating chains of events that carry positive meaning for others, positive emotions can trigger upward spirals that transform communities into more cohesive, moral and harmonious social organizations*
> (Fredrickson, 2003: 335)

Committing to using a strengths-based approach will mean that participants are given the opportunity to identify and express their emotional intelligence as well as rational thought. People are motivated to change not just by reason alone, but also by the exercise of emotion, imagination, engagement of the whole person, and opportunities for joyful celebration. To be able to generate the enthusiasm required to innovate and imagine new possibilities, many who use a strengths-based approach encourage the exercise of creative and artistic abilities. When introducing a strengths-based approach, they may use song, drama, drawing, and dance as part of the change process. These facilitation processes may generate positive energy for change at the beginning or celebrate an agreed vision/dream for the future. Arguing that the body and the mind are one, Dani Munggoro and Budhsi Kismadi, founders of Inspirit Innovative Circles in Indonesia, apply what they refer to as 'vibrant facilitation' to all their workshops and training. Vibrant facilitation actively encourages participants to sing, paint, and play throughout the learning process. Mac Odell also includes 'dance and drum' to celebrate success as part of an adapted Appreciate Inquiry practice.

A strengths-based approach incorporates insights about how and why it works from elements of the field of psychology, including positive psychology. The two fields have developed independently, with links between psychology and different strengths-based practices such as Appreciative Inquiry and strengths-based social work emerging only since the 2000s. The value of considering psychological aspects is relevant to facilitating behavioural and organizational change, which are common elements in international development and therefore worthy of consideration in this book. We acknowledge that this chapter is selective and offers only initial insights into connections between psychology and a strengths-based approach. We also recognize that positive psychology is dominant in western cultural contexts, with more work to be done in different cultures. We hope readers seek further insights into the inner workings of how and why a strengths-based approach works in motivating and catalysing change.

Connections between the field of psychology and international development are emerging, with many benefits to be gained. For example, behavioural science and behavioural economics are important in water, sanitation, and hygiene (WASH) projects as well as in health programming in order to influence behaviour change. Programmes which seek to strengthen organizations, networks, and sectors are also commonly addressing issues related to the psychology of individuals and groups as they navigate complexity and leadership, or engage with change agendas. These programmes involve consideration of the effects of psychological, cognitive, emotional, cultural, and social factors on the decisions of individuals and institutions, and how these influence change. These fields of practice are still relatively new and underdeveloped in international development. The introduction of different perspectives below is provided to stimulate further discussion, debate, and further research into the practice and value of positive psychology in international development.

Positive psychology

Like strengths-based practices, positive psychology is a reaction to, and intent to shift the weight of focus and inquiry of psychology from the negative side of the human experience to the positive. Seligman and Csikszentmihalyi (2000), who coined the term 'positive psychology', were reacting to the focus on treating psychological disorders in a disease framework (p. 6). They and others including Csikszentmihalyi (1990, 1996), Fredrickson (1998, 2001, 2009), and Peterson (2006) are critical of the focus of inquiry on the pathology of mental health with scant interest in what drives the state of 'normal' people and what enables individuals or groups to flourish. The term 'flourish' is explored below.

The field of psychology's focus on the negative is in part reflected in the growth of diagnosis of mental disorders. Since the first edition of the widely referenced Diagnostic and Statistical Manual of Mental Disorders (DSM) in 1952, the number of proclaimed mental disorders has risen from 60 to 157 in DSM-5, the updated 2013 edition. Seligman and Csikszentmihalyi wrote, 'this almost exclusive attention to pathology neglects the fulfilled individual and the thriving community. The aim of positive psychology is to begin to catalyse a change in the focus of psychology from preoccupation only with repairing the worst things in life to also building positive qualities' (2000: p. 5).

> The field of positive psychology at the subjective level is about valued subjective experiences: wellbeing and satisfaction (in the past); hope and optimism (for the future); and flow and happiness (in the present). At the individual level, it is about positive individual traits: the capacity of love and vocation, courage, interpersonal skill, aesthetic sensibility, perseverance, forgiveness, originality, future mindedness, spirituality, high talent and wisdom. At the group level, it is about the civic virtues and the institutions that move individuals toward better citizenship: responsibility, nurturance, altruism, civility, moderation, tolerance, and work ethic (Seligman and Csikszentmihalyi, 2000: 5).

Positive psychology is focused on inquiry into what works, the positive strengths or attributes of individuals, groups or institutions as a means of increasing individual and societal wellbeing. Like a strengths-based approach, positive psychology seeks to identify factors that generate positive experiences as a means of expanding and utilizing these to inform preferred futures.

The term 'positive psychology' covers a range of different theories and practices that share an interest in identifying ways that support positive life experiences. Positive psychology does not deny the experience of negative experiences, or negative emotions. While acknowledging these experiences or emotions, it chooses to focus on positive emotions, strengths, or the positive, as a means of creating change and enriching individual and community life. Positive psychology is not just about being happy. While there are numerous self-help guides with a focus on happiness, informed by positive psychology, there are other resources which emphasize the complexities of human life. There is a wealth of literature on positive psychology; robust and rigorous research, studies, and human trials informed by the science of psychology have advanced both the theory and practice.

Four streams of positive psychology, discussed below, are relevant to the practice of a strengths-based approach in international development: positive emotions; flourishing; motivations; and character strengths. While there is extensive literature on all of these, their application to international development still needs further research. Case studies of a strengths-based approach provided in this book provide illustration of these in practice.

Positive emotions

The contribution of positive emotions has been studied extensively in positive psychology. Studies led by Barbara Fredrickson highlight that the experience of a range of positive emotions has an effect on how we see the world and also provides a resource base that can be drawn upon at other times. She proposed the 'broaden-and-build' theory (Fredrickson, 2001) of positive emotions (Figure 7.1). The theory states firstly that the experience of certain discrete positive emotions 'broadens' one's perspective to consider creative, flexible, and innovative ways of thinking and acting. She refers to a list of 10 positive emotions: joy, gratitude, serenity, interest, hope, pride, amusement, inspiration, awe, and love. To strengthen experiences of positivity, the focus is not simply on an emotion but identifying levers or drivers which influence and turn on that specific positive emotion. For example, joy may be experienced by playing with grandchildren or pride might be associated with working with others to change a local government regulation on fishing. Positivity is strengthened by cultivating the experiences which will turn on the positive emotion. Inspiration might be gained by seeing young people take action to advocate for improved e-safety legislation and reduce bullying on social media. Another individual might foster emotions of hope by seeing infrastructure improvements to their local health clinic. Importantly the experience of positive emotions is unique to each individual.

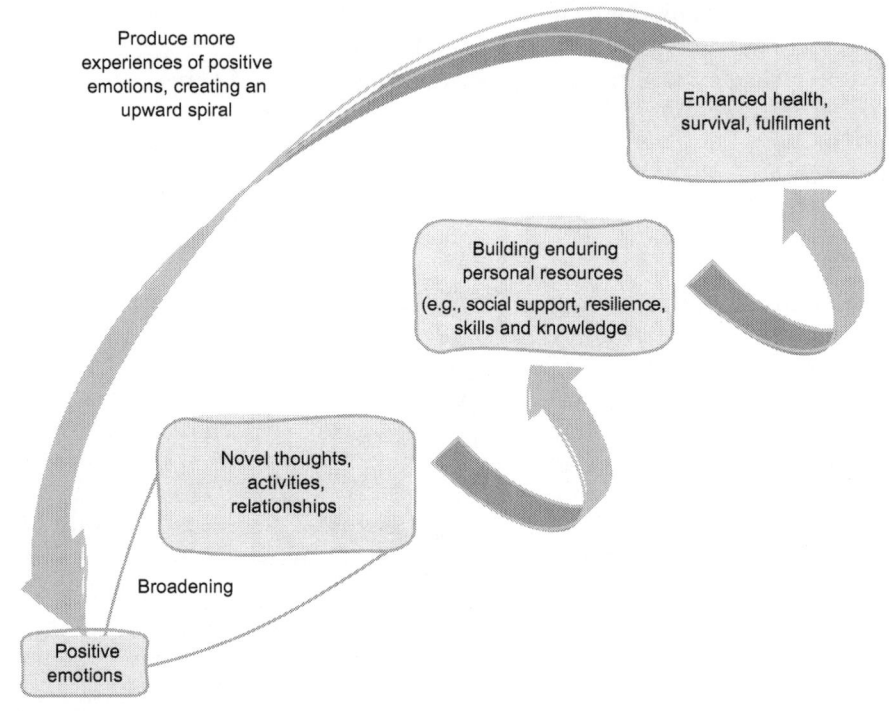

Figure 7.1 Broaden-and-build theory of positive emotions
Source: Fredrickson and Cohn, 2008: 783.

The second part of the theory states that the experience of positive emotions can be banked and drawn down to be used in the future. This bank of positive emotions 'builds' resilience. The past experience of positive emotions becomes a set of resources which can be used to help people to cope during a present negative experience. For example, past experience of an exam which generated a sense of pride (based on a good result) might strengthen one's resilience to cope with a future exam and potentially a poor grade. While the poor grade might be upsetting at the current time, one is better able to cope with this situation appreciating previous better results, and perhaps a belief that better grades are possible in future.

Fredrickson does not suggest that people need to be experiencing positive emotions all the time. She suggests that by experiencing positive emotions more than negative ones, people can build resiliency and trigger upward spirals towards improved emotional wellbeing (Fredrickson and Joiner 2002). Fredrickson proposes a 3-to-1 positivity ratio, where for every negative emotional experience, one should experience three positive emotions to ensure the tipping point to flourishing.

The relevance of positive emotions to a strengths-based approach in international development needs to be understood in the context of current limitations, whereby studies to date have a Eurocentric focus. There has been limited research in diverse cultural contexts, and cultural values clearly influence the expression of positive emotions. One study carried out by Leu et al. (2011) highlighted the role of culture in informing positive emotions. The study explored differences in association of positive and negative emotions and depression between European-Americans, Asian-Americans, and Asian immigrants. Their findings 'suggest that culture may moderate the role that positive emotions play in mental health' (p. 4). In explaining their results, they noted previous studies which showed that

> East-West differences in emotion reports are greatest in positive, and not negative, situations. While maximizing positive emotions may be a cultural goal in Western contexts, emotion moderation through balancing positive emotions with negative ones may be a cultural goal in Asian contexts (Leu et al., 2011: 5).

The view that cultural values influence emotions is also confirmed by others. Mesquita et al. (2014: 297) drew on a range of empirical studies to conclude 'there is substantial evidence of the cultural regulation of emotions'. That is, individuals regulate their emotions to conform with local cultural models. Regulation provides a way to ensure self-presentation as well as maintenance of relationships. Mesquita et al. also contend that emotions are more regulated not just at an intrapersonal level, but also through broader structures informed by the local context.

These few insights from the limited research on emotions and culture highlight the need for more research. The theory to date, the authors' experience, and that of other development workers of a strengths-based approach, confirm there are some potentially useful aspects which are explored below.

The value of a strengths-based approach for triggering positive emotions, and in turn the contribution of positive emotions to wellbeing, is widely evidenced in literature relevant to strengths-based practices. For example, the practice of Appreciative Inquiry seeks to increase positive emotions and recognizes the benefit of this outcome as a means to catalyse change (Bushe, 2007; Armstrong et al., 2020). An appreciative mindset opens possibilities and potential for generative change. This is in line with the broaden-and-build theory. Writing about the use of positive emotions within the practice of Appreciative Inquiry, Armstrong et al. (2020: 2) noted:

> Positive emotions not only make people more resilient and increase their ability to cope with occasional adversity, they also increase people's openness to ideas, creativity and capacity for action. Positive emotions can be cultivated to influence wellbeing and performance. Consider one positive emotion, that of gratitude. Gratitude has been found to be a predictor of mental health, with the ability to change the circuitry of your brain, increase happiness, boost the immune system, improve relationships and increase productivity.

A study of ABCD in the UK as part of a programme called *Your Neighbourhood* identified the value of the approach for catalysing positive emotions. The authors of the programme evaluation noted that 'evidence supports theories that an upward spiral of positive emotion and broadened thinking can overtime lead to "appreciable increases in emotional well-being", building resilience and helping individuals and communities to flourish' (van de Venter and Redwood, 2016: 28). The evaluation stated that, '*Your Neighbourhood* led to some early outcomes for residents in terms of promoting wellbeing. These have included skills development, including technical and interpersonal skills, increased confidence, providing a sense of purpose, promoted social interactions and developed pride; both pride in the local area and a personal sense of pride' (p. 27). The connection between strengths-based practice and positive emotions confirms the value to individual wellbeing as well as the contribution to potential generative and transformational change.

Anecdotal evidence of the value of a strengths-based approach for generating positive emotions is plentiful. For example, a group of chiefs in Vanuatu told Deborah Rhodes that they felt considerably more able and hopeful to proceed to navigate the complex interface between traditional and introduced government systems following their experience of a strengths-based design process. Another group of stakeholders in the disability sector reported that their confidence to advocate for changes in attitudes towards the rights of persons with disability had increased as a result of participating in a strengths-based planning process. In Solomon Islands, a group of NGO leaders whose applications for grants under the Solomon Island NGO Partnership Agreement programme (see Case Study 2) had not been successful were invited to a workshop facilitated by Deborah. They arrived disappointed and a little angry, but after participating in a strengths-based workshop, left proud and excited. They recognized their existing strengths and were hopeful about the prospect of using their own resources and working with each other to achieve shared development goals.

Keren Winterford experienced and documented the value of quick wins in her PhD research, which focused on citizen action for improved public service delivery. The research identified the value of quick wins in citizen-led advocacy. 'Because they had succeeded in achieving some change, citizens believed they could create more'. (Winterford 2013: 100). Achieving 'quick wins' increased citizens' sense of themselves and their abilities, and enabled a positive view of the future.

Flourishing

The notion of 'flourishing' is central to positive psychology. Seligman and Csikszentmihalyi (2000: 13) describe the aim of positive psychology is 'to understand and build those factors that allow individuals, communities and societies to flourish'. The notion of flourishing moves beyond happiness or wellbeing to a broader and multidimensional perspective. Seligman (2018) described the

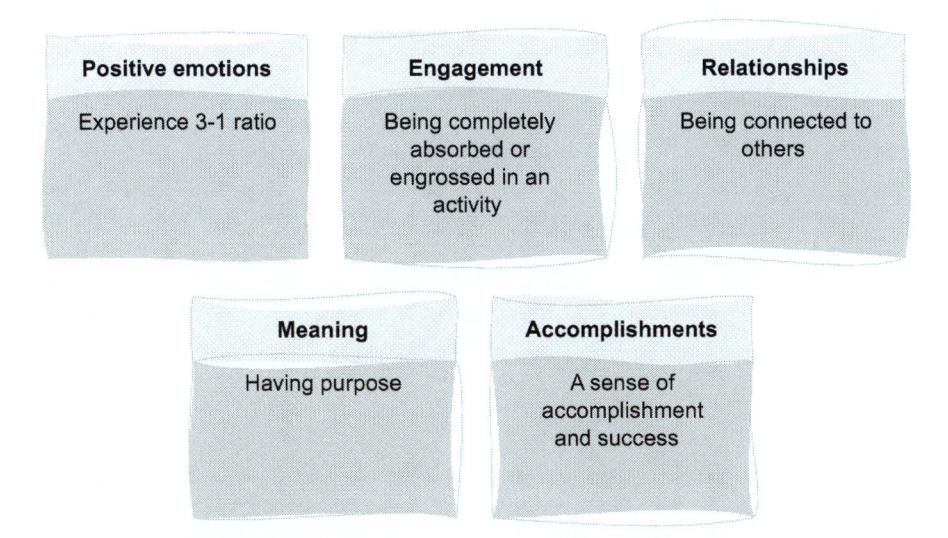

Figure 7.2 Five factors of flourishing

- **Positive emotions**: Experience 3-1 ratio
- **Engagement**: Being completely absorbed or engrossed in an activity
- **Relationships**: Being connected to others
- **Meaning**: Having purpose
- **Accomplishments**: A sense of accomplishment and success

PERMA model, an acronym of five factors that are the foundations of, or integral to a flourishing life. The five factors are shown in Figure 7.2.

Research and literature on flourishing grew exponentially in the 2000s (Haidt, 2003; Seligman, 2011; Rickman, 2013). Ways to foster and measure the extent to which individuals, groups, and organizations are flourishing have been proposed by various authors (Rickman, 2013; Seligman, 2011, Bono et al., 2011, Keyes and Haidt, 2003). In 2018, Harvard's Institute for Quantitative Social Science, which has the *Human Flourishing Program*, launched a Global Flourishing Study including researchers from multiple countries, which is likely to generate useful evidence.

In the international development field, there is little evidence of the application of the notion of flourishing. Why might that be? Is it because the sector is fixated on solving problems rather than contributing to flourishing communities? Is it because development workers work in sector silos, only focusing on one slice of people's lives (e.g. health, education, livelihoods)? Is it because international development is unable to grasp and engage with the full and holistic spectrum of people's lives as described in the PERMA model? Is the affirmative focus on future flourishing communities and organizations simply too great a leap from the dominant deficit perspective of development policy and programming?

The notion of flourishing and the foundations which support it strongly align with a strengths-based approach. A strengths-based approach seeks to strengthen relationships, emphasize meaning and purpose, and promote accomplishment and success of local actors. The practices used in a strengths-based approach trigger the experience of positive emotions. These experiences create a virtual and positive reinforcing experience for people as they decide and determine their own future. For example, in Appreciative Inquiry, the dream stage encourages participants to consider a world of abundance, where the best can happen, or the ideal future. This focuses attention on the potential for flourishing and what it would take to achieve this. Using a strengths-based approach to determine how to improve food security, for example, enables people to consider food abundance in a flourishing food production environment and thus generate hope and motivation, to begin to identify the steps that could be taken towards that improvement. The sense of hope and motivation in relation to food security can then also contribute to improved equity in supply chains, improved gender equality within families and institutions or any other desired change.

Motivation

People are actually growth oriented naturally and have a range of motivations within. Good motivation comes from inside. Poor quality motivation is when something is imposed from outside. A strengths-based approach supports this understanding because it recognises people's own motivation. (Ian Cunningham)

Motivation is clearly crucial for people and groups to achieve any change, and a strengths-based approach generates it at all levels. While not necessarily part of positive psychology, an area of research that seeks to bring together the strengths-based approach and the field of psychology is known as self-determination theory. Within his PhD research Ian Cunningham (2021) employed self-determination theory to investigate the motivation of community members in their roles in management of water services (boreholes) in rural Malawi. Ian was interested to test the oft-described statement that a strengths-based approach increases motivation and ownership of development agendas by local actors.

Self-determination theory is a field of psychology informed by numerous experiments and studies, similar to those of Fredrickson's broaden-and-build theory of positive emotions. The theory grew from the work of psychologists Edward Deci and Richard Ryan, who first introduced their ideas in their 1985 book *Self-Determination and Intrinsic Motivation in Human Behaviour*. This theory is concerned with human motivation and differentiates intrinsic (internal sources) and extrinsic (external sources) of motivation. Self-determination is fuelled by intrinsic motivators. Extrinsic motivation is where one acts to avoid punishment or earn a reward, and intrinsic motivation is for a personal reward or just to be or do. The theory suggests that people are able to become self-motivated when their needs for competence, connection, and autonomy are filled.

Motivation is fuelled by basic psychological needs:

- autonomy – the feeling one has choice or control;
- competence – capable, effective, dealing with a situation;
- connection – the feeling of belonging and relatedness to others.

Cunningham's (2021) research provides insights into the value of a strengths-based approach for catalysing motivation. He concludes:

> the tools used in the ABCD process were consistent with practice to support basic psychological needs. These tools include appreciative interviews, visioning, asset mapping, and planning and action phases. These tools are supportive of autonomy, competence, and relatedness as defined in Self Determination Theory. (Cunningham, 2021: 285).

Character strengths

An early representation of positive psychology was the definition of character strengths and virtue. The *Character Strengths and Virtues* handbook authored by Peterson and Seligman (2004) identifies and classifies positive psychological traits of human beings. Much like the DSM used in general psychology, the handbook provides a theoretical framework to assist in understanding strengths and virtues and for developing practical applications for positive psychology. The manual identified six classes of virtues (i.e. 'core virtues') underlying 24 measurable character strengths.

A conceptual pillar of positive psychology is the notion of strengths. In this context, strengths are defined as the 'pre-existing capacities that are authentic and energizing which lead to optimal functioning when they are employed' (Linley, 2008). Strengths represent a set of personal resources that individuals and groups can use to enhance individual and collective wellbeing.

The *Character Strengths and Virtues* handbook (2014) suggested six virtues have a historical basis in the vast majority of cultures and that these virtues and strengths can lead to increased happiness when built upon. The listed virtues and strengths are provided in Figure 7.3.

This model does not appear to have been applied in international development, though it has been applied in sectors such as education, leadership, and child and youth development. One multi-country study found cross-cultural similarity of the strengths:

> The results for 75 nations each represented by at least 150 respondents suggest substantial cross-cultural similarity in endorsement of the strengths. The most highly endorsed character strengths were Honesty, Fairness, Kindness, Judgment, and Curiosity, while the least endorsed were Self-Regulation, Modesty, Prudence, and Spirituality. Though the participants probably represent a biased sample for many of the countries examined in the study, these results suggest grounds exist for cross-cultural dialogue on how to advance the development of good character (McGrath 2015: 41).

In conclusion, this chapter has highlighted that the field of positive psychology has insights that can contribute to the quality and effectiveness of international development. This is particularly the case given that programmes

Wisdom	Courage	Transcendence	Humanity	Justice	Moderation
• creativity • curiosity • judgement • love of learning • perspective	• bravery • persistence • honesty • zest	• appreciation of beauty • gratitude • hope • humour • spirituality	• love • kindness • social intelligence	• teamwork • fairness • leadership	• forgiveness • modesty • prudence • self-control

Figure 7.3 Character strengths

generally engage people and groups of people in processes which seek to bring about some kind of behavioural, attitudinal, or organizational change. The research and practices associated with positive psychology contribute to understanding about the factors, levers, or drivers which contribute to motivation, which is a key ingredient in achieving change at any level. The value of taking an appreciative perspective, affirming strengths and confirming the validity of people's visions for the future, is evidenced in positive psychology and consistent with a strengths-based approach. It is easy to see how these elements from positive psychology are critical for achieving positive change, when people and groups are involved. A strengths-based approach taps into psychological foundations of individuals and groups and 'works with the grain', to encourage, motivate, and energize individuals and groups. Research and practice in positive psychology confirm the value of the strengths-based approach in building resilience and wellbeing as well as supporting flourishing individuals, communities, and countries, the ultimate goal of international development. We recognize that to date there is little evidence from diverse cultural contexts related to positive psychology and encourage further research.

CHAPTER 8
The development worker

> *Go to the people*
> *Live among them*
> *Learn from them*
> *Love them*
> *Start with what they know*
> *Build on what they have*
> *But of the best leaders*
> *When their task is done*
> *The people will remark:*
> *'We have done it ourselves'*
> (Lao Tzu, 6th century BCE)

This chapter explores the role of development workers when using a strengths-based approach. The mindset and practice of a strengths-based approach raise questions about traditional expectations of international development workers and transform this role in relation to others.

The term 'development worker' is used intentionally here, and throughout this book, since it captures the breadth of roles in international development, recognizing the diversity and scale of practice. The term includes those working directly with communities, often described as facilitators; project managers; technical or policy advisers; monitoring and evaluation specialists; and diplomatic personnel and individuals working directly in or with governments. While the major focus is on development workers, researchers in international development will also find the ideas to be relevant.

Mindset shift

As noted in Chapter 2, development workers have a choice to make: to take a deficit- or strengths-based perspective. Authors in the field of strengths-based social work suggest that working from a strengths perspective requires a shift in the 'automatic thoughts' of social workers and a 'paradigm shift or transformation of knowledge and practice' from the deficit-based practice of social work (Blundo, 2009: 42). A similar shift may be necessary for many development workers who have worked in the sector so deeply influenced by the deficit agenda.

It is not only one's own mindset that may need to be shifted, but also those of colleagues and partners. Bushe (2001: 7) writes, 'the most critical part of an appreciative process required for it to work is a change in the consciousness of the change agent'. Past experiences or ways of working may have ingrained a deficit mindset. As illustrated in Case Study 7, development workers need to develop respectful strategies and provide opportunities for individuals and groups to think about the strengths or assets they have and to aspire to a preferred future, and this may take time.

An international development worker should recognize their role as an outsider to the local change agenda. The appreciative attitude of an outsider is central to any strengths-based approach. The outsider should be a facilitator of locally led processes, when invited, to identify local knowledge, wisdom, and strengths, rather than a driver of externally determined agendas (Rhodes, 2022). The outsider's primary functions are to make enquiries in an appreciative manner, to support the process of mapping the assets a community or organization or network has at their disposal, and to facilitate a process to identify preferred visions of the future. Modelling a strengths-based approach through an appreciative perspective, active listening, and inclusion are important. It is difficult to fake or implement the processes of a strengths-based approach without truly embracing the philosophy.

Identity, role, and knowledge

> *What I now understand is that if you don't put a strengths-based approach into practice yourself it's very hard to apply it to your work and to the relationships and connections you need to achieve good work. If one focuses on one's own strengths and everybody else is doing the same, this results in greatly increasing your team's strength* (Soli Middleby).

A strengths-based approach redefines the role of a development worker in relation to those with whom they work: the 'identity' of a development worker and whose knowledge informs agendas for international development are discussed below.

Who is at the centre?

Taking a strengths-based approach redefines the people at the centre of the development agenda. Within development discourse, the development worker and their agenda (their job description, project objectives, or programme workplans) are often at the centre, with those within local contexts 'participating'. The latter are commonly described as 'counterparts' or 'beneficiaries', reflecting their role vis-à-vis the external project. This situates development workers and the programme, project, or change agenda at the centre of focus. Community members 'participate' in the project and representatives of local organizations are deemed to be stakeholders or partners to the development project. This focus in international development has dominated for decades and has raised multiple debates about the notion of participation in development (Chambers, 1997; Cornwall, 2000; Cooke and Kothari, 2001; Hickey and Mohan, 2005). The ladder of participation (Arnstein, 1969) has been commonly cited as a tool to assess types of participation in development, and denotes the focus on participation in the development programme.

A strengths-based approach premises a central leadership role for those who seek change (such as community leaders and members, staff of an organization) with no interest in degrees or levels of participation. It recognizes the change agenda is owned and led by individuals and groups themselves. The role of the development worker is to be a transitory visitor and supporter for a longer-term and endogenous change process.

More consideration has been given over time to participation as citizenship in development discourse. Cornwall (2000) outlined shifts in development thinking which have extended the notion of participation in projects or programmes to participation in governance and policy agendas. She noted, 'in recent years, concern with the relationship of citizens and the state has increasingly come to shape the practice of participation in development, particularly in the move towards engaging citizen participation in the policy process' (Cornwall, 2000: 60). These changing definitions of participation in international development are aligned with a strengths-based approach which places local relationships and processes at the centre of any change process. Yet in many contexts in the sector the term beneficiary is still described and used as a metric to measure progress of objectives in development programmes.

Who is the expert?

Use of a strengths-based approach redefines an expert in the international development sector. Development workers are often defined as technical or sector experts/advisers or as team leaders and managers who are responsible for guiding programming approaches or managing the implementation of plans, budgets, and timelines. A strengths-based approach gives expert status to those individuals situated within communities, groups, or organizations who are experienced in their own past, know their own context, and have a central stake in the future. The role of the international development worker to the 'local context' is to support and work with local agendas and priorities decided locally. Expertise is conferred in local stakeholders who should have power in decision-making, lead the change process, and are ultimately accountable to local actors. These ideas are explained briefly below.

Whose knowledge informs international development?

A critical examination of the 'role of the expert' raises the question 'whose knowledge counts in international development?' Outsiders' knowledge and perspectives might not provide the best vantage point to appreciate strengths of the past and aspirations for the future in other contexts. Case Study 10 below provides an example of the role of the development worker vis-à-vis the knowledge of citizens in countries where change happens. It is helpful to consider four aspects of 'knowledge' in international development.

First, the notions of expert knowledge or empiricist approaches to knowledge and knowledge owned outside the individual's control are problematic. Weick (1992), who wrote about strengths-based social work, calls for the 'recapturing' of 'lived experience and disqualified knowledge'. In taking this tack, 'people's knowledge of their lives is treated as a natural resource. The imposition of hierarchical knowledge structures in which professional knowledge is unquestionably superior to lay knowledge is overturned. In its place is the recognition of a multiplicity of knowledges' (Weick, 1992: 24).

Second, a strengths-based approach to knowledge aligns with the agenda of decolonizing knowledge, which challenges the dominance and claim of universality of western perspectives. A strengths-based approach emphasizes local prioritization of strengths and preferred futures informed by local knowledge. As described in Part A, a strengths-based approach emphasizes the centrality of context and culture and inherently prioritizes local knowledge over external or outsider perspectives.

Third, we should not wholly abandon knowledge of international development workers and outside perspectives. Broader sets of knowledge and perspectives are valuable and the contributions that international development workers offer in initial facilitation of strengths-based approaches are useful. Saleebey (1992), who wrote about strengths-based social work, questions the role of experts, but acknowledges the special knowledge and value that professionals and experts have. He wrote, 'while we may want to re-examine the notion of expert, especially the implicit paternalism that it abets, we do have special knowledge and it would be foolish to deny that. However, it might be very important to critically analyse the assumptions, the consequences of the use of this knowledge, as well as the cultural, racial, class and gender distortions and biases' (p. 8).

Fourth, a strengths-based approach brings together everyone's knowledge, and so individuals, groups, or organizations could draw on knowledge offered through external actors. Importantly, these knowledge sets are accessed and used on terms set by local actors, in line with their own agendas. As discussed in Chapter 5, external resources and knowledge can augment local assets, resources, and knowledge. In the field of research, this is described as transdisciplinary, whereby different knowledge sets (often from both non-academic and academic sources) are integrated in collaborative processes to achieve common goals, and in the process, new knowledge and theory are formed (Max-Neef, 2005; Wickson et al., 2006; Thompson Klein, 2017).

Case Study 10 Take your ego out of the equation

Godwin Yidana was born in a village in northern Ghana and in 2021 was undertaking PhD studies at the University of New England in Australia. This story of his journey confirms that the strengths-based approach enables development workers to contribute constructively in multiple roles. His experience exemplifies its benefits across many sectors and countries.

As a young man, Godwin started volunteering by helping prisoners to learn to read and write, realizing they were otherwise being 'left to rot'. Demand from prisoners quickly grew and more volunteers were needed, so he approached university students from a nearby campus to help. They found one of the prisoners had been a librarian and worked with him to set up a library. The word got out about this successful contribution to the rehabilitation process, but for political reasons, the volunteers' work was stopped by local authorities. However, Godwin's links with the university students led him to hear about Appreciative Inquiry and this began an ongoing interest.

In his own village, Godwin wanted to help women and men who wove baskets, the style and quality of which were well-regarded nationally. He had met an Australian, who had experience in fair trade. They collected discarded plastic bags around the village and turned them into strips suitable for weaving into baskets. He brought together five men and five women to discuss a new way of working, including ways to avoid their previous experience of being underpaid by 'middlemen'. The first 10 baskets were sent to a business in Accra with interests in recycled materials, then orders for many more came flooding in. On reflection, Godwin realized the business focused on the village's assets, including creative and open-minded women; the investment to mobilize them was relatively minor. Within two months, the number of women involved went from 5 to 70 and they agreed to allocate 10 per cent of the profits to manage the business.

On reflection, they had been working with the dynamics and strengths of the community, recognizing the values that existed in the community about the roles of men and women, and providing opportunities for these to change over time with a focus on positive outcomes for everyone. They were guided by what the individuals and communities have, rather than what they did not have. Godwin tried to help the women become economically independent but over time, he realized this was contributing to reducing gender-based violence. The experience of working together on the business led women to take action against men who committed violence, creating awareness and disincentives. Women talked about whether to allow more men to join the weaving group, since there was enough work to share around; they decided their criteria would be that men had to contribute to housework. Over time, this led to changing values, with more men involved in housework and the business. The funds raised have been used to fund girls' education.

Godwin moved to Australia to undertake a Master's degree at Sydney University. He took on a conflict transformation peace-building facilitation role in Myanmar, with an NGO. He worked with government officials and ethnic armed groups in conflict. Godwin helped the officials to see their own expertise, their leadership, and their skills, by acknowledging them and then mobilizing them to bring about

(Continued)

Case Study 10 Continued

positive change. He did this through running intensive one-week training courses in various parts of Myanmar. On many occasions, Godwin recalled that after the third day of the course the participants would realize that they had expertise, agency, and skills in transforming conflicts with farmers and ethnic armed groups, whereas before, they felt they had no ability to bring about change. He became aware of the importance of enabling individuals to see they have skills, to believe in themselves and use their abilities to bring about change.

Godwin quickly realized that women were not participating in equal numbers in peace-building processes. He decided to include a women's case study from Liberia, as an example of the role of women in peace, into the workshops. While the men dominated group work, he kept insisting on creating space for women to talk. Some men said that women were too emotional to be leaders, but he reminded them that diversity is a strength and women's contribution added to the overall strength of the community in addressing peace and conflict issues. Slowly the women became more involved, first in group work, then in leading groups, and then in presenting on various topics. By the end of 2015, it became apparent to the relevant national ministry in Myanmar that women can contribute to peace-building across the country: a major shift.

At the end of 2015, Godwin went to Sierra Leone to undertake a consultancy for a German NGO in the area of waste recycling. He was asked to train women who wanted to copy the weaving that had been undertaken in his own village in Ghana. The participants were women ex-combatants, very clear that they wanted to learn the same weaving style as had been used in Ghana. Godwin recommended they use their own strengths and materials to develop their own products, to get a much better result. This group is successfully creating products, drawing from their own assets.

Godwin has reflected on the importance of avoiding facilitator arrogance. He said 'ego is the main blockage on the path to change and it's important for facilitators to take their ego out of the equation. Where people are in poverty, there is often a strong belief they have nothing and have no future, so they live in a world of negativity: a development worker's role is to provide a pathway towards positive change'.

Back in Australia, Godwin was offered a role to develop new programmes in Africa with an Australian faith-based organization. He found the NGO's fundraising and communications elements portrayed Africans as hopeless victims who needed Australians to save them! He explained the reality of strong and capable Africans and insisted on shifting focus towards stories which describe differences made by funding rather than dependence and hopelessness of communities. After tentatively testing this approach on one donor, positive feedback about the strengths-based approach led to its widespread adoption.

Godwin's experience as a facilitator with a strengths-based approach led him to see his role as accompanying people on a journey in which the facilitator is a learner and local expertise is driving the change process. This, he said, is what a true development partnership should be about.

New ways of working

With new ways of defining knowledge, new working relationships are also formed between different actors engaged in the development process. These relationships are explored below.

Working in relationship

Taking a strengths-based approach requires those working in international development to listen, learn, and foster different types of relationships from those normally expected. As described by Glicken (2004: 6), who wrote about strengths-based social work, 'the binding elements of the strengths perspective include the recognition that the client, not the worker, is the primary change agent. The worker's role is to listen, help the client process, and facilitate by focusing on positive behaviours that might be useful in coping with the client's current life situation'.

The role of the international development worker is to reveal and surface existing strengths. Glicken (2004: 17) wrote: 'Our role is to reflect the strengths, assets and capacities of those that we are working with, we need to act as "mirrors" reflecting our client's sense of worth, strengths capacities and attraction'. This is the same for international development: in many instances individuals, groups, or communities may not appreciate their own strengths and assets, reflecting generational inequity, experience of colonization, or other forms of marginalization. The role of the international development worker is to champion and encourage the realization and appreciation of inherent strengths and assets.

To care for and respect those with whom we work means to listen, learn, and value local perspectives. This transforms paternalistic notions of international development. Rapp and Goscha (2008), who wrote about strengths-based social work, draw on the literature on resilience to argue that 'professional relationships need to convey a sense of caring and respect' (p. 26). Few could question the critical importance of quality relationships for international development. The importance of the relational aspect of international development is becoming increasingly recognized at long last (Horner, 2020; Peacifica, 2020; Spratt, 2020).

Strengthening local relationships commonly appears as a result of good quality international development practice, confirming the role of external facilitators in enhancing endogenous local relations. A broad range of relationships can be strengthened: within communities; between community members and other actors such as government representatives or service providers; or between private sector and non-governmental organizations. For example, working with a community in northern Uganda with World Vision, Keren Winterford asked questions framed through an Appreciative Inquiry perspective to generate conversations, connections, and strengthened relations between a variety of disparate community-based groups and government agencies.

The conversations surfaced a variety of existing efforts and initiatives for development and existing sets of relationships that could be used to support shared interests and commitment for future visions. Existing relationships included those between farmers and women's groups and between sub-county officials and the local primary school in this example.

Ensure space for local actors and stepping back

To enable a strengths-based approach, the development worker needs to purposely step back to create space for change agents to take the lead themselves. Development workers who are used to being in control and operating in a contractual context may see themselves as accountable for tasks and programme deliverables, so this might be hard and unnerving. To enable a strengths-based approach, the development worker needs to purposely step back to create space for change agents to take the lead themselves. It is within these spaces that change happens: the space between facilitated processes and local actors leading action towards their committed futures; and the space between local actors' relationships, where there are shared interests and where commitments and actions are made.

In a strengths-based approach, by stepping back, responsibility is continuously being shifted away from external programme stakeholders and intermediary implementing agencies to local organizations. This is achieved through a range of strategies described in Chapter 3, including emphasizing strengths, building self-esteem and confidence of local actors; revealing and using local strengths and resources to catalyse change; and promoting local leadership of the change agenda.

Confining the boundaries of the development worker is related to ensuring there is space for leadership roles by local actors. The development worker's role is limited to enabling space for inquiry, reflection, learning, and strengthening relations within and between local actors. The role of the development worker is only to support inclusive and participatory inquiry to reveal existing strengths and unrealized resources and support dialogue between citizens and organizations in each context.

As discussed in Chapter 1, a strengths-based approach requires letting go of the 'control, predict, and plan' processes of development project management. Such a radical conclusion is not new: it was reached by Robert Easterly (2006) in his book entitled: *The White Man's Burden: Why the West's Efforts to Aid the Rest Have Done So Much Ill and So Little Good.* Easterly attributes the failure of international development to the fact that most projects are designed and implemented by those he calls 'planners'. Planners are those who determine what is best for others and what will be implemented by an intermediary agency. He contrasts this approach of planners with that of 'searchers'. Searchers ask questions in a different way: 'What can foreign aid do for the poor people?' This approach is taken by countries that have not received much 'planned' development assistance and have been much more successful in their development efforts. These countries are described by Easterly as countries that searched for their own specific solutions to development goals. At the end of his book, Easterly (2006: 382) states: 'only the self-reliant effort of poor people and poor societies themselves can end poverty'. It is only when the practice of international development prioritizes a facilitator role for citizens searching for what works and what is being learned from success in their own context, that it will be in a position to contribute to change.

One illustration of the change in relationships between development workers and community actors can be found in a programme in Mozambique supported by the Australian Government and Australian Anglican Overseas Aid called *Towards Abundant Life*. The programme made a deliberate choice to use a strengths-based approach (Ascroft, 2016; Caulfield 2020). The *Equipa de Vida* (Teams of Life) are voluntary associations carrying out the programme's activities in villages. Reflecting on this programme, Burchardt et al. (2017) highlight the importance of using language that reflects the message of both the process and the end goal. The authors point out that programme managers can be seen as the agents of the change process if they play a directive role, and when they do this, they act in a way that is contrary to the longer-term objective. In this programme, the role of field staff is clearly defined as facilitator rather than active agent: 'the field workers walk alongside the *Equipas* as they achieve their own objective. The job title given to the programme field staff is *Adepto*, a Portuguese term referring to a "supporter" or "fan" – the one who is cheering on the players as in a sporting event'. Their role as *Adepto* is to cheer on the real players in this programme who are the *Equipa* to be found in each community.

Be comfortable with uncertainty

A strengths-based approach recognizes that change, particularly social change, is complex and highly uncertain: the opposite of the view that change is linear or time-bound. This is especially the case when change is catalysed by local strengths and led by local actors. Chapters 1 and 4 described the notion of complexity and its resonance with a strengths-based approach. Blundo (2009) recognizes that one of the consequences of a strengths perspective for social workers is 'the uncertainty, the not knowing and maybe the unfamiliarity of relying on the client to take the lead, in giving direction to the work to be done, that is so uncomfortable' (p. 42). This is similarly the case in international development. Facilitators of a strengths-based approach need to trust the process, and to respect and value local actors who are in the lead of the change process agenda.

Enable catalytic change

With knowledge of how change can work in a strengths-based approach, an international development worker can encourage catalytic change; that is, change that motivates continued activities and action for change. Over time, the achievement of change created through 'quick wins' offers the potential for future action and change. Research on strengths-based approaches has identified the value of quick wins (Winterford, 2013; Willetts et al., (2014)), and catalytic change is also described in relation to positive psychology (Peterson, 2006) and transformational change (Burnes, 2005). As noted in Chapter 7, Winterford's (2013) research on strengths-based social accountability identified that citizen-led advocacy to improve access to and delivery of quality public services was enabled through quick wins. The quick wins were described as local level improvements achieved by short-term actions by citizens. The consequences of achieving quick wins (changes to citizens' sense of self and view of the future) encouraged and motivated continued citizen action. Since they had succeeded in achieving some change, citizens believed they could create more. Using existing resources to achieve quick wins was valued as a way to sustain motivation for citizen-led advocacy towards the state.

Many examples of the concept of quick wins were mentioned by people interviewed for this book. For example, Ian Cunningham said 'a strengths-based approach provides a contrast with a problem-based approach where the maximum that can be achieved is a problem solved. A strengths-based approach enables people and communities to reach beyond a problem solved, to a better life overall, where their aspirations are elevated and progressed'.

Scott Martin, Program Manager for the Malawi Program of Caritas Australia said:

> The most important thing introduced by a strengths-based approach is the change in mindset of the communities themselves. The change in the community's mindset that they could control their own resources and use them to achieve their vision. Many times I have listened to the communities say: 'We can do this ourselves – we own the process' as communities began to recognize the fact that they have the skills, strengths and resources and management capacity within their reach. Every time we visited the community there would always be someone who stood up and said: 'We did not realize that we had so much – we are rich'. Change in community mindset to control their own resources and visions is a key to catalytic change.

Broaden span of strengths

The role of the development worker is to champion inclusion in the process, ensuring that everyone who can contribute does so safely, and that there is appropriate opportunity for everyone to describe their own strengths and contribute to visions about the future. It is valuable to have a broad perspective of who should be included in a strengths-based process, including ensuring that those not normally engaged in development initiatives are included. The role of the development worker is to model and champion inclusion and equity outcomes, to promote maximum opportunity for active participation for all.

As noted in Chapter 3, a critique of a strengths-based approach is that it does not acknowledge power and existing inequalities, which means that local actors are not able to equally participate and contribute to change processes. It is an important consideration that not all individuals or groups come equally to participate in a strengths-based process, just as they do not come equally to participate in any change process. The role of the development worker is to be cognizant of the local context and seek opportunities to maximize inclusion for future-orientated change.

When a change process begins with a deliberate and collective search for past contributions and existing strengths to catalyse future change, it is inevitable that prominent members turn their focus to those who are often hidden or ignored. The ongoing search for strengths and potential contributions of every community member continues and encourages the process of inclusion. In fact, the gradual discovery of potential strengths of women, children, and people with disabilities reinforces the value of ensuring that everyone has equal representation in both the process of change and the desired outcomes.

From the perspective of those in power, the discovery of gifts and strengths in every member of the community is not only a revelation but often seen as a lightening of the burden of responsibility and a sharing of the load of leadership. When men, in particular, discover that their partners and women in the community have talents and abilities they were not aware of, they often become more respectful and open to inclusion and equity. This has been the case in a World Vision Bangladesh project using a gender-transformative social accountability approach (Winterford et al., 2022) which has prioritized the inclusion of women and people with disabilities in WASH governance. Elected representatives and services providers who are responsible for WASH budgets and planning have been surprised and impressed by the 'new voice and role' of women and people with disabilities. Informed by their life experiences they are now recognized as best-placed to decide priorities for WASH improvements that will benefit the whole community. In turn, by listening and responding to community priorities, these government officials are more valued by the community.

Another important consideration for the development worker is to recognize broader structural or systemic challenges that may impede the utilization of strengths, assets, or resources to catalyse change. For example, a community or organization may have a strong desire to realize change and act towards preferred futures, but leaders or decision-makers in other parts of the system are not supportive. The role of the development worker is to work in ways that convince change in these actors, rather than being barriers, to be assets as well for the change. This may involve 'working around', 'crowding out', or simply ongoing direct advocacy to convince actors to change. For example, the authors have had numerous experiences where processes which sought to enable collective learning and visioning through a strengths-based approach have been thwarted by senior management in non-government organizations and ministries. As mentioned in the Preface, Keren Winterford had the early experience of using Appreciative Inquiry when a senior leader was not supportive of a participatory process. A commitment to the value of the process resulted in a strong plan of action to strengthen local programming approaches. Similarly, Keren has seen many community-led initiatives where government officials are reluctant to be part of the change process. The momentum of community and other actors means that those few who are not interested are left by the side. The momentum of a broad and connected set of strengths cannot be contained, and transformative change is realized.

Be equipped

This book seeks to encourage, motivate, and equip international development workers with some understanding of a strengths-based approach, but recognizes readers will need to learn more. Development workers need to be appropriately equipped to facilitate a strengths-based approach in diverse contexts. The Resource List in this book provides guides, materials, and links for this purpose. Drawing on the principles and practices set out in this chapter and others, employing a strengths-based approach requires humility, grace, and trust in the process and those with whom you are working, in every context.

Responding to expectations

New ways of working for development workers described above and in Case Study 11 include suggestions about the application of a strengths-based approach in reality. As noted earlier, the authors have successfully used this approach over decades and acknowledge that meeting others' expectations about the process of supporting developmental change can be challenging within the current paradigm and according to dominant systems.

There are three sets of expectations that may require navigation: those of development organizations (generally employers or sources of funding); those of governments and communities in which you are working; and development workers' own expectations about their efforts to 'make a difference'.

The first is addressed in Part A which describes how many development organizations, reflecting the broader systems in which they operate, expect development workers to be 'experts' in particular disciplines or areas of change. They develop terms of reference and job descriptions with lists of deliverables, such as 'revised legislation on x topic', 'drafted policy on y policy', 'new manuals for z process' or 'new project proposals'. This creates the momentum for the development worker to deliver such products, often to standards set by donors or offices in other countries.

> **Case Study 11** Learning to listen

Ian Cunningham has a professional background in water engineering and moved into the development sector after an 18-month placement with an international NGO, in his case Engineers Without Borders (EWB) Australia. Ian reflects on his use of a strengths-based approach:

> I use a strengths-based approach and I can't imagine using anything else ... A deficit framework seems totally inappropriate: it positions you as the one with the answers or power in a way which is unhelpful, an 'us' and 'them' kind of approach. In the philosophy of a strengths-based approach, it's 'us' plus 'us', and in my experience a shared direction of 'us' is necessary to bring about change. When we see people with dreams and strengths, it's very powerful. And it is this power that is necessary for change.
>
> This approach throws a spanner in the works for people who talk negatively about poverty, hopelessness and weakness, but it is what actually helps to make the world a better place. The approach helps to reframe views of the world that include people rather than pit one group against another. It is more collaborative and contradicts the idea of and language related to 'recipients' and 'donors' which I always feel very uncomfortable about. The organizations with money seem to think they have all the power: other sources of power are not sufficiently recognized, such as knowledge, time, dreams, agency, skills, commitment.

In 2007 and 2008, Ian worked on a WASH programme in Indonesia. He saw EWB's philosophy of community-led approaches to development practised by EWB's volunteers and staff. It was only later he found out EWB's practice was founded in ABCD principles, with many at EWB trained by Chris Dureau. He also later realized that this type of approach to development was not the norm. Ian reflected:

> The village water committee [in Indonesia] had a clear and strong vision: this was the driving force to progress their water aspirations. They knew what they wanted, and that was to be involved in every step of the project. The committee contrasted this with historical government-led water projects in the village that were, from their perspective, imposed. EWB's role, as outsiders, was to support the committee's vision. Sometimes this meant providing technical support and information when needed. It was a delicate balance to make sure we didn't encroach on their aspirations and their lead by being overly proactive. The Australian-based management team was on the whole very supportive, and provided a constant reminder that 'it is their project, not ours'. We quickly realized that often when we initiated an idea or training and it didn't respond to where the committee were at or what they wanted – it often fell flat. By contrast, whenever the local committee started something, and we fed into that process as needed, they owned the idea and made it work. Our contributions in those cases were much more valuable.
>
> There was one key moment when the water committee rejected a significant piece of engineering advice from the Australian team about water treatment.

(Continued)

Case Study 11 Continued

It initially caused some challenges for those who had spent their time investing in the design of the treatment element. But I took it as a positive sign of the committee's growing power and confidence in their technical capacity. They pushed back on the design as it didn't fit with where they were at. Later, we reflected it was absolutely the right decision to not implement the treatment element.

Ian remembers that his natural inclination was to use questions rather than directives, and this helped reveal existing strengths in each context. For example, asking about other elements of village governance revealed existing management approaches that were adapted to the water supply. Pitching different scenarios, 'how might you ...?' type questions provided an opportunity for the committee to consider their response to water-related scenarios using existing skills and structures.

After 18 months in Indonesia, Ian reflected on the 'foundations of a beautiful collaborative relationship' that were the basis for the success of the project. He noted that 'a strengths-based approach underpinned the way we worked together'. He said the approach particularly helped with both understanding, working with, and even changing power dynamics for the better, key for development effectiveness.

One of Ian's lessons relates to the limitations of a problem-based approach. He reflected: 'a strengths-based approach provides a contrast with a problem-based approach where the maximum that can be achieved is a problem solved. A strengths-based approach enables people and communities to reach beyond a problem solved, to a better life overall where their aspirations are elevated and progressed'.

When Ian returned to Australia in 2008, he continued to work with EWB. Besides establishing projects with partner organizations across the world, he has trained other overseas volunteers in a strengths-based approach. He mostly uses ABCD in his practice and uses the key premises of a strengths-based approach when working with young engineers to help frame and reframe their perceptions of poverty, justice, inequality, and their world.

Ian later pursued PhD research on the use of a strengths-based approach in the water sector, though was surprised to find few explicit applications of a strengths-based approach in the water sector.

To Ian, motivation is a key element of a strengths-based approach. In the water sector,

everybody needs and wants water, so there is a natural motivation. But when projects were pre-determined, or ideas around how to access water were felt to be imposed, then the natural reaction at the local level was to check out or push back. A strengths-based approach is good at flipping it round, so then the role of the facilitator is to provide spaces which nurture people's inherent energy or motivations, and help when needed, but not drive the change themselves. The community will come and ask for assistance when they hit roadblocks and the development partner can respond when requested. Then the communities can continue to follow their own trajectory.

(Continued)

> **Case Study 11** Continued
>
> Ian's PhD is:
>
>> an exploration of motivations in community-led water supply. People are naturally growth-oriented. Poor quality motivation is when something is imposed from outside, it can foster ill-being and ultimately this type of motivation often doesn't last. By contrast, higher quality motivation comes from inside, it's self-determined, and takes us towards things we care about or find interesting. A strengths-based approach supports this higher quality motivation because it recognizes what's inside people – their own motivation to work on things they care about. A strengths-based approach supports higher quality motivations by: focusing on projects people care about (and not imposing an external agenda), by focusing on the capabilities that people already have, and working with others to support change. These elements of a strengths-based approach mean it plays a key role in supporting motivation.
>
> Ian confirms that the power of a strengths-based approach is its philosophy as much as the tools. In his view, 'people could use the tools without understanding the philosophy, but it won't have the same effect'. When he discusses and explains the approach,
>
>> people (engineers are a good example of this) often focus disproportionately on fixing problems, but this can be limiting. A focus on problems doesn't provide a space to see or dream beyond the current reality. A problem-solving, fixing approach can be limiting. It means that only incremental steps are taken, which can be helpful but doesn't leave scope for transformation. Whereas when we use a strengths-based approach, there is the opportunity for people to dream, reflect on their own capacities, and move into a new way of doing or being. This type of thinking, feeling and doing can be transformative.
>
> Ian completed his PhD (2021) and is now in a strong position to contribute to global efforts to facilitate strengths-based change in the water sector, particularly reflecting his deep understanding about the concept of motivation, without which, change is really quite impossible!

Also, international development systems require proposals from development organizations with details about development worker deliverables before funding is provided. Engaging in front-end on-the-ground preparation is often not considered important enough to be funded. It is assumed that people know what they need or that 'expert advisers' can predict such needs, so that proposals are submitted for the 'doing' phase rather than for the groundwork and foundations. A strengths-based approach necessarily requires national level or community engagement from the beginning. Aid agencies can take some convincing to realize that this is key to the process of sustainable development. The irony is that the greater the investment in early local-level strengths-based facilitation, the shorter the overall life of the project will be and the more sustainable the benefits.

The authors and people interviewed for this book have all experienced the challenge of negotiating expectations of development organizations and have engaged with them at multiple levels on the use of a strengths-based approach. Respectful, collaborative, and evidence-based approaches tend to work best, though sometimes applying the approach 'under the radar' is possible. This can take time and effort, but will contribute to better results than continuing to 'deliver' products which do not contribute to relevant, locally driven, and sustainable changes.

Second, after decades of experience of 'receiving' international development programmes, many people in government and communities have learned to expect development workers to bring solutions and deliver results as well as write technical documents to suit their external audience. Case studies in this book illustrate how some may initially react negatively to the view that they have strengths and agency to lead and address their development goals, including in collaboration with people from other countries. If a well-facilitated initial interaction includes an exit strategy, it will be clear that once the fire has been lit (figuratively speaking), organizations and communities will take over. When given the language, space, and means to reflect on their strengths and vision for the future, the case studies confirm that people will always grasp the opportunity, at some stage.

Third, dealing with development workers' own expectations can be challenging. Societies, education systems, and families in countries that provide development programmes often expect development workers to 'change the world' and 'make a difference'. Such concepts are often internalized, so even experienced development workers tell themselves they must deliver results to be successful. Agency staff may say it is too risky to ask communities or organizations what they want; seeing an 'open menu' only raises expectations the agency will not be able to meet. Some who have learned about a strengths-based approach have simply refused to implement it because it contradicts their values and philosophical orientation as 'development worker'. In practice, learning the skills to ask, facilitate, listen, and support, using a strengths-based approach is like any other – with more practice, it becomes easier and with evidence of its benefits, it becomes obvious as the best way forward.

In summary, this chapter focused attention on the mindset and ways of working that, combined, will enable a development worker to successfully use a strengths-based approach. Challenging the controlling role of development workers over development processes and deliverables, the discussion encourages them to 'let go' and to focus on the critical importance of facilitating change led by the people and groups whose lives are changing. Modelling appreciative and inclusive facilitation is critical, alongside the ability to find comfort with uncertainty and recognize the limits of external contributors. While these ideas challenge contemporary international development systems which determine the role of development workers, a shift is possible. The authors have proven the significant value of this different mindset and new ways of working, 'within the system' albeit 'under the radar' for at least two decades. The process of writing this book has confirmed that many others, including Ian Cunningham (Case Study 11 above), have shared the experience and come to the same conclusions.

PART C
Application of a strengths-based approach in international development

> *For me, the value and advantage that a strengths-based approach brings to development has three elements:*
>
> 1. *It addresses the power imbalances that exist at many levels – between donor and recipient, between people with disabilities and those without disabilities – by empowering those whose lives are at the centre.*
> 2. *It places those whose lives are at the centre, as part of the solution, not the object of others' contributions.*
> 3. *It stops us in our tracks to give us time to think about how we are going to achieve the objectives/the vision we have, rather than just focus on how to deliver a particular result set by others*
>   (Setareki Macanawai)

Part C applies a strengths-based approach to the realities of how international development is currently organized. This Part offers an alternative approach to the current dominance of technical programme-driven and sector-driven approaches and provides many examples of how the approach is already applied in these contexts.

Chapter 9 acknowledges that most development funding is managed through a programme or project cycle, and therefore applies a strengths-based lens to the cycle. This includes the benefit of using a strengths-based lens at the stage of setting development policies within development organizations.

Chapter 10 applies a strengths-based lens to the work of analysing contexts and development processes, focusing on monitoring, evaluation, and research. It offers suggestions on the practicalities of using strengths-based practices to research and evaluative processes relevant to development, as well as to monitoring during a programme's implementation.

Chapter 11 links a strengths-based approach with dominant approaches which are currently used in international development, such as capacity development and gender and social inclusion. Beginning with a recognition that these approaches increasingly fit within the context of broader relationships between countries, in diplomatic and geo-political terms, this chapter invites readers to find opportunities to use a strengths-based approach in synergy with their current thinking and practice.

Chapter 12 begins by noting that a strengths-based approach does not sit comfortably with a sector-based way of working, which dominates international development funding and programmes, but then provides diverse and compelling examples of its application within the sectors which currently absorb most funding. Evidence of the use of a strengths-based approach is offered in examples of programmes in sectors as diverse as climate change adaptation and law and justice.

The concluding chapter (13) synthesizes key messages introduced throughout the book, linking them together to summarize the compelling arguments and evidence for a new approach to international development.

CHAPTER 9
A strengths-based approach and the programme cycle

> *A strengths-based approach gives clarity, a solid foundation and core grounding for international development practice in every context: it supports people in their right to be consulted, to be included and to achieve change* (Vicki Vaartjes)

A programme cycle is the commonly used system for organizing, funding, implementing, and evaluating international development. This chapter considers evidence from literature and development workers interviewed for this book, and discusses the use of a strengths-based approach at different stages of the cycle.

When considering the use of a strengths-based approach in practice, a question arises about whether it should be used as a single comprehensive approach across a programme cycle or as part of a mix of approaches. Some of those interviewed for this book stated that there should be consistency of application, since a mix of problem-based and strengths-based approaches contributes to confused messages as well as contradictory and dysfunctional practice. For example, Vicki Vaartjes, interviewed for this book, said, 'there is no point applying a strengths-based approach in the design, but then the implementers use a problem-solving approach, which focuses on weaknesses, problems and needs'. Proponents of a coherent approach confirm that the philosophy inherent in a strengths-based approach is critical, and that people's deeply held values about how change happens cannot be turned on or off to suit a particular context.

Others may argue that a strengths-based approach is just one of several methods that can be used in development practice in a mixed-methods way. This implies that a strengths-based approach is simply a tool, with benefits and limitations, like any other tool.

Proponents of a strengths-based approach believe that connections between the philosophical values and approaches mean that it is not just another tool, but a world-view or way of engaging with the world that cannot readily be turned on or off, or mixed with other world-views. We consider that if one holds a strengths-based philosophy, it is not feasible to practise in ways that contradict this approach. Similarly, if one holds a broader problem-solving perspective to how change happens, the potential for change is limited by the use of bits and pieces and discrete activities of a strengths-based approach. We consider that there should be coherence applying a strengths-based approach in all aspects of international development, whether a programme cycle is used or not.

Another interesting consideration when applying a strengths-based approach in relation to a programme cycle is that different stages of the programme cycle tend to be clearly demarcated, with only 'implementation' considered core to the change process. A strengths-based approach, informed by the perspective that when we ask a question we engage in a change process, does not engender such clear distinctions. We have deliberately used commonly used terms in this chapter so that readers can make sense of how a strengths-based approach can be applied in practice, while encouraging efforts to understand change as more holistic, beyond the confines of a donor-driven programme cycle.

Case Study 12 Trial project leads to whole organizational approach for Caritas Australia

This is a remarkable tale of how a small trial led to an organization taking a complete shift towards the use of a strengths-based approach. This case study describes what Caritas Australia discovered when it applied the approach in a few programmes in Africa: their learning subsequently changed the nature of their relationships with communities around the world.

The context
Caritas Australia is an international development and humanitarian organization working across 16 countries in Africa, Asia, the Pacific, and in Australia. Caritas Australia aims to promote integrated human development as reflected in Catholic social teaching. Most programmes are described as 'integrated community development', meaning they focus on multiple issues at the same time, driven by local circumstances and community aspirations. Caritas Australia is a member of the Australian Council for International Development and adheres to its guiding principles, codes of conduct, and professional standards.

In 2011, Caritas Australia chose to trial a strengths-based approach in integrated community development programmes in two African countries, Malawi and Tanzania, alongside traditional approaches. The results of the strengths-based approach trial were so outstanding that over the coming years Caritas Australia decided to adopt this approach across programmes in all countries where they operate.

Beginnings
Caritas Australia began using the strengths-based approach when it became a partner in the Australia Africa Community Engagement Scheme (AACES) (see Case Study 13), a partnership between the Australian Government and Australian non-governmental organizations (NGOs) working across multiple countries in Africa. The design for AACES itself applied a strengths-based approach by seeking out Australian NGOs and their African partners who were already doing development programming well and then resourcing them to do more. AACES applied a strengths-based approach in overall programme

(Continued)

Case Study 12 Continued

implementation over the following five years (DFAT, 2016). Caritas Australia continued funding these projects for a further two years following the end of Australian Government support.

While most of the 10 Australian NGO partners in the AACES programme used some form of a strengths-based approach in their project designs, Caritas Australia was one of the few which followed through with it during implementation. As Caritas Australia's Africa Programme Director, Scott Martin, explained:

> We initially thought that a strengths-based approach was a requirement of the grant application to AusAID. Initially I thought 'here is yet another set of buzz words and another new fashion for NGOs to adopt' that would last a couple of years. I wondered if this strengths-based approach was just another 'flavour of the month' idea. Now, we are so glad we adopted this approach. When we gradually learnt about the impact it was having on communities, we realized that a strengths-based approach was a fundamental change to our development thinking and at the same time it makes sense. It is logical and so radically different from the deficit approach we had been using. We thought we were being participative and bottom-up, but it's only now, after we have applied a strengths-based approach, that we realize we were actually creating dependency and applying a disguised top-down approach. I now think that when you find something that consistently works beyond expectations, there is no room for cynicism. The big questions for me now are: 'Why have we not been doing this before and why would anyone work in any other way in international development?'

The purpose of using a strengths-based approach

Many of the more experienced programme managers in Caritas Australia now see this approach is more likely to generate local ownership from the very beginning and is more sustainable in the long run. For example, Ivy Khoury reflected on Caritas Australia's work in southern Africa:

> For ten years before using ABCD, I often wondered where we were going because we stayed with the same communities, and they continued to be dependent on our funding. Now we engage with the local government and a selected community for just three years, encouraging them to take ownership and responsibility of the program so that we can move to other communities. What everyone notices is the commitment and enthusiasm of community members and local government partners. It is very satisfying and exciting once you see what happens when communities discover their assets and are convinced that they can manage their own development.

People often do not notice the value of resources in front of them. It is a slow process to help communities realize that they have assets they could use to reach their goals. In Dowa, Malawi, the strengths-based approach enabled the community to use the river and the floodplains they considered useless for agriculture and dangerous because of the crocodiles. They now use the floodplains to add three to four more crop rounds to their traditional high-ground corn harvest. The use of a

(Continued)

146 A STRENGTHS-BASED APPROACH FOR INTERNATIONAL DEVELOPMENT

Case Study 12 Continued

strengths-based approach enabled them to appreciate the value of existing assets. In its programmes, Caritas Australia engages with local government officials and service providers from the outset, reflecting a core principle of Appreciative Inquiry and ABCD. South of Blantyre, the government has helped communities operate an extensive irrigation system drawing from the traditionally unused river course.

Use of a strengths-based approach in Caritas Australia

Caritas Australia now initiates programmes by spending some time in a particular community, then developing a three-year agreement with community members and government agencies, incorporating a clear exit strategy. Caritas Australia contributes training in a strengths-based approach and technical inputs and then, once the three years is up, community members and government agencies continue to apply what they have learned and work together towards achieving their shared goals. Whatever the starting point, programmes usually include improvements in food security, savings, income generation, water, and sanitation and a very significant change in attitudes towards women and marginalized members of the community. This addresses gender-based violence, women's leadership, and inclusion of people with disabilities (Winterford and Cunningham, 2017).

At the end of collaboration with Caritas Australia, the community is well on the way to achieving their goals using their own skills, resources, and assets. In addition, local government officials and services are usually providing additional technical support. Instead of regretting the project has ended, communities celebrate that they are setting off on a new journey, with a solid foundation. Typically, Caritas Australia staff hear the message: 'we thank you for what you have done, but we can take it from here. We are going to be ok'. Scott Martin said, 'I have recently revisited some of the communities in Tanzania and Malawi we were working with during the five years of AACES and found that they are just as involved and fully functioning, with their clear plans and multiple use of resources. They had community signs about the progress they had made and the names of management committee members'.

Scott reflected the most important aspect is the change in mindset of the communities themselves. Those he revisited after the end of the project would say: 'We can do this ourselves now – we own the process and have the skills, strengths, resources and management capacity within our reach. We did not realize that we had so much – we are rich'.

Policy and strategy in international development

Between 2011–2018 we adopted a strengths- or asset-based community development model for our integrated development programmes. After the first two years of using this approach, I decided that the results were so outstanding that we would only use a strengths approach in all our future work. I went back to the key donors, in Norway, France, Holland and FAO and advised them that all future funded activities would use the strengths-based approach. (Casterns Mulume, Director of Social Development, Episcopal Conference of Malawi)

In every sector where we work, and in every task we do, we focus on the strengths. For example, when we recruit new staff, we focus on what they are good at, their passions, and how they can work in communities and what they can bring. We focus on bringing out the best in people and groups and the policies that are intended to support communities. (Anne Wuijts, SurfAid, Indonesia)

Organizations which operate in the international development sector produce policies and strategies to guide their external or global work with and through others. Such organizations include government donors, multilateral donors, international and other NGOs, as well as businesses and consultants contracted by donors. Their policies and strategies usually describe particular values and principles, and define preferred approaches and priorities. For example, national donor agencies generally specify which approaches will be prioritized and define what will and will not be funded and supported. NGO policies and strategies generally highlight their values and beliefs about relationships and change, the people with whom they collaborate, and their approaches and ways of working.

Since policies and strategies express organizational values and approaches, these are ideal places to specify use of a strengths-based approach, at philosophical and practical levels. Values associated with international development often change when new governments are elected or after major reviews. For example, more conservative governments may prioritize approaches used by the private sector, while more progressive governments may promote social justice and rights-based approaches and agendas. Similarly, NGOs, development banks, and development-focused organizations (including consulting companies, research institutes, umbrella bodies, faith-based organizations, and regional organizations for example) express their specific values and approaches in public statements. These all inform decisions about how international development is practised, how decisions are made about resource allocation, and how staff, partners, or volunteers are expected to work.

This section focuses only on the link between a strengths-based approach and development organizations' own policies and strategies about their role in international development, as these influence practice throughout the programme cycle. As noted in Part A, development organizations' policies and strategies are largely informed by a deficit-based approach and steer them towards a focus on finding solutions to problems. A strengths-based approach offers an alternative and constructive approach to creating change.

Applying a strengths-based approach at a development agency's policy level recognizes and centralizes the power of local actors in influencing and informing change. This moves the focus away from a situation where one group (from a donor country) sees the other group (in another country context) as having problems to be fixed, to a situation where the voices of those seeking change are heard by others who are interested in contributing. Policies and strategies which take a strengths-based approach also support others to use the approach.

Appreciative organizational vision and mission statements include the strengths and unique contributions of partner organizations and the broader contexts in which the organization works. Such statements generally articulate shared objectives at various levels, within collaborative and constructive partnerships. Three aspects of the use of a strengths-based approach in setting vision and mission statements are discussed here: the generation of a different analysis to inform the development of goals; the additional perspectives brought by people whose lives are expected to change; and the benefit of using the approach within organizations themselves.

First, priorities for organizations generally reflect their own frame of analysis of the world. The application of a strengths-based approach when decisions are made about policy and strategic priorities is likely to result in different outcomes from a problem or deficit-based approach. Starting with a philosophy that gives value to the achievements, strengths, and highlights of countries will likely reveal different analysis from that which appears in nearly all development strategies and reports. For example, considering the Pacific region as a place of considerable resources, deep maritime expertise, healthy environmental management, strong regional identity, and a remoteness which protects populations from global pandemics, will generate a different conversation from a deficit perspective. Considering Africa as a continent with resilient communities which have responded to significantly disruptive colonial and environmental challenges over centuries using a rich and diverse set of social assets and having much sought-after natural assets, will generate a different policy and strategic direction from that dominated by problem-based thinking.

Second, policy and strategy are often informed by the organizations themselves, rather than as a collaboration with others with whom they seek to work. Big questions in the development of policy and strategy relate to whose perspective counts and whose voices are listened to. A strengths perspective means that more value is placed on aligning policy and strategy with locally set agendas for future change. Leadership by local actors and inclusive processes ensures diverse perspectives inform decisions and are given greater priority. Giving prominence to leadership by local actors is in line with most aid effectiveness agendas as well as the growing localization agenda and calls for decolonizing knowledge within the international development sector.

From a donor country perspective, there may be value in maintaining that countries where their programmes are implemented have little if no agency in their development journeys. This is informed by the view that these countries are a mix of needs, weaknesses, problems, and often corruption and therefore that donor countries will 'fix' the situation through aid programmes. This perspective creates power imbalance and silences the perspectives of those who seek positive change in their country contexts. Of course, there are needs, weaknesses, problems, and corruption in all countries to varying degrees, with distinctions often made using colonialist and racist perspectives. As discussed earlier, a strengths-based approach does not deny such realities but it champions a means to address them through constructive and collaborative practice.

Third, using a strengths-based approach *within* development organizations could also support its use with others. As noted in Parts A and B, a strengths-based approach is already used widely in human resources management, staff engagement, partnership approaches, and other people-centred approaches. The quotes from SurfAid and the Episcopal Conference of Malawi at the beginning of this section, as well as Case Study 12 and others, illustrate that more than a few organizations are already applying the approach internally.

Chapter 11 addresses the important opportunity for international development organizations to support governments and others to strengthen their own policies and strategies related to developmental change, using a strengths-based approach. It includes an example of a strengths-based strategy at regional and country levels which is orientating perspectives about Pacific Islands, from 'small remote island states' to a vast and resourceful *Blue Pacific*. Chapter 12 also includes examples of the use of the approach to support policy change in various sectors.

Programme/project planning and design

An obvious point in the programme cycle to introduce a strengths-based approach and to make a substantive difference and contribution to development outcomes is the design stage. Examples of successful use of a strengths-based approach in the design of international development programmes, of all sizes, are not rare. The authors and other development workers interviewed for this book can list strengths-based designs in diverse sectors, countries, and contexts.

Most development organizations have an established programme management cycle which includes a design phase. The design phase is commonly based on a problem identification process and requires an analysis of the 'problem' and its causes. This analysis is then expected to inform decisions about how the designed programme or project will 'fix' the problem. The design phase is also often led by external actors who have demonstrated specialist project design skills, and employ various techniques and methods related to prediction and control as described in Chapter 4. This requirement makes development workers frame the situation or context of the project as a series of deficits to address. As described in Part A, such analysis provides a skewed perspective of the context and has negative consequences for those individuals and groups engaged in the project.

A project design informed by a strengths-based approach can benefit from the use of philosophical underpinnings described in Chapter 2 as well as processes, methods, and tools relevant to a strengths-based approach described in Chapter 3. A strengths-based approach has been used in the designs of programmes in many sectors and diverse contexts in the international development sector. The designs of programmes included in Case Studies 2, 14, and 16 explicitly applied and incorporated strengths-based approaches.

Projects and programmes are usually designed with a hierarchy of objectives, such as impacts, results, outcomes, outputs, or other statements of intent or expected changes. Both a problem-based and a strengths-based approach can produce these statements and, in some cases, may result in similar language, such as 'accessible law and justice systems', or 'flourishing and inclusive communities', or 'responsive accountability between citizens and public sector agencies'. It is the work undertaken before and behind such statements that differs.

Within the international development sector there is currently a dilemma that a design phase should be completed within a restricted period of time, so consultation is necessarily minimal, as funds to 'carry out the work' are yet to be provided. A strengths-based approach focuses on these early conversations and recognizes that any questions asked in these early phases are also part of the change process. The design phase in effect is 'part of the work' of contributing to change. Many examples of using a strengths-based approach in international development in this book illustrate the value of relatively long concept development or design timeframes which enable valuable processes of inquiry, learning, planning, and ultimately leadership of those at the centre of change.

'We have all done it', said Martin Wanjohi, a design consultant interviewed for this book, about how programme designs can be so arrogant and preconceived. 'The World Bank want us to design a project in a hurry with limited resources. We sit in our offices in Nairobi and put it all together. We don't need to speak to the potential beneficiaries because we know the answers the World Bank want, and we know they won't challenge us on whether these are relevant to the proposed beneficiary group'.

By contrast, a strengths-based approach was used in the design of the Australian Government's Samoa Disability Programme in 2013, the first national bilaterally funded programme in this sector in Samoa. The approach was applied in the context of the design team's knowledge of existing organizations, interests, and experiences, which were expected to provide a foundation for collaborative work. The design process brought people together from varied civil society and government organizations to generate a shared understanding of existing strengths in the context and a jointly negotiated set of objectives and processes. As is the case with all design processes, there were limitations and some unresolved challenges; however, the strengths-based approach generated a high degree of engagement and interest, including from stakeholders with responsibility but little prior knowledge of disability inclusion. The valuing of existing expertise, particularly in the national disabled person's organization, Nuanua O Le Alofa, was critical for the generation of early collaboration with the ministry responsible for disability inclusion.

A design process informed by a strengths-based approach is different from traditional deficit-based approaches in a variety of ways. First, design processes informed by a strengths-based approach are inclusive, participatory, and locally owned, informed by locally created knowledge and locally driven sense-making. Of course, the same could be said of common design processes, but within a strengths-based approach local knowledge is explicitly premised and informed by an appreciation of strengths and assets which can be used as a foundation to catalyse change. This is coupled with identifying preferred futures which orientate action towards change.

Second, and this is particularly unique to a strengths-based approach, the design process itself is part of the change process. The design process generates energy, motivation, collaboration, leadership, and ownership of the change agenda. A design process is traditionally focused on the documentation of the programme design, but a design process informed by a strengths-based approach is just as, if not more important than the documentation for catalysing change.

Third, rather than the design process being led by external development workers with expertise and sole responsibility for producing the design, their role is one of facilitator only. The nature of a development worker's role, considered in Chapter 8, applies to design within the programme cycle.

Finally, a strengths-based design process opens up new possibilities for transformational and generative change. It questions the reality that is commonly taken for granted (e.g. that communities, organizations, or countries are poor and lacking agency) and enables participants to see the world anew with different and alternative possibilities. Transformative change includes reflecting on and challenging existing assumptions, prevailing norms, and interests and acting in new ways. Transformative change encompasses a paradigm shift – new ways of thinking and acting shape action towards preferred futures.

Case Study 13 Designing to maximize a strengths-based approach across Africa

The Australia Africa Community Engagement Scheme (AACES) was a five-year partnership between the Australian Government and 10 Australian NGOs together with their 23 Africa-based partner organizations. The participating Australian NGOs were ActionAid, AFAP (Australian Foundation for the Peoples of Asia and the Pacific, now Action on Poverty), Anglican Overseas Aid, CARE, Caritas Australia, Marie Stopes, WaterAid, Burnet Institute, Oxfam, and World Vision. Between 2011 and 2016, the Scheme operated in 11 countries (Ethiopia, Ghana, Kenya, Malawi, Mozambique, Rwanda, South Africa, Tanzania, Uganda, Zambia, and Zimbabwe). The Australian Government contributed A$83 m, and a further $28 m was contributed by the NGOs. The Scheme's activities affected the lives of more than 2.3 million women and marginalized people. The objective was to reach out to more remote communities across Africa with a broad focus on improving food security, maternal and child health, and water, sanitation, and hygiene. The Scheme used community-based interventions with particular attention on women, youth, and people with disabilities.

(Continued)

Case Study 13 Continued

The AACES design team was interested in using non-traditional approaches, in contrast with logframe and problem tree analysis: one of these was a strengths-based approach. This approach to design had been used successfully in other programmes of collaboration between the Australian Government and NGOs, such as the Churches Partnership in Papua New Guinea and the Solomon Islands NGO Partnership Agreement (see Case Study 2). The design's starting point was to identify/select Australian NGOs already working successfully with remote communities in Africa. The focus was not on 'what could be done?' but on 'what has been done so far?' and 'how can this be enhanced?'

Power relations were addressed both in the design process and in a specific focus on greater gender inclusion and engagement with people with disabilities. At the overall programme management level, the design moved away from the donor–contractor–subcontractor relationship towards a partnership at every level, inclusive of communities themselves (AusAID, 2011: 22). Donor agency officials willingly relinquished their traditional power to sit with the funded agencies and community representatives around the table of learning and adaptation (DFAT, 2014b: 5). Although it took time, this shift was reflected in relationships between staff of the Australian and Africa-based agencies who felt empowered to speak out with suggestions about how to increasingly draw from the strengths of communities themselves. There was also a significant shift in the relationship between communities and their own local governments, whereby communities became more vocal about their development rights and governments came to see the communities as partners in carrying out their own development plans.

The design process provided an opportunity for donors and implementers to build collaborative relationships, trust, and collective learning (DFAT, 2016) during six months of consultation and partnership building. The staged planning process was integral to the strengths-based approach. Before any specific objectives and activities could be determined, agencies and their local partner organizations needed time within communities to jointly identify strengths, assets, and resources and then to give the whole community time to determine what they might achieve in the future based on these locally available competencies and assets (DFAT, 2016).

Many of the agencies were unfamiliar with this approach, so the Australian Government arranged a five-day workshop on the theory and practice of a strengths-based approach for the Australian and African organizations. The workshop also introduced partners to locally available advisers with experience of using a strengths-based approach and resources to learn more about various perspectives of the approach. One participant said: 'We have not used a strengths-based approach before. It changed the whole relationship with partners. Now we've introduced this approach to all our African programmes. We are seeing the changes and the differences where people are not dependent' (personal communication with a staff member of Caritas Australia).

The deliberate inclusion of women in decision-making and service delivery at the community level, was in part enhanced by a strengths-based approach. The approach ensured the gifts and talents of every individual were included in a collective inquiry, recognizing every individual has something to offer, including those most marginalized. Programme progress reports provided evidence

(Continued)

Case Study 13 Continued

of benefits for women and girls. These included increased access to and use of sexual and reproductive health services; improved school toilets; time saving from improved access to water; and increased incomes and diversity of food intake. As the role of women in public life and the voices from women became stronger, this led to reductions in domestic violence, more influence on the use of available assets, and increased opportunities for income generation as well as increased leadership positions in the community (DFAT, 2014b). The same principle applied to deliberate attempts to include people with disabilities. In some agencies, the success of the whole plan was based on ensuring that marginalized groups had first access to intended benefits.

As with all strengths-based approaches, the focus of monitoring was more on mutual learning than auditing progress. Indeed, the second objective of AACES was to provide input into policy direction for development work and international cooperation in the African context. Bi-annual learning workshops brought together people from Australian and African NGOs with Australian Government representatives to share programme strategies, learning, and challenges. These were important processes to facilitate shared learning and collaboration. This included peer review and field visits to each other's projects.

Programme implementation

Programme implementation from a strengths-based approach incorporates a strong focus on learning and cycles of continuous improvement, so implementation is informed by successful practices, reflection, and refinements to visions for the future. Thinking about change as complex and with uncertainty (see Chapter 1) prioritizes learning and adaptation. Action research and adaptive management, explored more in Chapter 10, are examples of approaches that support acknowledgement of these realities.

Following approval of design, implementation occurs, usually within a complex set of management processes. Importantly, from a strengths-based approach, approval of a design document is not simply an act by the responsible personnel and funding organizations of a programme, but also a commitment from those individuals and groups at the heart of change, who own the change process.

A central aspect of a programme is mobilization of human resources to support or implement change. A strengths-based approach helps to identify and map existing assets and strengths in local contexts to enact change. These assets should include competencies among participants required for various activities, such as training, mobilizing groups, or initiating new processes or construction. This is critical for ownership and leadership of the change initiative by local actors. Programme implementation is also about connecting local assets with external resources.

A strengths-based approach generates the kinds of respectful, trust-based relationships that are required for team work, particularly in complex, cross-cultural, and dynamic contexts. Ensuring that each team member's strengths are recognized and valued and their contributions are respected and used, contributes to successful teamwork. Soli Middleby, former CEO and Australian Diplomat to the Pacific, led a team of over 300 people at the Australia Pacific Technical Coalition (APTC). She reflected that her efforts to create a positive environment, to believe in others, and to focus on the strengths of her team, 'have been an important factor in creating the energy and motivation needed for the APTC's success to date'.

While a strengths-based approach actively promotes the leadership and ownership of the change agenda by local actors, common practice tends to prioritize leadership by the externally appointed project leaders and managers. Highly experienced programme team members interviewed for this book reflected that when working in some cultures, local team members have deferred to the expatriate, international team members when new programmes commence. A strengths-based approach can overcome the hesitancy of local team members to express their existing expertise, share their knowledge of what works in each context, and feel confident to speak up about appropriate ways forward. For example, Soli Middleby increasingly adopted a strengths-based approach in her role and reflected, 'when I talk to [local] people about what they can do, they often downplay their strengths. However, a good proportion of the senior leadership team here can achieve amazing things and now have the authority to do so much more than in the past'.

A strengths-based approach provides an important base on which to inform action for change and is an appropriate means to build high functioning teams, manage performance (Aguinis et al., 2012), assess and develop staff (Garcea et al., 2014), develop caring workplaces (Henry and Henry, 2007), maximize quality engagement, and retain team members. Since the success of international development programmes is often tightly linked to the quality of personnel, this is a significant contribution to aid effectiveness.

To achieve international development outcomes multi-stakeholder engagement is usually required and a strengths-based approach is a positive way to bring diverse groups and perspectives together. The building of successful collaborative relationships between programme teams and officials from government agencies, staff from NGOs, and other partner organizations or community leaders is one of the most critical elements in any successful programme. As noted in Chapters 4 and 6, a strengths-based approach contributes to the achievement of trust and respect-based relationships which support positive collaboration in all contexts, particularly across cultures. A strengths-based approach gives energy to the factors that actually bring about change during programme implementation: people, teamwork, energy, and commitment.

There are numerous case studies in this book that highlight the effective practices of programme implementation through a strengths-based approach, demonstrating the value of shared commitment and action and leadership of those at the centre of the change agenda.

Managing risk

Risk management is a key feature of international development particularly for donors and implementers of development programmes. Risk management is often associated with preventing financial problems, such as misuse of funds, as well as environmental protection and social safeguards such as child protection and the prevention of sexual harassment in workplaces. Risks are also related to project effectiveness and the extent to which planned objectives can be achieved within local contexts. Risk management frameworks are established as part of designs and implementation strategies; they are reviewed and updated periodically. It is usually the responsibility of implementing organizations to manage this process, even if they played no part in the design or have limited understanding of the complexities in the particular context. Risks are managed as part of prediction and control thinking, which is central to results-based management. Implementing agencies, whether bilateral, multilateral, commercial, or from civil society are often risk averse, reflecting expectations about 'achieving results'. These results are defined in contracts and are the responsibility of the implementing organization, again, often when they have had little or no participation in the design process or connection with the local stakeholders. In simple terms, such transactions make little sense. Control over and responsibility for change should not rest with these organizations, but with those whose lives or contexts are at the centre of change. Instead, in current practice, external actors are being expected to 'deliver' change in the lives and contexts of others.

Risk management is a form of control, but this does not necessarily lead to positive and transformative development outcomes. Development organizations and development workers need to 'let go' and recognize where risks are actually held – by those who seek to change their own lives and contexts.

Risk management from a strengths-based approach is grounded in leadership and ownership by local actors and is enabled through reflective practice and iterative cycles of planning and action. Risk management is framed in relation to preferred futures and continuous learning and improvement. It reflects a programme's ability to change course when required and to continue to strive for improvement. For example, Soli Middleby said, 'I have managed to enable the best risk thinkers to be more positive lately to focus on what is possible. This ability to be more positive is a gift and it's where the good stuff happens, bringing together a combination of understanding risk and being positive.'

While a strengths-based approach is not dominant within international development and donor systems, there are sufficient examples of where the practice has worked to invite more mainstream practice across the programme cycle. This chapter has identified practical ways in which the approach could be championed and operationalized through bilateral and multilateral funding agencies. For example, this could be undertaken by ensuring the programme cycle is informed and grounded in strengths-based inquiry and led by definitions of the future decided and prioritized by local actors, not external people. Programme implementation can be understood not as prescribed linear exercises but rather emergent change processes that are informed by earlier rounds of collaborative activity and joint learning. Chapter 10 offers further insights on how this can happen in practice.

Programme management in the 21st century is not for the faint-hearted. The complexities involved in juggling multiple agendas, integrating commonly competing drivers and responding to diverse and dynamic expectations, require excellent collaboration, leadership, and flexibility. They also require optimism and positive thinking. When a strengths-based approach underpins the collaboration required for the management of any development programme in most contexts, a positive contribution can be made. Those involved in programme management who find the maturity to achieve humility, who recognize they cannot be responsible for change, but can make a positive contribution to the changes achieved by others, and who recognize the strengths in themselves, their teams, and their world, will be successful by most measures.

CHAPTER 10
Rethinking monitoring, evaluation, and research

> *The questions that will help us achieve our future are not those that accuse, find fault and condemn, but those that create energy, hope, motivation* (Preskill and Catsambas, 2006)

Monitoring and evaluation are central to international development practice and key drivers of international development approaches since the 1990s. This chapter considers implications of a strengths-based approach for the practices associated with monitoring and evaluation. Implications for research in international development are also addressed, since research informs understanding and ways to influence policy and programming changes. Ways of monitoring, evaluating, and researching strengths-based practice are also offered.

Consideration of monitoring, evaluation, and research through a strengths-based perspective is important since these practices inform what knowledge is valued, whose knowledge counts and which types of knowledge influence ongoing international development discourse, policy, and programming. While various strengths-based practices (see Chapter 3) guide strengths-based monitoring and evaluation, these are not currently the norm in international development. Practices are evolving, aligned to a strengths-based approach, but a radical shift in monitoring and evaluation is still required. There is a wealth of literature and resources on monitoring and evaluation in international development and this chapter does not seek to provide a comprehensive overview or engage in debates on best practice monitoring and evaluation. Rather, it explores practice through the perspective of a strengths-based approach.

Monitoring, evaluation, and research in international development

Definitions

There are countless descriptions and labels given to monitoring and evaluation (M&E) in international development, including: MEL (monitoring, evaluation, and learning), MERL (monitoring, evaluation, research, and learning), MEAL (monitoring, evaluation, accountability, and learning), and MERLA (monitoring, evaluation, research, learning, and adaptation) (described by DFAT in *Partnerships for Recovery* 2020). By the time this book is published, there may be more labels.

Importantly though, these terms have similar meanings and practices; common understandings of key terms can be found. In this chapter, since the focus is on discussing the relationship between a strengths-based approach and M&E, only brief descriptions of relevant terms are provided here.

Monitoring

Monitoring is generally described as the process of collecting and analysing information about the performance of a project or programme during implementation. It is focused on the process of checking to assess if activities have been completed as planned, so commonly addresses compliance and achievement of predetermined plans and indicators of achievement. Monitoring occurs concurrently with the implementation of activities and when done well, is useful for those involved in the process to support and inform decision-making, including by managers. Monitoring is often associated with single loop learning (Argyris and Schön, 1978) and focuses on the question, 'are we doing things right?'

Evaluation

Evaluation is a more clearly defined term in international development, influenced by the OECD DAC. Evaluation criteria, definitions, and principles are set by the OECD DAC Network on Development Evaluation. OECD member countries are obliged to employ this guidance to evaluate their development and humanitarian programmes.

For OECD DAC, evaluation is defined as:

> The systematic and objective assessment of an on-going or completed project, programme or policy, its design, implementation and result. Evaluation also refers to the process of determining the worth or significance of an activity, policy or program. An assessment, as systematic and objective as possible, of a planned, on-going, or completed development intervention (OECD DAC 2002).

In 2019, evaluation criteria were updated: five original criteria were preserved and refined and an additional criterion, 'coherence' added.

- *Relevance* – is the intervention doing the right things?
- *Coherence* – how well does the intervention fit?
- *Effectiveness* – is the intervention achieving its objectives?
- *Efficiency* – how well are resources being used?
- *Impact* – what difference does the intervention make?
- *Sustainability* – will the benefits last?

As defined by the OECD DAC guidance, the criteria are used in evaluation to support accountability, including the provision of information to the public, and learning, through generating and feeding back findings and lessons.

Within the sector, numerous debates have raged about the relative weight and merit of accountability and a learning focus of evaluation. There has been no definitive resolution, with both viewed as important, depending on one's position in the sector.

Evaluation is commonly understood to be separate from the change process and those involved. Central to the notion of evaluation as defined by the OECD DAC is that it should be 'transparent and independent from programme management and policy-making, to enhance credibility' (OECD DAC, 2010: 6). The practice of evaluation is taken away from those involved in development. 'Evaluators are independent from the development intervention, including its policy, operations and management functions, as well as intended beneficiaries' (OECD DAC, 2010: 11). The separation of evaluation from the change process does not accord with a strengths-based approach.

Research

Research is described as different from evaluation in international development. While a project or programme is the subject of the evaluation, research is not constrained by this focus and can explore empirical or theoretical topics. Research is an 'investigation undertaken to gain knowledge and understanding or to train researchers' (NHMRC, 2018: 6). Evaluations share the same interaction with 'human subjects' as other research activities; however, the purpose of evaluations often links more directly to policy and programming decisions.

While differences are stated, there are clear practical similarities between evaluation and research, as they are understood within contemporary international development discourse. They both require information to be gathered systematically, thoroughly, and carefully and evaluation uses methods and tools similar to other research processes.

Key characteristics of international development M&E and research

Focus on prediction and control of results

A core feature of contemporary international development is prediction and control, which underpins a focus on results and related practices, such as results frameworks and results-based management. Results-based management, a 'strategy focusing on performance and achievement of outputs, outcomes and impacts' (OECD DAC, 2002: 34), is a key foundation of international development and how it is assessed.

Logical frameworks, programme logic, and theory of change are some of many terms used to describe results frameworks, central to the practice of results-based management. These frameworks are commonly accompanied by indicators, as a means to 'measure' results achieved relative to plans. They are also based on often unquestioned assumptions relating to past performance, pre-conceptions of the local context, and how future behaviour is expected to occur.

The logical framework, or logframe, has had a significant influence on the international development sector and has been the most commonly used results framework for decades. As noted below there have been shifts to different types of approaches; however, the logframe is still employed in many instances. OECD DAC defines the logframe as:

> Management tool used to improve the design of interventions, most often at the project level. It involves identifying strategic elements (inputs, outputs, outcomes, impact) and their causal relationships, indicators, and the assumptions or risks that may influence success and failure. It thus facilitates planning, execution and evaluation of a development intervention (OECD DAC, 2002: 27).

The focus on results and results-based management assumes that predetermined pathways between 'cause and effect' can result in change and be achieved within set time frames, inputs, and budgets. It is assumed that if the project is 'fit for context' and managed efficiently, these predetermined changes can be achieved. The basis of these cause and effect type frameworks can be useful and applicable to technical or engineering activities, but are inadequate for projects that involve complex social changes shaped by various sets of relationships. Cause-and-effect-type frameworks can be useful and applicable to technical or engineering activities, but are inadequate for projects that involve complex social change informed by sets of relationships.

Evolving practices of international development M&E and research

In response to critiques of logframes in international development, there is evidence of evolving design, monitoring, and evaluation practices, though the underlying interest in prediction and control still dominates. Macro perspectives on programme theory have not yet translated to shape day-to-day operations of international development programming and project management focus.

Critiques of the logframe have been numerous and prevalent for decades. A few of these critiques highlighted below help confirm the potential of a strengths-based approach. The linear logic of the logframe operates within a closed system (i.e. the situation is defined at the start of the programme or project and is assumed to stay static throughout its duration). This logic is challenged in thinking about how change happens, including notions of complexity thinking (see Chapter 1). Another critique of the logframe questions its reductionist nature, which dismisses the diverse realities of people's lives. The logframe's origins in infrastructure projects and military planning explain the delivery of simple inputs and activities which do not consider the dynamics associated with working with individuals, groups, or communities and their many relationships.

Another important critique of results frameworks and results-based management relates to the professionalization of international development, whereby development workers, external to the local context, are expected to control design, monitoring, and evaluation processes and produce deliverables. The development of logframes and associated M&E frameworks is so complicated that they are seen to require expertise beyond the scope and interest of community-based individuals or organizations in countries where change is expected to occur.

Increasing disquiet about results-based management and logframes has led to new thinking and practices. For example, adaptive management is now widely promoted as a strategy to manage uncertainty over time (Honig, 2018). At its core are flexibility, continuous re-adaptation, and programming adjustment depending on context. USAID's Learning Lab defines adaptive management as 'an intentional approach to making decisions and adjustments in response to new information and changes in context' (USAID, 2021: 1). Other researchers argue the crucial difference between classical results-based management and adaptive management concerns the relationship between ends and means. 'In classical results-based management the outputs are fully specified at the outset and there is a fixed logic ... (whereas) in an adaptive approach the desired outcomes are fixed but programme outputs are not' (Booth et al., 2018: 9).

A range of concepts is included in the broad idea of adaptive management. For example, Valters et al. (2016) focus on the adaptive approach which 'involve(s) experimentation, in particular where the overall objective is clear but how to achieve it in a given context is unknown or uncertain' (p. 5). They emphasize learning at the centre of adaptive development programming and argue 'that a focus on learning and adaptation demands a focus on development relationships; that is, how learning for adaptation can take place within and across development programmes' (p. 5) (see Case Study 20). Problem-Driven Iterative Adaptation (PDIA) is an extension of this approach, operating in some contexts. The Building State Capability Faculty at Harvard University developed PDIA, orientated to flexible learning and adaptation. PDIA is described as a step-by-step approach which helps to break down problems into their root causes, identify entry points, search for possible solutions, take action, reflect upon what has been learned, adapt, and then act again. It is promoted as a dynamic process with tight feedback loops that allows teams to build solutions to identified problems that fit local contexts. Though there are various iterations of adaptive management in international development, these practices are not yet mainstream, with prediction-control methods still dominating.

Recognizing that M&E thinking and practices are constantly evolving, there are opportunities to extend this evolution, using a strengths-based approach. Insights on monitoring, evaluation, and research informed by a strengths-based approach are discussed below.

Monitoring, evaluation, and research through a strengths-based approach

> *I am shocked by how little is already written about the use of a strengths-based approach. I am surprised by the lack of material out there on its intricacies. I also wonder why it is not taken up more in the development sector, and what's needed for this to happen?*
> (Ian Cunningham)

Numerous examples in international development and established fields of practice in other disciplines provide insights and confidence in the practicality and value of a strengths-based approach in monitoring, evaluation, and research. This section applies these insights to practice in international development, with examples.

Informed by philosophical underpinnings

Philosophical underpinnings of a strengths-based approach described in Part A are clearly relevant to monitoring, evaluation, and research. From the perspective of a strengths-based approach, knowledge is vested in people whose lives will change rather than independent external actors who carry out monitoring, evaluation, or research of projects or programmes. This contradicts current perspectives which prioritize 'independent' external actors' assessment of development programmes and projects. This process can be extractive, whereby knowledge is sourced from local contexts and reported by independent, external evaluators. In a strengths perspective, knowledge and expertise are valued within the local context. Knowledge gained through the process of monitoring or evaluation is used by local actors in their own change process. In a strengths-based approach, people are at the centre of the change process and also at the centre of enquiry, learning, and benefits of monitoring, evaluation, and research. M&E processes are primarily intended to support change agendas and local people's actions towards these, rather than primarily for external audiences.

From a strengths perspective, asking a question automatically represents engagement in a change process. Yet M&E, a key part of international development, is defined as separate and works alongside the development process. For a strengths-based approach, monitoring, evaluation, and research are not separate from the development agenda or the change process, but linked to, part of, and contributing to the development agenda. Case Study 12 is a good example of this integrated connection.

For a strengths-based approach it is important that the agenda for change is determined locally. Monitoring, evaluation, and associated inquiry therefore should follow this focus. This means that indicators of change are set locally, not by external actors as part of a pre-planned process. Since change is emergent, indicators of success will have to be defined and assessed progressively through the process, rather than set like concrete at the outset.

A strengths-based approach values transformative and generative change, meaning it is not only focused on solving problems of the past, but seeking alternative and preferred futures. M&E are currently focused on assessing relative achievement of planned results, and by definition assessing past performance. Dominant approaches in M&E are focused on what has been predicted and controlled rather than informing, influencing, and advancing transformative and generative change for the future. There is a major missed opportunity: the opportunity to contribute to preferable futures.

Monitoring, evaluation, and research informed by a strengths-based approach focus on complementing and supporting the transformative and generative change agenda. To evaluate is usually understood to judge, but could also mean to identify and value an activity. In this sense, from a strengths-based approach, the exercise of evaluation is to find what has occurred that is of particular value for achieving the desired change agenda. Appreciative evaluation supports and encourages an organization to focus on what is likely to lead to more successful outcomes. As discussed below, there are various research frameworks which enable this potential.

Linked to broader research frameworks

Monitoring, evaluation, and research through a strengths-based approach is not an abstract idea, but has connections to existing frameworks for research and knowledge creation. These connections provide a theoretical basis and give confidence about how this can work in practice. Reed (2007) wrote about Appreciative Inquiry as a research practice, stating that it 'can be linked to a number of different ideas and traditions across a range of methodologies, but it cannot be said to fit exclusively or exactly to any one school' (p. 45). In this book, we have defined a strengths-based approach for international development to be broader than Appreciative Inquiry, but these linkages equally apply.

A strengths-based approach links to a strong body of evidence and theoretical foundations. Without going into detail here, there is a wealth of philosophical, theoretical, and practical literature. Readers are encouraged to follow their own self-directed inquiry. Reed (2007) highlights that a strengths-based approach has connections to critical inquiry (interest in developing challenges to ways of thinking and acting) as well as social constructionism (concern with meaning and interpretation rather than measurable facts). A strengths-based approach has a strong appreciation of the local context in line with case study methodology which focuses on specific settings or situations, and ethnography which, as a research approach, has an interest in complexity of the social world and understanding of it in its entirety. A strengths-based approach seeks to inform change which aligns with action research (interest in facilitating change). The connections of a strengths-based approach to established research frameworks and approaches demonstrate that this approach is a legitimate and evidence-based means of understanding inquiry and change.

Examples of using a strengths-based approach in evaluation and research

Examples of the use of strengths-based approach in monitoring, evaluation, and research activities within international development are included here to illustrate its broad applicability and future potential. The application of a strengths-based approach to research is already highly developed, with most literature linked to Appreciative Inquiry and Positive Deviance and to a lesser extent strengths-based social work and Asset-Based Community Development.

Numerous journals and books are available to guide research practice using Appreciative Inquiry. For example, Jan Reed's (2007) *Appreciative Inquiry: Research for Change* explores the use of Appreciative Inquiry as a research framework, rather than an approach to organizational management for which it was originally developed. The *International Journal of Appreciative Inquiry* records experiences of applying Appreciative Inquiry to diverse learning contexts. Dewar (1997) also provides a guide to evaluating Asset-Based Community Development.

Appreciative Inquiry has also been applied more specifically to research in international development, confirming its value to inform improved development practice and development outcomes. For example, a paper, 'Can positive inquiry strengthen obstetric referral systems in Cambodia?' (Lee et al., 2018: 89) described research which 'took an alternative approach and rather asked what works in contemporary obstetric referral in a low-income setting to find out if positive inquiry could generate original insights on referral that could be transformative'.

Case Study 14 illustrates the significant benefits of using a strengths-based approach in agricultural research in Papua New Guinea.

Case Study 14 Research that gives back in rural Papua New Guinea

This case study illustrates the value of using a strengths-based approach in development-related research. Both the researcher and the subjects of the research benefit from an engagement that starts with what people have, rather than what is missing in the local context (ACIAR, 2019).

The Australian Centre for International Agricultural Research (ACIAR) receives Australian Government funds for research and field work into improving agricultural practice in a range of countries. ACIAR noticed the absence of women attending agricultural extension activities and approached the Centre for Sustainable Communities, at the University of Canberra, Australia to explore this issue and develop an alternative approach. In 2012 the Centre started the Papua New Guinea Family Farm Teams programme and since then, has been examining, developing, and facilitating ways to build the business acumen, skills, and knowledge of women farmers in Papua New Guinea (https://www.canberra.edu.au/research/faculty-research-centres/csc/action-research-for-development/family-farms-teams-program).

(Continued)

Case Study 14 Continued

Professor Barbara Pamphilon AM, the Head of the Centre and chief researcher, when interviewed for this book, recounted the team's first finding was that women self-selected themselves out not only because of their busy lives managing farm, family, and cultural responsibilities but also because they had low literacy levels. Thinking about this from a Freire model of education (Freire, 1970), she designed an approach which affirmed that people as learners would be critically aware of their own context, albeit often unknowingly. Barbara decided to start with validating people's existing knowledge of their context; one that accessed and re-affirmed (retained) their indigenous learning. In this context, the team considered strengths-based methodologies such as Appreciative Inquiry and ABCD, combining these with other relevant approaches such as experiential and place-based learning (Pamphilon, 2017).

As a highly experienced community development academic, Barbara Pamphilon had often asked students to reflect on a deficit model of research. She suggests this model does not provide the researcher with an understanding of the learning edge of participants because it focuses on articulating weaknesses which disempowers participants. On the other hand, a strengths-based model, such as Appreciative Inquiry or ABCD, engages and energizes participants and encourages them to join their strengths through networking together for an agreed way forward. Barbara asked, 'what is the value of research that collects information without leaving anything behind?' A strengths-based approach has a dual result: it collates data by asking the community to talk about what they have, what they want, and who they are; and, at the same time, leaves them with both a direction for their own future and a greater understanding of the means to get there.

The programme sought to ensure key messages were always 'place-based' and drew from stories of past success or accepted wisdom in each location. The Australian facilitators gave examples from their own context relating to key learning outcomes, and then asked the volunteer community educators to find parallels from their experience. These peer educators in turn would engage in the same process when working with each community, eventually modifying the order of exercises, the type of exercises to be included, and the examples to illustrate them. Sometimes this meant a team developed a completely new exercise that matched the different contexts and priorities of participants. The programme used the same process in producing local training manuals where the contents were adapted from this type of exchange rather than being a pre-prescribed set manual. This model of 'roll out and adapt' before deciding the final training process always drew from the local and cultural strengths of the participating community and the shared collective experiential learning process.

An Appreciative Inquiry process was used for carrying out baseline surveys which began not with answering survey questions but with workshops that explored a community's previous successes and mapped their assets. In this way, the team members built trust with community members and established the foundation for a true partnership. 'Relationship' in a Melanesian society is a gift bestowed only when the community is ready to engage. It was only after a community had reflected on what was important to them and were confident in the 'outsiders' that a baseline survey was able to be collectively completed.

(Continued)

Case Study 14 Continued

Pamphilon (2017) wrote about this experience: 'Following asset-based community development (ABCD) principles (Green & Haines, 2012), the project used a strengths-based philosophy that understood individuals and local communities as knowledgeable, resilient and resourceful, rather than as "needy"'. The programme used ABCD to identify community physical assets, social assets, and indigenous knowledge. This method has been criticized for dissecting a community, but Barbara sees it as asking key questions – the why, how, and which – about assets that can be used to move people forward. Sometimes this knowledge was no longer current or was only relevant to certain contexts. For example, older people described how, in times of drought, it was important never to eat the last remaining root crop, but rather to bury some root stock for use when the drought breaks: this was their version of a food bank. Another example was the challenge of oil palm plantations encroaching on traditional lands and ways of agriculture. In this case the facilitators did not offer solutions but worked with the community to find ways to stay strong and share their strengths collectively among themselves to face the challenges.

Appreciative Inquiry was consistent with the action research learning cycle used by the programme. Sometimes the best insights the researcher initially formed were not right for a particular community. In the end, it is the people in the community who are going to make change happen and they know what is going to work for them. That is why the approach must be to nudge the process of learning 'like rolling a stone all together rather than standing up in front and teaching', reflected Barbara. A good example was an Australian understanding of an emerging market economy, compared with that of families in rural Papua New Guinea. Their economy included time to maintain a collective identity even if it meant forgoing opportunities for income generation.

This programme has been so successful, it has been extended to other Pacific Islands. The approaches used have also been adopted by other organizations. A report of the programme (Pamphilon, 2019: 66) concluded:

> A number of Papua New Guinea agencies have integrated the FFT approach and learning activities in their work: FPDA Village Extension Worker program and Gender Equity and Social Inclusion policy, Oxfam Sustainable Livelihoods program, PanAust Women in Mining (Extractives), and Voice for Change Women's Economic Empowerment program. It has also been adapted by Oxfam and Femili Papua New Guinea for their gender justice, violence prevention and recovery programs.

The use of Appreciative Inquiry in evaluation practice is widely documented and applicable to international development. For example, in *Reframing Evaluation Through Appreciative Inquiry* (Preskill and Catsambas, 2006) the authors describe the potential that Appreciative Inquiry offers to evaluators:

> We suggest that Appreciative Inquiry offers evaluators at least two options – it may be simply understood and used as one more evaluation method, approach or strategy, or it may be viewed and used more

ambitiously as a means for challenging the foundations of evaluation practice by shifting evaluation from something that can, at best, produce incremental positive changes, to something that can generate exponential, radical changes in organizations and communities (Preskill and Catsambas, 2006: ix).

An example of Appreciative Inquiry in evaluation is provided by Donnelly (2010). He described the benefits of engaging stakeholders in evaluation, enabling effective conversations and learning as well as a bridge to the future beyond the life of the project:

> Another outcome is that when the focus of the discussion focuses on the gains/benefits (outcomes) obtained from the project, this process helps to ensure sustainability of the project outcomes. The end of a project can often be perceived to be the end of a discrete event within developing communities. However, Appreciative Inquiry-guided, participatory evaluation can be the bridge that links the intervention of the project to the future lives of the people by clearly linking outcomes with the future rather than to a discrete event in the past. This process is the core of the strengths-based approach: identifying the good, the strengths and the valued aspects that exist within people/communities and carrying them forward to build the future (Donnelly, 2010: 48).

Research informed by a strengths-based approach also promotes local learning and action. Willets et al. (2010) conducted research on gender and water, sanitation, and hygiene (WASH) initiatives across Pacific countries, using a focus on strengths and appreciation. The authors reported their research approach 'sought to empower non-governmental organization staff and community participants to address gender equality' and 'to expose and build on the existing strengths of NGO staff and community participants, to promote learning and action as a result of the inquiry process and to maintain a constructive focus in the dialogues that took place' (Willets et al., 2010: 166). The researchers noted that 'the research methodology proved successful in allowing gender conceptions to be shaped by the community participants themselves. It also supported constructive reflection and learning for community participants and for NGO staff' (p. 175). Application of a strengths-based approach to the WASH sector in international development is discussed more in Chapter 12.

Positive Deviance was established as a practice and research method within international development, as described in Chapter 3. Numerous research activities and studies employ a Positive Deviance approach in national and regional contexts and sectors. A review of Positive Deviance literature by Herington and van de Fliert (2018: 675) concluded that 'a positive deviance strategy shows promise for addressing some of the most challenging of problems confronting modern society'.

In summary, a strengths-based approach connects with established research frameworks, so is not new or radical. While this practice can be seen to counter established results-based management and the deficit focus of international development, there are already shifts within the sector towards more flexible and responsive approaches. The relatively quick uptake of approaches such as adaptive management, by some development organizations, suggests there is realistic potential for the use of strengths-based monitoring, evaluation, and research in international development more broadly.

How to assess a strengths-based practice

How might a strengths-based approach for international development be assessed? This area of thinking is still underdeveloped, and it is hoped this book will make a useful contribution. It does not make sense to assess programmes or projects which employ a strengths-based approach with an externally driven problem-based evaluation approach. Monitoring, evaluations, or research of programmes or projects which employ a strengths-based approach should employ a strengths perspective. Aspects of this practice are proposed below.

1. Interwoven with the ongoing change agenda

Use of a strengths-based approach and its evaluation should not be viewed separately. This is in line with the philosophical underpinnings of the strengths-based approach stated in Chapter 2. As described by Van der Haar (2004 1032), 'Appreciative Inquiry and responsive evaluation are interwoven, ongoing processes' rather than understood as two separate and independent activities.

2. Cyclical forms of learning

Learning and assessment of a strengths-based approach for international development should be practised through cycles of learning, recognizing the iterative nature of change. Insights from monitoring, evaluation, and research activities become data sources and information to guide and progress change agendas and actions. Action research methodology, already introduced in this chapter as aligned to a strengths-based approach enables this practice. The cycle of plan, act, observe, reflect, plan, illustrated in Figure 10.1 supports this practice.

3. Led by locals

Those for whom change is expected or sought should be at the centre of any monitoring, evaluation, or research activity of a strengths-based approach. The role of a development worker is to support this local leadership. Equipping local change agents to be learners, reviewers, and assessors of their own achievements will enable them in turn to ensure any monitoring, evaluation, or learning inform future change agendas.

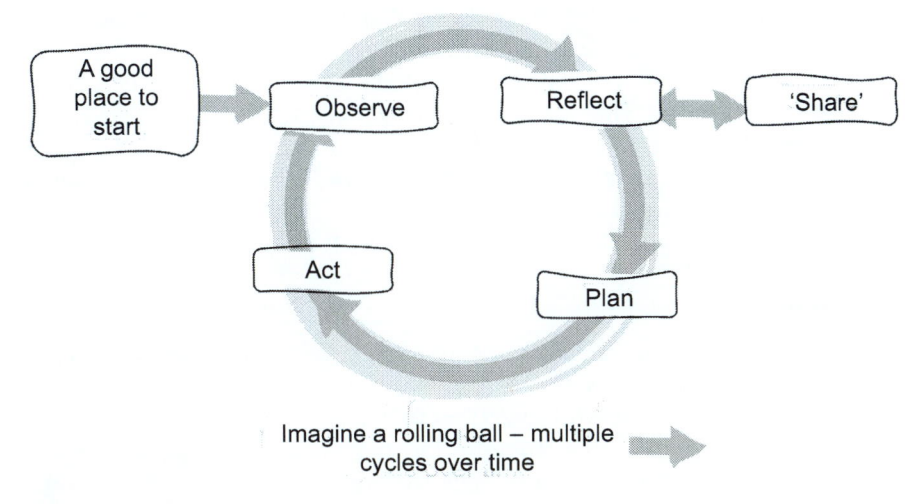

Figure 10.1 Action research cycle

4. Accountability and learning for generative and transformative change

Assessment of a strengths-based approach is not simply about focusing on what is working well. This view of a strengths-based approach does not take into account the future-focus orientation and critical perspective which seek to contribute to change towards preferred futures. Assessment of a strengths-based approach as part of a change agenda seeks to focus on ongoing and continuous improvement of the practice. It is through progressive assessment of the plan, re-orienting the preferred future (informed by the changing context), and deciding relevant actions to take, that generative change is realized. Accountability is enabled through a collective process of inquiry and re-confirmation of preferred futures and stakeholder commitment and action to achieving this. The task of assessing whether the process is working well and whether expected outcomes are being achieved offers a means of querying whether all relevant actors who signed on to commit to change and action are still committed and whether the plan is still relevant to all. This inquiry enables an accountability of stakeholder actions, but also acknowledges that things change, and what was once a key priority and preferred future might change. For example, people might plan for five years ahead, but once they are part way there or reach that time, they might want something different.

There are six key questions that can be used to assess strengths-based practice as part of the M&E process. These are:

1. Have the project participants been able to recognize and utilize life-giving patterns of success in their own past?
2. Have the project participants been able to identify and effectively mobilize their own assets and potential assets (skills, competencies, operating systems, and resources)?

3. Have internal management structures and associations become more numerous, effective, and efficient?
4. Have participants been able to negotiate more equitable relationships between genders, with vulnerable sections of the community, and with duty bearers?
5. Have project participants been able to articulate, own, and work towards a desirable future or picture of success?
6. Have participants' clarity of vision and purposeful use of their own assets been able to leverage suitable and adequate additional outside resources to achieve common goals?

In this chapter we considered assessment of a strengths-based approach, offering insights as to how this would work in practice. A strengths-based approach is needed to assess this practice – to strengthen practice and potential change outcomes achieved. A strengths-based approach to assessing international development was also considered, highlighting that there are relevant approaches emerging in contrast and opposition to traditional control and predict processes. This further establishes the value and practicality of a strengths-based approach for international development.

CHAPTER 11
A strengths-based approach and development themes

> *Since a strengths-based perspective is primarily a lens through which to see the world, there is no real limit to its potential application* (Willetts et al., 2014)

A strengths-based approach complements, supports, and enables most widely used approaches and ways of working in international development. Without seeking to explain or describe each of these current development themes in detail, this chapter explores the relevance and value of a strengths-based approach in the following:

- geo-political relationships;
- partnerships;
- capacity development, including organizational development, leadership development, community organizations, and skills development;
- community development;
- gender and social inclusion, including disability-inclusive development;
- governance.

In most international development programming, approaches have been borrowed from other fields of practice, but they share a central focus on effective collaboration between different individuals, stakeholder groups, organizations, and countries. Trust and mutual respect are crucial for any type of collaboration, and a strengths-based approach is an effective means to achieve these. Collaboration also provides the means to bring together and capitalize on diverse sets of assets and resources to bring about change. One Pacific leader reflected on the various aspects of a collaborative approach:

> A strengths-based approach provides a positive approach to getting into the right frame of mind to be able to make progress on any issue. A strengths-based approach is critical for advocating the change, for inclusion and for equality in contexts where the playing field is not level: when I think about it, that means in every context (Setareki Macanawai, CEO of Pacific Disability Forum).

The authors and development workers interviewed for this book who use a strengths-based approach in their practice highlight different elements and apply it in diverse areas of work, but are united in their valuing of its benefits. A clear message is that the thinking and practice is applicable in a wide range of settings and contexts in international development.

In this chapter we have selected broad approaches most commonly used in international development to illustrate that a strengths-based approach is applicable and that it supports and enables what might be other, more familiar ways of working and areas of international development. A strengths-based approach is most often associated with community development, but it is important to dispel any misunderstanding that it is only a community-based approach. This chapter and the following chapter illustrate and showcase the relevance of a strengths-based approach across all aspects of international development. These approaches and ways of working in international development have their own extensive literature, reviews, and debates and this is not the place to examine them in detail. Any application of these approaches needs to be relevant to the local context and informed by commitments to change outcomes decided by local actors.

Geo-political relationships

International development has always been practised within the context of broader foreign relations between countries, to varying degrees. In the 2020s, the convergence of development and foreign affairs agendas has perhaps become more obvious than in previous decades. Within the past decade, the separate international development agencies of all English-speaking countries have merged or been amalgamated into national foreign ministries or departments. The UK Department for International Development was merged into a new Foreign, Commonwealth and Development Office in 2020. In Australia, AusAID was incorporated into the Department of Foreign Affairs and Trade in 2013. While this section is necessarily broad, the key point is that a strengths-based approach supports effective relationships between countries, the context for most contemporary international development programming.

Geo-political relationships are central to national and shared agendas and seek to maximize agreement and contribute to joint commitments for change. All countries experience challenges and have problems to address in order to achieve planned national and international development goals. Increasingly these are shared across borders, and require multilateral, regional, and bilateral collaboration. Examples include people trafficking, terrorism, cyber security, border control, climate change effects, and pandemics. Countries and institutions are at varied stages of understanding and addressing these. A strengths-based approach does not deny the reality of the myriad challenges and problems but provides appropriate means to work towards the achievement of improvements, within effective collaborative geo-political relationships.

National governments in all countries are responsible for developing new legislation, policies, and strategies to address their myriad development issues. A significant focus of the work of donor countries and development agencies is support for or commitment to driving policy and strategic change, to address perceived needs or problems. International collaboration commonly focuses on the development of new legislation and intersectional collaboration to address new or shared issues, such as cross-border cyber-crime, money laundering, people trafficking, or disability rights. A strengths-based approach is directly useful for generating the level of respectful collaboration required for agreed policy shifts and for informing the processes required to generate new policies.

A strengths-based approach provides a means to develop collaboration which is based on respect for each party's contributions. Identifying strengths and assets across different country and regional contexts means that many contributions can be made to address shared priorities. Geo-political development challenges are usually complex and require multi-faceted responses to achieve change. A strengths-based approach provides an effective means to identify and connect diverse contributions across nation-state boundaries to meet regional and global priorities.

A strengths-based approach enacts a decolonization perspective in response to recognition that a neo-colonial approach has underpinned international development and contemporary geo-political relations. Pacific governments are increasingly rejecting negative statements made about them by the Australian Government (Nunn and Kumar, 2019). Sweeping negative portrayals of African countries are being rejected (Jamme, 2010). Anna Gero, who works in the area of climate change adaptation in Pacific countries, for example, commented, 'I think one of the reasons why a strengths-based approach will make a difference in international development is because it will counter this idea that the Pacific has lots of aid that doesn't work. The idea that donors will be able to fix up a problematic Pacific is wrong and old-fashioned.'

While some government leaders in donor countries may consider their national interests are served by consistently and publicly portraying countries that receive overseas development assistance as weak, lacking capacity, needing resources, or deprived, vulnerable or fragile, this is increasingly less likely to be the case. For example, if a government is aggrieved by the label applied to them, such as 'fragile state', they may turn away from the donor country and towards alternative partners, thus denying opportunities for dialogue and potential shifts towards a shared positive future. While acknowledging the complexities of inter-country diplomacy, and the need to call out globally unacceptable behaviour, donor countries that demonstrate some appreciation for the strengths of other countries in their development-related collaboration and participate in partnerships focused on shared definitions of a preferred future may find positive change and mutually achieved development outcomes are more achievable. Similarly, a donor agency may seek to work with civil society or particularly strong elements in a country where there are shared definitions of a positive future.

A strengths-based approach offers insights into how countries which have been negatively labelled can shift descriptions, metaphors, and tropes within geo-political relationships. Negative adjectives used to describe the Pacific have a very damaging impact on relationships and aid programme effectiveness. For example, the Pacific is commonly described in terms of small, low-lying islands, remoteness, and low resources. Since the 2010s, efforts by Pacific communities to flip this analysis to focus on the enormity of the ocean and its resources, the strengths of Pacific Islanders as mariners, and the strong regional identity which underpins Pacific life are examples of the power of language. While land-based countries such as Australia and New Zealand may critique the absence of land in the Pacific, this does not mean that the Pacific does not have alternative strengths.

The Pacific Island Forum's *2050 Strategy for the Blue Pacific Continent* exemplifies a strengths perspective in geo-political relations. The notion of the 'Blue Pacific' seeks to reframe how Pacific Island countries are understood by others, and how islanders see themselves. The Strategy states:

> The Blue Pacific seeks to recapture the collective potential of our shared stewardship of the Pacific Ocean based on an explicit recognition of our shared ocean identity, ocean geography, and ocean resources. The Blue Pacific aims to strengthen collective action as one 'Blue Pacific Continent' by putting The Blue Pacific at the centre of the regional policy making process and the requisite collective action for advancing the Forum Leaders' Vision for the Region (Pacific Islands Forum, 2017).

Blue Pacific is a powerful generative metaphor that redefines Pacific Island nation-states and their geo-political relations. Hon. Tuilaepa Sailele Malielegaoi, previous Prime Minster of Samoa and Pacific Islands Forum Chair, said, as he opened the 2018 Pacific Islands Forum meeting:

> I see the Blue Pacific as a powerful narrative to call us together, drawing on our shared ocean identity, ocean geography, and ocean resources. It serves to empower us – reminding us of the value and potential of our region, encouraging us to think and act from a position of strength (Pasifika Rising, 2018).

Diplomats and international development workers may have different frames of reference but overlaps in their respective agendas mean that there are inevitable benefits associated with shared understanding about countries' strengths. If those diplomats who are now responsible for determining the distribution and nature of international development funding use a strengths-based approach, then both they and development workers are likely to find that relationships and development programmes are more effective in achieving their respective goals. Soli Middleby, former CEO and Diplomat to the Pacific, reflected on her extensive experience in Pacific countries:

> Donors, media and foreign governments continue to regularly use negative language when describing the Pacific region, instead of focusing on its many strengths, as a basis for addressing the shared development priorities. If they focused more on existing capacity, the successes that

have been achieved and the immense human, social, environmental and economic assets that are there, they would be more effective and this will be in their own interests. Pacific people and governments are asking to be treated more respectfully.

Partnerships

Collaborative multi-sector or inter-organizational partnerships are increasingly prioritized and included in contemporary approaches to international development. Growth in partnership approaches used by the Partnership Brokers Association and the Partnering Initiative, for example, confirms this shift. Current research, such as the project on partnerships for advancing the Sustainable Development Goals (SDGs) (Graduate Institute Geneva, 2022; Andonova et al., 2022) as well as other work by Winterford (2017) on partnerships for international development research, also illustrates increasing attention to this topic.

A strengths-based approach is highly relevant to the development of respect-based and effective collaboration within partnerships, particularly across cultures (see Chapter 6). A range of partnerships in international development have used and continue to use a strengths-based approach as illustrated below.

A partnership between a University and a school in a rural area of South Africa was studied by two researchers in 2014. After analysing the use of a strengths-based approach in the partnership, the researchers concluded 'that the asset-based approach has great potential as a way of achieving school-community partnership'. They found 'a focus on strong leadership, greater clarity on the aims and thrust of any partnership, as well as coordinated asset-mapping strategies constitute some of the key areas requiring nurturing if this approach is to be useful' (Myende and Chikoko, 2014).

Within a partnership setting, a strengths-based approach enables each partner to identify the strengths and assets they bring. Importantly, it encourages each partner to understand and give value to those strengths and assets, often underplayed and even undermined by the partner with the greater funds and perceived power. A partnership context also suggests, but is not necessarily completely consistent with the idea of Co-production (see Chapter 3).

The alignment of development partnerships with existing local assets, processes and structures is much better understood from a strengths-based perspective than a problem-based approach. For example, asking 'what processes have worked well here on previous occasions?' generates a richer understanding of previous experience and a better foundation for collaboration, than asking 'what failed here previously?' Simply acknowledging that partners have previous positive experience and 'lessons learned' can make a substantial difference to the quality of interaction. Vicki Vaartjes, interviewed for this book, recalls meeting colleagues in Solomon Islands within a partnership programme, and realizing her new colleagues did not reveal their substantial expertise for some time. In their previous experience with other development workers, these strengths and assets had neither been sought nor valued. Once this expertise was revealed and valued, the partnership became much more relevant, vibrant, and successful.

A strengths-based approach is an opportunity to generate more respectful shared language between partners. Particularly since people involved in international cooperation often come from diverse disciplinary backgrounds, many are professionally trained to be problem solvers and to critique the weaknesses of others. Strengths-based development workers report that when they formally stop using negative language associated with a problem-based approach, then a substantial shift occurs in the quality of partnerships. The importance of language as a foundation of international development generally and a strengths-based approach particularly was highlighted in Chapter 2. Development workers interviewed for this book confirmed the importance of language as a foundation of their development partnerships. For example, Soli Middleby said, 'Language at all levels is very important and we must move beyond post-colonial terms and post-colonial language. A new framing, based on a strengths-based approach would help enable this much deeper and most critical change.'

A key theme in successful partnerships is the promotion of mutual responsibility for achieving outcomes, usually portrayed as shared benefits and shared risks. A strengths-based approach supports the application of this principle, by valuing existing strengths and contributions within partners' communities, organizations, and leaders, all essential for maximizing benefits. It also generates the kinds of confidence, commitment, and motivation required to mitigate and respond to risks, as described in Chapter 9.

While the power of partnerships in bringing about positive change is widely promoted and celebrated, the process cannot be assumed to be straightforward or easy. Specific skills and dedicated efforts are required to promote effective partnerships, beyond the actual content or technical aspects of the collaborative work. A strengths-based approach to partnerships, including the use of respectful language, will further enhance their quality, relevance, and value.

Capacity development

Almost all international development approaches, partnerships, and programmes, either explicitly or implicitly include some element of capacity development. In practice, the term is interpreted in diverse ways. The assumption is that contributions to stronger capacity through development interventions will support local actors to identify and manage their own development priorities in the future. Once the concept moves from the general level to something more specific, the influence of different world-views and perspectives starts to shape understanding about 'capacity' and particularly how to bring about stronger capacity. As noted earlier, a strengths-based approach recognizes that capacity exists and has the potential to be strengthened in all contexts and in many dimensions – individual, community, team, organizational, sectoral, national, and global – and development programmes can contribute at any level and in many forms.

It is useful to focus for a moment on what is meant by the term 'capacity', before considering how it may be strengthened and the role of a strengths-based approach in international development practice. The term is complex, particularly through a cultural values lens (Rhodes, 2014) (see Chapter 6). Capacity can be a means to an end or an end in itself and is often understood in vastly different ways depending on the nature of the technical or sectoral programme. Capacity can include a substantial list of elements, from desks and buildings, to personal qualities, national policies and systems, technical skills, or even national military power. It can refer to a community's assets, personnel, expertise, or other elements which enable the community to exist, survive, thrive, or change. It can refer to the components of an organization – such as policies and strategy, leaders and staff, structure, skills, and shared values as described in McKinsey's 7S model (Waterman et al., 1980) – as if it were an engine and needed these fixed and moving parts to succeed. It can include the elements of an organization's efforts – its ability to set a vision and work towards it, to deliver technical work, to network and attract resources, to balance core work and new ideas, and to adapt and self-renew in a changing environment, as identified by Baser and Morgan (2008). Capacity can also refer to physical elements, as in the capacity of a stadium to seat a certain number of sports fans, or the capacity of a pipe to carry so much water per minute. The fact that capacity can also include the concept of 'potential', as in 'she has the potential capacity to be a leader', adds complexity to the word's use.

Diverse interpretations of the term, particularly when translated into languages other than English, mean that identifying, measuring, and assessing capacity is not straightforward in international development contexts. It is not surprising therefore, that efforts to contribute to others' capacity can be approached in diverse ways. A strengths-based approach to understanding existing capacity and developing shared definitions of preferred future capacity can help overcome some of this confusion.

Capacity development in international development carries a great deal of power and judgement. Describing another person, organization, or country as 'lacking capacity' is not just a technical matter, but one which raises inequalities and assessment of others through a particular lens. When an aid donor says to a partner government 'we are here to build the capacity of the Ministry of X', the implication is that the aid donor considers that the ministry lacks capacity to enable it to achieve its own objectives or some other objectives and that the donor has the power and skills to change that situation. It also implies the donor country has more capacity (than simply funds to focus attention on the topic) and the requisite expertise to strengthen the capacity of another government's ministry including in terms of policy and strategy development.

Portraying one partner's lack of capacity vis-à-vis another partner's capacity leads to the kinds of problem-solving approaches which are then incorporated into development programmes. The negative consequences associated with such a problem-solving approach are described in Part A of this book. A strengths-based approach to capacity development complements, supports, and enables a positive change agenda in four key ways.

Firstly a strengths-based approach enables trusting relations and respect-based partnerships to develop, both of which are key to contemporary practices of development. The approach provides the foundational basis for mutual respect and potential for collaboration. A strengths-based approach to capacity recognizes that in every context there are strengths in capacity and that the recognition and mobilization of these are critical for any next steps towards positive change. Contemporary approaches to development recognize that cooperation is key to success, and any analysis of cooperation will confirm that trust and respect are the critical elements. Thus, where the relationship is unequal and where one party sees another as 'lacking capacity' and the other party sees that the donor has the 'solution' to the lack of capacity, it is hard to imagine how mutual respect, and thus genuine collaboration, can flourish.

Secondly change is enabled by focusing on objectives or goals for the future; that is, preferred futures, rather than seeking to address deficits or problems of the current situation. The desired level of future capacity can be easily expressed in the form of objectives for the purpose of defining an aid programme or partnership arrangement. For example, a donor may consider they are seeking to address a problem such as 'weak governance' and spend considerable effort on analysing this topic, describing just how weak governance is, through their lens, while in the country context, stakeholders may be more focused on a future which is described as 'stronger accountability systems' or 'increased evidence-based decision-making'. In another example, a community-based NGO may portray an area as 'lacking access to water', whereas a strengths-based approach will enable community members and local officials to express their interest in 'mobilizing existing resources to increase water flows'.

Thirdly a strengths-based approach enables potential for transformative changes beyond solving a problem. If one considers the broader definition of capacity – the capacity for an entity to manage themselves and their future – then taking a strengths-based approach has the potential for much bigger changes beyond a problem-based approach. As noted by Ian Cunningham (see Case Study 11), a problem-based approach is limiting, in that it seeks only to 'fix the problem' rather than to envision a bigger or better future more broadly. A problem-based approach might fix the first problem (or not), but does not necessarily contribute to the entity's capacity to address the next challenge, to envision a better future beyond the existing problem, or to succeed in much broader ways.

To illustrate this, consider the example of a problem-based approach which focuses on the exclusion of children with disabilities from accessing education. It could seek to fix the problem in myriad ways, including training teachers, raising community awareness of the rights of children or building ramps. A strengths-based approach can enable schools, education authorities, and communities to consider existing strengths in the education system and recognize the potential for a preferred future where all children, regardless of disability, race or ethnic identity, gender or sexual identity, family order, or location are included, welcomed, and able to achieve their educational potential in schools. In this case, the strengths-based approach would not only increase participation of children with disabilities but contribute to a more inclusive education system overall, including through stronger policies and strategies.

Finally a strengths-based approach can help to measure changes in capacity. If it is deemed necessary to develop a framework for assessing capacity, a process which generates a locally relevant framework is recommended. This means asking participants, for example, 'what kinds of capacity are valued here?' as a basis for self-assessing the extent to which capacity already exists and what priorities exist for future development. This contrasts with the imposition of an externally determined model against which local priorities may not be valued. Organizational capacity assessments are a common but problematic tool commonly used in international development, based on externally determined measures of capacity. Working without a preconceived framework is quite feasible, with the emphasis on engaging stakeholders and applying strengths-based tools to stimulate conversations, determine plans and priorities, and then assess progress.

Donor agencies generally seek to measure existing capacity as a basis for measuring changes over time, to prove the effectiveness of their 'investments', assuming that there will be 'low' capacity at the beginning and 'higher' capacity at the end. The potential complications with this approach are limitless, including challenges associated with who defines capacity, whose capacity is being judged and by whom, who does the measurement, how the capacity of one person can be added to others to make a meaningful total, who does the analysis of the data, and who owns the data. A negative approach to capacity may justify a donor's financial commitment and generate a great deal of data about what is deemed to be missing, usually by some externally defined measure; however, this approach generates negative feelings associated with being deemed to 'lack capacity'. This often leads to demotivation and, over time, withdrawal by those whose capacity is deemed poor, low, weak, or missing.

Using a strengths-based approach to assess capacity may not only avoid the threatening and demotivating aspects of a needs-based analysis, but also have many other benefits, consistent with findings included in this and other chapters. It may generate a greater sense of self-assurance and self-confidence required to initiate and follow through with particular actions and priorities, and unleash a vision for the future beyond that determined using existing measures of capacity. Interviewees for this book consistently confirmed the role of a strengths-based approach in building energy and motivation for individuals and groups to achieve the changes they seek; that is, their capacity to achieve their objectives.

Two examples illustrate the use of a strengths-based approach to capacity development in areas such as organizational development, leadership development, and skills development.

Firstly the Pacific Disability Forum, a regional member-based organization, uses a strengths-based approach to achieve its objectives for a more disability – inclusive Pacific. The quote at the beginning of this chapter from CEO Setareki Macanawai confirms the centrality of a strengths-based approach for the work of the organization to bring about change.

Secondly a Pacific Literacy Project, funded by the New Zealand Ministry of Foreign Affairs and Trade, supported teachers and ministries of education in several countries to achieve changes in capacity prioritized by each country. One member of the implementation team, Rebecca Spratt, interviewed for this book, reflected on how a strengths-based approach changed the relationship in which teaching skills were expected to develop. She said:

> Definitely, the approach made a significant difference. In particular, it made a foundational difference to the quality of the relationships we had with educators, and to the motivation they showed towards the changes. They had been used to previous aid programmes which had focused on their weaknesses: their teaching was criticized or they were regularly told they were inadequate. When we came in, we said 'we really value your knowledge and skills as a basis for our collaboration', and we were told that this was a completely new experience for them. They told us and we could also see for ourselves that this approach resulted in a high level of involvement and a much greater comfort with experimenting with new ideas.

Many official development assistance programmes seek to introduce or update government legislation, policies, and strategies as means to increase capacity for achieving developmental change. Approaches for producing such documents commonly include the placement of highly specialized experts as 'advisers.' Policies which reflect a population's interests or a government's priorities can be quite different from those written to suit an external agenda, which often tick someone's box but sit on a shelf once the adviser has left. Use of a strengths-based approach offers the means to identify existing valued elements of legislation and policy, structures, and systems, as well as to generate a shared understanding of the future that will be described in the new documents. A facilitated, collaborative, strengths-based approach to legislative change, policy, and strategy development is more likely to contribute to the levels of ownership necessary for these to actually contribute to sustainable benefits at national and population levels.

Community development

Strong established links between community development and a strengths-based approach were described in Chapter 3. A strengths-based approach has been informed by insights emerging from practice of community development and community organizing, particularly ABCD.

The United Nations (1995) defines community development as 'a process where community members come together to take collective action and generate solutions to common problems'. The International Association for Community Development (IACD) has a more expansive description set out on its website:

> Community Development is a practice-based profession and an academic discipline that promotes participative democracy, sustainable development, rights, economic opportunity, equality, and social justice, through the organization, education, and empowerment of people within their communities, whether these be of locality, identity, or interest, in urban and rural settings (IACD, n.d.).

Community development has a strong connection to international development and, as indicated by the UN definition, a solid tradition in identifying and addressing needs and solving problems. International development approaches such as participatory rural appraisal seek to engage community members in identifying their own needs and problems which community-orientated projects can address.

Despite this historical practice and focus on addressing needs, key concepts central to community development of community leadership, organization, and self-determination, are also enabled through a strengths-based approach, and the practice of a strengths-based approach in community development is well-entrenched.

Numerous examples of successful application and positive outcomes through a strengths-based approach are documented in literature as well as described by many individuals interviewed for this book. Mathie and Cunningham (2008) detail examples from around the world of the use of strengths-based practice at community level. Nicolau and Delpont (2015) describe its use in rural South Africa. Also Linley et al. (2011) draw on experiences reported by the ABCD Institute and LASA Development as well as their own work with The Strengths Project, to conclude:

> Adopting and applying strengths-based approaches to community development can be a powerful and transformative force for positive social change. By building on the strengths (however broadly defined) of the individuals, families, groups that make up these community

populations, as well as those of their wider social networks, it is possible to harness an intrinsic motivation for change that was always there, but latent, and in doing so, to inspire people with a passion for their own potential, a belief in their own capabilities and what they can achieve (Linley et al., 2011: 153).

A New Zealand NGO, SurfAid, working mainly in Indonesia and Solomon Islands, undertakes a range of community development activities in remote locations, usually near surf beaches. The Programme Director, Anne Wuijts, interviewed for this book, reflected:

> Communities who learn to focus on their strengths and their abilities to get things done can achieve great results, often not predicted at the outset. It does take a bit of time to get the message across that communities have the abilities to achieve what they want, including getting governments to provide services, but not a long time, and then they are off and away on their own development journey.
>
> In SurfAid now, we use a strengths-based approach explicitly in our work in remote locations in Indonesia. We use Appreciative Inquiry almost always in our work and have used Sustainable Livelihoods when working on food security issues. Appreciative Inquiry works well when working with village-owned enterprises in Indonesia, because all villages need to have a plan, and Appreciative Inquiry is the perfect means to develop these plans. Once villages have a plan, then they can access funding from the Government. We use Appreciative Inquiry to help villages determine their assets and to give them the confidence to approach Government with their priorities.

Another example of strengths-based community development comes from LASA Development, an organization in Nepal. In one of LASA's projects in Phakhel, Nepal, the team was interested in using the strengths-based principles of Appreciative Inquiry to work with villagers. The project was led by Mac Odell who had adapted Appreciative Inquiry to work with villagers. At the outset of the project, drawing from Appreciative Inquiry (Cooperrider and Srivastva, 1987), LASA ran a mini-4D cycle (Discovery, Dream, Design, and Delivery) in two hours, all the time the subsistence-level farmers had to give them. Throughout the project, they held meetings every few months, visiting villagers about three times a year to support the process. They separated the men, women, and children into different groups and came together to share information and go through the Appreciative Inquiry cycle.

Using Appreciative Inquiry as a means of community building, significant outcomes have been achieved, including raising substantial funds to build school foundations, accessing a grant from an international NGO to build the first model secondary school, and raising funds for school registration fees, teachers' salaries, equipment, and books. The village has moved from strength to strength with these outcomes. The project reflected strong community organization, led by a woman in her 40s, a 70-year-old grandfather, and another man in his 40s whose children attend secondary school far away from home in Kathmandu. A village man was quoted as saying:

> This really brings it home to me. We've been bloody lazy! For the past 40 years we have been holding our hands out for aid from the government and what do we get? We fight, we can't agree on anything, and we don't feel good about ourselves. 40 years ago, we did a lot together because there was no one else to help us and you know what? We were proud of what we did! We were proud of our village. Are any of you proud now? No? Well, let's do this together and be proud again! (Linley et al., 2010).

When given the opportunity, most communities and organizations can find examples of using what they already have to achieve what they want in the future. Most can look into their past and find strategies that have helped them address daily or organizational challenges. Most can also find people who seem to be achieving their goals and so have found approaches that could be applied more widely. Case Study 15 illustrates the use of ABCD in a government and citizen partnership in Vietnam, with widespread community benefits.

Case Study 15 A government–citizen partnership using ABCD in Vietnam

This case study illustrates how ABCD can be useful at a whole town level when used by local authorities and community members. It shows how the approach can be easily aligned with existing governance practices and quickly bring about economic, social, and cultural changes prioritized at local levels.

This is an edited version of a story communicated from Vinh Nguyen, Director of the Centre for Research, Training and Consultancy on Local Development, Vietnam for this book, based on conversations with Le Minh Hien, Vice Chairperson of the An Khe Town's People's Council, and other community members in 2018.

The town of An Khe in central Vietnam has a population of 66,000 living in 11 administrative units, called communes or wards. Bahnar and Cham ethnic minorities have lived in An Khe for a long time. The town has a rich history and features several important cultural sites. The town is particularly renowned for its food production and flower-growing industries. Located on a unique geological structure, An Khe is seeking to be recognized by UNESCO as a global geological park. The town promotes sustainable development by combining scientific research, historical-cultural preservation, archaeological, and geological heritage with local economic development for local residents based on tourism.

An Khe was made aware of ABCD through the Deputy Chairperson's family connection with an ABCD trainer associated with the Center for Educational Exchange with Vietnam (CEEVN), a US Foundation. The town's leaders say that some core concepts had been applied before they heard of this practice.

(Continued)

Case Study 15 Continued

They shared many stories of mobilizing community assets which they are very proud of, such as the preservation of An Khe Truong, a historic cultural site from the Tay Son dynasty (1771–1802). Maintenance and preservation of the site was previously carried out by the town's cultural officers, but when senior citizens took over this task, a significant change occurred. They revived traditional processions and festivals by training village youth in traditional music. The town leaders reflect that this demonstrates the ABCD spirit of asset-mobilization and community-driven action, even before ABCD was introduced.

The first ABCD training was held in An Khe in May 2017 with the participation of the Town People's Committee, Communist Party Committee, People's Council, Fatherland Front, town officials, and members of six communities. The training inspired participants to identify all of their assets for community development via mobilization of internal resources. In the first training, many participants said that they had applied ABCD without knowing it; and now, after the training, they recognized that their community was very rich. For example, Mr Dinh, who established the An Binh clean vegetable cooperative, said he realized that the community has all kinds of assets. Another community member emphasized that 'whatever we intend to do from now on, we will first ask what the local people have, before asking for support from the Government'. The participants started to develop action plans based on their assets and the Secretary of the town's Communist Party Committee was excited and surprised to note that nobody asked the town leaders for financial support. The leaders confirmed that the development-orientation of the town somewhat reflected ABCD principles with their motto of 'people know, people discuss, people do and people supervise'.

After the training, the town's leaders supported activities in six communities which applied ABCD. For example, in the Ngo May ward, officials ran a three-day ABCD training session for 70 people from seven residential sub-wards. The training led to significant results which bring inspiration to and high appreciation from local residents: participants recognized new opportunities from their strengths and assets such as flower growing, livestock raising, trading and services, and irrigation scheme construction. They happily told success stories of their community as well as how they identified their assets. In another ward, An Binh, a cooperative was established to produce clean vegetables according to national agricultural standards and the cooperative comprising 21 households now produces 3 tonnes of fresh vegetables for the local market each day. Local authorities and residents have been continuously discussing how to mobilize and link up all assets for further development of the town.

The success of the first ABCD training has spread across the town, creating significant change and contributing to cultural and socio-economic development. The most significant change is that ABCD has fundamentally changed awareness among the town's officials and core community members of their assets. They are now aware that An Khe has many potential advantages and internal resources which need to be identified, mobilized, and used in socio-economic and community development. The local authorities make their best efforts and have become more determined and more confident in supporting development. Second, local communities are more deliberately creating connections and sharing what

(Continued)

Case Study 15 Continued

they have in a more appropriate, intensive, and effective manner. This includes establishment of new cooperatives, improvement of existing cooperatives, and formation of interest groups in farming, flower growing, calligraphy, martial arts, dragon dance, and Ayurveda in various communities.

Realizing that ABCD is an approach to help local people discover their potential and strengths for development, local authorities now consider this as one of the tasks in An Khe's development plan. Town leaders affirmed that to reach their development goals, mobilizing existing resources is a must. They want ABCD to be introduced in other communities and in new sectors such as education and culture. The leaders want An Khe to shift from being agriculturally based to incorporating more industry, construction, trading, and services. In addition, they want the agriculture sector to shift towards organic farming and high-technology plantations. Local authorities say that to achieve this in reality, all internal resources, potential, and advantages need to be mobilized.

An Khe's town leaders want to develop different models of ABCD application in the town, to cooperate more with CEEVN and its consultant group to conduct research on successful models, and to continue to build up the capacity of the town's officials and core members of communities. This is an important asset-building or human capital building strategy for ABCD expansion. To realize these plans, with support from the consultant group, An Khe will continue to improve the working capacity of the town's officials in applying ABCD and to form ABCD task groups in different communities in order to adopt and apply ABCD in their community development activities.

Gender and social inclusion

> *Strengths-based approaches do not address gender rights head on. We have found that men quickly become alienated, 'waiting to hear that they are to blame'. When they are asked to talk about how they can contribute to making their family strong and peaceful there is a sense of common purpose and inclusion that they appreciate. Tools like Appreciative Inquiry are an enabling rather than a divisive process. Men realize that they have an important role to play. Men often refer to this as 'the Papua New Guinea way' as opposed to the outsiders' way* (Barbara Pamphilon, University of Canberra).

Approaches which prioritize consideration of gender equality and social inclusion have been a key feature of international development since the 1980s. This both recognizes that development programmes had not and do not automatically benefit all equally, and that there is increasing global interest in addressing universal issues of discrimination and inequality. Every development initiative has an influence on gender relations and gender equality, whether intentional or not. Programmes may reinforce existing marginalization or discrimination without realizing.

A continuum of approaches to gender and social inclusion approaches can be identified. At one end, programmes can ignore or cause harm to gender and social inclusion. Along the continuum, programmes may be aware, responsive, or accommodating to gender and social inclusion. At the other end of the continuum programmes may be transformative (described in Chapter 4). Gender-transformative change influences the systems or structures which inform gendered relations (Cornwall, 2003; Cornwall and Rivas, 2015). MacArthur et al. (2022) provide an excellent summary of the trajectory towards gender-transformative approaches.

Gender-transformative approaches have been employed by large international NGOs such as CARE, Plan International, and Oxfam since the 2010s. Gender-transformative change seeks to address discrimination against gender and sexual minorities. These approaches seek to contribute towards shifting power relations and social structures to enable marginalized communities to have equal access to decision-making, resources, and opportunities.

There are challenges in implementing a gender-transformative change approach within current parameters of international development. A gender-transformative approach is dynamic and adaptive, yet donors typically expect linear and predefined change outcomes to be achieved in a short time period. Change is also multi-dimensional, multi-level, multi-scale, long-term, non-linear, multi-actor, and relational, all of which can be challenging to reconcile with donor-driven practices of development influenced by result-based management thinking. Transformative change was described in detail in Chapter 4.

A strengths-based approach complements perspectives of a gender-transformative approach in four ways. First, it enables all people to be involved in structural and systems level change. For example, Willetts et al. (2013) found a strengths-based approach 'generated both meaningful findings to improve development practice as well as insight on how an SBA could enable women and men to identify, to value, and to discuss positive gender outcomes and safely identify priorities for future change' (p. 1004). The authors of this research 'proposed that SBAs may be used to address (not just assess) gender equality' (Willetts et al., 2013: 1004). Through constructive conversations, people of all genders are engaged in necessary change outcomes for gender equality.

A strengths-based approach invites conversations about how gendered relations might be improved in the future by focusing on what has worked well in the past. The approach enables stakeholders in any context to generate the energy and motivation to bring about immediate and often transformational change towards more egalitarian and inclusive societies and organizations.

Second, a key assumption of a strengths-based approach is that all people have something to contribute and the whole community is richer when each potential contribution is recognized, regardless of gender or other characteristics. Identifying and mobilizing everyone's contributions, both individually and as a group, is part of any thorough strengths-based approach. Everyone's ability to contribute, economically, socially, and politically, is recognized through this lens; this is potentially empowering for all, thus minimizing the commonly held premise that for women to be empowered, men must be comparatively disempowered, or when people with disability are empowered, people without disability are disempowered. When undertaken deliberately, a strengths-based approach can showcase the benefits of inclusion for and to all participants in a development process. As noted by Willetts et al. (2013: 999), 'the strengths-based process placed significance on both women's and men's views of what they value, and what they would both like to change in the future. Often, enquiry into gender equality, or even practice to address gender equality, involves a stronger focus on women than on men'.

Third, a strengths-based approach focuses on local leadership to leverage change and is more culturally appropriate than imposed agendas from external agencies. For example, Jayne Curnow, interviewed for this book, said: 'I like how the strengths-based approach addresses gender relations and enables gender transformation, not by imposing or forcing ideas, but by encouraging an awakening'.

A strengths-based approach reinforces the value and contribution of women in transformative change, and through this, gender equality outcomes.

Finally, consistent with the theme of the power of positive language (see Chapter 2), a strengths-based approach can contribute to changes in self-perception and power which underpin gender relations and roles. For example, in Nepal, Odell (2004) found that the use of a strengths-based approach (described as appreciative planning and action) 'has shown positive results in replacing the fatalism and resignation of women, with pride in their achievements, self-confidence in their ability to set attainable goals, and success in achieving them' (p. 1).

In Indonesia, in the ACCESS programme (see Case Study 16), recognizing and unleashing the potential that women have to contribute to decision-making and leadership in the public domain, has been found to significantly decrease the incidence of domestic and gender-based violence. In this context, as women's contribution to the public domain was increasingly recognized, they were more respected and more likely to be treated equitably. ACCESS Programme reports referenced the benefits of a strengths-based approach for women's leadership and wellbeing. For example, in one village called Kayuloe Barat in South Sulawesi, a leader reported that 'when we started listening to the women and they became engaged in all aspects of rice production, our rice production rose from 2–3 tonnes per hectare to 5–6 tonnes. Women brought discipline and consistency to our work'. In another village in West Timor, called Noelbaki, women looked at the potential of their natural assets and formed themselves into women farmer groups. Thinking of their priorities and what was available, they decided to help each other use the land in front of each house, however big or small, to grow all sorts of vegetables and fruits and raise more chickens. They also learned how to make organic fertilizer. Before long they were able to provide added nutrition and a source of regular income. From this experience they were given a certificate of appreciation and additional resources from the local government to train women in surrounding villages.

Disability-inclusive development

> In the disability context, a strengths-based approach has an important role to play and fits very well because it focuses on the strengths of people with disabilities as well as their representative organizations. A strengths-based approach focuses on abilities rather than on disabilities (Setareki Macanawai, CEO of Pacific Disability Forum).

Since 2006, when the United Nations adopted the Convention on the Rights of Persons with Disabilities (CRPD), governments have signed up to promote, protect, and ensure the full enjoyment of human rights by persons with disabilities and ensure persons with disabilities enjoy full equality under the law. CRPD serves as a major catalyst in the global disability rights movement enabling a shift from viewing persons with disabilities as objects of charity, medical treatment, and social protection towards viewing them as full and equal members of society, with human rights.

There are strong links between contemporary, rights based approaches to disability inclusion and a strengths-based approach. Dignity, respects, and rights enshrined in CRPD also underpin a strengths-based approach. People with disabilities and their representative organizations, organizations of persons with disabilities (OPDs), call for: a focus on abilities rather than disabilities; to be included in decisions that affect their lives; and to be respected for their contribution to development. Focusing on a person's abilities leads to a sense of feeling valued, included, and holding potential. A strengths-based approach to disability inclusion focuses on the strengths of OPDs to represent the voices of their members and the experiences of communities, movements, and programmes that have successfully included people with disabilities in all aspects of their work. This approach was employed in the design of AusAID's Samoa Disability Program (2013). As described in the design, 'a collaborative and holistic approach is appropriate in Samoa. This would build on existing strengths, reflect the complexity of relationships and interactive factors and facilitate mutual learning about what works best in this relatively new area of work' (AusAID, 2013: 1).

The emphasis on contributions that can be made to developmental change by everyone was echoed by Setareki Macanawai, interviewed for this book, who said:

> People with disabilities are commonly brought up to believe they have little value and thus have nothing to contribute. A strengths-based approach enables them to focus on what they can do in contrast with

the perception that they cannot do anything. This recognizes that people may start with a little to contribute, but then they can build on this overtime. I tell the OPDs that it does not matter what size of contribution they make, whether it's a spoonful or a bucket size contribution, their contribution is valuable and they deserve a place at the table.

Consistent with the themes described throughout this book, the role of a strengths-based approach in disability inclusion relates particularly to issues of power, partnership, self-worth, and self-determination. These themes are evidenced in the work of the Pacific Disability Forum, an umbrella body for Pacific OPDs since 2002. The reflections of Setareki Macanawai on the value of this approach for disability inclusion in the Pacific region include the following:

I first heard about a strengths-based approach when undertaking a major piece of research on the capacity of Pacific organizations of persons with disabilities in 2011–12 (Rhodes et al., 2013). We encouraged these organizations to reflect on their own strengths rather than give us a wish list of what they wanted from outsiders. In a post-colonial context, this way of thinking requires a huge change of mindset, particularly in terms of giving value to cultural assets in each place. People have felt marginalized and countries have been disempowered for a very long time. This means for people with disabilities to see themselves as having value is a huge shift. In some cases, a person with a disability may need to be supported to be able to recognize their own strengths and worth. It also takes time, as some people with disabilities have been told their whole lives they have very little value. There are now many people in the Pacific, after decades of advocacy in this area, who feel empowered and confident to speak up about their rights and priorities.

The evidence we have that this approach is effective is our ability to now challenge the systems that continue to exclude us. Recognition of our own strengths has enabled us to engage with government agencies and others who make decisions, to test the waters or to challenge the status quo, for example in relation to inclusive budgeting and disaster risk reduction. We are using our strengths to change the systems that need to change.

Within inclusive education programmes, a strengths-based approach has also proven to be powerful. For example, Garwood and Ampuja (2019) reported on the value of the 'growth-mindset approach' for students with learning disabilities, emotional and behavioural disabilities. Approaches which engage people with intellectual disabilities based on their character strengths have been studied (for example, see Niemiec et al., 2017) and offer examples of the benefits. This is consistent with the broader value of strengths-based approach in education as described in the next chapter (Education section).

Governance

The strengths-based approach also creates a more democratic process ...
(Erin Anderson).

Improved governance as a means to achieve development outcomes has been prioritized in international development since the 1990s. Governance can be understood as structures and processes by which an entity is directed and controlled. Importantly governance does not equate to government, but encapsulates wider processes of decision-making, control, and behaviours. International agencies such as the United Nations Development Programme, World Bank, the OECD DAC, and others define governance as the exercise of authority or power in order to manage a country's economic, political, and administrative affairs.

Within international development discourse the notion of 'good governance' has been defined as a priority-enabling environment for poverty reduction and sustainable human development. Kofi Annan, when UN Secretary-General in 1998, declared that 'good governance is perhaps the single most important factor in eradicating poverty and promoting development'. Good governance is characterized by an accountable and responsive state and the participation of citizens in the process of government. Good governance can be defined as structures and processes that are designed to ensure accountability, transparency, responsiveness, rule of law, stability, equity and inclusiveness, empowerment, and broad-based participation.

The focus on good governance in international development has been characterized by a deficit perspective, whereby countries are blamed for their inefficiencies, mismanagement, corruption, and lack of leadership and management capacity. This frame of reference leads to generalized efforts to fix inefficiencies and strengthen management and leadership, often using models and methods which are developed in other contexts and are not necessarily relevant. A quick review of the programmes of multilateral, regional, and bilateral donors will find those which seek to improve governance related to service delivery, including law and justice, health and education, infrastructure and procurement, for example, as well as parliamentary and electoral systems. A problem-based approach, which pitches others' approaches to governance as being poor, weak, lacking capacity, or otherwise inadequate through the eyes of donor agencies, has arguably contributed to less than successful collaborative efforts in this context.

The reasons why dominant approaches to strengthening governance may not work reflect many of the points raised earlier in this book. Which government organization is comfortable being critiqued by another government, being told that they lack capacity and being treated as if they lack agency, authority, and self-determination? What leader responds well to being portrayed as weak and corrupt or being ignored and disempowered, regardless of their strengths and merit? Which community organization values and responds well to being demeaned through negative language about their governance capacity and authority?

A strengths-based approach recognizes that in every context, there are governance and leadership strengths on which to base collaborative efforts to plan for and bring about positive change. For example, a strengths-based approach was used as part of Joint Organizational Assessments for applicants to an Australian Government-funded programme, called the Papua New Guinea Democratic Governance Program (2010–2014). This approach enabled organizations to reflect on their own strengths as the basis for future collaboration and priority setting, rather than rate themselves against an externally determined framework about what makes a good organization. While it may be easy for an outsider to nominate an organization's weaknesses, through their own cultural or theoretical framework, this does not achieve the kinds of change that will actually help an organization achieve its own objectives.

A strengths-based approach does not deny the need for change in governance in certain contexts, but focuses on ways to catalyse change building on potential, assets, and resources as well as actors interested and active in creating positive change. Chapter 4 identified a range of ways change happens within a strengths-based approach, including crowding out which is relevant to improving governance outcomes.

A strengths-based approach is particularly useful for sector-wide or regional collaborative governance efforts, since it helps build respect between organizations which may otherwise operate in silos or in competition with others for scarce resources. It potentially reduces the negative aspects of 'us vs. them' feelings that are often implied in problem-based approaches. The example of the Parties to the Nauru Agreement (see Chapter 12) illustrates the power of collective bargaining with the strengths of governments at a regional level.

Case Study 16 Strengthening civil society for improved governance in Indonesia

A major community development programme in eastern Indonesia contributed to significant positive changes across 1,000 villages after integrating a strengths-based approach. The Australian Community Development and Civil Society Strengthening Scheme (ACCESS) began in 2003 and concluded in 2012 after two phases (Aragón and Pakpahan, 2015). Throughout this period the Scheme became increasingly aligned with the strengths-based approach and was regarded by the Australian Government's Aid Programme Performance Review as an example of high quality and sustainable development (DFAT, 2014a: 72).

ACCESS Phase 2 (ACCESS II) worked in partnership with 70 civil society organizations, 3,500 citizen associations, and reached 1,118 village communities in 20 districts from four provinces across eastern Indonesia. The strengths-based approach became the way of engaging with communities, civil society organizations, and governments.

(Continued)

Case Study 16 Continued

The design of ACCESS II included three intentional directions. First, it strengthened relationships between all development actors. This meant the primary focus was on interactions between government, civil society organizations, and local communities. This contrasted with other programmes which prioritize the relationship between 'donor' and 'recipient'. Second, ACCESS II encouraged the use of a strengths-based approach as the strategic basis for all its operations and training with all stakeholders. In practice, this included both a holistic approach described as empowering citizens and their organizations for democratic governance, and the application of various strengths-based methodologies including Appreciative Inquiry, ABCD, Positive Deviance Initiative, and Positive Imaging. Third, the overall design introduced a more iterative approach to implementation, creating the space and providing the opportunity in a continuous learning process. The programme was not so much implementing a plan as facilitating a process of democratization at multiple levels.

According to the design of ACCESS II, 'an assets-based approach fosters endogenous processes, inclusive participation, and community leadership'. In the context of community building, the design noted that the approach 'perceives residents and other community stakeholders as active change agents rather than passive beneficiaries or clients' (AusAID, 2007). The Scheme helped communities to determine the appropriate enabling environment as it began with what is present in the neighbourhood, and relied heavily on the efforts of internal agents, such as residents, associations, and institutions: an inside-out perspective.

Over 8 years, ACCESS II drafted and applied 14 different products or processes described in 60 different books, manuals, case studies, and research articles. They all focused on strengthened civil society–government partnerships in development. Various strengths-based methods are reflected throughout these products relating to:

- Provincial and district planning and budgeting engaging with and building on community voice and assets.
- Village citizens taking initiatives and using their skills to improve overall village life.
- Local civil society organizations gaining higher stakeholder participation in village level projects and becoming facilitators and linkers rather than project managers.
- Multi-stakeholder District Citizen Engagement Plans leading to improvements in economic development, participatory poverty assessment, pro-poor planning and budgeting, and public service delivery in education, health, utilities, and agriculture.
- Citizen-initiated improvements optimizing the local resources which served to confirm the village community as a worthy recipient of government agency support.
- Citizens' increased self-esteem, greater participation of women in public life, mobilization of local assets, strengthening of internal associations, and greater space for public advocacy.

(Continued)

A STRENGTHS-BASED APPROACH AND DEVELOPMENT THEMES 193

Case Study 16 Continued

Table 11.1 summarizes some of the many processes where strengths-based approaches were applied in ACCESS II.

While not all Australian Government aid officials accepted communities determining their own priorities (one noted in a private conversation with an author of this book that many in AusAID thought the design was 'wishy-washy and lacked cohesion'), overall, ACCESS II became one of the more successful democratizing and capacity development schemes. Its success is now recognized at the highest levels as noted by this Australian Government internal review:

> The now complete ACCESS program proved to be an excellent example of a sustainable program whose gains have been institutionalized at a local level. It was clear that, close to two years after its completion, the program has achieved sustained improvements in civil society capacity and local poverty data quality. The Bupati (District Head) with whom we met suggested that, when he was elected in 2009, ACCESS data was the basis on which he identified priorities for targeting poverty and he drew upon ACCESS-trained personnel to deliver his reform agenda (email communication between Jakarta-based DFAT official and the Project Director, Paul Boon (2021)).

Table 11.1 Strengths-based processes used in ACCESS II in Indonesia

ACCESS II event	Strengths-based strategies	Explanation/Purpose
National Appreciative Summit	Appreciative Inquiry; Positive Imagining of the Future; Social Capital Analysis	Multi-stakeholder summit to rehearse and plan district-level action
District Appreciative Summit	Appreciative Inquiry; Asset Mapping; identification of change champions through Positive Deviance Initiative	Week-long strategic planning with identified change agents from every sector for whole district coordinated actions
Identifying best practice in service delivery	Positive Deviance Initiative used as a research tool to identify and showcase best practice	In multiple locations to improve service delivery in education, utilities, clinics, health posts
Village Administrative Information System	Appreciative Village Mapping using OpenStreetMap; Asset Mapping	What works, what are the gaps, and how to mobilize assets for national and district planning
Citizen Action Plans	ABCD; Appreciative Inquiry; Social Capital	Rich storytelling in gender and age-specific groupings
Outcome mapping and continuous learning	Appreciative Evaluation; Inclusive visioning as a force for social change	Focus on how much of the vision has been achieved and what assets could be better mobilized
Civil Society Index and Advocacy	Citizen voice as an asset; Constructive dialogue, generating a surplus of desired behaviour	Power analysis and advocacy through growing power within systems and individuals

The concept of social accountability, broadly defined as ways in which citizens directly seek increased state accountability, is clearly related to governance. The term social accountability describes a broad range of citizen-led activities and initiatives to increase state accountability and improvements in delivery of public services (Sharma, 2008).

Social accountability gained prominence in the early 2000s linked to the view that lack of accountability was a primary reason for service delivery failure in low-income countries. The *World Bank Development Report 2004, Making Services Work for Poor People* (World Bank, 2003), promoted citizen engagement as a means of addressing poor accountability, and in turn improving services for the poor.

Early writing on social accountability described a contest or confrontation between citizens and the state. Joshi (2007: 14) described it as 'the confrontational nature of accountability demands'. The discourse used to describe social accountability practice informs a citizen–state relationship which is contested and divided with contrary positions.

However, as the field of practice evolved, more nuanced perspectives emerged which offered insights into collaborative practice. Literature since 2010 challenges the dichotomous view of the citizen–state relationship which is aligned to and enabled through a strengths perspective. Research found that change happened through the 'blurring of boundaries' (Citizenship DRC, 2011) between state and citizens. This research also aligned with research on World Vision's Citizen Voice and Action approach (Winterford, 2013), which demonstrated the process and value of dialogue (Bohm, 2004) strengthening relations between service users, providers, and local government to strengthening delivery of basic services such as education and health.

In summary, a strengths-based approach complements and supports commonly used approaches in international development cooperation. It is already applied in many contexts around the world and there is increasing research documenting its benefits for effective processes and for achieving desired developmental outcomes. It is explicitly promoted by those who use it already as the best approach to achieve sustainable development goals and any other positive change in almost all contexts, particularly where people, organizations, and cross-cultural collaboration are involved.

A strengths-based approach is suitable for maximizing the quality of interaction and engagement between people from different cultures who are collaborating to address mutually agreed objectives. It is ideal for planning that involves people and organizations. It has potential in any kind of process associated with strengthening policies, programmes, and service delivery, from education to police development. It is perfect for supporting people who work collaboratively in teams, networks, associations, communities, and movements to generate energy, respect, and motivation towards positive change.

Examples of the use of a strengths-based approach have been researched and found to offer positive contributions to the achievement of international development outcomes. The examples included in this chapter, in countries in Asia, Pacific, and Africa, illustrate the diversity of contexts in which they offer value. The following chapter considers the use of a strengths-based approach in the sectors in which current international development programmes are directed.

CHAPTER 12
A strengths-based approach and development sectors

> *I believe there is neither a sector nor a place where a strengths-based approach does not apply* (Soli Middleby)

A strengths-based approach has been widely used and proven to be effective in almost all sectors and disciplines relevant to international development. For readers interested in how they might use a strengths-based approach in practice, this chapter provides links and examples from various sectors and countries to get started. The chapter does not seek to describe or explain each sector in any depth, but to explore the intersection between a strengths-based approach and some of the many sectors in which the approach is applied.

The notion of 'sectors' can be problematic in international development, and the complex nature of change requires consideration of both synergies and trade-offs related to development outcomes. There is increasing recognition of the value of considering the nexus of sectors which have dominated international development, and in fact breaking down the notion of sectors. There is also increasing awareness that change is complex with various feedback loops and positive and negative consequences to other parts of the system (context). For example, building a dam to support agricultural activities and improve food security might in fact negatively impact the natural ecosystem and long-term health of the environment. The dam construction might not take into account climate change projections of less rainfall in the area, and ultimately not strengthen agricultural yields. Farmers may instead consider the uptake of drought-resilient crops, to transform agricultural practices and achieve food security objectives. Another example of synergies in development outcomes across sectors is initiatives to improve health delivery. Providing better pay and work conditions may encourage more health professionals to join the sector and, as women tend to dominate health professions, the focus on improving health delivery can result in improved gender equality outcomes.

There is increasing recognition of the benefit of working in ways that prioritize the nexus between sectors. While professionalization in international development has reinforced 'working in silos' and the dominance of disciplinary cliques, there are signs of movement towards bringing different disciplines together, in some areas. For example, there is increasing use of transdisciplinary thinking whereby inquiry and action are informed by a strategy that crosses many disciplinary boundaries to create a holistic approach. This way of thinking is concerned with knowledge that transcends disciplines to create an overarching perspective in relation to a specific context. Another critical defining characteristic of transdisciplinary practice is the inclusion of stakeholders at the centre of a change process in defining objectives and strategies. This strong emphasis on collaboration with stakeholders is akin to a strengths-based approach for international development. The collaboration between disciplines and different types of stakeholders enables new ways of knowing the world and offers potential for collective action for change.

Another example of working beyond sectors is the humanitarian-development nexus. Strengthening this nexus was identified as a top priority at the World Humanitarian Summit in 2016 by the majority of stakeholders, including donors, NGOs, and crisis-affected states, among others. The nexus describes 'the transition or overlap between the delivery of humanitarian assistance and the provision of long-term development assistance' (Strand, 2020: 104). For many decades these fields of practice have been separated in funding arrangements, implementation approaches, and organizational structures and staffing. Described as a 'new way of working' the nexus is informed by collective outcomes; recognition that different organizations are not defined by specific roles; and that multi-year time frames are required. This 'new way of working' demonstrates efforts to break down silos.

This chapter is structured according to sectors currently dominating international development, but we encourage readers to consider connections and combinations between them. This presentation is similar to the SDGs: while 17 goals are described, the goals are expected to be connected in recognition of the linkages between social, economic, and environmental goals.

This chapter is not intended to be exhaustive in its coverage of sectors, but to situate a strengths-based approach with current dominant sectors. We recognize that many readers see themselves as specialists within particular sectors, many organizations identify themselves as sector-specific, and most programmes funded by donors are classified into sectors. Readers are encouraged to take these examples and consider how to use a strengths-based approach in their own practice. Application of a strengths-based approach offers insights into the importance of taking a multi-sectoral approach and working in the nexus of sectors. Use of a strengths perspective as well as methods and tools associated with a strengths-based approach enable development workers and organizations to apply a holistic perspective on change beyond a single sector perspective.

This chapter includes evidence drawn from the authors' own experiences as well as the perspectives of those interviewed for this book and broader literature. Application of a strengths-based approach in the following sectors, listed alphabetically, is considered:

- climate change action and disaster risk reduction;
- economic development;
- education;
- food security and agriculture;

- gender-based violence, domestic violence, and child protection;
- governance and social accountability;
- health systems strengthening and health security;
- humanitarian responses and recovery after disaster;
- law and justice;
- water, sanitation, and hygiene.

Climate change action and disaster risk reduction

Efforts to support communities, industries, and countries to adapt to climate change and cope with increased natural disasters have grown exponentially since the 2000s. Climate change is disrupting national economies and affecting lives. Weather patterns are changing, in some cases dramatically, sea levels are rising, and extreme weather events are becoming more frequent. Development initiatives must increasingly consider the current and potential impact of climate change to ensure goals and intended changes are achieved.

Key to climate change and disaster risk reduction in international development is the notion of vulnerability and the use of vulnerability assessments. A plethora of definitions of vulnerability are used within the sector. The Intergovernmental Panel on Climate Change described vulnerability to climate as the degree to which a system is susceptible to, and unable to cope with, adverse effects of climate change, including climate variability and extremes. Vulnerability is a function of the character, magnitude, and rate of climate change and variation to which a system is exposed, its sensitivity, and its adaptive capacity. Thinking about extreme weather events such as cyclones, floods or storm surges by the coast, 'exposure' marks the extent to which people, the environment, and physical assets could be affected by such events. 'Sensitivity' defines the degree to which people and the environment might be positively or negatively affected. 'Adaptive capacity' describes the type of response to cope and adjust (Schneider et al., 2007).

Responses to climate change and disaster risk are grounded in deficit-based language which, as described earlier, has negative consequences for enabling positive change. When meeting government officials, community leaders, and members as part of her early work in climate change adaptation, in several Pacific Islands, Anna Gero recalls the discomfort she felt when asking for responses to questions about vulnerability. Years later, she understood why. Once she became aware of a strengths-based approach, she began to use different language and methods in her engagement with Pacific leaders and communities. She said: 'people use the wrong language – such as vulnerability assessment and deprivation measure – and it is so grating. The deficit discourse is so dominant and this is strongly linked to disempowerment'. She recalls:

> In subsequent events, we used the Sustainable Livelihoods Framework, which talks about available resources as 'the five capitals' at the beginning of each session. It was a small shift, but it clearly influenced

the rest of the process and the outcome. It shifted the thinking from 'what can we get the donors to pay for?' to 'what can we do ourselves?' Recognising climate justice aspects, a strengths-based approach does not ignore challenges and problems caused by countries which are also donors, but the process reminded the participants of the cultural strengths of their communities. These strengths include their history of rebuilding houses after disasters and adjusting their practices to suit changes in their environment. This was my first intentional attempt to bring in strengths-based approach, and I have not gone back since.

The use of language and methods which demonstrate an interest in the strengths and assets held by people and organizations is clearly more respectful and beneficial than a singular focus on what is missing. Anna Gero now reflects how inappropriate it was to ask people to focus entirely on the negative aspects of their lives, recalling the impact of the shift to the strengths-based approach:

When we got to identifying activities to respond to the community's priorities, it was clear that some could be done immediately, using existing networks and community strengths. In retrospect, it is about enhancing the resilience that is already there, rather than focusing on what the donor project funding will do to fill in the gaps. The donors were needed for the infrastructure side of things, but that is only one part of the broader picture of adaptation and resilience. The focus shifts.

Others also question the notion of vulnerability-related language and approaches in climate change and disaster risk. Barnett (2020: 1174) points out, 'vulnerability is a matter of complex power relations rather than fate', and focusing on individuals, rather than systems and broader power systems, is likely to perpetuate disempowerment rather than find ways to support positive change. Barnett considers the connection between vulnerability and powerlessness in depth, noting that when a vulnerability lens is applied, the implication is that 'solutions can only ever come from powerful institutions and actors, and done to the vulnerable, because they cannot by definition *address* their own powerlessness' (p. 1175). Vulnerability to climate change is a matter of political economy, according to Barnett (2020), including how 'powerful institutions and interests that create vulnerability are themselves adapting by appropriating the cause of the vulnerable' (p. 1179). The concept of power is described earlier in Chapter 5.

Climate change clearly has negative consequences and there is no denying the harm caused. This discussion focuses on how people and organizations in the international development context respond to and act on the crisis. Responses can take two forms. One, a deficit-based approach, defines individuals as disempowered and at risk, with lack of potential to act or respond to the situation. Alternatively, a strengths-based approach respects the agency and potential of individuals, groups, and communities, fuelled by local assets and strengths, and supports them to achieve their own definitions of the future.

Communities' and countries' responses to climate change can be supported through use of a strengths-based approach by valuing and mobilizing existing assets and supporting locally led efforts which are required to address change. A strengths-based approach has the potential to recognize and address political economy aspects of climate change adaptation, by explicitly handing over the power to respond to those whose lives are affected. By focusing on what national governments, communities, and civil society already have, what they want to achieve, and can do to increase resilience and to collectively and inclusively manage responses to disasters, much more can be achieved than by focusing on gaps, weaknesses, and vulnerability.

A strengths-based approach has the potential to bring about better results to climate change response, as confirmed by extensive analysis of activities in Pacific countries. Research by McNamara et al. (2020) highlighted the value of locally determined and locally led efforts to address the impacts of climate change through assessment of community-based adaptation initiatives in Pacific Island countries. This extensive research, covering 32 programmes in 20 rural communities, found that 'locally-funded initiatives were, for example, proportionately more evident among high-and medium performing initiatives ... (In contrast) internationally funded initiatives ... dominated the low performing category' (McNamara et al., 2020: 631). The researchers found 'instead of external actors attempting to foster local approval and ownership, initiatives need to be driven by the community, where approval and ownership are inherent' (p. 636). They concluded that 'rather than experiments in communities to improve their adaptive capacity deficit, communities would, in community-led adaptation, build on their strengths and design/drive their own adaptation aspirations on the basis of local knowledge, experiences and coping mechanisms' (p. 638).

McNamara et al. (2020: 638) noted that 'the role that implementors and donors should and can play is to become "facilitators" of the desired adaptation aspirations for communities, rather than "doing" adaptation "to communities" under the guise of community-based adaptation'. These research findings align with a strengths-based approach as described in earlier chapters of this book.

McNamara et al.'s (2020: 638) research concluded:

> Despite the supposedly development deficit that is projected on communities from the outside, such communities have always been resilient, and there is still much that the community-based adaptation field can learn from traditional governance systems, coping strategies and Indigenous knowledge. Our findings suggest that it is time to support these communities' diverse capacities and allow their situated and tacit resources to flourish.

The authors' own experience of working with communities on the topic of climate change also accords with McNamara et al.: Pacific Island communities use a wealth of expertise, experience, and local assets to adapt to climate change.

In another context, Fuchs et al. (2019) present the 'building assets and agency' approach taken by the Accelerating Adoption of Agroforestry project in Kenya, the objective of which is to scale the adoption of context-specific adaptation and mitigation options. They conclude 'that the approach fosters sustainable engagement of rural community groups in self-driven development by providing a people- and community-centred, socially acceptable model, which gives groups ownership of the contents, and to some extent, of the process in the context of externally supported development projects' (Fuchs et al., 2019: 704).

In the context of climate change adaptation work, communities' ability to envision their own future and work towards it, with support if and where required, is critical, as echoed in the strengths-based practices described in Chapter 3. Anna Gero described how she now incorporates a strengths-based tool, a future visioning exercise, during her workshops. She recalled,

> I didn't realize it was a strengths-based approach. It just seemed a positive way to finish. I did it in Yap in the Federated States of Micronesia. I asked a group of people (chiefs, dignitaries and community members) to close their eyes and think about their vision for the next 20 years. In the end, they really got into it and said it was a really positive experience to collectively envision their preferred vision for the island, and it drew on their strengths and assets. They used pictures to communicate their messages. Creative expression clearly opens up a different part of one's brain and helps people think about what's possible in different ways.

There have been shifts in some quarters to both theorize and practise climate resilience in ways which recognize the potential to respond based on existing assets. Climate resilience can be generally defined as the adaptive capacity for a socio-ecological system to: 1) absorb stresses and maintain function in the face of external stresses imposed upon it by climate change and 2) adapt, reorganize, and evolve into more desirable configurations that improve the sustainability of the system, leaving it better prepared for future climate change impacts (Folke, 2006). The notion of resilience as a focus on what is possible within the existing system as opposed to what is lacking, is well-aligned to thinking and practice of a strengths-based approach.

Development worker experience, research, and the development of new theoretical frameworks all demonstrate the application of a strengths-based approach to climate change and disaster risk, and highlight its future potential to address global and local consequences of the climate crisis.

Economic development

Economic development is a common agenda within international development and can be focused at different scales from community to national levels. At community level, the focus is usually on livelihoods, micro-credit, entrepreneurship, and improved efficiency and effectiveness of agriculture or other small-scale businesses. At national levels, programmes seek to strengthen institutions and links between them as well as economic policies which influence market processes, private sector efficiency, and growth. Programmes can be designed within an economic growth agenda or in the interests of reducing inequalities and increasing economic justice.

Increasing and more widespread use of a strengths-based approach is evident at the community level, with its emphasis on strengthening household and community livelihoods, but less obvious at national programming levels. There is scope for economists to learn about the value of this approach for their work in strengthening economic development institutions and systems. Potential applications and implications are discussed here.

A strengths-based approach is of considerable value at the community level. Major and proven contributions of a strengths-based approach include extending and improving efficiencies and effectiveness of existing livelihoods, mobilizing local assets to achieve shared economic goals, and strengthening community ownership and leadership of change agendas. Case studies 2, 13, and 16 all illustrate the contributions made to livelihoods and related community-level economic development.

Numerous other examples of a strengths-based approach have been documented in community livelihood projects. For example, a detailed study of economic development in the island province of Bohol in the Philippines (Cahill, 2010) documents implications of a strengths-based approach for community enterprise. Cahill's research considered the contested nature of power relations in community development related to a programme called *Jagna Community Partnering Project*. This programme applied participatory, strengths-based, and action research approaches to build on informal economic practices to establish community enterprises. Cahill found the programme 'disrupted the hegemony of local development discourses, catalysing profound changes in the lives of project participants who moved from perceiving themselves as passive and dependent recipients of development to self-reliant and active decision-makers' (Cahill, 2010: iii). Such a shift confirms the value of supporting citizens to see their power over their lives differently, including in terms of economic productive capacity.

Another example is an evaluation of a savings and literacy-led alternative to financial institution building in Nepal. The evaluation by Ashe and Parrott (2001) identified the value of local ownership and control in line with a strengths-based approach. The authors noted: 'The poor can meet most of their credit needs through internally generated savings. Access to credit from an external source of credit supplements internally generated savings if available' (Ashe and Parrott, 2001: 11).

In another example in Solomon Islands, a community in the Nggela Islands group participated in a strengths-based approach workshop facilitated by Anglican Board of Mission Australia in partnership with a local NGO, *Inclusive*

Communities Program, as part of the Australian Government-funded Solomon Islands NGO Partnership Agreement (SINPA) (Case Study 2). Following the identification and mapping of their assets, the community realized that their most valuable asset was their reef which was being overfished and destroyed by their own community. As part of their vision for the future they collectively decided to stop fishing the reef for six months followed by a much more sustainable set of fishing and reef harvesting practices. They sent a delegation to the capital Honiara to find technical expertise and advice on best practice for sustainable sea farming. They also decided to set up a cooperative to collect fish and engage one local family to take it to market in the capital and sell it rather than continuing the practice of each family taking the two-hour boat journey to the capital to sell their individual catches.

A special issue of the *International Journal of Appreciative Inquiry* titled 'The Impact of Appreciative Inquiry on International Development' (2011) includes articles describing the practice's value in economic development-focused initiatives. For example, women's saving and loan groups linked to a community-based organization in India employ Appreciative Inquiry to craft visions for the future. Visions cover economic development, social development, clean villages, and environmental development. Actions to achieve these visions are decided and carried out. Through the process women 'start talking and sharing stories of their past and present capacities, they highlight their achievements, unexplored potentials, core values, innovations, strength, best practices, moments of high point and competencies' (Singh et al., 2011: 22). This process fuels ongoing commitment and action of the group. In another article, Mann et al. (2011) describe the use of Appreciative Inquiry in the design of a forestry project in Liberia, highlighting the value of the processes to engage all key actors and use available strengths and assets from this group.

At a national level, a strengths-based approach offers a range of benefits for progressing economic development outcomes. These include taking a systems perspective, which ensures all actors who can contribute to change are brought into the process. The appreciative focus of inquiry provides a constructive platform for engagement and collaboration between different groups. It also draws out and uses local strengths and assets. Ownership and authority of local actors are premised within a strengths-based approach. The approach legitimizes the role of government in leading policies for economic development.

These same benefits from a strengths-based approach can also be realized regionally. An example of the power of self-driven economic development, linked to a focus on strengths, is found in the fisheries sector in the Pacific region (Aqorau, 2019). In *Fishing for Success* Aqorau (2019) described Pacific Government efforts to improve benefits to the region from tuna fishing. The report told 'how a group of eight countries, considered to be small, vulnerable and dependent on others, managed to establish the most sustainable and profitable tuna venture in the world' (Aqorau, 2019: xiii) through their efforts as Parties to the Nauru Agreement (PNA). In the preface to the book, the Secretary General to the Pacific Islands Forum, Dame Meg Taylor, stated:

> This book articulates the remarkable journey of commercial innovation and ingenuity, and transformation of power structures against the odds. ... At its core, the Parties to the Nauru Agreement (PNA) emerged from a shared vision for self-determination through an unwavering commitment by 'the right set' of personalities who had a clear understanding of the regional environment and its culture to ensure that this collective fishing initiative not only took hold, but thrived.
>
> The success of the PNA is a stellar example of the unswerving commitment by resource owners to take control of their fishery rights on their own terms and conditions. Since its establishment, the agreement has grown from strength to strength – testament to the political strength and ownership behind this industry shown by the eight PNA states. The fact that they have transformed the value of economic returns from the tuna fishery from US$60 million in 2010 to around US$500 million in 2019 is no mean feat, especially when it relates to small island developing states (Aqorau, 2019: xiii).

Education

Application of and positive outcomes achieved from a strengths-based approach in the education sector in western country contexts are well-evidenced. However, despite the high profile of education programmes in international development, little documented evidence has been found that a strengths-based approach has been applied. A UK-focused book titled *Celebrating Strengths: Building Strengths-based Schools* (Fox Eades, 2008) described the practice and success of applying a strengths-based approach in schools and success in building flourishing school communities, flourishing staff, and flourishing pupils. Lopez and Louis (2009) described the principles of a strengths-based approach in the education sector. Meier (2020) provided a theoretical analysis and practical guide on the use of a strengths-based approach for pre-school literacy. A book about a donor-funded education programme in Pacific countries also emphasized the value of a strengths-based approach (Johansson-Fua et al., 2020).

A strong alignment of the philosophical underpinnings of the strengths-based approach can be found in concepts which are central to education. In particular these include a focus on the inherent potential within each individual student, and the value of drawing together strengths and assets of different actors, recognizing that the education system is made up of students, teachers, parents, and government ministries: that is, a school community.

Focus on education within the international development sector encompasses different levels or scales. Some programmes address systems to promote institutional change and longer-term benefits. Others focus on local and community-based initiatives where students and teachers interact in classrooms. The SDG focus on education illustrates the broad range of desired education outcomes. Goal 4 is to 'ensure inclusive and equitable quality education and promote lifelong learning opportunities for all' and it comes with seven associated targets. Example targets include primary and secondary school completion rates, access to education, elimination of gender disparity, upgrading school facilities, and increasing numbers of teachers. These example targets are mirrored in education programmes in international development.

A strengths-based approach has been applied in the education sector in many national contexts, and in international development programmes in this sector, positive results have been significant. For example, in Papua New Guinea, a strengths-based approach was explicitly used in part of a large Australian Government-funded programme, the Basic Education Development Program (see Case Study 17). A component sought to rehabilitate long-neglected education facilities across remote locations through community engagement. Large numbers of District Women's Facilitators were trained in the use of a strengths-based approach. They visited over 3,000 schools with Ministry of Education inspectors across most provinces, many in villages which had not previously been accessed by education authorities. Together, they supported community members to identify their own abilities, resources, and interests in improving education facilities, using a customized variation of Appreciative Inquiry. The women facilitators reported extraordinary responses to this process, with many village members immediately taking action to fix classrooms using existing resources, even before their visit was over. With such actions, using locally available resources, only a small contribution from the programme, the cost of a few iron sheets for a new roof for example, was required. Beyond financial benefits, the approach generated pride and ownership of schools.

In an education programme in Laos titled 'Schools of Quality' implemented by UNICEF and the Ministry of Education (MoE) and funded by various donors from 2005 to 2012, a strengths-based approach was applied to supporting ongoing quality improvements at school level. An independent evaluation of the programme in 2009 identified a wide range of benefits associated with this approach. For example, it found:

> MoE noted that they are able to provide support to schools in ways that match the needs of schools, rather than insist on a 'one-size-fits-all' approach. ... with the implementation guidelines written by MoE, decisions can be made to respect and build upon existing strengths, provide different inputs to suit different schools' needs and histories and adjust approaches based on feedback and experience. For example, at Provincial level, the MoE has promoted the identification of model schools for demonstrating to other schools how SoQ [schools of quality] dimensions can be integrated. At the school level, the use of school self-assessments, a key step in the SoQ approach, promotes local decision-making about priorities based on community participation (UNICEF, unpublished: 20).

Government donor-funded aid programmes in the education sector tend to focus on strengthening national institutions and infrastructure, both of which benefit from a strengths-based approach. Just as all students have existing talents which can be nurtured for their future wellbeing, all countries' education systems have assets and strengths, which can be recognized and mobilized as a means to strengthen the delivery of education services. When development agencies support the recognition and mobilization of these assets, rather than paint a picture of missing elements and weaknesses, the potential for strengthening education systems and achieving SDG 4 can be achieved. As described in Chapter 11, capacity development which is central to strengthening institutions should and can employ a strengths-based approach as a means to catalyse positive change and strengthened educational outcomes.

Case Study 17 Using local assets to improve school infrastructure in Papua New Guinea

A large, multi-year national education programme in Papua New Guinea, called the *Basic Education Development Program* (BEDP), began using a strengths-based approach to fully engage the whole community in the management of primary schools. During its first five years, the programme was regarded by the donor, AusAID, as 'gold standard' due to the use of a strengths-based approach and excellent results. However, for the last two years of the project, the donor shifted focus from community involvement to infrastructure development and as a consequence the programme was critically reviewed (Packer et al., 2009: 28–29).

BEDP was the second phase of an Australian Government-funded collaboration to improve the quality of primary-level education across Papua New Guinea. An evaluation of the first phase identified there had been little progress, especially because of a lack of community ownership. The second phase, implemented from 2004 to 2010, covered all 3,000+ primary schools in Papua New Guinea. It aimed to enhance the capacity of school boards to manage school infrastructure and improve the learning environment for primary school children. A specific focus of the managing contractor, Coffey International, was to put the community at the centre of managing primary education facilities.

A 2008 review concluded that the project was:

> a path-breaking project in terms of community engagement and gender mainstreaming. It was found to be well-designed with sufficient flexibility to evolve during implementation. A high level of stakeholder participation and ownership was noted, especially at the school and community levels, and capacity was being built in ways likely to lead to significant improvements in the delivery of primary and community infrastructure maintenance (Tagagau and Pettit 2006: 28).

Two key features of the programme's approach to capacity development were the introduction of a strengths-based approach and a focus on local women's leadership. It was envisaged that school boards would facilitate a whole-of-community asset mapping and mobilizing process in each location. This process was expected to

(Continued)

Case Study 17 Continued

identify past and existing strengths and set a vision for a favourable education environment for each community's children. Local women leaders, chosen through the National Women's Association, were expected to drive the process and act as links with the respective Provincial Departments of Education.

Within two years, the initial process rolled out across Papua New Guinea. In each location, a two-day event led by trained local women and the respective education inspector enabled representatives from the whole community to come together to consider the future of their schools. This included parents, leaders, business and trades people, youth, and local government representatives. The use of Appreciative Inquiry and ABCD included stories of past community achievements, active listening, group engagement, asset mapping, role plays, drama, and focused social inclusion. This mix of elements ensured everyone's potential talents were included to generate community consensus on actions needed, both immediately and later. Each community agreed upon their own 'picture' of the most desirable-looking primary school environment and what potential resources they could immediately access to achieve that vision.

Women were selected on the basis of their prior experience as change agents and focus on good educational outcomes, though they were neither educational experts nor paid workers. They were trained in leadership and supported through collaborative networking. Some used their experience and learning to achieve many other positive benefits.

Helping communities learn how to use their available assets, skills and resources, traditional values, and existing management structures began with stories of success. These were experiences of each community's previous achievements; this directly built self-confidence and motivation. Working separately with youth, women, and men in groups provided the opportunity for everyone to be heard and to identify their respective contributions.

To further enhance community capacity, a training strengths analysis was undertaken (in contrast with training needs analysis). This produced increased confidence and a list of existing skills among teachers, parents, and school board members; those with skills became the core group for in-service district-level peer-to-peer training, supplemented by outside expertise only when appropriate.

Outcomes and impact

As a result of the strengths-based work undertaken, all communities became involved in multiple changes to improve their school environment, both immediately after the visits and for the foreseeable future. This included repairs and building new classrooms using only locally sourced material and volunteer labour. It also included noticeable improvements in discipline, gardens, security, sanitation, and welcoming and support for teachers from other parts of the country. The benefits were obvious both inside and outside the classroom. As reported in many of the monitoring visits, some communities began to shift their attitude towards ongoing education for girls.

The messages behind the strengths-based approach such as: 'we can do it ourselves', 'change starts from within', everyone has something to offer', 'when shared, we have abundant resources', 'everyone can have a dream', and 'women

(Continued)

Case Study 17 Continued

play an equal role in change' all started to be integrated into the school curriculum and other parts of community life. This was confirmed in reports of six-monthly meetings of volunteer women coordinators, and stories of change generated through monitoring.

The educational impact of a fully engaged school community taking responsibility to ensure the educational environment was most favourable to learning for all became particularly obvious in remote schools. It takes days of travel from even the smallest of towns to reach some villages. In one change story collected as part of programme monitoring, where teachers had been absent for an extended period from a remote school in Bougainville, parents used textbooks to help children learn, and as a result every child passed the final national examination, for the first time in their school history.

In terms of value for money, one quantitative survey in 2007 showed that financial contributions by communities were typically up to three times more than those provided by the programme. Community members donated wood, labour, equipment, and expertise as managers, carpenters, and engineers. Authorities at the provincial level were astounded to find there were no cases of stolen goods or pilfering of supplies left on roadsides or near the schools. In many villages, the same approach was then used by community members for other aspects of life such as income generation, agriculture, and health improvements.

Towards the end of the programme, the Australian Government changed focus to fund only prefabricated classroom blocks with no community input. Communities were sidelined and their involvement discouraged. All activities were carried out by sub-contractors from urban centres. The lack of community ownership and engagement simply reaffirmed that education was no longer a whole-of-community responsibility. Consequently, like killing the goose that laid the golden eggs, a subsequent evaluation unsurprisingly concluded that there were 'weak links with broader reforms in the education sector', and like other big projects that responded to need alone 'there is a lot of activity for a few years and then there is nothing' (Packer et al., 2009: 29).

Food security and agriculture

Efforts to secure food security through agriculture-focused projects have been core to international development for decades. Food security is of central concern to communities dependent on subsistence farming, as well as crucial for many others. The Food and Agriculture Organization (FAO) defines food security as when 'all people, at all times, have physical, social and economic access to sufficient, safe and nutritious food that meets their dietary needs and food preferences for an active and healthy life' (FAO, 1996). Food security has four interrelated elements: availability (quantity, quality, and diversity of food); access (economic and physical access to food); utilization (means to use nutrients of food through broader community and household conditions); and stability (food security at all times). This multi-dimensional perspective of food security means that international programmes and projects must take on a broad remit to be able to influence change.

There is clear alignment between a strengths-based approach and ways to influence food security. Recognizing the multiple dimensions of food security, there is clear value in including broad and multi-stakeholder perspectives. A strengths-based approach has a strong focus on engaging with stakeholder groups and drawing on diverse sets of knowledge and strengths to inform action towards change. A strengths-based approach also enables inquiry into what has worked well in the past, to identify cultural values and priorities for agricultural practices and sustainable livelihoods. For example, in Pacific Island countries many communities are prioritizing traditional land and marine systems management to ensure food security from their natural resources. A strengths-based approach seeks to identify and elevate local values as a means to support constructive change and development. Pacific farmers are encouraged to maintain healthy diets through traditional staples such as taro, yams, sweet potato, and cassava instead of imported foods of rice, flour or noodles. The Handbook *The Staples We Eat* produced by the Pacific Community noted, 'traditional staple foods play a very important role in the life of Pacific Islanders. Despite early food colonization and influence of western lifestyles on food habits, traditional staple foods are highly regarded, not only as a means for sustenance but as the basis for meaningful exchanges of culture' (Malolo et al., 1999: 9). Yet as noted by the Asian Development Bank (2011: viii), 'food security, which was once highly associated with local and traditional agriculture and fishery products, has assumed a different connotation for the Pacific countries, as it has in the rest of the world. It is now closely influenced by trends of rapid urbanization, increasing food importation, and shifts away from traditional and subsistence (food) production systems'.

Focus on what has worked well in the past is evident in *Towards a Food Secure Pacific: Framework for Action on Food Security in the Pacific*, endorsed in 2010 by the Pacific Island Forum leaders. The framework promotes local and traditional production and supply of nutrient-rich foods and emphasizes greater community involvement as part of institutional capacity development for implementing food security and climate change adaptation.

A strengths-based approach is appropriate to identify and champion local and traditional practices of food production, embedded in local values and practices. The authors and many interviewed for this book have extensive experience using a strengths-based approach in agriculture- and food-security-focused programmes. For example, Martin Wanjohi, Senior Consultant based in Nairobi, Kenya, when interviewed for this book, said:

> I recall you (Chris Dureau) were helping design the Food Security aspect of our program in Malawi and Tanzania. You said that we should stop talking about 'food security' and start talking to the communities about how to reach 'food abundance'. I thought that is an incredible paradigm shift from the way we have been thinking in the past. Yes, I thought, the soil is there, the water is there, and we have our own strengths – why not think about what we can do with our own hands, why not dream about how we can be eating healthily, not only meeting relevant SDG targets

but producing and making food available in abundance. It is in our own hands and will come from our own efforts to change our own cultural practices about gender inequality and live healthy, wholesome lives.

The experience of the Family Farm Teams programme in Papua New Guinea is another strong example of how a strengths-based approach has been used to strengthen food security outcomes (Pamphilon, 2015) (see Case Study 14). The programme has been examining, developing, and facilitating ways to build the business acumen, skills, and knowledge of women farmers in Papua New Guinea. Recognizing connections between food security, leadership, gender relations, and other factors, a programme report noted, 'All women leaders reported an improvement in their skills and knowledge from their involvement in the leadership training (Building leaders from the inside out). The strengths-based approach that began the course helped women identify and value their leadership roles in the family and the community' (Pamphilon, 2019: 34).

Gender-based violence, domestic violence, and child protection

Programming to address gender-based and domestic violence and child protection is a key feature of contemporary international development. Family violence is a serious societal issue in every country in the world (Garcia-Moreno et al., 2006). It may seem counter-intuitive to apply a strengths-based approach to domestic violence, but its relevance and application demonstrate the core essence of this approach. A strengths-based approach does not deny the presence of negative experiences, tragic circumstances, social injustice, or criminal activity. These negative realities are acknowledged and need to be sanctioned by law. One of a suite of potential contributions to respond to such situations is recognition of inherent human strengths. In the context of family violence, strengths of women and children are at the centre of catalysing change. Importantly, this discussion does not underplay the seriousness and extent of violence and abuse and it does not seek to portray the victims or survivors of violence and abuse as 'lacking strength' or needing to strengthen themselves. Rather this section seeks to draw on experience of the use of a strengths-based approach in responding to violence and abuse.

As described in Chapter 2, language matters and there has been a historical shift in terms used to describe gender-based violence from 'victim' to 'survivor'. Advocates argue that the term victim, while relevant in court proceedings, may contribute to a sense of powerlessness. The term survivor positions the focus on the power inherent within each individual and seeks to enable an individual to take control of their future life, when they are ready and with support, as appropriate. Of course, it is imperative to follow the lead of the person seeking support and use the term preferred by them. A strengths-based approach premises the capability of an individual to determine their own future.

Programming that seeks to influence change in gender-based violence, domestic violence, and child protection operates in many ways: at systemic and individual levels; and in both formal and informal spheres. A framework to guide programmes commonly used is the Gender at Work Framework (Rao et al., 2016). This framework recognizes the importance of multiple dimensions of change. At the broader society level, it includes informal levels (norms, attitudes, and behaviours) and formal levels (legal frameworks, laws, and policies). At the individual level, it includes focus on women and men (to have awareness and appreciation of gender equality). In addition, it refers to women having resources and access to rights to realise their potential for equality.

A strengths-based approach enables change in both individual and systemic spaces. For example, the emphasis on language central to a strengths-based approach drives consideration of key terms and phrases which have a deep impact on individuals' lives. Language affects self-esteem, self-assessment, and human agency. This and other key elements of a strengths-based approach are highlighted in Case Study 18, about Imarisha Maisha, a programme in Kenya focused on justice and equality.

At a systemic level, a strengths-based approach provides a practical means to engage a broad range of actors in realizing change for gender equality. Transformative change is required to end domestic and gender-based violence. A strengths-based approach emphasizes and enables transformative change by seeking to engage all stakeholders and recognize efforts made by organizations, networks, activists, support programmes, and carers to prevent violence. Transformative change seeks to enable new possibilities for gendered relations.

A strengths-based approach has been used extensively to address and respond to gender-based and family violence in many country contexts. Case Study 7 is an excellent example of this, describing an anti-violence programme in South Africa, called the *Sinakho Safe Community Network*. The programme is supported by a group of organizations including Australian Anglican Overseas Aid and has effectively used a strengths-based approach in achieving its objectives. The programme began with a focus on helping women address domestic violence. The strategy initially sought to identify a network of 'safe persons' but after realizing violence was part of many aspects of community life, they turned to creating a vision of a safe community network. The Department of Social Responsibility of the Diocese of Grahamstown are implementing the programme and finding their approach is contributing to significant positive changes.

An example of the use of a strengths-based approach in child protection is the *Pacific Children's Program*, initially funded by AusAID and then continued by UNICEF. The first phase of the programme worked in Fiji, Samoa, and Vanuatu, with interested partner organizations, both government and civil society. Informed by a strengths-based approach, a community-based programme for child protection was grounded in respect and value of Pacific cultures in the protection of children. The programme sought to engage families and communities in conversations about how love, care, and protection for children were demonstrated. The programme illustrated how change happens within a strengths-based approach, by 'crowding out' negative behaviour and elevating preferred practice. The package has since been adopted by the Fiji Ministry of Women, Children and Poverty Alleviation (previously known as Department of Social Welfare) which is responsible for child protection. The 'Children are a Gift from God' manual has been used in child protection outreach activities by the Ministry for many years. Using a strengths-based approach, the manual has proven to be an effective facilitation tool in encouraging community participation around potentially contentious issues (UNICEF, n.d.). The programme is described as 'tapping into community values to support child protection' (UNICEF, n.d.).

There is extensive literature on the use of a strengths-based approach in gender-based violence and child protection in western country contexts. For example, a Canadian-focused book *Investing in Children, Youth, Families, and Communities: Strengths-Based Research and Policy* (Maton et al., 2004) advocates a strengths-based approach to family-based research and social policy. Instead of deficit-based models of social problems, resiliency models are advocated. Resiliency models identify and promote factors associated with competence and positive developmental outcomes. In the UK and other high-resource countries, the benefits of a strengths-based approach in social work, including in child protection and domestic violence prevention, have been researched widely and supported by government policy (for example, see Baron et al., 2019).

This discussion confirms that a strengths-based approach has already been successfully applied in multiple settings to address violence and has the potential to contribute more. While not the only approach that can usefully contribute to positive change, a strengths-based approach can support individuals, as well as direct community engagement on improving policing and justice processes. It can also play a useful role in the development of systemic changes, including gender relations, strengthened governance, and reconciliation processes.

Case Study 18 Generative change in addressing gender-based violence in Kenya

The *Imarisha Maisha Project*, focused on gender-based violence and child protection, is currently managed by Anglican Overseas Aid (AOA) with funding through the Australian NGO Cooperation Program. In Swahili, *Imarisha aisha kwa kuzingatia haki na usawa* means 'strengthening lives by promoting justice and equality'. Building on a partnership since 1996, this phase began in 2017 in Chaka and Thangathi in Nyeri County, central Kenya. A strengths-based approach was applied in design and implementation, consistent with AOA's use of this in all its work.

The stated aim of the Project is 'to improve community self-reliance and identify strategies that improve the quality of life for all'. This vision for a better future was intentionally chosen instead of a negative description of gender-based violence and child neglect. The project aims to improve family harmony, increase economic activities for both women's and men's groups, and indirectly remove many of the triggers for domestic violence and child neglect. The project involves improving relationships and communications within and between families; strengthening existing community structures; and opening avenues for engagement with schools and government officials.

(Continued)

Case Study 18 Continued

Strengths-based training is the foundation and starting point in all participating communities. This focuses on mobilizing existing resources and skills and encourages participants to use their own local knowledge to achieve a shared vision of the future.

Florence Nderita, the previous Programme Coordinator for the Anglican Diocese of Mt Kenya West, learned about the strengths-based approach in 2010 as a result of AOA's involvement in AACES (see Case Study 13). Florence was about to retire from her community development work when she first learned about ABCD and the whole mindset of strengths-based approaches. When in Melbourne for a work visit, she said: 'this approach so completely re-invigorated me that I decided to continue as I could see it had a much greater ability to achieve effective results'. The Project Officer, James Senjura, a Masai Elder, recalls how the Masai community became aware for the first time that they had bountiful knowledge about priorities and could quantify their valuable assets such as cows, goats, land, and labour. In an interview for this book, James Senjura said: 'Development can only happen when it comes from the community itself and the community needs to start by realizing their assets'. He said, 'the people realized these assets can become the power base to advocate for improved government support and endorsement, especially in promoting human rights and enforcing adherence to national legislation on child protection and gender equality'.

Communities are best suited to identify their own strengths, rather than outsiders. In fact, explains the current Programme Coordinator, Millicent Wambugu, 'now that communities are empowered, they are finding that they are better at coming up with solutions to suit their situation. When they were depending on outsiders to make decisions for them, they found that they do not address what is actually happening in the community'.

Imarisha strengthens the role of local leadership and community-level institutions. This includes engaging and enhancing the role of the *Nyumba Kumi* (community police force). The *Nyumba Kumi* changed from simple policing to advocating for human rights and a safer, equitable, and just community. Men and women re-examined their respective roles, looking for existing and potential skills development towards a more equitable distribution of labour. Now, home duties and income generation are shared between men and women. Stronger agriculture and livestock support groups emerged, with shared resources. Savings and loan groups (known as *tabletop banking*) and a programme to purchase and then loan out communally owned assets (known as *merry-go-round*) were also established. Community members allocated their own excess resources such as land and physical assets for communal purposes, thereby strengthening community cohesion and helping people to rely on each other. This approach particularly connected with vulnerable individuals and families.

Drawing on local practice, traditional homes, called *manyattas*, were built alongside the government's health facility, where women from distant villages could stay before and after giving birth. *Manyattas* have cooking facilities, a bed for a helper to stay, and added warmth for cold weather. As a result, the number of women giving birth in health facilities increased from 10 to 40 per cent since the project began, leading to a remarkable decrease in infant mortality (von Kalm, 2018).

(Continued)

Case Study 18 Continued

Millicent Wambugu said: 'Compared with the more traditional approach that we used previously and is still being used by other agencies, the project objectives of *Imarisha* are realized very quickly because communities are able to be the champions of their own development course'. She listed the key outcomes of the approach as: greater self-reliance from the use of their own assets; greater agency to determine what is best for the future; stronger sense of ownership; stronger and many more local associations; the resurrection and adaptation of indigenous structures; and the sustainability of initial efforts demonstrated by an ever-expanding network of functional groups within and outside the community.

An evaluation report prior to the latest phase concluded: 'The project is working towards a system of community-based protection, strengthening accountability in the community for one another's safety, and equipping grassroots structures to act on abuse and the findings suggest that this innovative approach is providing an appropriate and effective method to reducing violence against women, men and children, and promoting safer, more resilient communities' (Caulfield, 2016: 34).

Governance and social accountability

The term social accountability describes a broad range of citizen-led activities and initiatives to increase state accountability and improvements in delivery of public services. Originally framed as a contest between citizens and states, in practice effective social accountability approaches embody a strengths-based approach.

Social accountability emerged within the development sector in response to a view that traditional forms of accountability, through political and institutional mechanisms, were failing to ensure the accountability of states to their citizens. The World Bank Development Report 2004, *Making Services Work for Poor People*, was influential in identifying lack of accountability as a primary reason for service delivery failure in low-income countries. This report promoted citizen engagement as a means to address poor accountability, and in turn improve services for the poor (World Bank, 2004).

The language of social accountability initially portrayed a dichotomy between citizens and states, whereby citizens demanded accountability from governments. Joshi (2008) described this as 'the confrontational nature of accountability' (p. 14). The emergence of social accountability was also informed by recognition of citizen participation within a rights-based approach to development (Gaventa, 2004), as a means of achieving good governance and improving aid effectiveness. Since then, research, including Keren Winterford's PhD research, highlighted that the simple dichotomy between citizen and state does not take into account the ways in which collaborative action works within social accountability activities. 'There is a need to go beyond the simplistic dichotomy of supply and demand towards a recognition that state and society do not exist in isolation from one another. In practice, the lines between them are blurred; they may be interdependent and mutually constructive' (Citizenship DRC, 2011: 39).

A strengths-based approach is evident in the practice of social accountability. For example, Citizen Voice and Action is a social accountability approach which aims to increase dialogue and accountability between service users and government for the improved delivery of basic services (World Vision UK, 2016). The approach was initially piloted by World Vision International in nine countries from 2005 to 2010 and is now being implemented in more than 30 countries in Africa, Asia, Eastern Europe, and South America. Keren's PhD research was conducted between 2007 and 2012, based on interviews in Uganda and Armenia with local government officials, service providers, and service users who had participated in Citizen Voice and Action activities. Six senior World Vision staff, responsible for coordinating Citizen Voice and Action in Armenia, Uganda, Brazil, and India, were also interviewed. The experiences of Citizen Voice and Action revealed the practice and benefit of a strengths-based approach.

Citizen Voice and Action practitioners described a strengths perspective as a foundation for their facilitation, as illustrated in the following example: 'I think maybe every human being has some potential insights. The important thing is ... facilitation. It tries to release this potential, creates space, creates a condition, [and] creates an environment to release this potential' (Citizen Voice and Action Practitioner, Armenia). Government representatives were engaged through the Citizen Voice and Action approach; they were invited on the expectation they would engage constructively with solutions and action for improved service delivery. Participants in the process noted:

> Even when we invite the Government to come, I will do this with the perspective that the Government will bring solutions to help and not we will invite them to kill them or to blame them (Citizen Voice and Action Practitioner, Brazil).

> So it's not all about 'you've done wrong'. You – it's all about you, but it's about okay, I have this to do and you have this. So where have we gone wrong and how can we put the things together and then we move on (Citizen Voice and Action Practitioner, Uganda).

Citizen strengths were also described as the base from which citizens were able to advocate and influence government action. One World Vision staff member said: 'when we strengthen the base, they can also advocate for themselves'. Another Citizen Voice and Action facilitator confirmed this, noting that strengths were the foundation from which citizens were able to advocate to the state:

> The strength is the foundation. Before you solve the deficit, the problem. Just like when you are beginning a house, it's the foundation that matters ... So you begin with the strength. If those people are not strong enough, they can't solve this deficit because they won't be able to go and demand for it. When they work on their strengths that they have, then they will be able to demand from others (Citizen Voice and Action Practitioner, Uganda).

Keren's PhD research highlighted a connection between a rights-based approach and strengths-based practice, which is also described in literature on strengths-based practices. For example, Mathie (2006: 3) wrote: 'belief in one's own capacity inspires the confidence to bring about change, to seek out opportunity. Confidence in one's own capacity to act is also the basis for people to claim the rights to which they are entitled by virtue of citizenship, or to exercise influence through the political processes'.

Social accountability practice, through a strengths-based approach, seeks to reveal and catalyse all assets and resources from citizens and the state for improved service delivery. It seeks to strengthen relations, dialogue, and shared commitment for action, blurring the divide between contested relations for joint action. A Citizen Voice and Action Practitioner in India told Keren Winterford: 'Whereas in other [approaches], like social auditors it's just like blame shifting. But that's the point where you break the relationship between the service provider and the service user. But in this CVA [Citizen Voice and Action] entire approach, the whole thing is built on the relationship, even those service providers not providing services, but how we can approach them'.

Citizens are able to advocate for change informed by their own action and increased self-esteem and hope for the future, as described in the practice of Citizen Voice and Action. For example, one woman community member in Armenia told Keren:

> We are very happy and we started to believe in ourselves ... It wasn't to happen before because we always were waiting that someone would come and establish something for us. We didn't think that we could also do this [advocate to local government for a kindergarten] ... you had to believe in yourself, you have to believe in good future ... I feel so good. When I think that the building has already been worked on and I feel so great.

Health systems strengthening and health security

A strengths-based approach is applicable to all aspects of health, international cooperation in the strengthening of health systems, and global health security. The COVID-19 pandemic shines a spotlight on the critical nature of national health systems' ability to respond to emergencies. It also highlighted the critical role for high-resource countries to extend existing capacity to other parts of the world, in many different and varied ways. Starting with existing strengths and supporting all aspects of a health system, from aged care workers to national emergency response planning systems, to reflect on lessons learned and mobilize towards a shared vision for the future, is an appropriate way to improve health systems across the globe.

In the international development sector, increasing focus is being given to health systems strengthening. Efforts to contribute to strengthening health systems are inevitably complex and long term, given the many parts of the system and need for all to work in synergy with each other. Every country in the world is continually striving to respond to existing and changing health priorities of citizens over time, with vastly varied levels of resources.

A strengths-based approach to collaborating with other countries in the health sector recognizes efforts made by health practitioners and officials over decades as a basis for achieving ongoing changes. Global commitment to universal health care, for example, will require collective efforts, based on respectful collaboration, which will be achieved much more efficiently through a strengths-based approach.

An example of the use of a strengths-based approach in improving health services is found in 44 village community centres in West Lombok, Indonesia (see Case Study 4). These community health centres have established agreements with 15 government clinics to improve health services and revitalize government initiatives involving citizens, achieved through a strengths-based approach.

Another important shift in public health programming relates to language about the factors which make people unhealthy or healthy. Historically and understandably, language in the health sector focuses on illness, health burden, and factors that contribute to ill health and disease. Traditionally, therefore, it is not surprising that problem-based approaches have dominated work in the health sector, both within countries and in international development programming. Salutogenesis, an approach coined by Antonovsky (1979) to describe actions that support human health and wellbeing, has emerged as a valid and valued concept in health care (Bauer et al., 2020). It highlights the benefits of focusing on and maximizing the factors that contribute to good health, such as good diet, exercise, regular testing, prevention of communicable diseases, and managing stress. This contrasts with pathogenesis, which focuses on the factors that cause disease. A salutogenic perspective provides an opportunity to use a strengths-based approach to bring about health and wellbeing at global, national, and local levels.

Some public health and preventive health efforts which seek to bring about positive changes in social and individual behaviour, known as health-seeking behaviour, also use a strengths-based approach. Successful examples of public health campaigns achieve their goals by generating the levels of motivation and energy for people to behave in positive ways.

Community health services which aim to prevent or minimize the harmful effects of illness also benefit from the use of a strengths-based approach. Consistent with the positive psychology aspects of a strengths-based approach (Chapter 7), the promotion of positive health-related behaviour has a much greater response than demands for the cessation of negative behaviour.

There are many examples of the use of a strengths-based approach and health projects in international development. For example, Dewi et al. (2018) studied use of an asset-based approach to tuberculosis (TB) leadership groups in three villages in Flores Island, Indonesia, with positive outcomes. The approach generated 'significant changes in the TB groups' view of outsiders and their relationship with the villagers, built dialogue between group members, strengthened local initiatives that could reduce the rates of TB and encourage early diagnosis and therefore treatment, and encouraged community engagement' (Dewi et al., 2018: 340). A community-led health and wellbeing project in Mozambique also employed this approach. As stated in an evaluation of the project, 'using a strengths-based approach, the program is enabling communities to define their own assets and use them to address core health and well-being priorities. There is also strong community ownership and engagement in the program' (Ascroft, 2016: 1).

Case Study 19 Positive Deviance study of health clinics in eastern Indonesia

In 2013–2014 a large health provider called CD Bethesda received funding to identify ways to improve the effectiveness of village health posts (*Posyandu*) in Sulawesi Tenggara, a province in eastern Indonesia. With guidance from Chris Dureau, the Positive Deviance approach was chosen as the method for part of this research.

CD Bethesda was set up in 1974 as a community development outreach programme for the Bethesda Hospital in Yogyakarta, Central Java. Its aim is to provide a primary health care service, especially for marginalized community members 'outside the walls of a hospital'. It is now a national programme, providing services across the Indonesian archipelago.

The Integrated Health Service Post (*Pos Pelayanan Terpadu* or *Posyandu*) was decreed in the 1980s by the Government of Indonesia to be set up in every village as an entirely voluntary local organization. While the focus was to reduce infant mortality, the *Posyandu* became responsible for monitoring several aspects of community health including maternal and early childhood health; nutrition; health promotion; immunization; and disease control. *Posyandu* operations are supported by a doctor and staff from the servicing clinic at the sub-district level and volunteer village health cadre. In the beginning these volunteer '*kader*' were young women with little authority or access to resources. Their lack of influence or their ignorance of traditional health practices and disconnection with traditional birth attendants were among early criticisms of the system. Notwithstanding these issues, the system flourished until the 1997 financial crisis when communities became extremely poor and their focus on meeting basic needs meant support for *Posyandu* was reduced. In the early 2000s the Ministry of Health called for a 'revitalization' of the *Posyandu* across Indonesia. It is within this context that CD Bethesda decided to consider how Positive Deviance and a focus on mobilizing local assets might be used as a driver for that revitalization process. According to one international review of similar community health programmes, the *Posyandu* is today perhaps the largest and longest running community-driven health initiative in the world (Perry et al., 2017: 58).

Research carried out by CD Bethesda in 2013–2014 sought to answer the question, 'What opportunities are there to revitalize the *Posyandu* using local assets in the District of Sulawesi Tenggara?' The research explored the potential assets, opportunities, and challenges of *Posyandu* across four districts in the province. Sample locations were chosen in each of the four districts, and nearly 1,000 interviews were conducted with individuals and groups. The study compared poor families whose children were well nourished with families whose children were

(Continued)

Case Study 19 Continued

suffering from malnutrition. This second group comprised both poor families and relatively well-resourced families.

The study also compared activities of the village health cadre who played a facilitation role in the *Posyandu* programme and identified examples of effective cadre behaviour compared with others; that is, positive deviants. At the conclusion of the research, the findings and recommendations were presented to district-, provincial-, and national-level forums to improve health care at the village level.

While it is not possible to determine the long-term impact of these studies, it is clear that following this research many more *Posyandu* in this part of Indonesia are now functioning well. In an interview for this book, Christa Dewi who visited some of the communities in 2016 reported that, 'many communities are both proud of what they have achieved to revitalise their communities and full of enthusiasm to continue their efforts, especially in their use of locally available traditional crops to improve their nutrition, such as "daun kelor" or moringa, a plant that grows in everyone's backyard'. Also the use of Positive Deviance and the desire to identify and mobilize local assets have demonstrated a clear path towards improved effectiveness and better resourcing of community-driven maternal child health care.

In comparison with other programmes where the revitalization of *Posyandu* has been considered (Luthfa, 2019; Sari, 2018), this research focused on how the *Posyandu* system can better use various local social, physical, natural, and financial assets for its continued operations. This focus is consistent with the objectives of using a Positive Deviance approach. There is limited space here to describe all the recommendations that emerged from the research but the following examples relating to 'revitalization' illustrate key findings for health workers, health clinic staff, and community leaders responsible for *Posyandu*.

- Active and committed volunteer health workers who are also aware of traditional health practices and how to supplement food intake with traditional sources.
- Health workers and leaders promote collaboration and integration with other women's village networks.
- Health workers and participants of *Posyandu* acquire the ability to access and to promote traditional medicines including practising how to grow them.
- Health workers and community leaders work with traditional birth attendants and integrate their work with that of the *Posyandu*.
- Community leaders foster the use of traditional and nutritious food sources, such as papaya flowers and leaves, fish, and crustaceans including crabs both from the rice fields and from the sea.
- Health workers and community leaders access government subsidies provided to the village so that they are directed to improving *Posyandu* services.
- Government Health Clinic staff and sub-district leaders utilize monthly sectoral meetings to promote the *Posyandu*.
- Key village leaders and their partners at sub-village, village, and sub-district levels ensure that the *Posyandu* is well patronized and personally supported.

(Continued)

Case Study 19 Continued

As a result of the success of the use of Positive Deviance in this research, Christa Dewi used her doctoral research a few years later to challenge CD Bethesda's traditional approach to treating TB. Working with three village communities in Sikka District of Flores Island, Dewi applied an asset-based approach with considerable success (Dewi et al., 2018). 'The big difference was in the transfer of the ownership of the process from the NGO to the people themselves and the sustainability of the efforts when the community learned that they could manage the treatment and future prevention through their own efforts', Christa said when interviewed for this book. So substantial was the change brought about by both these examples that today CD Bethesda's focus is the design and implementation of primary health care programmes that are entirely based on the mobilization of local assets.

Humanitarian responses and recovery after disasters

While a strengths-based approach has been most relevant to development programming to date, it is also relevant and practised in disaster responses and support for recovery processes.

It is helpful to consider humanitarian responses in relation to the notion of the 'humanitarian-development nexus' mentioned at the beginning of this chapter or a 'humanitarian-development-peace nexus'. The nexus challenges the status quo which distinguishes long-term project-based development and humanitarian interventions. The increased focus on this nexus seeks to build from and reinforce long-running efforts in the humanitarian and development fields, such as 'disaster risk reduction'; 'linking relief rehabilitation and development'; the 'resilience agenda'; and the embedding of conflict sensitivity across responses.

Humanitarian responses, particularly in relation to extreme weather events due to climate change, are often associated with separate though linked phases: preparedness, response, and recovery. Increasingly each of these phases is connected to and benefits from a strengths-based approach.

A strengths-based approach is particularly advantageous in preparedness and disaster responses as it is founded on recognition that communities and countries have often experienced disasters previously and have recovered in many ways before. Obvious questions such as 'what worked well to minimize harm when a community or country was affected by a previous disaster', or 'what worked well in the recovery last time', provide rich information as well as motivation and energy required to plan preparedness for future disasters.

The current emphasis on localization of disaster responses illustrates the critical importance of a strengths-based approach, since local responders need to be motivated and energized to achieve their objectives, rather than portrayed as lacking and falling short of externally imposed standards. Emphasis on localization also recognizes and respects the role of preparedness and response being primarily in the hands and control of local actors, especially those directly affected by disasters.

A body of work on the use of strengths-based thinking in disaster and humanitarian contexts has emerged since the 2000s. For example, a major New Zealand review of approaches to psychological recovery from disasters (Mooney, 2011: 31) found:

> Historically, the psychosocial needs of individuals and families/whānau have been seen from a vulnerability perspective (i.e., pathology such as post-traumatic stress, anxiety states and depression). ... Needs or strengths assessment of active local community participation is a challenging but necessary component of recovery efforts. Active community participation and using individuals' own capacities and resources can reduce perceptions of having recovery imposed without any consultation process.

Recovery after disasters often requires more community-based or national leadership and local motivation and effort than external technical responses. Thus, support for communities to acknowledge their own strengths and to mobilize them to recover after disasters can be a major contribution to long-term results and to future recovery. The example of Vanuatu's response to Cyclone Harold in 2020, without considerable external support, confirmed the reality that local responders and locally led responses are both possible and effective, even if they do not necessarily match externally determined standards and measures of success. Kenni and Wijewickrama (2020: 1) found,

> While not flawless, the Cyclone Harold response in Vanuatu proved the viability of the localization concept, even as it highlighted the vast challenges that come with delivering a complex humanitarian response amid enormous constraints. For this reason, it will likely be a point of no return for humanitarian response in Vanuatu. After demonstrating that they can manage a major disaster response with limited external capacity, in a global pandemic, heavy reliance on international experts is a thing of the past.

An example of the use of Appreciative Inquiry in recovering from a natural disaster occurred as part of the Japanese humanitarian response to the Great East Japan Earthquake and Tsunami in 2011. In an interview for this book, Shinko Tana, the then Advisor to the International Rescue Committee, said she applied the approach in her work in Ishinomaki City, Miyagi Prefecture. Shinko Tana previously worked on the ACCESS programme (see Case Study 16) as a staff member of IDSS based in Melbourne, Australia. During this time, she became aware of a strengths-based approach. In monitoring visits to ACCESS, she was struck by the level of energy, enthusiasm, and delight the villagers showed when reporting on their activities: 'I remember the faces of these people; how their eyes lit up when they talked about their successes'. Years later, when confronted with what was happening to the elderly people in the fishing community in Ishinomaki in Japan, Shinko realized that Appreciative Inquiry would be useful to give them hope and a way to plan their future. Modifying the words and phrases to suit the circumstances of

Case Study 20 Rebuilding with the community after a natural disaster in Indonesia

This case study demonstrates that it is more important to have a strengths-based way of thinking than to set out to apply any specific methodology or tool. It also shows how outsiders with a 'help the victim' mentality can miss the mark in terms of lasting and effective reconstruction work.

The Aceh Rehabilitation Program was the Australian Government's response to the massive earthquake and tsunami in December 2004. The Local Governance and Infrastructure for Communities in Aceh (LOGICA) programme was part of this response. Banda Aceh, the northernmost province of Sumatra in Indonesia, was the worst-hit region, with 170,000 deaths, widespread destruction of infrastructure, and 500,000 displaced people. LOGICA was an immediate effort to assist local communities and authorities to respond to the situation where more than 110,000 houses were completely destroyed along with 3,000 kilometres of road, 14 seaports, 11 airports, 2,000 school buildings, 8 hospitals, and 120 bridges (Nazara and Resosudarmo, 2007).

LOGICA demonstrated all aspects of a strengths-based approach without specifically using a particular methodology. It was designed to build back from the inside out, in contrast with more traditional development approaches which plan interventions from outside. It also explicitly included those who were expected to benefit from the project in design and delivery, in contrast to approaches which separate the implementers from the beneficiaries. The project sought to 'give the people a voice' in what was prioritized and how activities were implemented. The design used existing and proven successful management structures and processes from pre-tsunami. Although it was not described as such at the time, this project was a good example of adaptive development programming design, where the intention and initial inputs were clear but the direction changed in response to ongoing results and the challenges presented in the emerging context (Valters et al., 2016).

The project also built on the strengths of existing networks and engaged with people who best knew the local context. Implementation began with a search for agencies and individuals who were having success on the ground and then developed collaborative arrangements with them to do more of what they had found to be useful. It engaged community resources where they could be found and drew on traditional knowledge in building construction. In contrast to a logical framework design, implementation was undertaken using an adaptive and 'learning by doing' theory of change.

In response to the observation that local people affected by the tsunami of December 2004 were not engaged or even being consulted about the reconstruction programmes, AusAID official Bernadette Whitelum and her colleagues chose to recognize the competencies of the survivor community and to support them to re-engage and reorganize so that they could take the lead in rebuilding and reorganizing their lives. The programme began by providing space and resources for local leaders to engage with their devastated population, so they could be registered and organized and then contributions from external donors could be appropriately coordinated.

LOGICA started small and grew exponentially while remaining flexible to emerging challenges. Over time the initially identified 'entry points' became less relevant than the mobilization of local resources to meet emerging needs. LOGICA

(Continued)

Case Study 20 Continued

supported communities to act quickly and collectively on issues that needed to be addressed immediately. For example, as a result of the tsunami, not a single building was left standing which meant there were no indications of who owned what land. The Indonesian Government commissioned the World Bank to carry out a land survey using the latest equipment and methods. However, while the survey was being designed in New York, the community were not in a position to know where to start rebuilding. Rather than wait for the survey results (which could have taken years), under LOGICA, each household negotiated land boundaries with their surrounding neighbours and had that agreement at least temporarily endorsed by local authorities. This made it possible for them to rebuild their houses and community service buildings. When the 'official' surveying project finally arrived, they did not need to do anything other than endorse the decisions of the local community.

Where other projects brought in engineers and builders from across the globe to rebuild houses according to foreign designs drawn up in far-away places such as the UK, USA, Germany, and Australia, LOGICA provided up to 70 'roaming technical advisers' who were available to support traditional reconstruction efforts so that local tradespeople could rebuild for themselves. LOGICA also trained more than 2,400 village cadres who had nothing tangible to offer the communities but were there to facilitate the community's own efforts at reconstruction. Unlike many other programmes working with village volunteers, the cadre recruited and trained by LOGICA had no specific agenda or sector plan to be implemented. During a mid-term evaluation, Chris Dureau inquired about the contribution of LOGICA to village reconstruction, and villagers all said, 'well nothing really because we did it all ourselves, but we could not have done it without them'.

Where most other projects focused on the enormous 'needs' created by the devastating tsunami, LOGICA looked for remaining assets. Other projects engaged the beneficiary community through a 'hand over' event after infrastructure had been constructed, whereas LOGICA engaged the community as integral partners from the start of any reconstruction work. Most other projects ignored or bypassed local leadership structures, whereas LOGICA chose to strengthen these as the first priority. Most projects designed their interventions in remote places, whereas LOGICA provided local people with the resources to design their own recovery. Most projects had fixed designs, while LOGICA used an adaptive design: even after 10 months of operation, the activity flow chart was markedly different from that of the original design.

Mohammad Najib, the Team Leader, reflected on the programme in an email communication with Chris Dureau. He wrote:

> The strengths-based approach we used in LOGICA strongly influenced our whole way of working and all our activities right up to the end. At the time we considered this approach most appropriate for a humanitarian response because it was based on mobilizing local capacity and assets and AusAID gave us the policy framework to apply this approach. Looking back now I can see that it was very successful because what came out of LOGICA's work in local governance was eventually taken up not only across the Aceh Province but also applied nationally in governance reforms at the sub-district (Kabupaten) level.

local partners, Shinko realized that 'ai' is the word for love in Japanese and so it not only became the approach but the theme for the whole programme. Each community recalled the roles they played and how they had gained expertise through years of experience. They looked at what was left after the tsunami and what assets and competencies they could use. They considered where they thought they could get back to, including what they could sell to restore their livelihoods and what they needed to do to reach their goal of attracting tourists back to the region. She concluded, 'the Appreciative Inquiry process was a mutual learning opportunity for everyone. All the NGOs really appreciated the chance to learn from rather than teach the communities they were working with'.

Law and justice

A strengths-based approach in law and justice has an important role in contributing to stronger organizations, effective collaboration, respectful engagement, evidence-based planning, and strengthening team work and motivation within and between institutions in the sector. While clearly not appropriate in the actual process of arresting and prosecuting criminals, a strengths-based approach contributes to the respect, energy, and motivation required within judicial agencies and police services to bring about the kinds of change sought by governments themselves, including those supported by development programmes. Changes ranging from stronger legislative frameworks and better functioning judicial systems to effective community policing and correctional services can be achieved through use of a strengths-based approach. The approach can also support community justice systems, through emphasizing communities' abilities to manage conflict and crime and to settle disputes in locally relevant ways. A strengths-based approach is also useful in contexts where human rights issues are the focus of attention (for example see Landry and Peters, 2018).

In the area of legislative drafting, a strengths-based approach is a means to ascertain the strengths of existing laws and engage with communities about existing resources. It is also an approach for mobilizing collective will and energy towards new laws.

In the area of strengthening judicial agencies – courts, prosecutions offices, inter-government anti-corruption groups, for example – a strengths-based approach is useful for recognizing and valuing existing assets and resources as the basis for future planning and for generating the levels of inter-agency respect and collaboration needed to bring about systemic change.

Policing services around the world clearly experience a range of challenges, often as very large workforces working with and between governments and communities. As they respond to issues and events, the levels of expertise required in planning, mobilizing, and motivating large groups of people are particularly high, so a strengths-based approach can be relevant. Police development programmes in Pacific countries, for example, currently seek to strengthen selected aspects of police expertise, from cross-border cyber-crime to community violence prevention. Therefore, methods which support staff learning, institutional change, and rapid responses through valuing past efforts and motivating positive energy are relevant.

Engaging in complex human rights conversations can be supported by use of a strengths-based approach, particularly in contexts where different understandings of human rights prevail. While much is written about the universality of human rights agreements, different countries' legal systems interpret responsibilities under these agreements in different ways. In Solomon Islands, the former team leader of a major programme in the justice sector, Alice McGrath, found value in the use of a strengths-based approach when engaging on issues associated with holding people in prison after they allegedly broke rules associated with the COVID-19 lockdown, when there were insufficient resources to expedite their cases through the judicial system, resulting in overcrowding. The team leader recounted that by focusing on previous success by the judicial system to address overcrowding in the corrections system, conversations led to a different approach in the second lockdown and reduced incarceration rates.

Where communities and governments are interested in enabling people who have been involved in the criminal justice system to return to community life, a strengths-based approach has been found useful. For example, research in the Australian context highlights the role of a strengths-based approach in social work in criminal justice settings (Harvey and Petrakis, 2019). In cross-cultural justice settings, a strengths-based approach is included in training run by the National Criminal Justice Training Center in the US for those involved in corrections in indigenous communities (National Criminal Justice Training Center, n.d.). The course description states:

> Promote healing, enhance public safety, and reduce recidivism in your role as a tribal community corrections professional. During this training, you will explore strengths-based supervision strategies and case management skills for the following populations on probation: probationers with mental illness, alcohol and substance abuse addiction, and domestic violence offenses. Engage in a variety of activities to enhance your ability to effectively case manage high risk populations.

Water, sanitation, and hygiene

A strengths-based approach is useful in all aspects of water, sanitation, and hygiene (WASH). Globally, WASH is recognized as critical for human and economic development and the foundation of sustainable development, as well as other development goals, including health and gender equality. Where there is human life, a foundation exists on which efforts to improve access to safe drinking water and sanitation can be based. Improving access to water and sanitation, and increasing hygiene, involves the interaction of people, institutions, and policies, as well as the natural environment and infrastructure. The SDG targets related to WASH include: 'by 2030, achieve universal and equitable access to safe and affordable drinking water for all' (Target 6.1) and 'by 2030, achieve access to adequate and equitable sanitation and hygiene for all and end open defecation, paying special attention to the needs of women and girls and those in vulnerable situations' (Target 6.2). A strengths-based approach will contribute to achieving these goals, building on existing knowledge and assets in each context.

The intersections between WASH and other sectors, particularly health and nutrition, are well known. Access to clean water and sanitation helps reduce diseases and mitigates under-nutrition (Checkley et al., 2008). Access to WASH also contributes to health security, as evidenced during the COVID-19 pandemic in countries where low access to clean water exacerbated transmission. The global economic return on funds invested in the provision of WASH is reported to be high, given that it contributes to reduced health care costs, increased productivity, and opportunity for growth of new industries (WHO, 2012). Providing access to water and sanitation has been documented to increase girls' attendance at school (Jasper et al., 2012) and women's time used for productive and reproductive tasks, among other benefits.

As is the case with other development sectors, issues associated with WASH are as political and cultural as they are technical and economic, and are often portrayed in the negative. The way these elements interact, in the form of social accountability systems, power dynamics, gendered relations, and organizational responsibilities, confirms there is scope for a strengths-based approach, not just to support better service delivery but also to enhance coherence between WASH and other aspects of human life.

Extensive evidence of the use of a strengths-based approach in WASH can be found in Africa, Asia, and Pacific contexts. A World Bank paper from the 1990s, reviewing evidence from over 120 rural water supply projects around the world, highlighted the critical importance of community participation for project success (Narayan-Parker, 1995). While not explicitly referring to the use of a strengths-based approach, Narayan-Parker's analysis confirmed the centrality of positive engagement which is generated by respectful collaboration. The report found 'beneficiary participation was more significant than any other factor in achieving functioning water systems and in building local capacity. The degree of participation depended on local demand and organization, and particularly important were agency autonomy and the degree to which agencies accepted and monitored the goal of achieving local participation' (Narayan-Parker, 1995). Given the role of a strengths-based approach in contributing to positive beneficiary participation and effective local organizations, the connection is obvious.

Another example of use of a strengths-based approach in the WASH sector is evident from Engineers without Borders (EWB) Australia, a large NGO which champions a strengths-based approach. Each year EWB Australia partners with universities and a different community-based organization to develop and deliver the EWB Challenge programme (Engineers Without Borders, 2021). Students are encouraged to design creative solutions to real-world, community-identified projects. Representatives from the partner organization are invited to view the top student work at a showcase event, and all ideas are shared back with the potential for future development. One participant reflected on the use of a strengths-based approach in a Cambodia-based programme:

> When I went on the Humanitarian Design Summit, I'd just graduated as a software engineer. I was more comfortable around computers than people. I knew a bit about working with people to make good computer programs. I realized how important it was to be respectful guests of the community, realising at each step how little we knew. I learnt obvious questions were sometimes the most interesting, because we'd often get a reply I didn't expect. The experience helped me work with people's strengths, which also meant discovering where we weren't useful. I also learnt to be curious. Understanding the tiniest details is thrilling when that understanding can change people's lives for the better. But, it's important that it is by their own definition of better, not mine (https://ewbchallenge.org/ewb-challenge).

In conclusion, the examples provided in this chapter confirm that a strengths-based approach is relevant to and useful in every sector of international development cooperation that involves people and organizations. It is already being used in many contexts around the world. There is increasing research documenting its benefits for effective processes and for achieving desired developmental outcomes. It is clearly promoted by those who use it already as the best means to achieve the sustainable development goals and any other positive change in any sector, particularly where cross-cultural collaboration is required.

Case Study 21 Value for money in a WASH project in Tanzania

Scott Martin has been an Africa Program Manager for Caritas Australia for more than 17 years. He was interviewed for this book about his conversion to using a strengths-based approach in all his work.

In 2010, Caritas and its partners in Tanzania and Malawi received a grant from the Australian Government to work with remote communities in water supply and sanitation under AACES (see Case Study 13). When it was decided to use a strengths-based approach, Scott was initially not that convinced, but it did not take long before Scott and his whole team realized this approach was far superior to any used before.

This case study has been well documented in Caritas Australia programme reports and was provided by Scott at the time of the interview as an example of the sustainability and value for money that a strengths-based approach demonstrates. Scott explained this is particularly important since AusAID was subsumed

(Continued)

Case Study 21 Continued

into the Australian Department of Foreign Affairs and Trade (DFAT) and 'the major concerns were about value for money and sustainability'.

Endashang'wet is a remote village in Tanzania, over an hour's drive from the closest town. It is a place that the District Government officials thought was 'too remote, backward and too challenging'. So, when the Tanzanian Government asked Caritas to work there, given their own repeated failures, 'it was a natural fit for the AACES program of Caritas', reported Scott.

Following an introductory period during which a field officer stayed in the community to get to know and develop trust with the community members, the District Government and all relevant service providers joined the whole village for a week-long workshop using Appreciative Inquiry and ABCD. This was followed up by several community-run meetings to explore disused and potentially useful assets, skills, and resources in the environment. A range of support workshops including on Community-Led Total Sanitation and permaculture practices were also organized.

After this, the village-elected development committee set out to mobilize the whole community in the following activities:

- A long-disused water tank on the top of a hill near the community was repaired and connected to multiple community water outlets.
- A small electric generator pump house to take water from the river spring to the hilltop tank was installed.
- All families contributed labour to build clay bricks and some donations to construct a large, four room community centre, including water catchment from it.
- A sanitation demonstration centre was established around the community centre and included six model latrines and washstands, starting from no external cost to fully subsidized and all costed. Similarly, four models of septic tanks were designed. Community members were trained in how to build each.
- Recycling, composting, and organic fertilizing pits were dug and used for demonstration purposes.
- The land where the tank is located was converted from a dusty and cactus-covered mound to a tree and native grass-planted terraced area resulting in better water catchment and irrigation.

At the end of the five-year partnership between Caritas, the District Government and the community, a day-long celebration took place in which the community thanked Caritas for 'putting a fire under them' and getting them started on their own journey. The community also thanked Caritas for 'showing them they no longer needed aid from the rest of the world' because they have discovered so many resources they can use themselves.

Three years after Caritas finished working in Endashang'wet, Scott decided to return to see what remained. He found that 'the impact for the village was a total transformation at many levels':

- The Community Development Committee is active and engaged in the prosperity of the whole community and is ready to give a full report to visitors.

(Continued)

Case Study 21 Continued

- The community centre has now become a WASH Training Centre for people from surrounding villages and districts and is a significant source of income and endorsed by local government sponsorship.
- The community has its own song describing how beautiful Endashang'wet has become.
- The dusty cactus-filled surrounds of the village have become a cash-crop and vegetable-growing area.
- The health of the community has improved and together with an increase in local crop-growing has resulted in far more young people remaining.
- Toilets and washing facilities (tippy tap) have been set up at each house.
- Village-appointed 'caretakers' receive a stipend from the community for maintenance of the water system.
- The District Government now shows considerable interest in the community, providing ongoing support services (which did not exist before) and they have integrated this village's development into their own achievements.
- The National Government was so impressed with the efforts of this remote community that it provided the community with mains electricity for the pump house, the community centre, and for surrounding houses: a contribution of over A$100,000.

For Scott Martin, the initial agency investment comprised funds for a water pump (A$24,000) but this leveraged a government investment of A$102,000 and an ongoing partnership between government and community that is priceless. Scott concluded:

> The difference between what we did before a strengths-based approach and now is that a strengths-based approach is so much more effective, so much more owned by the community themselves and so much more sustainable in that it sets up the community and the District Government on a development partnership where both own the vision, commit to mobilizing assets and mutually manage the outcomes.

CHAPTER 13
Conclusion

> *I cannot see why anyone would want to go back to a needs-based approach. ... I have noticed that people sometimes appreciate what we are doing but immediately say that such an approach would not fit with the work they are doing. I would encourage people with this reaction to just go and look at the impact of the projects that are using strengths-based approaches. Talk to the people who have changed their lives in ways that fitted for them and for the futures they valued.*
> (Barbara Pamphilon)

We wrote this book to support those involved in international development to understand a strengths-based way of thinking and to show that it is a valuable and practical approach for engaging with the world and contributing to social justice and sustainable development. Our hope is that the book will contribute to a paradigm shift in international development, away from needs-based, problem-based, and expert-led approaches to a locally led, strengths-based approach. This is consistent with current movements towards localization and decolonization in the sector. It is also consistent with recognition of shared humanity and the necessity for global cooperation. While donors and development organizations have clung to the problem-based approach to date for various reasons, this is now discordant with contemporary agendas. External control of international development processes by donors and the primacy of western knowledge are not serving the interests of sustainable development outcomes and are no longer relevant. For the efforts of development organizations to become useful, it is time to change their approach.

We are confident that everyone will have found something of relevance to their life and work in this book. We are optimistic, consistent with our strengths-based approach, that some readers will make a substantial shift in their life and work. We acknowledge that, for some, the concepts may be a 'step too far', but as Barbara Pamphilon suggested, we encourage steps in this direction of a strengths-based approach.

This book explicitly seeks to reframe the core premise and practice of international development. At one level, the reframing shifts from a focus on problems to be fixed to a focus on strengths to be recognized and mobilized to bring about positive change. At another level, applying a strengths-based approach actually means the work of international development is understood quite differently. In this challenging third decade of the 21st century, there is no doubt that a significantly new way of thinking and working is necessary!

There is a commonly used saying about a new idea that it is 'a solution in search of a problem'. This book challenges the idea that offering solutions and searching for problems are meaningful concepts and approaches in this dynamic and complex world. The authors offer a way of thinking and engaging with the world which is relevant to the 21st century, recognizing the interconnectedness of humanity, shared development challenges, and priorities. The book affirms the reality that no single person, development programme, discipline, or country 'has the solutions' to another's problems. It offers a way forward that expands the size of the power pie so that more people have agency over their development future. It provides a way of working that enables communities, partners, organizations, movements, and people to achieve positive change, relevant to their contexts and desired futures.

Over 70 years since Truman described the role of high-resource countries to address the 'needs' of other countries (see Chapter 1), it is now clear that distinctions are way more blurred and problems cannot be solved through the transfer of funds or expertise from one country to another. In addition, there is shared recognition that issues and goals are shared, not limited to one group of countries or another. A strengths-based approach is about 'us all' bringing about change *for* 'us all', rather than 'us' bringing change to 'them'. As the stories in this book confirm, a strengths-based approach is a way of thinking and working that has universal value and application, at least wherever there are people involved in a change process. Recognizing that no one knows what the future holds, we suggest that a strengths-based approach will help us to constructively engage in whatever it is, since we will bring all of our strengths, resources, and what we uniquely have to offer to jump in and respond.

The dominant paradigm underpinning most international development policies and programmes is that countries comprise a set of problems, weaknesses, gaps, or challenges, and that development programmes are the means to fix a problem, address a weakness, fill a gap, and meet a challenge. The whole sector is based on mechanisms to organize such a process, from the initial analysis of specific problems to the construction of evaluation structures to identify the extent of contribution or attribution to results. Whole organizations are created to arrange the flow of funds and other resources to support this process. Whole careers are built on professionals' ability to undertake needs analysis, construct problem trees, or research/define the causes of problems, or conduct a ranking of vulnerability, inequality or poverty.

This book has revealed and promoted a different way of thinking and working, as well as showcased a set of organizations and a wide range of professionals who are already applying this on a daily basis. Stories from countries in Africa, Asia, and the Pacific confirm that the approaches are universal. Examples from sectors as diverse as governance, water and sanitation, economic development, and community health confirm that the approaches are relevant in most contexts. Reflections by people at all stages of their career and in diverse roles confirm that everyone can use and benefit from this approach. Illustrations from each step in a programme cycle confirm that a strengths-based approach generates different ways of working at all stages.

At the conceptual level, a strengths-based approach highlights some of the key themes relevant to international cooperation in the 2020s, particularly the importance of agency by those whose development is at stake. This is manifested in calls for greater localization in development programming and for greater ownership and leadership of people responsible for their own development. It is also central to the movement towards decolonizing knowledge and development. While these principles are not particularly new – they were clearly articulated in the Paris Declaration of 2005, for example – they are now much more central to mainstream development discourse.

A strengths-based approach also highlights the reality that sustainable, long-term developmental change is more likely to be the result of self-determined, locally led, and long-term processes of change among those whose development is at the centre, rather than short-term projects controlled by external interests. Again, this is not new: researchers, international agencies, and development workers around the world have regularly called for rethinking the development cooperation approaches which have dominated for decades. In the 2020s, with so many significant shifts occurring in global issues and power relationships, respectful and feasible collaboration are more necessary than ever. A strengths-based approach is a way of working that will contribute to effective collaboration as well as developmental change.

This book provides a weight of evidence and legitimacy for a strengths-based approach. The examples provided demonstrate that this approach is not a passing fad, but a serious reframing of development practice, underpinned by research in many sectors. International development approaches have not kept up with thinking and practice about how best to bring about change. A strengths-based approach to collaboration for change means revealing and catalysing existing strengths, visioning preferred futures, and working together towards these visions. When such processes are led by those at the centre of a change process and who have the vision for the future, supported by external collaborators, then success is achievable. Strengths-based support for and from each other to achieve shared visions helps to break down the 'us' and 'them' distinctions, replacing them with 'us' and 'us'.

The current problem-based approach which underpins international development practice is simply not suitable for achieving successful collaboration for change, across cultures and in every corner of the world. Successful collaboration requires trust and respect. Trust and respect require recognition of everyone's agency and potential, understanding of diverse cultural values, localization of goal-setting and decision-making, and decolonization. A strengths-based approach contributes to all of these layers.

As experienced international development workers and thinkers, we are not naïve about the extent to which shifts need to be made and perspectives about how 'development is delivered' need to be transformed. Perspectives on national interests from donor countries and concern about control need to be recalibrated with trust and respect for those whom you might be working with. Evidence from the past demonstrates the need for change. This book highlights that change is already under way.

Consistent with our strengths-based approach, we are optimistic that the many people who work in the international development sector have agency and influence on the way in which programmes are conceptualized, designed, implemented, and reviewed. We see increasing recognition of the importance of recognizing local voices in determining development pathways, of the value of cultural understanding and respect in change-oriented partnerships, and of the benefits of listening to development protagonists – that is, people and communities whose development is central – about what works from their perspective.

We are obviously not unique in calling for action to address collective global challenges. Clearly, governments which run development cooperation programmes should not be undertaking activities that threaten the global environment or increase poverty and inequality in other countries. Recognizing that we are all responsible for the future of the planet and that action is urgent requires a global response and much greater collaboration than ever before. A strengths-based approach will help us with these responsibilities.

A strengths-based approach, as illustrated by examples in this book, is relevant to and can operate at different levels and scales, from national development agendas to village-level interactions. Multinational organizations will find value in applying the approach, when negotiating complex global strategies to address shared change agendas. Bilateral agencies will benefit from engaging more effectively with the governments and organizations they implement programmes with. Governments determining and driving development programmes need to take this approach seriously to generate the changes that we all know need to happen, including improved national security. Use of a strengths-based approach by governments implementing aid programmes will have positive benefits because countries where programmes are operating will be acknowledged as sources of potential strengths to address issues. Developmental changes are clearly possible with a shift to using a strengths-based approach. The process of shifting approach will not be easy, but this book provides a foundational and proverbial kick in the right direction, an alternative pathway associated with reframing development. Ultimately, use of a strengths-based approach will contribute to donor countries and development agencies being seen as better global partners and neighbours.

At the level of development programming, the strengths-based approach will contribute to greater effectiveness through more trust-based connections with leaders and organizations in countries, and since they are ultimately responsible for change, their achievements might reflect positively on relationships with donor countries. The approach will save money, by avoiding spending on programmes that will not work because of poor cooperation and disrespectful relationships. The approach can certainly contribute to motivation, essential for achieving positive change, as well as ongoing efforts to tackle the long list of challenges faced by everyone in every context. The approach can also take the pressure off development organizations in high-resource countries that feel that sense of needing to 'rescue' others, the other side of the colonial coin.

For individuals working in international development, the strengths-based approach can be life-changing, invigorating, liberating, and motivating. The authors encourage readers from all corners of the international development sector to try using the approach. We suggest that a good development worker is open to shifting thinking and reflecting on their own ways of seeing and interacting with the world. We recommend you test it, work with others who have used it, reflect on how different your relationships and work are when you use a strengths-based approach, and share your experiences with others. Our experience and that of many who have told their story throughout this book is that the conviction of the worth of this approach comes after it has been tried and is based on results that are consistently beyond expectation.

At first, using a strengths-based approach may appear to be counter-intuitive, especially for those from the 'helping' sectors and those steeped in critical analysis methods. It may appear to some to be irresponsible. In reality, as evidenced by the research and stories captured in this book, a strengths-based approach is the opposite – your job will be much easier if you work in true partnership using this approach. Using a strengths-based approach lifts a huge weight off your shoulders, because you become less conscious of your own expectation that you can solve problems like poverty and injustice and 'save the world'. We simply cannot solve these problems, but we can work with others to address them, on a transformative change pathway. Our job is to support people, communities, and organizations to identify their own pathways and achieve their own goals. We can do this by enabling people to change their own perceptions of their strengths, enabling them to convert wicked problems (e.g. exclusion and inequality) into future visions and collective objectives (e.g. increased inclusion and equality). We can also support them to collaborate with others who can contribute to their own goals, and facilitate change processes with the combined expertise found in specialist and collaborative partnerships.

As long-experienced development workers, the authors know that big challenges such as gender inequality or water insecurity cannot be addressed by a three-year project or a two-way partnership. However, we are confident that reframing international development will help take us in that direction much faster than if we continue to take a problem-based approach.

The time has come and there is now unstoppable momentum to reframe the core of the international development sector. If we use a strengths-based approach in international development, we unlock the potential of shared global efforts and motivate collective action to realize positive change.

Websites and training manuals applying strengths-based approaches

Appreciative Inquiry (AI)

There are many resources available on the Appreciative Inquiry website of Case Western Reserve University in Ohio, USA. This website is referred to as Appreciative Inquiry Commons and has access to books, articles, research, bibliographies, practice tools, management, stories from the field, contact lists, and the best websites associated with AI. <https://appreciativeinquiry.champlain.edu/>

The *International Journal of Appreciative Inquiry* offers a constant flow of articles and examples relevant to a wide range of sectoral and geographical contexts. <https://aipractitioner.com>

The following guides have been developed for change practitioners:

>Ashford, G. and Patkar, S. (2001) *The Positive Path: Using Appreciative Inquiry in Rural Indian Communities*, DFID, IISD, MYRANA <https://www.iisd.org/system/files/publications/ai_the_positive_path.pdf> (Accessed 4 November 2021).

>Chowdhury, M.R. (2021) 4 Appreciative Inquiry Tools, Exercises and Activities, <https://positivepsychology.com/appreciative-inquiry-tools/>

>CSR (2005) *The Partnership Toolkit – A Facilitator's Guide to Partnership Dialogue.* <https://www.fsnnetwork.org/sites/default/files/partnership_toolbox.pdf> (Accessed 4 November 2021).

>CARE Nepal (2000) Appreciative Planning and Action: A Trainer's Guidebook <https://dokumen.tips/documents/care-nepal-trainer-guidebook.html> (Accessed 4 November 2021).

>The Mountain Institute (2000) *Community-based Tourism for Conservation and Development: A Resource Kit*, The Mountain Institute. <https://www.servicevolontaire.org/livres/developpement/projet_community_dev_manual.pdf> (Accessed 4 Nov 2021)

>O'Dell, M. (2000) The "Do it Now!" Appreciative Tool Kit, see downloadable doc at <https://aicommons.champlain.edu/educational-material/the-do-it-now-appreciative-tool-kit-a-collection-of-short-exercises/> (Accessed 4 Nov 2021)

The following website highlights some of the publications by Gustave Bushe, including academic discussions, guides and tools for applying Appreciative Inquiry. <http://www.gervasebushe.ca/appinq.htm>

Asset-Based Community Development (ABCD)

Useful and downloadable training resources can be found on the following ABCD website: <https://resources.depaul.edu/abcd-institute/Pages/default.aspx>

This includes publications such as basic manuals, training guides and introductory videos, podcasts, and toolkits. Generic tools in languages other than English are also available.

See also: McKnight, J. (undated) *A Basic Guide to ABCD Community Organizing*, Asset Based Community Development Institute, Northwestern University. <https://resources.depaul.edu/abcd-institute/publications/publications-by-topic/Documents/A%20Basic%20Guide%20to%20ABCD%20Community%20Organizing(3).pdf> (Accessed 4 November 2021).

Altogether Better (2019) 'Altogether better: helping health services and communities finding new ways of working' together [website] <https://www.altogetherbetter.org.uk> [accessed 27 January 2022].

The Coady Institute's work with ABCD is an extension of its philosophical roots in the Antigonish Movement, a people's movement for economic and social justice which reshaped the economy of north-eastern Nova Scotia (Canada) in the 1920s and 1930s. Coady Institute at St Francis Xavier University, Nova Scotia, Canada, conducts short courses on ABCD and related subjects. Some of its training materials can be found on the website <https://coady.stfx.ca/coady-publications/>. In particular the following is the course-based manual for ABCD training at Coady:

> Mathie, A. and Cunningham, G. (2008) *Mobilizing Assets for Community Driven Development*, Diploma Course, Coady International Institute, St Francis Xavier University, Antigonish, Nova Scotia, Canada. <https://www.academia.edu/727934/mobilizing_assets_for_community-driven_development> (Accessed 4 November 2021).

More specific project-oriented manuals can be found at:

> SEWA (2005) *An Asset-based Approach to Community Development: A Manual for Village Organizers*, Self Employed Women's Organization Jeevika project in association with the Coady International Institute. <https://coady.stfx.ca/wp-content/uploads/pdfs/SEWA_ABCD_Manual.pdf> (Accessed 4 November 2021).

> *The Jambi Kiwa Story* provides a guide to mobilizing assets in a rural community in Colombia. See <https://coady.stfx.ca/wp-content/uploads/pdfs/JAMBIenglishfin1(1).pdf> (Accessed 4 November 2021)

> Fuchs, L.E., Kipkorir, L., Apondi, V. and Orero, L. (2020) *Facilitating an Asset-Based Community-Driven (ABCD) Approach for Holistic Community Development: A Manual for Community Organising*, World Agroforestry (ICRAF), Nairobi, Kenya. <http://apps.worldagroforestry.org/downloads/Publications/PDFS/MN20057.pdf> (Accessed 4 November 2021).

Indianapolis Neighborhood Resource Center (2012) *Organizer's Workbook: Tools to Support Your Awesome Neighbourhood.* <http://www.inrc.org/files/file/inrc-book-2012update-web.pdf> (Accessed 4 November 2021).

Positive Deviance

The Positive Deviance Collaborative was launched in 2017 in place of the Positive Deviance Initiative. The main website contains access to resources, examples, locations of programmes, and toolkits. See: <http://positivedeviance.org>. To find guides and tools, visit the 'How to Get Started' tab on this website: <http://positivedeviance.org/guides> (both accessed 4 November 2021).

Community Economies

The Community Economies Institute is a research and action network that promotes this variant of a strengths-based approach. <https://www.communityeconomies.org/about/community-economies-research-and-practice> (Accessed 4 November 2021).

Perhaps the most practical website related to processes for promoting 'diverse community economies' is <http://www.communitypartnering.info/conducting76.html> (Accessed 4 November 2021).

Co-production

There are multiple articles and examples of Co-production related to health and social services especially across the UK. One such example is the Social Care Institute for Excellence (SCIE). Information on how to conduct Co-production can be found via its website: <https://www.scie.org.uk/publications/guides/guide51/> (Accessed 4 November 2021).

The Think Local Act Personal network also offers a practical guide to carrying out Co-production entitled *Public Services Inside Out* at this website: <https://media.nesta.org.uk/documents/public_services_inside_out.pdf> (Accessed 4 November 2021).

Positive psychology

From the perspective of a psychologist or counsellor, the following is a useful introduction:

Stoerkel, E. (2019) What is a Strengths-based Approach? <https://positivepsychology.com/strengths-based-interventions> (Accessed 4 November 2021).

References

Ackerman, P. and Duval, J. (2000) *A Force More Powerful: A Century of Nonviolent Conflict*, Palgrave, New York.

Aguinis, H., Joo, H. and Gottfredson, R.K. (2012) 'Performance management universals: think globally and act locally,' *Business Horizons* 55(4): 385–92 <https://doi.org/10.1016/j.bushor.2012.03.004>.

Ailon, G. (2008) 'Mirror, mirror on the wall: "Culture's consequences" in a value test of its own design', *The Academy of Management Review* 33(4): 885–904. <https://doi.org/10.5465/AMR.2008.34421995>.

Aldred, R. (2011) 'From community participation to organizational therapy? World Café and Appreciative Inquiry as research methods', *Community Development Journal*, 46(1): 57–71. <https://doi.org/10.1093/cdj/bsp039>.

Alsop, R., Mette, B. and Holland, J. (2005) *Empowerment in Practice: From Analysis to Implementation*, World Bank Publications <https://doi.org/10.1596/978-0-8213-6450-5>.

Anderson, M.B. (1999) *Do No Harm: How Aid Can Support Peace – or War*, Lynne Rienner, Boulder, CO.

Andonova, L., Faul, M. and Dario Piselli, D. (2022) *Partnerships for Sustainability in Contemporary Global Governance: Pathways to Effectiveness*, Routledge, London.

Anglican Board of Mission (2018) 'Philippines asset-based community development', Anglican Board of Mission [website] <https://www.abmission.org/projects/the-philippines/asset-based-community-development-project-vimrod/> [accessed 8 May 2023].

Anglican Board of Mission Australia (2018) 'IFI VIMROD Asset-Based Community Development (ABCD) Project in the Philippines' [video]. Available from: <https://www.youtube.com/watch?v=mPiqAWtkLrI> [accessed 6 February 2022].

Anglican Overseas Aid (2019) *Sinakho Safe Community Network: Evaluation Terms of Reference (TOR)*. Available from: <https://anglicanoverseasaid.org.au/wp-content/uploads/2019/10/Sinakho-Safe-Community-Network-Evaluation-Terms-of-Reference.pdf> [accessed 24 October 2021].

Antonovsky, A. (1979) *Health, Stress, and Coping*, Jossey-Bass Inc., San Francisco.

Aqorau, T. (2019) *Fishing for Success: Lessons in Pacific Regionalism*, The Australian National University, Canberra.

Aragón, A.O. and Pakpahan, D. (2015) *ACCESS II: Asset-based capacity building for local development: How do asset-based CB approaches uniquely support local empowerment?* Packard Foundation Capacity Development Study: Indonesia, Root Change, Washington DC. Available from: <https://www.researchgate.net/publication/286918595_ACCESS_II--Asset-based_capacity_building_for_local_development_How_do_asset-based_CB_approaches_uniquely_support_local_empowerment> [accessed 6 February 2022].

Arendt, H. (1958) *The Human Condition*, University of Chicago Press, Chicago.
Arendt, H. (1972) *Crises of the Republic*, Penguin Publishing, London.
Argyris, C. and Schön, D.A. (1978) *Organizational Learning: A Theory of Action Perspective*, Addison-Wesley Publishing, Boston, MA.
Armstrong, A.J., Holmes, C.M. and Henning, D. (2020) 'A changing world, again. How Appreciative Inquiry can guide our growth', *Social Sciences & Humanities Open* 2(1): 100038 <https://doi.org/10.1016/j.ssaho.2020.100038>.
Arnstein, S. (1969) 'A ladder of citizen participation', *Journal of the American Planning Association* 35(4), July 1969: 216–24.
Ascroft, J. (2016) *Community-led Health and Well-being Project Evaluation: Diocese of Niassa, Mozambique: An Executive Summary: November 2016*, Anglian Overseas Aid. Available from: <https://anglicanoverseasaid.org.au/wp-content/uploads/2017/01/2016-Moz-Exec-FINAL.pdf> [accessed 25 October 2021].
Ashe, J. and Parrott, L. (2001) *'Impact Evaluation, PACT's Women's Empowerment Program in Nepal: A Savings and Literacy Led Alternative to Financial Institution Building'*, PACT. Available from: <https://www.rfilc.org/wp-content/uploads/2020/08/1126180840123_PACT_s_women_s_empowerment_in_Nepal.pdf> [accessed 11 November 2021].
Asian Development Bank (ADB) (2011) *Food Security and Climate Change: In the Pacific - Rethinking the Options*, ADB Pacific Studies Series, Manila.
Australian Agency for International Development (AusAID) (2007) *Project Design Document ACCESS 2 Annexes*, AusAID, Canberra, Australia.
AusAID (2010a) *AIPRD Yogya Reconstruction Program Yogyakarta – Central Java Community Assistance Program (YCAP) Independent Completion Report*. Available from: <https://www.dfat.gov.au/sites/default/files/ycap-independent-completion-report.pdf> [accessed 24 October 2021].
AusAID (2010b) *Learning Assistance Program for Islamic Schools (LAPIS): Independent Completion Report*. Available from: <https://www.dfat.gov.au/sites/default/files/lapis-icr.pdf> [accessed 24 October 2021].
AusAID (2011) *Australia Africa Community Engagement Scheme: Program Design Document*. Available from: <https://www.dfat.gov.au/sites/default/files/aus-africa-community-engagement-design-doc.pdf> [accessed 24 October 2021].
AusAID (2013) *Samoa Disability Program: Final Design Document*, Government of Samoa and Government of Australia. Available from: <https://www.dfat.gov.au/sites/default/files/samoa-disability-program-design-document.pdf> [accessed 3 October 2021].
Australian Centre for International Agricultural Research (ACIAR) (2019) 'Improving opportunities for economic development for women smallholders in rural Papua New Guinea'. Available from: <https://www.aciar.gov.au/project/ASEM-2014-095> [accessed 25 October 2021].
Barnett, J. (2020) 'Global environmental change II: political economies of vulnerability to climate change', *Progress in Human Geography* 44(6): 1172–84 <https://doi.org/10.1177/0309132519898254>.
Baron, S., Stanley, T., Colomina, C. and Pereira, T. (2019) *Strengths-based Approach: Practice Framework and Practice Handbook*, UK Department of

Health and Social Care, London. Available from: <https://assets.publishing.service.gov.uk/government/uploads/system/uploads/attachment_data/file/778134/stengths-based-approach-practice-framework-and-handbook.pdf> [accessed 22 January 2023].

Barrett, F. and Cooperrider, D. (1990) 'Generative metaphor intervention: a new approach for working with systems divided by conflict and caught in defensive perception', *The Journal of Applied Behavioral Science* 26(2): 219–23 <https://doi.org/10.1177/0021886390262011>.

Baser, H. and Morgan, P. (2008) *Capacity, Change and Performance Study Report*, ECDPM Discussion Paper 59B, ECDPM, Maastricht.

Bauer, G.F., Roy, M., Bakibinga, P., Contu, P., Downe, S., Eriksson, M., Espnes, G.A., Jensen, B.B., Juvinya Canal, D., Lindström, B., Mana, A., Mittelmark, M.B., Morgan, A.R., Pelikan, J.M., Saboga-Nunes, L., Sagy, S., Shorey, S., Vaandrager, L. and Vinje, H.F. (2020) 'Future directions for the concept of salutogenesis: a position article', *Health Promotion International* 35(2): 187–95 <https://doi.org/10.1093/heapro/daz057>.

Bingley, K. (2014) *A Review of Strategic Foresight in International Development*, Institute of Development Studies, Brighton. Available from: <https://www.ids.ac.uk/publication/a-review-of-strategic-foresight-in-international-development> [accessed 20 January 2023].

Blundo, R. (2009) 'The challenge of seeing anew the world we think we know: learning strengths-based practice', in D. Saleebey (ed.), *The Strengths Perspective in Social Work Practice*, 5th edn, Pearson Education Inc, Boston, MA.

Bohm, D. (2004) *On Dialogue*, Routledge, London.

Bono, J.E., Davies, S.E. and Rasch, R.L. (2011) 'Some traits associated with flourishing at work', in K.S. Cameron and G.M. Spreitzer (eds), *The Oxford Handbook of Positive Organizational Scholarship*, Oxford University Press, Oxford.

Booth, D., Balfe, K., Gallagher, R., Kilcullen, G., O'Boyle, S. and Tiernan, A. (2018) *Learning to Make a Difference: Christian Aid Ireland's Adaptive Programme Management in Governance, Gender, Peace Building and Human Rights*, Overseas Development Institute, Christian Aid, Irish Aid. Available from: <https://cdn.odi.org/media/documents/12387.pdf> [accessed 3 October 2021].

Boulton, J., Allen, P. and Bowman, C. (2015) *Embracing Complexity: Strategic Perspectives for an Age of Turbulence*, Oxford University Press, Oxford.

Burchardt, M., Patterson, A.S. and Rasmussen, L.M. (2017) 'The politics and anti-politics of social movements: religion and HIV/AIDS in Africa', in M. Burchardt, A. Patterson, and L.M. Rasmussen (eds), *The Politics and Anti-Politics of Social Movements Religion and AIDS in Africa*, Routledge, Abingdon, UK.

Burnes, B. (2005) 'Complexity theories and organizational change', *International Journal of Management Reviews* 7(2): 73–90 <https://doi.org/10.1111/j.1468-2370.2005.00107.x>.

Burns, D. and Worsley, S. (2015) *Navigating Complexity in International Development: Facilitating Sustainable Change at Scale*, Practical Action Publishing, Rugby.

Burr, V. (1995) *An Introduction to Social Constructionism*, Routledge, London.

Bushe, G. (1995) 'Advances in appreciative inquiry as an organizational development intervention', *Organizational Development Journal* 13(3): 14–22. Available at: <http://www.gervasebushe.ca/aiodj.htm> [accessed 27 January 2021].

Bushe, G. (2001) 'Five theories of change embedded in appreciative inquiry', in D. Cooperrider, P. Sorenson, D. Whitney, and T. Yeager (eds), *Appreciative Inquiry: An Emerging Direction for Organization Development*, pp. 117–27, Stipes Publishing Company, Champaign, IL.

Bushe, G.R. (2007) 'Appreciative inquiry is not about the positive', *OD Practitioner* 39(4): 30–35. Available at: <https://appreciativeinquiry.champlain.edu/wp-content/uploads/2016/01/Appreciative-Inquiry-is-not-just-about-the-positive-Bushe.pdf> [accessed 5 February 2022].

Bushe, G.R. (2011) 'Appreciative inquiry: theory and critique', in D. Boje, B. Burnes, and J. Hassard (eds), *The Routledge Companion to Organizational Change*, Routledge, Oxford.

Bushe, G.R. (2013) 'Generative process, generative outcome: the transformational potential of appreciative inquiry', in *Organizational Generativity: The Appreciative Inquiry Summit and a Scholarship of Transformation* (Advances in Appreciative Inquiry, Vol. 4), pp. 89–113, Emerald Group Publishing Limited, Bingley <https://doi.org/10.1108/S1475-9152(2013)0000004003>.

Cahill, A. (2010) *Playing with power: a strengths-based approach to local economic development in the Philippines*, thesis (PhD), Australia National University <https://doi.org/10.25911/5d51541974cff>.

Cahn, E.S. (2004) *No More Throw-Away People: The Co-Production Imperative*, Essential Books, London.

Caulfield, T. (2016) *Evaluation Report: Imarisha maisha kwa kuzingatia haki na usawa: Just and Resilient Communities Project: Gender-based Violence and Child Protection*, Diocese of Mt Kenya West, Anglian Overseas Aid. Available from: <https://anglicanoverseasaid.org.au/wp-content/uploads/2017/10/Imarisha-Evaluation-Report-November-2016.pdf> [accessed 24 October 2021].

Caulfield, T. (2020) *Towards Abundant Life Program Evaluation: Diocese Missionária de Nampula, Mozambique, May, 2020*. Available from: <https://anglicanoverseasaid.org.au/wp-content/uploads/2020/07/Final-Eval-Report-Towards-Abundant-Life-22-May-2020-web.pdf> [accessed 25 October 2021].

Chambers, R. (1997) *Whose Reality Counts? Putting the First Last*, Intermediate Technology Publications, London.

Chambers, R. (2006) 'Transforming power: from zero-sum to win-win?', *IDS Bulletin* 37(6): 99–110 <https://doi.org/10.1111/j.1759-5436.2006.tb00327.x>.

Checkley, W., Buckley, G., Gilman, R.H., Assis, A.M., Guerrant, R.L., Morris, S.S., Mølbak, K., Valentiner-Branth, P., Lanata, C.F. and Black, R.E. (2008) 'Multi-country analysis of the effects of diarrhoea on childhood stunting', *International Journal of Epidemiology* 37(4): 816–30 <https://doi.org/10.1093/ije/dyn099>.

Citizenship DRC (2011) *Blurring the Boundaries: Citizen Action Across States and Societies: A Summary of Findings from a Decade of Collaborative Research on Citizen Engagement*, The Development Research Centre on Citizenship,

Participation and Accountability, Brighton. Available from: <https://assets.publishing.service.gov.uk/media/57a08aea40f0b64974000854/cdrc.2011-blurring.pdf> [accessed 22 January 2023].

COMPAS (Project) (2007) *Learning Endogenous Development: Building on Bio-cultural Diversity*, Practical Action, Rugby, UK.

Cooke, B. and Kothari, U. (2001) *Participation: The New Tyranny?* Zed Books, London.

Cooperrider, D. (1990) 'Positive image, positive action: the affirmative basis of organizing', in D.L. Cooperrider and S. Srivastva (eds), *Appreciative Management and Leadership: The Power of Positive Thought and Action in Organizations*, pp. 91–125, Jossey-Bass Publishers, San Francisco.

Cooperrider, D. and Srivastva, S. (1987) 'Appreciative inquiry in organizational life', in W. Pasmore and R. Woodman (eds), *Research in Organizational Change and Development*, Vol. 1, pp. 129–69, JAI Press, Greenwich.

Cooperrider, D. and Whitney, D.K. (2005) *Appreciative Inquiry: A Positive Revolution in Change*, 1st edn, Berrett-Koehler Publishers, Oakland, CA.

Cooperrider, D. and Whitney, D. (2007) 'Appreciative inquiry: a positive revolution', in S. Cady, T. Devane, and P. Holman (eds), *The Change Handbook*, 2nd edn, Berrett-Koehler Publishers, San Francisco.

Cooperrider, D., Sorenson, P., Yeager, T. and Whitney, D. (eds) (2005) *Appreciative Inquiry: Foundations in Positive Organization Development*, Stipes Publishing, Champaign, IL.

Cooperrider, D., Whitney, D. and Stavros, J. (2008) *The Appreciative Inquiry Handbook for Leaders of Change*, 2nd edn, Berrett-Koehler Publishers, San Francisco.

Cornwall, A. (2000) *Beneficiary, Consumer, Citizen: Perspectives on Participation for Poverty Reduction*, SIDA studies no.2, Swedish International Development Agency, Stockholm. Available from: <https://www.alnap.org/help-library/beneficiary-consumer-citizen-perspectives-on-participation-for-poverty-reduction> [accessed 5 June 2021].

Cornwall, A. (2003) 'Whose voices? Whose choices? Reflections on gender and participatory development', *World Development* 31(8): 1325–42 <https://doi.org/10.1016/S0305-750X(03)00086-X>.

Cornwall, A. and Rivas, A.M. (2015) 'From "gender equality" and "women's empowerment" to global justice: reclaiming a transformative agenda for gender and development', *Third World Quarterly* 36(2): 396–415 <https://doi.org/10.1080/01436597.2015.1013341>.

Csikszentmihalyi, M. (1990) *Flow: The Psychology of Optimal Experience*, Harper and Row, New York.

Csikszentmihalyi, M. (1996) *Creativity: Flow and the Psychology of Discovery and Invention*, Harper Perennial, New York.

Cunningham, I. (2021) *Designing for motivations in community-managed rural water supply*, thesis, UTS Digital Thesis Collection, Sydney.

Deci, E. and Ryan, R. (1985) *Intrinsic Motivation and Self-determination in Human Behaviour*, Springer, New York.

de Jouvenel, H. (2004), *Invitation à la Prospective*, Edition Futuribles, Paris.

Department of Foreign Affairs and Trade (DFAT) (2014a) *Aid Program Performance Report 2012–13 Indonesia*, DFAT, Canberra, Australia. Available from: <https://www.dfat.gov.au/sites/default/files/indonesia-appr-2012-13.docx> [accessed 22 January 2023].

DFAT (2014b) *Australia Africa Community Engagement Scheme: Mid Term Review*. Available from: <https://www.dfat.gov.au/sites/default/files/australia-africa-community-engagement-scheme-mid-term-review.pdf> [accessed 24 October 2021].

DFAT (2015) *Australia Africa Community Engagement Scheme: Effective Partnerships for Sustainable Development Program 2013–2014 (Annual Report)* DFAT, Canberra, Australia. Available from: <http://dfat.gov.au/about-us/publications/Pages/aaces-annual-report-2013-14.aspx> [accessed 24 October 2021].

DFAT (2016) *The Australia Africa Community Engagement Scheme: Effective Partnerships for Sustainable Development: Program review 2011–2016*, DFAT, Canberra, Australia. Available from: <https://www.dfat.gov.au/sites/default/files/aaces-program-review-2011-2016.pdf> [accessed 24 October 2021].

DFAT (2020) *Partnerships for Recovery: Australia's COVID-19 Development Response*, DFAT, Canberra, Australia.

Dewar, T. (1997) *A Guide to Evaluating Assets-based Community Development: Lessons, Challenges and Opportunities*, The Asset-Based Community Development Institute, Chicago.

Dewi, C., Barclay, L., Wilson, S. and Passey, M. (2018) 'An asset-based intervention with tuberculosis groups in rural Indonesian villages: overview and lessons learned', *Community Development Journal* 53(2): 340–57 <https://doi.org/10.1093/cdj/bsw037>.

Donnelly, J. (2010) 'Maximising participation in international community-level project evaluation: a strength-based approach', *Evaluation Journal of Australasia* 10(2): 43–50 <https://doi.org/10.1177/1035719X1001000206>.

Easterly, W.R. (2006) *The White Man's Burden: Why the West's Efforts to Aid the Rest Have Done So Much Ill and So Little Good*, Penguin Press, London.

Elgström, O. (1990) 'Norms, culture, and cognitive patterns in foreign aid negotiations', *Negotiation Journal* 6(2): 147–59 <https://doi.org/10.1111/j.1571-9979.1990.tb00565.x>.

Elgström, O. (2009) 'Trade and aid? The negotiated construction of European Union policy on economic partnership agreements', *International Politics (Hague, Netherlands)* 46(4): 451–68 <https://doi.org/10.1057/ip.2009.2>.

Ellerman, D. (2007) 'Helping self-help: the fundamental conundrum of development assistance', *The Journal of Socio-Economics* 36(4): 561–77 <https://doi.org/10.1016/j.socec.2006.12.014>.

Elliott, C. (1999) *Locating the Energy for Change: An Introduction to Appreciative Inquiry*, International Institute for Sustainable Development, Manitoba, Canada.

Engineers Without Borders (2021) 'EWB Challenge', Engineers Without Borders [website] <https://ewbchallenge.org/ewb-challenge> [accessed 20 October 2021].

Escobar, A. (2007) 'Worlds and knowledges otherwise', *Cultural Studies* 21(2): 179–210 <https://doi.org/10.1080/09502380601162506>.

Esteva, G. (1992) 'Development', in W. Sachs (ed.), *The Development Dictionary*, Zed Books, London.

Finegold, M., Holland, B. and Lingham, T. (2002) 'Appreciative inquiry and public dialogue: an approach to community change', *Public Organization Review* 2(3): 235–52 <https://doi.org/10.1023/A:1020292413486>.

Fitzgerald, S.P., Oliver, C. and Hoxsey, J.C. (2010) 'Appreciative inquiry as a shadow process', *Journal of Management Inquiry* 19(3): 220–33 <https://doi.org/10.1177/1056492609349349>.

Folke, C. (2006) 'Resilience: The emergence of a perspective for social–ecological systems analyses', *Global Environmental Change* 16(3): 253–67 <https://doi.org/10.1016/j.gloenvcha.2006.04.002>.

Food and Agriculture Organization of the United Nations (FAO) (1996) *World Food Summit 1996*, FAO, Rome.

Fowler, A. and Biekart, K. (2008) 'Civic driven change – implications for aided development', in A. Fowler and K. Biekart (eds), *Civic Driven Change: Citizen's Imagination in Action*, Institute of Social Studies, The Hague.

Fox Eades, J.M. (2008) *Celebrating Strengths: Building Strengths-Based Schools*, Capp Press, Coventry.

Fredrickson, B.L. (1998) 'What good are positive emotions?', *Review of General Psychology* 2(3): 300–319 <https://doi.org/10.1037/1089-2680.2.3.300>.

Fredrickson, B.L. (2001) 'The role of positive emotions in positive psychology: the broaden-and-build theory of positive emotions', *The American Psychologist* 56(3): 218–26 <https://doi.org/10.1037/0003-066X.56.3.218>.

Fredrickson, B. (2003) 'The value of positive emotions: The emerging science of positive psychology is coming to understand why it's good to feel good', *American Scientist* 91(4): 330–35 <https://doi.org/10.1511/2003.4.330>.

Fredrickson, B. (2009) *Positivity*, Crown Publishers, New York.

Fredrickson, B.L. and Cohn, M.A. (2008) 'Positive emotions', in M. Lewis, J.M. Haviland-Jones, and L.F. Barrett (eds), *Handbook of Emotions*, The Guilford Press, New York.

Fredrickson, B.L. and Joiner, T. (2002) 'Positive emotions trigger upward spirals toward emotional well-being', *Psychological Science* 13(2): 172–75 <https://doi.org/10.1111/1467-9280.00431>.

Freire, P. (1970) *Pedagogy of the Oppressed*, Penguin, London.

Friedli, L. (2013) '"What we've tried, hasn't worked": the politics of assets based public health', *Critical Public Health* 23(2): 131–45 <https://doi.org/10.1080/09581596.2012.748882>.

Fuchs, L.E., Peters, B. and Neufeldt, H. (2019) 'Identities, interests, and preferences matter: fostering sustainable community development by building assets and agency in western Kenya', *Sustainable Development* 27(4): 704–12 <https://doi.org/10.1002/sd.1934>.

Garcea, N., Harrison, R. and Linley, A. (2014) 'Living the future: a strengths-based example of restructure and culture at Boehringer Ingelheim', *Strategic HR Review* 13(3): 111–17 <https://doi.org/10.1108/SHR-02-2014-0010>.

Garcia-Moreno, C., Jansen, H.A., Ellsberg, M., Heise, L. and Watts, C.H. (2006) 'Prevalence of intimate partner violence: findings from the WHO multi-country study on women's health and domestic violence', *The Lancet* (British Edition) 368(9543): 1260–69 <https://doi.org/10.1016/S0140-6736(06)69523-8>.

Garwood, J. and Ampuja, A. (2019) 'Inclusion of students with learning, emotional, and behavioral disabilities through strength-based approaches', *Intervention in School and Clinic* 55(1): 46–51 <https://doi.org/10.1177/1053451218767918>.

Gaventa, J. (1980) *Power and Powerlessness: Quiescence and Rebellion in an Appalachian Valley*, University of Illinois Press, Urbana, IL.

Gaventa, J. (2004) 'Towards participatory local governance: assessing the transformative possibilities', in S. Hickey and G. Mohan (eds), *Participation: From Tyranny to Transformation*, pp. 25–41, Zed Books, London.

Gaventa, J. (2006) 'Finding the spaces for change: a power analysis', *IDS Bulletin* 37(6): 23–33 <https://doi.org/10.1111/j.1759-5436.2006.tb00320.x>.

Gelfand, M.J. and Brett, J.M. (eds) (2004) *The Handbook of Negotiation and Culture*, Stanford University Press, Stanford, CA.

Gergen, K.J. (1978) 'Toward generative theory', *Journal of Personality and Social Psychology* 36(11): 1344–60 <https://doi.org/10.1037/0022-3514.36.11.1344>.

Gergen, K.J. (1982) *Toward Transformation in Social Knowledge*, Springer-Verlag, New York.

Gergen, K.J. (1999) *An Invitation to Social Construction*, 1st edn, Sage Publications, London.

Gergen, K.J. (2009) *An Invitation to Social Construction*, 2nd edn, Sage Publications, London.

Gibson-Graham, J.K. and the Community Economies Collective (2008) *Cultivating Community Economies*, Next System Project. Available from: <https://www.communityeconomies.org/sites/default/files/2019-03/Next%20System%20Project%2C%20Community%20Economies%2C%20Final.pdf> [accessed 19 January 2023].

Giotis, C. (2022) *Borderland: Decolonizing the Words of War*, Oxford University Press, New York.

Glavas, A., Senge, P. and Cooperrider, D.L. (2010) 'Building a green city on a blue lake: a model for building a local sustainable economy', *People & Strategy* 33(1): 26–33.

Glicken, M.D. (2004) *Using the Strengths Perspective in Social Work Practice: A Positive Approach for the Helping Professions*, Pearson Education Inc, Boston, MA.

Glouberman, S. and Zimmerman, B. (2002) *Complicated and Complex Systems: What Would Successful Reform of Medicare Look Like?* Commission on the Future of Health Care in Canada, Discussion Paper No.8. Available from: <https://publications.gc.ca/collections/Collection/CP32-79-8-2002E.pdf> [Accessed 21 May 2021].

Goffman, E. (1963) *Stigma: Notes on the Management of Spoiled Identity*, Simon & Schuster, New York.

Graduate Institute Geneva (2022) 'Effectiveness of partnerships for advancing the SDGs: behavioural pathways and impacts' [website] <https://www.graduateinstitute.ch/research-centres/centre-international-environmental-studies/effectiveness-partnerships-advancing> [accessed 27 January 2022].

Gray, M. (2011) 'Back to basics: a critique of the strengths perspective in social work', *Families in Society* 92(1): 5–11 <https://doi.org/10.1606/1044-3894.4054>.

Green, D. (2008) *From Poverty to Power: How Active Citizens and Effective States can Change the World*, Practical Action Publishing Ltd in association with Oxfam GB for Oxfam International, London.

Green, D. (2016) *How Change Happens*, Oxford University Press, Oxford.

Green, G. and Haines, A. (2012) *Asset Building & Community Development*, Sage Publications, Thousand Oaks, CA.

Gronemeyer, M. (1992) 'Helping', in W. Sachs (ed.), *The Development Dictionary: A Guide to Knowledge as Power*, Zed Books, London.
Hammond, W. and Zimmerman, R. (2012) *A Strengths-Based Perspective*, Resiliency Initiatives, Canada. Available from: <https://www.esd.ca/Programs/Resiliency/Documents/RSL_STRENGTH_BASED_PERSPECTIVE.pdf> [accessed 11 November 2021].
Harvey, S. and Petrakis, M. (2019) 'Forensic social work (including criminal justice settings) in Australia: The role of social work to promote human rights and social perspectives', abstract from *9th International Conference on Social Work in Health and Mental Health 2019, York, United Kingdom*.
Henkel, H. and Stirrat, R. (2001) 'Participation as spiritual duty: empowerment as secular subjection', in B. Cooke and U. Kothari (eds) *Participation: The New Tyranny?*, pp. 168–84, Zed Books, New York.
Henry, L.S. and Henry, J.D. (2007) 'Using a strengths-based approach to build caring work environments', *Workplace Health & Safety* 55(12): 501–503 <https://doi.org/10.1177/216507990705501204>.
Herington, M.J. and van de Fliert, E. (2018) 'Positive deviance in theory and practice: a conceptual review', *Deviant Behavior* 39(5): 664–78 <https://doi.org/10.1080/01639625.2017.1286194>.
Hickey, S. and Mohan, G. (2005) 'Relocating participation within a radical politics of development', *Development and Change* 36(2): 237–62 <https://doi.org/10.1111/j.0012-155X.2005.00410.x>.
Hiroto, D. and Seligman, M. (1975) 'Generality of learned helplessness in man', *Journal of Personality and Social Psychology* 31(2): 311–27 <https://doi.org/10.1037/h0076270>.
Hofstede, G. (1980) *Culture's Consequences: International Differences in Work-related Values and Organizations*, SAGE, Beverley Hills, CA.
Hofstede, G. and Hofstede, G.J. (2005) *Cultures and Organizations: Software of the Mind* (2nd edn), McGraw-Hill, New York.
Honig, D. (2018) *Navigation by Judgment: Why and When Top-Down Control of Foreign Aid Doesn't Work*, Oxford University Press, Oxford.
Horner, R. (2020) 'Towards a new paradigm of global development? Beyond the limits of international development', *Progress in Human Geography* 44(3): 415–36 <https://doi.org/10.1177/0309132519836158>.
House, R.J., Hanges, P.J., Javidan, M., Dorfman, P.W. and Gupta, V. (eds) (2004) *Culture, Leadership, and Organizations: The GLOBE Study of 62 Societies*, Sage Publications, Thousand Oaks, CA.
Illich, I. (1973) *Deschooling Society*, Penguin Books, London.
Inayatullah, S. (2008) 'Six pillars: futures thinking for transforming', *Foresight* 10(1): 4–21 <https://doi.org/10.1108/14636680810855991>.
International Association for Community Development (IACD) (no date) About [website] <https://www.iacdglobal.org/about/> [accessed 3 October 2021].
Jamme, M. (2010) 'Negative perceptions slow Africa's development', *The Guardian*, 10 December. Available from: <https://www.theguardian.com/global-development/poverty-matters/2010/dec/10/africa-postcolonial-perceptions> [accessed 3 October 2021].
Jasper, C., Le, T.T. and Bartram, J. (2012) 'Water and sanitation in schools: a systematic review of the health and educational outcomes', *International Journal of Environmental Research and Public Health* 9(8): 2772–87 <https://doi.org/10.3390/ijerph9082772>.

Johansson-Fua, S., Jesson, R., Spratt, R. and Coxon, E. (eds) (2020) *Relationality and Learning in Oceania: Contextualizing Education for Development*, Brill Publishing, Leiden.

Joshi, A. (2007) 'Producing social accountability? The impact of service delivery reforms', *IDS Bulletin (Brighton, 1984)* 38(6): 10–17 <https://doi.org/10.1111/j.1759-5436.2007.tb00414.x>.

Kelm, J.B. (2015) *Appreciative Living: The Principles of Appreciative Inquiry in Daily Life*, Venet Publishers, Charleston, SC.

Kenni, L. and Wijewickrama, E. (2020) 'Vanuatu: a real test for local emergency response', *theinterpreter*, The Lowy Institute. Available from: <https://www.lowyinstitute.org/the-interpreter/vanuatu-real-test-local-emergency-response> [accessed 18 January 2023].

Keyes, C.L.M. and Haidt, J. (eds) (2003) *Flourishing: Positive Psychology and the Life Well-Lived*, American Psychological Association, Washington, DC.

Khanyile, S. (2020) *A New Country* [documentary film], Anaphora Films, South Africa.

Klein, J.T. (2017) 'Typologies of interdisciplinarity: the boundary work of definition', in R. Frodeman (ed.), *The Oxford Handbook of Interdisciplinarity*, pp. 21–34, Oxford University Press <https://doi.org/10.1093/oxfordhb/9780198733522.013.3>.

Kollmair, M. and Gamper, St. (2002) *The Sustainable Livelihood Approach: Input Paper for the Integrated Training Course of NCCR North-South*, Development Study Group, University of Zurich. Available from: <https://www.alnap.org/help-library/the-sustainable-livelihoods-approach-input-paper-for-the-integrated-training-course-of> [accessed 8 February 2022].

Kothari, U. (2005) *A Radical History of Development Studies: Individuals, Institutions and Ideologies*, Zed Books, London.

Kretzmann, J. and McKnight, J. (1993) *Building Communities from the Inside Out: A Path Toward Finding and Mobilizing a Community's Assets*, The Asset-Based Community Development Institute, Institute for Policy Research, Northwestern University, Evanston, IL.

Kretzmann, J. and McKnight, J. (1997) *A Community Building Workbook*, ACTA Publications, Chicago.

Landry, J. and Peters, B. (2018) *Assets on the Right(s) Track? Reflections at the Intersection of Human Rights-Based Approaches and Asset-Based and Citizen-Led Development*, Innovation Series No. 19, Coady International Institute. Available from: <https://coady.stfx.ca/wp-content/uploads/2019/04/IS19.pdf> [accessed 6 February 2022].

Lee, G., Heng, M., Nou, K., So, P. and Ensor, T. (2018) 'Can positive inquiry strengthen obstetric referral systems in Cambodia?', *The International Journal of Health Planning and Management* 33(1): e89–e104 <https://doi.org/10.1002/hpm.2385>.

Leu, J., Wang, J. and Koo, K. (2011) 'Are positive emotions just as "positive" across cultures?', *Emotion* 11(4): 994–99 <https://doi.org/10.1037/a0021332>.

Levy, A. and Merry, U. (1986) *Organizational Transformation: Approaches, Strategies, Theories*, Greenwood Publishing Group, New York.

Lewis, S., Passmore, T. and Cantore, S. (eds) (2008) *Appreciative Inquiry for Change Management*, Kogan Page, London.

Linley, A. (2008) *Average to A+: Realising Strengths in Yourself and Others*, CAPP Press, Coventry.

Linley, P.A., Bhaduri, A., Sharma, D.S. and Govindji, R. (2011) 'Strengthening underprivileged communities: strengths-based approaches as a force for positive social change in community development', *Positive Psychology as Social Change*, pp. 141–56, Springer, Netherlands <https://doi.org/10.1007/978-90-481-9938-9_9>.

Lopez, S. and Louis, M. (2009) 'The principles of strengths-based education', *Journal of College and Character* 10(4) <https://doi.org/10.2202/1940-1639.1041>.

Lucas, B., Hiele, L., Folasi, K. and Samosani, M. (2016) *SINPA: Final Evaluation Report*. Available from: <https://www.dfat.gov.au/sites/default/files/solomon-islands-ngo-partnership-agreement-final-report.pdf> [accessed 24 October 2021].

Ludema, J.D. (2002) 'Appreciative storytelling: a narrative approach to organization development and change', in R. Fry, F. Barrett, J. Seiling, and D. Whitney (eds), *Appreciative Inquiry and Organizational Transformation: Reports from the Field*, pp. 239–61, Quorum, Westport, CT.

Ludema, J.D., Whitney, D., Mohr, B.J. and Griffin, T.J. (2003) *The Appreciative Inquiry Summit: A Practitioner's Guide for Leading Large-Group Change*, Berrett-Koehler Publishers, San Francisco.

Lukes, S. (1974) *Power: A Radical View* (2nd edn), Palgrave Macmillan, Basingstoke.

Luthfa, I. (2019) 'Revitalisasi Posyandu sebagai upaya peningkatan kesehatan anak dan balita di Posyandu Manggis Kelurahan Karang Roto Semarang', *Indonesian Journal of Community Services* 1(2) <http://dx.doi.org/10.30659/ijocs.1.2.202-209>.

Luttrell, C., Sitna, Q., Scrutton, C. and Bird, K. (2009) *Understanding and Operationalising Empowerment*, Overseas Development Institute, London.

MacArthur, J., Carrard, N., Davila, F., Grant, M., Megaw, T., Willetts, J. and Winterford, K. (2022) 'Gender-transformative approaches in international development: A brief history and five uniting principles', *Women's Studies International Forum* 95: 102635 1–11 <https://doi.org/10.1016/j.wsif.2022.102635>.

Mackintosh, U.A.T., Marsh, D.R. and Schroeder, D.G. (2002) 'Sustained positive deviant child care practices and their effects on child growth in Viet Nam', *Food and Nutrition Bulletin* 23: 16–25 <https://doi.org/10.1177/15648265020234S204>.

Malolo, M., Smith, T.M. and Hughes, R. (1999) *Pacific Foods: The Staples We Eat*, SPC Handbook No. 35, Secretariat of the Pacific Community, Noumea. Available from: <https://spccfpstore1.blob.core.windows.net/digitallibrary-docs/files/fb/fb0721565ed28e6cf962cb5fa94fb12d.pdf?sv=2015-12-11&sr=b&sig=V0diF4ZypI1LKLN%2B8vJ9oX6lF7pJaiC%2FPFDiN6XVrPc%3D&se=2023-07-17T10%3A42%3A14Z&sp=r&rscc=public%2C%20max-age%3D864000%2C%20max-stale%3D86400&rsct=application%2Fpdf&rscd=inline%3B%20filename%3D%2227128_1999_Pacific_foods_the_staples_we%20eat_col.pdf%22> [accessed 18 January 2023].

Malunga, C. and Holcombe, S. (2014) 'Endogenous development: naïve romanticism or practical route to sustainable African development?'

Development in Practice 24(5–6): 615–22 <https://doi.org/10.1080/09614524.2014.938616>.

Mann, A.J., Sibert, J. and Carazas, D. (2011) 'From seed to forest', *International Journal of Appreciative Inquiry* 13(3): 32–38 <https://issuu.com/aipractitioner/docs/aipaug2011-ai-and-international-development> [accessed 5 February 2022].

March, C., Smyth, I. and Mukhopadhyay M. (1999) *A Guide to Gender-Analysis Frameworks*, Oxfam GB, London.

Mathie, A. (2006) 'Does ABCD deliver on social justice?' panel discussion for the *International Association of Community Development CIVICUS Conference*, Glasgow. Available from: <https://coady.stfx.ca/wp-content/uploads/pdfs/resources/publications/Does_ABCD_deliver_on_social_justice.pdf> [accessed 22 January 2023].

Mathie, A. and Cunningham, G. (2003) 'From clients to citizens: asset-based community development as a strategy for community-driven development', *Development in Practice* 13(5): 474–86 <https://doi.org/10.1080/0961452032000125857>.

Mathie, A. and Cunningham, G. (2008) *From Clients to Citizens: Communities Changing the Course of their Own Development*, Practical Action Publishing, Rugby.

Mathie, A., Cameron, J. and Gibson, K. (2017) 'Asset-based and citizen-led development: using a diffracted power lens to analyze possibilities and challenges', *Progress in Development Studies* 17(1): 54–66 <https://doi.org/10.1177/1464993416674302>.

Maton, K.I., Schellenbach, C.J., Leadbeater, B.J. and Solarz, A.L. (eds) (2004) *Investing in Children, Youth, Families, and Communities: Strengths-based Research and Policy*, American Psychological Association, Washington, DC <https://doi.org/10.1037/10660-000>.

Max-Neef, M.A. (2005) 'Foundations of transdisciplinarity', *Ecological Economics* 53(1): 5–16 <https://doi.org/10.1016/j.ecolecon.2005.01.014>.

McGrath, R.E. (2015) 'Character strengths in 75 nations: an update', *The Journal of Positive Psychology* 10(1): 41–52 <https://doi.org/10.1080/17439760.2014.888580>.

McKnight, J. (1995) *The Careless Society and Its Counterfeits*, Basic Books, New York.

McKnight, J. and Russell, C. (2018) *The Four Essential Elements of an Asset-Based Community Development Process: What is Distinctive about an Asset Based Community Development Process*, ABCD Institute, Northwestern University. Available from: <https://www.nurturedevelopment.org/wp-content/uploads/2018/09/4_Essential_Elements_of_ABCD_Process.pdf> [accessed 27 January 2022].

McNamara, K.E., Clissold, R., Westoby, R., Piggott-McKellar, A.E., Kumar, R., Clarke, T., Namoumou, F., Frances, A., Francis, J.E., Warrick, O. and Nunn, P. (2020) 'An assessment of community-based adaptation initiatives in the Pacific Islands', *Nature Climate Change* 10(7): 628–39 <https://doi.org/10.1038/s41558-020-0813-1>.

McNamee, S. and Gergen, K.J. (1999) 'Preface: situating the conversation', in S. McNamee and K.J. Gergen (eds), *Relational Responsibility: Resources for Sustainable Dialogue*, Sage Publications, Thousand Oaks, CA.

McSweeney, B. (2002) 'Hofstede's model of national cultural differences and their consequences: a triumph of faith – a failure of analysis', *Human Relations* 55(1): 89–118 <https://doi.org/10.1177/0018726702551004>.

Meadows, D. (1999) *Leverage Points: Places to Intervene in the System*, The Sustainability Institute, Hartland, VT. Available from: <http://www.donellameadows.org/wp-content/userfiles/Leverage_Points.pdf> [accessed 27 January 2022].

Meadows, D.H., Meadows, D.L. and Randers, J. (2004) *The Limits to Growth: The 30-Year Update*, Chelsea Green Publishing Company, White River Junction, VT.

Meier, D.R. (2020) *Supporting Literacies for Children of Color: A Strengths-based Approach to Preschool Literacy*, Routledge, New York.

Mesquita, B., De Leersnyder, J. and Albert, D. (2014) 'The cultural regulation of emotions', in J.J. Gross (ed.), *Handbook of Emotion Regulation*, The Guilford Press, New York.

Mezirow, J. (1997) 'Transformative learning: theory to practice', *New Directions for Adult and Continuing Education* 74: 5–12 <https://doi.org/10.1002/ace.7401>.

Michael, S. (2005) 'The promise of appreciative inquiry as an interview tool for field research', *Development in Practice* 15(2) April: 222–30 <https://doi.org/10.1080/09614520500042094>.

Moncrieffe, J. (2006) 'The power of stigma: encounters with "street children" and "Restavecs" in Haiti', *IDS Bulletin* 37(6): 34–46 <https://doi.org/10.1111/j.1759-5436.2006.tb00321.x>.

Moncrieffe, J. (2007) 'Labelling, power and accountability: how and why our categories matter', in J. Moncrieffe and R. Eyben (eds), *The Power of Labelling*, Earthscan, London.

Mooney, M.F. (2011) 'Psychosocial recovery from disasters: a framework informed by evidence', *New Zealand Journal of Psychology* 40(4): 26–38.

Moser, C. (1993) *Gender Planning and Development: Theory, Practice, and Training*, Routledge, London.

Munggoro, D.W. and Kismadi, B. (2013) Pandual Fasilitator Pertemuan Apresiasi Multiaktor ACCESS. Available from: <https://www.academia.edu/34761940/Panduan_Fasilitator> [accessed 25 October 2021].

Murphy, J.B. (2011) 'Perspectives on power', *Journal of Political Power* 4(1): 87–103 <https://doi.org/10.1080/2158379X.2011.555961>.

Mwenda, A. (2012) 'Africa: The Next Chapter', Part 3 TED Talk, 'A New Look at Africa', TED Radio Hour. Available from: <https://www.npr.org/2012/06/29/155904209/africa-the-next-chapter> [accessed 5 June 2021].

Myende, P. and Chikoko, V. (2014) 'School-university partnership in a South African rural context: possibilities for an asset-based approach', *Journal of Human Ecology* 46(3): 249–59 <https://doi.org/10.1080/09709274.2014.11906724>.

Narayan-Parker, D. (1995) *The Contribution of People's Participation: Evidence from 121 Rural Water Supply Projects*, World Bank, Washington, DC. Available from: <http://documents.worldbank.org/curated/en/274861468767096877/The-contribution-of-peoples-participation-evidence-from-121-rural-water-supply-projects> [accessed 6 February 2022].

National Criminal Justice Training Center, US (no date) 'Strengths-based approaches to supervising high-risk populations' [website] <https://ncjtc.fvtc.edu/trainings/TR00002875/tribal-probation-supervision-series> [accessed 5 February 2022].

National Health and Medical Research Council, Australian Research Council (NHMRC) and Universities Australia (2018) *Australian Code for the Responsible Conduct of Research 2018*, Commonwealth of Australia, Canberra. Available from: <https://www.nhmrc.gov.au/about-us/publications/australian-code-responsible-conduct-research-2018> [accessed 5 February 2022].

Nazara, S. and Resosudarmo, B. (2007) *Aceh-Nias Reconstruction and Rehabilitation: Progress and Challenges at the End of 2006*, Asian Development Bank Institute, Tokyo. Available from: <https://www.adb.org/sites/default/files/publication/156708/adbi-dp70.pdf> [accessed 22 January 2023].

Ngunjiri, E. (1998) 'Viewpoint participatory methodologies: double-edged swords', *Development in Practice* 8(4): 466–70 <https://doi.org/10.1080/09614529853486>.

Nicolau, M. and Delpont, C. (2015) 'A community asset mapping programme for roots-driven sustainable socio-economic change in rural South Africa', *The International Journal of Social Sustainability in Economic, Social, and Cultural Context* 10(1): 1–11 <https://doi.org/10.18848/2325-1115/CGP/v10i01/55254>.

Niemiec, R.M., Shogren, K.A. and Wehmeyer, M.L. (2017) 'Character strengths and intellectual and developmental disability: a strengths-based approach from positive psychology', *Education and Training in Autism and Developmental Disabilities* 52(1) March: 13–25.

Nunn, P.D. and Kumar, R. (2019) 'Cashless adaptation to climate change: unwelcome yet unavoidable?' *One Earth* 1(1): 31–34 <https://doi.org/10.1016/j.oneear.2019.08.004>.

Obama, B. (2020) *A Promised Land*, Viking, New York.

O'Brien, K. (2012) 'Global environmental change II: From adaptation to deliberate transformation', *Progress in Human Geography* 36(5): 667–76 <https://doi.org/10.1177/0309132511425767>.

Ochieng, C.M.O. (2007) 'Development through positive deviance and its implications for economic policy making and public administration in Africa: the case of Kenyan agricultural development, 1930–2005', *World Development* 35(3): 454–79 <https://doi.org/10.1016/j.worlddev.2006.04.003>.

Odell, M. (2004) *Women's Empowerment: The Role of Appreciative Planning and Action in Women's Empowerment/WORTH*. Available from: <https://nanopdf.com/download/apa-summary-pact-the-appreciative-inquiry-commons_pdf> [accessed 18 January 2023].

Oliver, C. (2017) *Strengths-Based Child Protection: Firm, Fair, and Friendly*, University of Toronto Press, Toronto.

Organisation for Economic Co-operation and Development – Development Assistance Committee (OECD DAC) (2002) *Evaluation and Aid Effectiveness No. 6 - Glossary of Key Terms in Evaluation and Results Based Management* (in English, French and Spanish), OECD Publishing, Paris <https://doi.org/10.1787/9789264034921-en-fr>.

OECD (2010) *Quality Standards for Development Evaluation: DAC Guidelines and Reference Series*, OECD Publishing, Paris <https://dx.doi.org/10.1787/9789264083905-en>.

Ostrom, E. (1996) 'Crossing the great divide: coproduction, synergy, and development', *World Development* 24(6): 1073–87 <https://doi.org/10.1016/0305-750X(96)00023-X>.

Pacific Islands Forum (2010) *Towards a Food Secure Pacific: Framework for Action on Food Security in the Pacific*, Suva. Available from: <https://pafpnet.spc.int/pafpnet/attachments/article/180/Draft%20Towards%20A%20Food%20Secure%20Pacific.pdf> [accessed 5 February 2022].

Pacific Islands Forum (2017a) 'The Blue Pacific: Pacific countries demonstrate innovation in sustainably developing, managing, and conserving their part of the Pacific Ocean', Pacific Islands Forum [website] <https://www.forumsec.org/2017/06/07/the-blue-pacific-pacific-countries-demonstrate-innovation-in-sustainably-developing-managing-and-conserving-their-part-of-the-pacific-ocean/> [accessed 5 February 2022].

Pacific Islands Forum (2017b) *'The 2050 Strategy for the Blue Pacific Continent'*. Available from: <https://www.forumsec.org/2050strategy/> [accessed 18 January 2023].

Packer, S., Emmott, S. and Hinchliffe, K. (2009) *Improving the Provision of Basic Education Services to the Poor in Papua New Guinea: A Case Study, May 2009*, The Office of Development Effectiveness, AusAID, Canberra, Australia. Available from: <https://www.dfat.gov.au/sites/default/files/improving-provision-basic-education-services-poor-png-case-study-may-2009.PDF> [accessed 24 October 2021].

Palmer, L. and Barnes, S. (producers) (2021) 'Holding Tightly: Custom and Healing in Timor-Leste' [short film]. Available from: https://www.roninfilms.com.au/feature/17333/holding-tightly-custom-healing-in-timor.html [accessed 4 February 2022].

Pamphilon, B. (2015) 'Weaving knowledges: the development of empowering intercultural learning spaces for smallholder farmers in Papua New Guinea', *Multicultural Education Review* 7(1–2): 108–21 <http://dx.doi.org/10.1080/2005615X.2015.1061921>.

Pamphilon, B. (2017) *The Farmer-to-Farmer Adult Learning Manual: A Process and Resources for the Development of Farmers as Peer Educators*, ACIAR Monograph No. 198, Australian Centre for International Agricultural Research, Canberra.

Pamphilon, B. (2019) *Final Report: Improving Opportunities for Economic Development for Women Smallholders in Rural Papua New Guinea*. Available from: <https://www.canberra.edu.au/research/faculty-research-centres/csc/family-farm-teams-program/publications/ASEM-2014-095-Published-Final-Report.pdf> [accessed 25 October 2021].

Pamphilon, B. and Mikhailovich, K. (2017) *Examining Women's Business Acumen in Papua New Guinea: Working with Women Smallholders in Horticulture - Final Report*, ACIAR, Canberra. Available from: <https://www.aciar.gov.au/publication/technical-publications/examining-womens-business-acumen-papua-new-guinea-working-women-smallholders> [accessed 5 February 2022].

Pascale, R.T., Sternin, J. and Sternin, M. (2010) *The Power of Positive Deviance: How Unlikely Innovators Solve the World's Toughest Problems*, Harvard Business School Press, Boston, MA.

Pasifika Rising (2018) 'Blue Pacific is a powerful narrative to call us together', Pasifika Rising [website] <https://www.pasifikarising.org/blue-pacific-powerful-narrative-to-call-us-together/> [accessed 28 January 2022].

Patton, M.Q. (2003) 'Utilization-focused evaluation', in T. Kellaghan and D.L. Stufflebeam (eds), *International Handbook of Educational Evaluation*, Springer, Dordrecht <https://doi.org/10.1007/978-94-010-0309-4_15>.

Patton, M.Q. (2011) *Developmental Evaluation: Applying Complexity Concepts to Enhance Innovation and Use*, Guilford Press, New York.

Peacifica (2020) *Pacific Perspectives on the World: Listening to Australia's Island Neighbours in Order to Build Strong, Respectful and Sustainable Relationships*, Whitlam Institute within Western Sydney University, Sydney, Australia. Available from: <https://www.whitlam.org/publications/2020/2/13/pacific-perspectives-on-the-world> [accessed 18 November 2022].

Pellini, A., Maesy, A. and Purnawati, E. (2014) *Improving Health Services through Knowledge Sharing and Communication: A Story of Change from the Regency of Lombok Barat*, DFAT. Available from: <https://www.ksi-indonesia.org/assets/uploads/original/2020/01/ksi-1580302322.pdf> [accessed 6 February 2022].

Perry, H., Crigler, L., Lewin, S., Glenton, C., LeBan, K. and Hodgins, S. (2017) 'A new resource for developing and strengthening large-scale community health worker programs', *Human Resources for Health* 15(1), 13–13 <https://doi.org/10.1186/s12960-016-0178-8>.

Peters, B. and Landry, J. (2018) *Human Rights Based Approaches and Citizen-Led, Asset-Based and Community Driven Development' Discussion Paper*, Coady Institute, St Francis Xavier University, Nova Scotia, Canada. Available from: <https://coady.stfx.ca/wp-content/uploads/2019/04/HRBA-and-CLABCD-Discussion-Paper.pdf> [accessed 4 November 2021].

Peterson, C. (2006) *A Primer in Positive Psychology*, Oxford University Press, New York.

Peterson, C. and Seligman, M.E.P. (2004) *Character Strengths and Virtues*, Oxford University Press, New York.

Positive Deviance Initiative (2010) *Basic Field Guide to the Positive Deviance Approach*, Tufts University, Boston, MA. Available from: <https://static1.squarespace.com/static/5a1eeb26fe54ef288246a688/t/5a6eca16c83025f9bac2eeff/1517210135326/FINALguide10072010.pdf> [accessed 19 January 2023].

Prakash, B.N. (2011) 'Recognition and support for traditional anti-malarial programmes', in W. Hiemstra (ed.), *Endogenous Development Magazine* 7: 22–24.

Preskill, H. and Catsambas, T. (2006) *Reframing Evaluation through Appreciative Inquiry*, Sage Publications, Thousand Oaks, CA.

Preskill, H. and Coghlan, A. (eds) (2003) 'Appreciative inquiry and evaluation', *New Directions for Program Evaluation* 100, Jossey-Bass, San Francisco.

Pritchett, L. and Sandefur, J. (2014) 'Context matters for size: why external validity claims and development practice do not mix', *Journal of Globalization and Development* 4: 2 <https://doi.org/10.1515/jgd-2014-0004>.

Public Health UK (2018) *Health Matters – Community Centred Approaches to Health*. Available from: <https://www.gov.uk/government/publications/health-matters-health-and-wellbeing-community-centred-approaches/health-matters-community-centred-approaches-for-health-and-wellbeing> [accessed 27 January 2022].

Ramalingam, B. (2013) *Aid on the Edge of Chaos: Rethinking International Cooperation in a Complex World*, Oxford University Press, Oxford.

Rao, A., Sandler, J., Kelleher, D. and Miller, C. (eds) (2016) *Gender at Work: Theory and Practice for 21st Century Organizations*, Routledge, Abingdon.

Rapp, C.A. and Goscha, R.J. (2008) *The Strengths Model: Case Management with People with Psychiatric Disabilities*, 2nd edn, Oxford University Press, New York.

Reason, P. (2020) 'Action research as spiritual practice', prepared for the University of Surrey Learning Community Conference, 4–5 May 2020. Available from: <https://peterreason.net/Papers/AR_as_spiritual_practice.pdf> [accessed 27 January 2022].

Reed, J. (2007) *Appreciative Inquiry: Research for Change*, Sage, Thousand Oaks, CA.

Research for Development Impact Network (2021) *Principles and Guidelines for Ethical Research and Evaluation in International Development, Updated August 2021*, Research for Development Impact Network, Australian Council for International Aid, Canberra. Available from: <https://rdinetwork.org.au/wp-content/uploads/2021/08/Updated-Aug-2021_ACFID-RDI-Network-Ethical-Principles_Accessible.pdf> [accessed 3 October 2021].

Rhodes, D. with Macanawai, S., Tawaka, K. and James, R. (2013) 'Capacity Development for Effective and Efficient Disabled People's Organizations in Pacific Island Countries', Pacific Disability Forum, Suva.

Rhodes, D. (2014) *Capacity Across Cultures: Global Lessons from Pacific Experiences*, Inkshed Press, Fairfield, Australia.

Rhodes, D. (2022) *Facilitating Change Across Cultures*, Practical Action Publishing, Rugby.

Rickman, C. (2013) *The Flourish Handbook: How to Achieve Happiness with Staying Power, Boost your Well-Being, Enjoy your Life More and Reach your Potential*, CreateSpace, Scotts Valley, CA.

Rogers, P.J. and Fraser, D. (2003) 'Appreciating appreciative inquiry', *New Directions for Evaluation* 100: 75–83 <https://doi.org/10.1002/ev.101>.

Rosenthal, R. and Jacobson, L. (1992) *Pygmalion in the Classroom: Teacher Expectation and Pupils' Intellectual Development*, Irvington Publishers, New York.

Sachs, J. (1997) 'The limits of convergence: nature, nurture and growth', *The Economist* 343(8021): 24.

Saleebey, D. (1992) *The Strengths Perspective in Social Work Practice*, Longman Publishing Group, New York.

Saleebey, D. (1996) 'The strengths perspective in social work practice: extensions and cautions', *Social Work* 41(3): 296–305 <https://doi.org/10.1093/sw/41.3.296>.

Saleebey, D. (2009) *The Strengths Perspective in Social Work Practice*, 5th edn, Allyn and Bacon/Pearson, Boston, MA.

Sari, P. (2018) 'Evaluasi pelaksanaan revitalisasi posyandu dan pelatihan kader sebagai bentuk pengabdian masyarakat (studi kasus di rw 06 desa cileles kecamatan jatinangor tahun 2017)', *Jurnal Unpad* 2(2): 1–5.

Schneider, S.H., Semenov, S., Patwardhan, A., Burton, I., Magadza, C.H.D., Oppenheimer, M., Pittock, A.B., Rahman, A., Smith, J.B., Suarez, A. and Yamin, F. (2007) 'Assessing key vulnerabilities and the risk from climate change', in M.L. Parry, O.F. Canziani, J.P. Palutikof, P.J. van der Linden and C.E. Hanson (eds), *Climate Change 2007: Impacts, Adaptation and Vulnerability. Contribution of Working Group II to the Fourth Assessment Report of the Intergovernmental Panel on Climate Change*, pp. 779–810, Cambridge University Press, Cambridge, UK.

Schön, D.A. (1979) 'Generative metaphor: a perspective on problem-setting in social policy', in A. Ortony (ed.), *Metaphor and Thought*, Cambridge University Press, Cambridge.

Schwandt, T.A. (2000) 'Three epistemological stances for qualitative inquiry: interpretivism, hermeneutics, and social constructionism', in N.K. Denzin and Y.S. Lincoln (eds), *Handbook of Qualitative Research*, 2nd edn, pp. 189–213, Sage Publications, London.

Schwartz, P. (1998) *The Art of the Long View: Planning for the Future in an Uncertain World*, Wiley, Hoboken, NJ.

Seligman, M.E.P. (2011) *Flourish: A Visionary New Understanding of Happiness and Well-Being*, John Murray Press, London.

Seligman, M.E.P (2018) 'PERMA and the building blocks of well-being', *The Journal of Positive Psychology* 13(4): 333–35 <https://doi.org/10.1080/17439760.2018.1437466>.

Seligman, M.E.P. and Csikszentmihalyi, M. (2000) 'Positive psychology: an introduction', *The American Psychologist* 55(1): 5–14 <https://doi.org/10.1037/0003-066X.55.1.5>.

Sen, A. (1985) 'A sociological approach to the measurement of poverty: a reply to Professor Peter Townsend', *Oxford Economic Papers* 37(4): 669–76 <https://doi.org/10.1093/oxfordjournals.oep.a041716>.

Sen, A. (2001) 'Economic development and capability expansion in historical perspective', *Pacific Economic Review* 6(2): 179–92 <https://doi:10.1111/1468-0106.00126>.

Sharma, B. (2008) *Voice, Accountability and Civic Engagement: A Conceptual Overview*, Commissioned by Oslo Governance Centre, Bureau for Development Policy, UNDP. Available from: <https://www.undp.org/sites/g/files/zskgke326/files/publications/2008_UNDP_Voice-Accountability-and-Civic-Engagement_EN.pdf> [accessed 22 January 2023].

Shiva, V. (1997) 'Western science and its destruction of local knowledge', in M. Rahnema and V. Bawtree (eds), *The Post-Development Reader*, Zed Books, London.

Singh, A., Patkar, S., Ramesh, R. and Babu, T. (2011) 'Social capital and MYRADA's pioneering approach: the power of women in community-based organizations in southern India', *International Journal of Appreciative Inquiry* 13(3): 16–23.

Slaughter, R.A. (2008) 'Integral futures methodologies', *Futures: The Journal of Policy, Planning and Futures Studies* 40(2): 103–108 <https://doi.org/10.1016/j.futures.2007.11.011>.

Spratt, R. (2020) 'What does relationality mean for effective aid?' in S. Johansson-Fua, R. Jesson, R. Spratt, and E. Coxon (eds), *Relationality and Learning in Oceania: Contextualizing Education for Development*, Routledge, Leiden.

Strand, A. (2020) 'Humanitarian–development nexus' In A. de Lauri (ed.), *Humanitarianism*, Brill, Leiden.

Sullivan, P.W. and Rapp, C. (2009) 'Honoring philosophical traditions: the strengths model and the social environment', in D. Saleebey (ed.), *The Strengths Perspective in Social Work Practice*, 5th edn, Pearson Education Inc, Boston, MA.

Sultana, F. (2019) 'Decolonizing development education and the pursuit of social justice', *Human Geography* 12(3): 31–46 <https://doi.org/10.1177/194277861901200305>.

Tagagau, S. and Pettit, J. (2006) *A Successful Strength-based Approach in PNG Education: From Strength to Strength – Building on Strengths to Build Strong School-community Partnerships*. Available from: <https://www.researchgate.net/publication/237232175_A_successful_strength-based_approach_in_PNG_Education_From_strength_to_strength_-_Building_on_strengths_to_build_strong_school-community_partnerships> [accessed 13 February 2023].

Truman, H.S. (1949) *Inauguration Speech*. Available from: <https://avalon.law.yale.edu/20th_century/truman.asp> [accessed 5 June 2021].

United Nations (1995) *United Nations Terms*, United Nations. Available from: <https://web.archive.org/web/20140714225617/http://unterm.un.org/DGAACS/unterm.nsf/8fa942046ff7601c85256983007ca4d8/526c2eaba978f007852569fd00036819?OpenDocument> [accessed 3 October 2021].

United Nations (2015) *Resolution Adopted by the General Assembly on 25 September 2015*, United Nations, New York. Available from: <https://www.un.org/en/development/desa/population/migration/generalassembly/docs/globalcompact/A_RES_70_1_E.pdf> [accessed 18 January 2023].

United Nations Development Programme (UNDP) (2018) *Foresight Manual: Empowered Futures for the 2030 Agenda*, United Nations, New York.

UNICEF (no date) *Child Protection Case Study: Tapping into Community Values to Support Child Protection in Fiji: 'Children Are a Precious Gift from God': Community-Based Facilitation Manual*. Available from: <https://www.unicef.org/pacificislands/media/976/file/Case-Study-Fiji.pdf> [accessed 3 October 2021].

UNICEF and WHO (2011) *Drinking Water Equity, Safety and Sustainability: Thematic report on drinking water – 2011*. Available from: <https://reliefweb.int/report/world/drinking-water-equity-safety-and-sustainability> [accessed 18 January 2023].

USAID (2021) *Discussion Note: Adaptive Management*, USAID, Washington, DC. Available from: <https://usaidlearninglab.org/sites/default/files/resource/files/dn_adaptive_management_final2021.pdf> [accessed 3 October 2021].

Valters, C., Cummings, C. and Nixo, H. (2016) 'Putting learning at the centre: Adaptive development programming in practice', Overseas Development Institute, London. Available from: <https://odi.org/en/publications/putting-learning-at-the-centre-adaptive-development-programming-in-practice/> [accessed 3 October 2021].

van der Haar, D. and Hosking, D.M. (2004) 'Evaluating appreciative inquiry: a relational constructionist perspective', *Human Relations* 57(8): 1017–36 <https://doi.org/10.1177/0018726704045839>.

van de Venter, E. and Redwood, S. (2016) 'Does an asset-based community development project promote health and wellbeing?', *The Lancet (British Edition)* 388: S108–S108 <https://doi.org/10.1016/S0140-6736(16)32344-3>.

Van Otterloo-Butler, S. (ed.) (2007) *Learning Endogenous Development. Building on Bio-cultural Diversity*, Compas, Practical Action Publishing, Rugby.

Van't Hooft, K. (ed.) (2010) *Endogenous Development in Practice: Towards Well-being of People and Ecosystems*, ETC Compas, Leusden, Netherlands. Available from: <https://edepot.wur.nl/534539> [accessed 27 January 2022].

VeneKlasen, L. and Miller, V. (2002) *A New Weave of Power, People & Politics: The Action Guide for Advocacy and Citizen Participation*, World Neighbors, Oklahoma City, OK.

Von Kalm, N. (2018) *A Visit from our Kenya Partners. (Interview with James Sanjura) at Anglican Overseas Aid Office*, Melbourne. Available from: <https://anglicanoverseasaid.org.au/a-visit-from-kenyan-partners/> [accessed 18 November 2021].

Vunisea, A., Leduc, B., Bernard, K., Duaibe, K., Cleary, L., Manley, M. and Leavai, P. (2015) *The Pacific Gender and Climate Change Toolkit: Tools for Practitioners*, UN Women. Available from: <https://www.unwomen.org/sites/default/files/Headquarters/Attachments/Sections/Library/Publications/2015/Toolkit%20booklet%20pages.pdf> [accessed 5 February 2022].

Waterman, R.H., Peters, T.J. and Phillips, J.R. (1980) 'Structure is not organization', *Business Horizons* 23(3): 14–26 <https://doi.org/10.1016/0007-6813(80)90027-0>.

Weick, A. (1992) 'Building a strengths perspective for social work', in D. Saleebey (ed.), *The Strengths Perspective in Social Work Practice*, pp. 18–26, Longman, New York.

Weick, A., Rapp, C., Sullivan, P. and Kisthardt, W. (1989) 'A strengths perspective for social work practice', *Social Work* 34(4): 350–54 <https://doi.org/10.1093/sw/34.4.350>.

Whitney, D.K. and Trosten-Bloom, A. (2003) *The Power of Appreciative Inquiry: A Practical Guide to Positive Change*, Berrett-Koehler Publishers, San Francisco.

Wickson, F., Carew, A. and Russell, A. (2006) 'Transdisciplinary research: characteristics, quandaries and quality', *Futures: The Journal of Policy, Planning and Futures Studies* 38(9): 1046–59 <https://doi.org/10.1016/j.futures.2006.02.011>.

Willetts, J., Halcrow, G., Carrard, N., Rowland, C. and Crawford, J. (2010) 'Addressing two critical MDGs together: gender in water, sanitation and hygiene initiatives', *Pacific Economic Bulletin* 25(1): 162–76. Available from: <https://openresearch-repository.anu.edu.au/bitstream/1885/30589/2/PEB25_1_Willets%20et%20al.pdf> [accessed 22 January 2023].

Willetts, J., Carrard, N., Crawford, J., Rowland C. and Halcrow, G. (2013) 'Working from strengths to assess changes in gender equality', *Development in Practice* 23(8): 991–1006 <https://doi.org/10.1080/09614524.2013.840564>.

Willetts, J., Asker, S., Carrard, N. and Winterford, K. (2014) 'The practice of a strengths-based approach to community development in Solomon Islands', *Development Studies Research* 1(1): 37–41 <https://doi.org/10.1080/21665095.2014.983275>.

Winterford, K. (2003) *Sharing Stories: A Participatory Approach to Monitoring and Evaluation in the Pacific*. Available from: <https://www.pacific-climatechange.net/sites/default/files/documents/Sharing-Stories-A-participatory-approach-to-monitoring-and-evaluation-in-the-Pacific.pdf> [accessed 27 January 2022].

Winterford, K. (2013) *A strengths perspective on social accountability: informing citizen and state action for improved services and development*, thesis, UTS Digital Thesis Collection, Sydney. Available from: <https://opus.lib.uts.edu.au/handle/10453/21817> [accessed 30 October 2021].

Winterford, K. (2016) 'A positive notion of power for citizen voice and state accountability', *Development in Practice* 26(6): 696–705 <https://doi.org/10.1080/09614524.2016.1195793>.

Winterford, K. (2017) *How to Partner for Development Research*, Research for Development Impact Network, Canberra, Australia. Available from: <https://rdinetwork.org.au/wp-content/uploads/2017/01/How-to-Partner-for-Development-Research_fv_Web.pdf> [accessed 31 August 2022].

Winterford, K. and Cunningham, I. (2017) *Strengths-based Approaches in Malawi and Zimbabwe*, prepared for Caritas Australia by the Institute for Sustainable Futures, University of Technology Sydney. Available from: <https://www.caritas.org.au/media/josdiuhm/sba-research-report.pdf> [accessed 6 February 2022].

Winterford, K., Baroi, H., Ahsan, K., Pranay, P., Megaw, T., Willetts, J. Roy, P., Ferdows, H. and Ray, S. (2022) *Gender-Transformative Social Accountability for Inclusive WASH: Outcome Assessment*, report prepared by Institute for Sustainable Futures at the University of Technology Sydney, University of Rajshahi and World Vision Bangladesh.

World Bank (2003) *World Development Report 2004: Making Services Work for Poor People*, World Bank and Oxford University Press, Washington, DC.

World Health Organization (WHO) (2012) *Global Costs and Benefits of Drinking-water Supply and Sanitation Interventions to Reach the MDG Target and Universal Coverage*. Available from: <https://apps.who.int/iris/handle/10665/75140> [accessed 13 February 2023].

World Humanitarian Summit (2016) *Commitments to Action: World Humanitarian Summit, 23–24 May 2016, Istanbul, Turkey*. Available from: <https://agendaforhumanity.org/sites/default/files/resources/2017/Jul/WHS_Commitment_to_Action_8September2016.pdf> [accessed 5 June 2021].

World Vision (2016) *Citizen Voice and Action Guidance Notes*, World Vision, Milton Keynes. Available from: <https://www.wvi.org/sites/default/files/2023-01/CVA%20Guidance%20Notes%20-New%20English.pdf> [accessed 22 January 2023].

Zander, R.S. and Zander, B. (2000) *The Art of Possibility*, Penguin Books, New York.

Zeitlin, M., Ghassemi, H. and Mansour, M. (1990) *Positive Deviance in Child Nutrition - with emphasis on Psychosocial and Behavioural Aspects and Implications for Development*, United Nations University Press, Tokyo.

Zimmerman, B., Lindberg, C. and Plsek, P. (1998) *Edgeware: Insights From Complexity Science for Health Care Leaders*, VHA Inc., Irving, TX.

Zulkifli, M.S.I. (2003) *Posyandu dan kader Kesehatan*. Available from: <https://repository.usu.ac.id/bitstream/handle/123456789/3753/fkm-zulkifli1.pdf;jsessionid=F5D58896CB73BC496BF3E0BE9CBFB821?sequence=1> [accessed 18 January 2023].

Index

AACES *see* Australia Africa Community Engagement Scheme
ABCD *see* Asset Based Community Development
ABM *see* Anglican Board of Mission
ACCESS *see* Australian Community Development and Civil Society Strengthening Program
accountability 158–9, 169
  social 76, 132, 133, 194, 215–7
Aceh Rehabilitation Program 223
ACIAR *see* Australian Centre for International Agricultural Research
ADRA *see* Adventist Development and Relief Agency
Adventist Development and Relief Agency 42–3
advocacy 32, 92, 94, 107, 118, 132, 193
agricultural research 20–1
  case study 164–6
agriculture 145, 166, 185, 209–10
Anderson, Erin 99, 190
Appreciative Inquiry 17, 49–55, 67, 75, 78, 204
  case studies 20–1, 44–5, 53–5, 164–6, 192–3
  critiques of 66–72
  definition 49
  elements 50
  evaluation method 164, 166–7
  examples 93, 96, 182, 208, 222, 229
  figure 51
  gender and social inclusion 185
  origin 49–50
  positive emotions in, 117
  research practice 163
  resources 204, 237

Asset-based Community Development 46–9, 67, 70
  case studies 44–5, 48–9, 145–6, 165–6, 183–5
  critiques 66–71
  definition 46
  examples 96, 118, 121, 192, 208, 218
  figure 47
  in evaluation and research 164
  origin 46
  resources 238
  steps 48
assets 18, 26, 39, 43–4, 46–8, 61–2, 171
  definition 18, 26
  mobilising 92
Australia Africa Community Engagement Scheme 39, 144–6
  case study 151–3
Anglican Board of Mission 32, 48–9, 203
Anglican Overseas Aid 81, 131, 151, 212–3
Australian Centre for International Agricultural Research 20–1, 164–6
Australian Community Development and Civil Society Strengthening Program 43, 62, 187
  case studies 53–55, 191–93

balance of power 70, 87–8, 91
Basic Education Development Program 43, 206
  case study 207–9
behaviour change 67, 114
Boon, Paul 53, 193

Cambodia 68, 164, 228
capability approach 11
capacity development 5, 176–81

child protection 211–3
Cleary, Lisa 1
climate change 199–202
Coady Institute 46, 48, 238
collective inquiry 36, 39–41, 43, 67, 93, 152
community development 48, 72, 144, 181–5, 191–2, 219
complexity 14–6, 73
conflict 68, 92, 127–8, 221, 225
co-production 17, 61–3, 70
  case study 63–4
  definition 61
  elements 62
  origin 61
  resources 239
cross-cultural collaboration 99–102, 194
Crowding out 76, 135, 212
cultural value differences 8, 13, 14, 57, 99–105
Cunningham, Ian 23, 33, 120, 132, 135–7, 162, 178
Curnow, Jayne 20–1, 187

decolonization 13, 173, 231, 233
decolonizing knowledge 13, 126, 148, 233
deficit discourse 8, 199
deficit-based approach 6–10, 18, 32–4, 46, 148–50, 200
Dewi, Christa 220–1
disability inclusion 150, 188–9
disaster response 96, 221–2
disaster risk reduction 199–202, 221
domestic violence 109, 153, 211–3

earthquakes 41, 95,
  case study 222–3
economic development 20, 54, 183–4, 192, 202–5
education 10, 26, 179–80, 189, 205–7
  case studies 63–4, 207–9
empowerment 88–9
Endogenous Development 57–9
  case study 58–9
  definition 57
  elements 58
  origin 57

environment 197, 199–200
  enabling 11, 77, 192
  social 77
evaluation 27, 50, 53, 162–70
exclusive focus on strengths 16, 37
expanding power 88, 94–5
  case study 95–97

facilitation 42–4, 52, 67, 103–5, 109, 113, 138
Fiji 212–3
flourishing 118–20, 205
food security 56, 120, 145, 151, 182, 197, 209–11
foresight/futures thinking 17, 65–7
  definition 65
  elements 66–7
  origin 65

gender based violence 81, 127, 146, 187, 211–5
gender equality 4, 89, 120, 185, 186–7, 197, 212, 214, 226
generative change 30–1, 38, 79–80, 108, 169, 213
  definition 31, 78
geo-political relationships 172–4
Gero, Anna 173, 199–200, 202
Ghana 127–8
governance 5, 80, 125, 178, 190–3, 215–7

health service delivery 92–3, 219–21
health systems strengthening 217–21
history of strengths-based approaches 17
human rights 4, 70, 94–5, 107, 188, 214, 225–6
humanitarian response 12, 221–5

IDSS see International Development Support Services
inclusion 39–40, 45, 70, 77, 91, 107, 108, 132–3, 185–8
  disability 150, 188–9
  diversity and inclusion 107–8
  social 53, 185–9
India 57, 204, 216–7
  case study 58–9

Indigenous knowledge/learning 57, 59, 164–6, 201
Indonesia 41, 147, 182, 218,
   case studies 53–5, 63–4, 92–3, 95–7, 135–6, 191–3, 219–21
infrastructure 5, 17, 227
   case studies 207–209, 223–4
International Development Support Services 95, 222

Japan 222
justice *see* law and justice

Kenya 202, 210,
   case study 213–215
Khoury, Ivy 145

language (strengths-based) 27–8, 32, 34, 68, 174, 176, 199–200, 211–2
   (spoken) 99–102
Laos 206
LAPIS *see* Learning Assistance Program in Islamic Schools
law and justice 190, 225–6
leadership 190–1
   case study 48–50
   local 13, 42, 125, 130, 148, 150–1, 153–4, 168, 187
   women's 44, 146, 207–9, 211
Learning Assistance Program for Islamic Schools 63–4
livelihoods 20, 44, 97–8, 202–3,
localization 12–3, 110, 148, 231, 233
   in humanitarian responses 221–2
logframe 152, 160–1

Macanawai, Setareki 13, 73, 141, 171, 180, 188–9
Magallanas, Lina 32, 49
Malawi 31, 120, 132, 144–7, 151, 210, 228
Martin, Scott 39, 132, 145–6, 228–30
McGrath, Alice 226
Middleby, Soli 73, 74, 124, 154–5, 174, 176, 197

motivation 16, 30, 45, 87, 103, 120–1, 132, 157
   case study 135–7
   in different cultures 108
   in humanitarian responses 222
multi-stakeholder engagement 54, 81, 154, 192–3, 210
Mulume, Carsterns 31, 147
Myanmar 127–8

Najib, Mohammad 224
Nderita, Florence 214
Nguyen, Vinh 183
nutrition 55–6, 219–20, 188, 227

ownership 35, 49, 122, 145, 151. 153–5, 201–6, 233
   case studies 53–5, 82–3, 207–209

Pamphilon, Barbara 34, 71, 165–6, 185, 231
Papua New Guinea 40, 43, 71, 103, 185, 191, 211
   case studies 20–1, 152, 164–6, 207–9
Papua New Guinea Democratic Governance Program 191
participatory approaches 16–8
Participatory Rural Appraisal 17–8, 27, 181
partnerships 12, 16, 21, 148, 173, 175–6, 178, 234, 5
Philippines 20, 32, 203
   case study 48–9
positive deviance 15, 17, 55–7, 67, 71, 164, 167
   case studies 192–93, 219–21
   definition 55
   elements 55–6
   origin 55
   resources 239
positive psychology 114–115
   resources 239
preferred future/s 30–32, 38–9, 43, 51–2, 67, 68, 75–7, 169
problem-based approach 7, 72, 190, 218, 231, 233, 235
   contrast with strengths-based approach 39, 43–4, 103, 105, 132, 136, 150, 178–9

Quick wins 44, 79, 118, 132

risk management 106, 155–6

Samoa 103, 150, 174, 188, 212
Samoa Disability Program 150, 188
Schnell, Tony 37, 81
schools 179, 205–7
  case studies 63–4, 95–7, 207–9
Seda, Sulis 55
Segu, Stefanus 55
self-reliance 70, 213–5
Senjura, James 214
SLA *see* Sustainable Livelihoods Approach
Solomon Islands 21, 37, 40–5, 118, 176, 152, 182, 203–4, 226
South Africa 37, 78, 81–3, 151, 175, 181, 212
Spratt, Rebecca 180
strengths
  definition 26, 121
  see also assets
strengths-based social work 17, 26, 32–3, 59–61
  definition 59
  elements 60
  origin 59
sustainability 32, 49, 50, 158, 167, 215, 221, 228–9
  environmental 4
Sustainable Livelihoods Approach 16, 18, 96
  definition 18
  elements 18
  origin 18
systems thinking 52, 79

Tana, Shinko 222, 225
Tanzania 39, 144–6, 151, 210, 228–30
theory of change 159, 223
Timor-Leste 20, 58–9
Transdisciplinary 126, 197–8
transformative change 28, 30–1, 34, 48–9, 69, 79–81, 151, 169–70, 178
  case study 81–3
  gender transformative change 133, 186–7, 212

Vaartjes, Vicki 85, 143, 175
value for money 209, 228–9
Vanuatu 118, 212, 222
Vietnam 183–5

Wambugu, Millicent 214–5
Wanjohi, Martin 150, 210
WASH *see* water, sanitation, sanitation, and hygiene
water, sanitation, sanitation, and hygiene 113, 133, 146, 151–3, 167, 226–8
  case study 135–7, 228–30, 228–30
waves of development thinking 5–6
Whitelum, Bernadette 223
whole system summit 39, 51–2, 70, 77
World Vision 76, 129, 133, 151, 194, 216
Wuijts, Anne 147, 182

Xavier University, Philippines 46, 48, 238

Yidana, Godwin 127–8
Yogyakarta-Central Java Community Assistance Program 95–7
youth 44–5, 60, 121, 184, 208